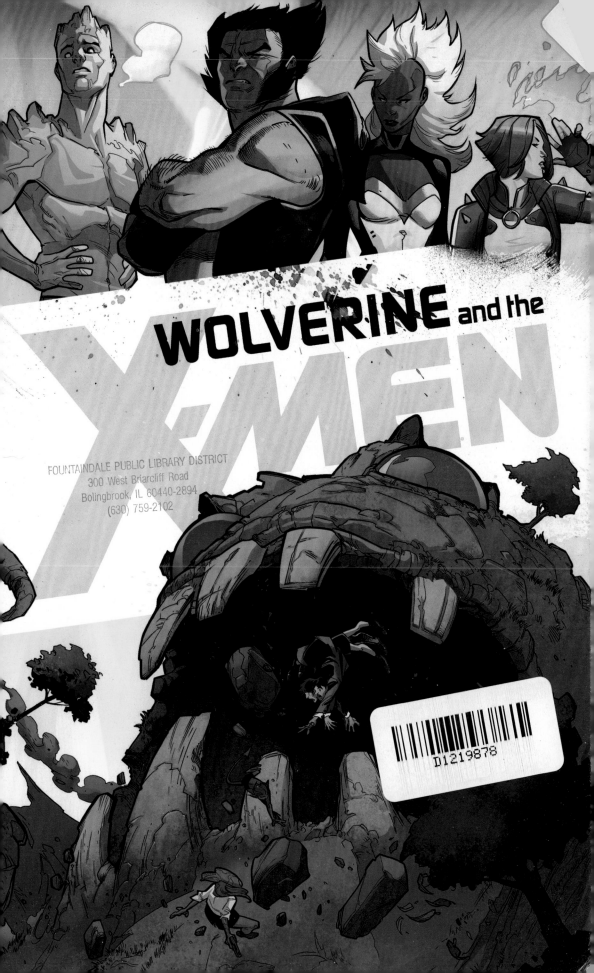

WOLVERINE and the X-MEN

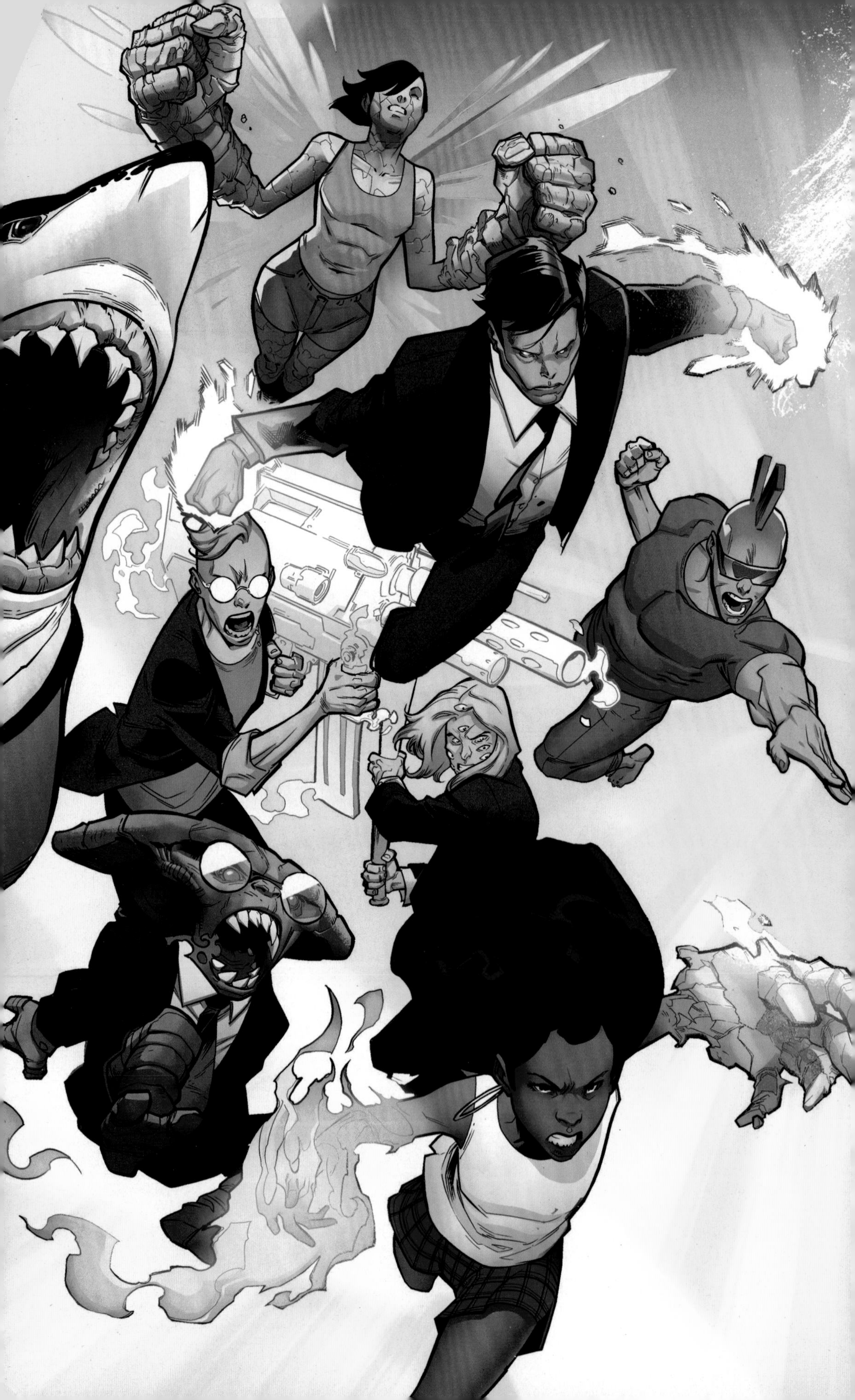

WOLVERINE and the X-MEN

WRITER: **JASON AARON**

ANNUAL #1

PENCILER: **NICK BRADSHAW**

INKERS: **WALDEN WONG, KARL KESEL, VICTOR OLAZABA & NICK BRADSHAW**

COLORIST: **JAMES CAMPBELL** COVER ART: **NICK BRADSHAW & LAURA MARTIN**

ISSUES #38-40

ARTIST: **PEPE LARRAZ** COLORIST: **MATT MILLA** WITH **PETE PANTAZIS** (#39)

COVER ART: **NICK BRADSHAW & LAURA MARTIN**

ISSUE #41

ARTISTS: **PEPE LARRAZ & TODD NAUCK** COLORIST: **MATT MILLA**

COVER ART: **NICK BRADSHAW & ISRAEL SILVA**

ISSUE #42

ARTISTS: **NICK BRADSHAW, PEPE LARRAZ, RÁMON PÉREZ, SHAWN CRYSTAL, STEVE SANDERS, NUNO ALVES, TIM TOWNSEND & CHRIS BACHALO**

COLORISTS: **MATT MILLA & LEE LOUGHRIDGE**

COVER ART: **NICK BRADSHAW & ISRAEL SILVA**

LETTERER: **VC'S JOE CARAMAGNA** ASSISTANT EDITOR: **FRANKIE JOHNSON**

ASSOCIATE EDITOR: **TOM BRENNAN** EDITOR: **NICK LOWE**

COLLECTION EDITOR: **JENNIFER GRÜNWALD**
ASSOCIATE MANAGING EDITOR: **ALEX STARBUCK**
EDITOR, SPECIAL PROJECTS: **MARK D. BEAZLEY**
SENIOR EDITOR, SPECIAL PROJECTS: **JEFF YOUNGQUIST**

SVP PRINT, SALES & MARKETING: **DAVID GABRIEL**
BOOK DESIGNER: **RODOLFO MURAGUCHI**

EDITOR IN CHIEF: **AXEL ALONSO**
CHIEF CREATIVE OFFICER: **JOE QUESADA**
PUBLISHER: **DAN BUCKLEY**
EXECUTIVE PRODUCER: **ALAN FINE**

WOLVERINE & THE X-MEN BY JASON AARON VOL. 8. Contains material originally published in magazine form as WOLVERINE & THE X-MEN #38-42 and ANNUAL #1. First printing 2014. ISBN# 978-0-7851-6601-6. Published by MARVEL WORLDWIDE, INC., a subsidiary of MARVEL ENTERTAINMENT, LLC. OFFICE OF PUBLICATION: 135 West 50th Street, New York, NY 10020. **Printed in Canada.** ALAN FINE, EVP - Office of the President, Marvel Worldwide, Inc. and EVP & CMO Marvel Characters B.V.; DAN BUCKLEY, Publisher & President - Print, Animation & Digital Divisions; JOE QUESADA, Chief Creative Officer; TOM BREVOORT, SVP of Publishing; DAVID BOGART, SVP of Operations & Procurement, Publishing; C.B. CEBULSKI, SVP of Creator & Content Development; DAVID GABRIEL, SVP Print, Sales & Marketing; JIM O'KEEFE, VP of Operations & Logistics; DAN CARR, Executive Director of Publishing Technology; SUSAN CRESPI, Editorial Operations Manager; ALEX MORALES, Publishing Operations Manager; STAN LEE, Chairman Emeritus. For information regarding advertising in Marvel Comics or on Marvel.com, please contact Niza Disla, Director of Marvel Partnerships, at ndisla@marvel.com. For Marvel subscription inquiries, please call 800-217-9158. **Manufactured between 3/7/2014 and 4/14/2014 by SOLISCO PRINTERS, SCOTT, QC, CANADA.**

10 9 8 7 6 5 4 3 2 1

ANNUAL 1 GLADIATOR ZERO

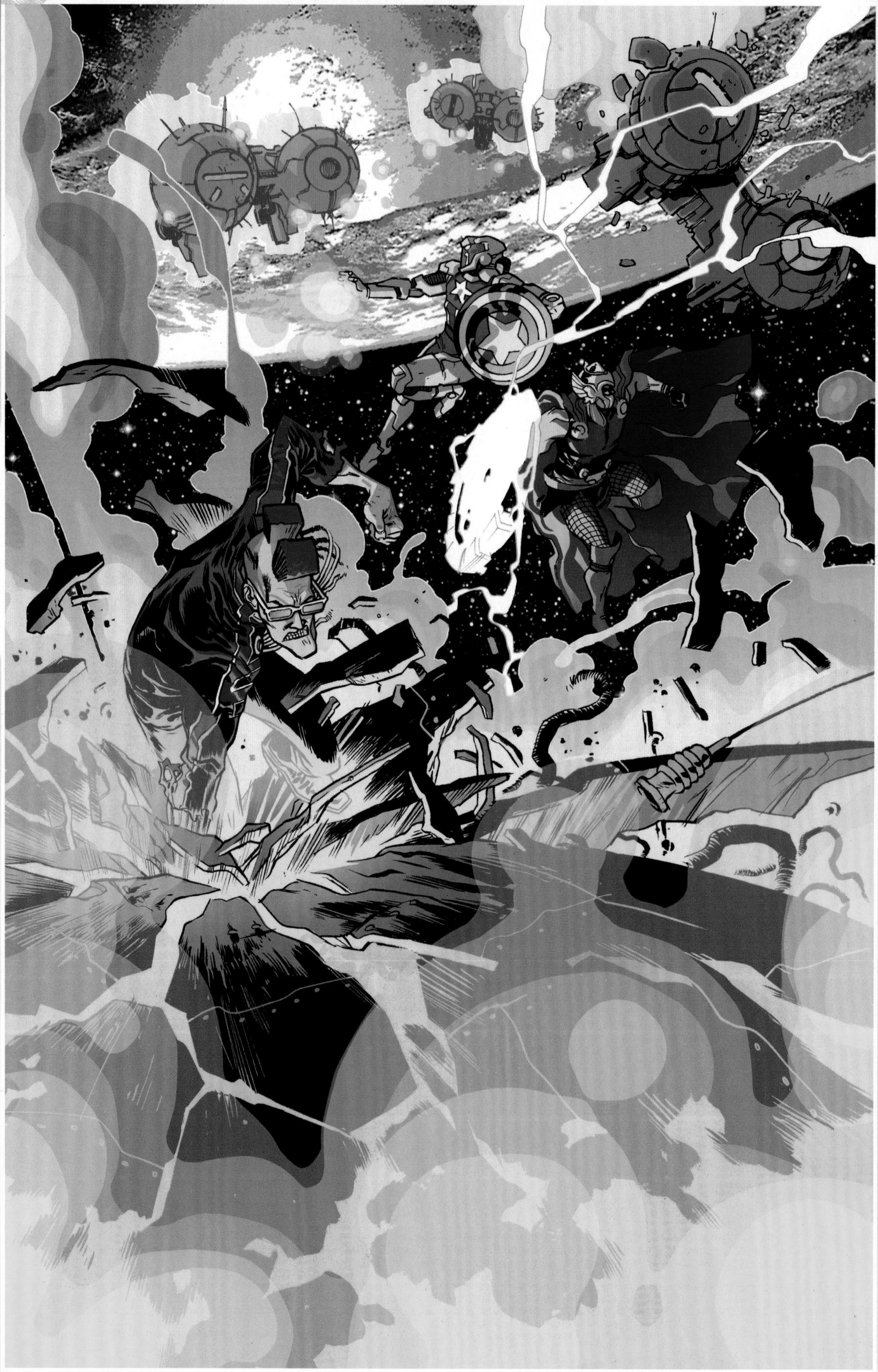

If you were born different with mutant super-powers, the Jean Grey School for Higher Learning is the school for you. Founded by Wolverine and staffed by experienced X-Men, you will learn everything you need to know to survive in a world that hates and fears you.

WOLVERINE and the X-MEN

PREVIOUSLY

KUBARK IS A NORMAL KID — A LITTLE FULL OF HIMSELF, A LITTLE UNAWARE OF HIS OWN STRENGTH, AND HAS A TOUGH RELATIONSHIP WITH HIS DAD.

HE'S ALSO "KID GLADIATOR" — A SUPERSTRONG ALIEN AND SON OF GLADIATOR, A.K.A. KALLARK, EMPEROR OF THE SHIAR EMPIRE, ONE OF THE MOST POWERFUL BEINGS IN THE UNIVERSE.

KID GLADIATOR WAS BANISHED TO EARTH AND ENROLLED IN THE JEAN GREY SCHOOL FOR HIGHER LEARNING, AN INSTITUTE DEDICATED TO EDUCATING YOUNG MUTANTS — HUMAN BEINGS BORN WITH INCREDIBLE POWERS — AS WELL AS OTHER SUPERPOWERED STUDENTS. IT'S NORMALLY NOT A PEACEFUL PLACE — IT'S EVEN LESS PEACEFUL AS THE FORCES OF THANOS OF TITAN LAY SIEGE TO THE EARTH.

RECENTLY, KUBARK WAS BROUGHT BACK TO THE SH'IAR EMPIRE TO RESUME HIS TRAINING WITH THE IMPERIAL GUARD. BUT THE FORCES THAT THREATEN EARTH WILL BECOME THE UNIVERSE'S PROBLEM SOON ENOUGH. KID GLADIATOR IS GOING TO WAR.

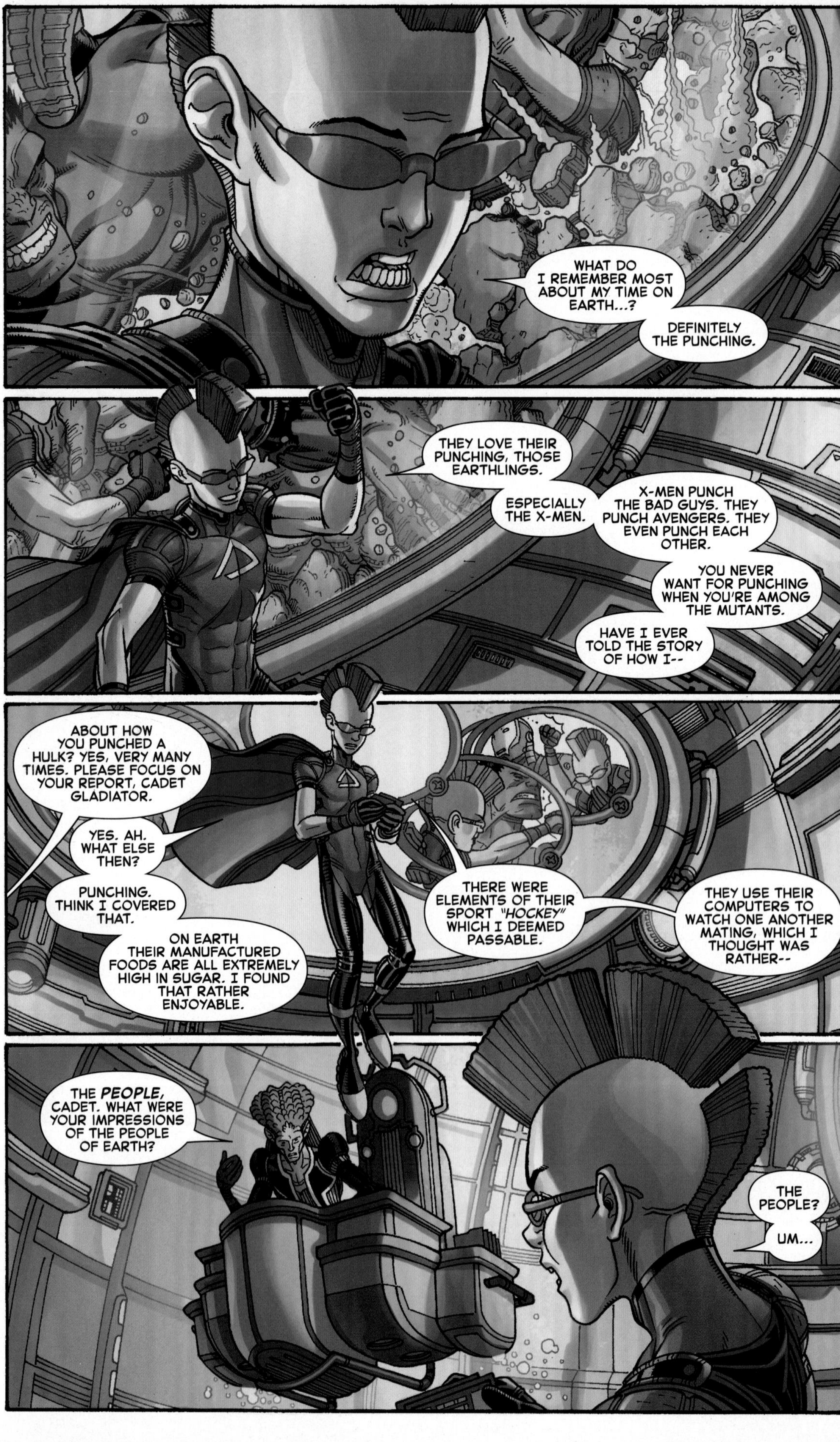
WHAT DO I REMEMBER MOST ABOUT MY TIME ON EARTH...?
DEFINITELY THE PUNCHING.
THEY LOVE THEIR PUNCHING, THOSE EARTHLINGS.
ESPECIALLY THE X-MEN.
X-MEN PUNCH THE BAD GUYS. THEY PUNCH AVENGERS. THEY EVEN PUNCH EACH OTHER.
YOU NEVER WANT FOR PUNCHING WHEN YOU'RE AMONG THE MUTANTS.
HAVE I EVER TOLD THE STORY OF HOW I--
ABOUT HOW YOU PUNCHED A HULK? YES, VERY MANY TIMES. PLEASE FOCUS ON YOUR REPORT, CADET GLADIATOR.
YES. AH. WHAT ELSE THEN?
PUNCHING. THINK I COVERED THAT.
ON EARTH THEIR MANUFACTURED FOODS ARE ALL EXTREMELY HIGH IN SUGAR. I FOUND THAT RATHER ENJOYABLE.
THERE WERE ELEMENTS OF THEIR SPORT *"HOCKEY"* WHICH I DEEMED PASSABLE.
THEY USE THEIR COMPUTERS TO WATCH ONE ANOTHER MATING, WHICH I THOUGHT WAS RATHER--
THE *PEOPLE,* CADET. WHAT WERE YOUR IMPRESSIONS OF THE PEOPLE OF EARTH?
THE PEOPLE?
UM...

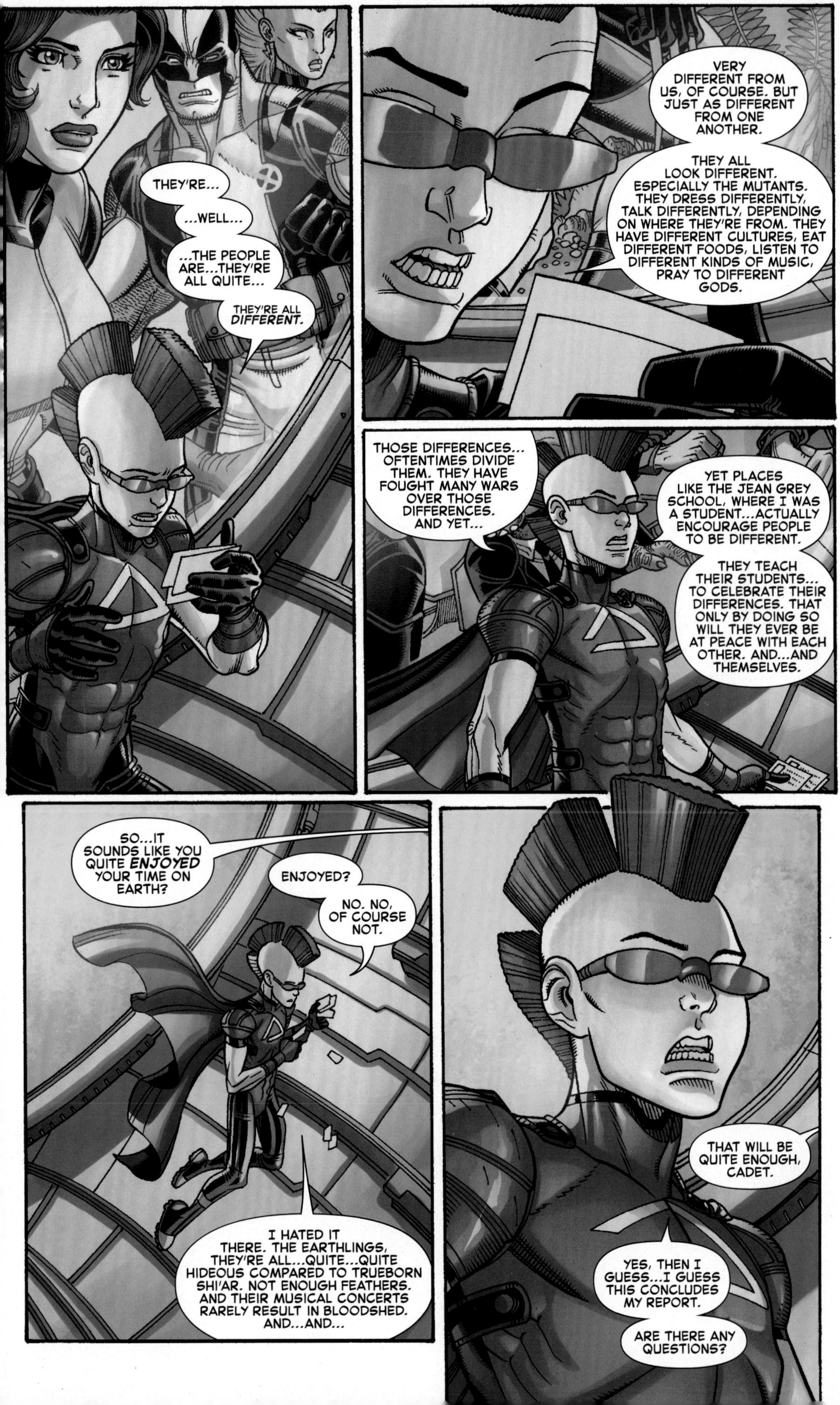
THEY'RE...
...WELL...
...THE PEOPLE ARE...THEY'RE ALL QUITE...
THEY'RE ALL DIFFERENT.
VERY DIFFERENT FROM US, OF COURSE. BUT JUST AS DIFFERENT FROM ONE ANOTHER.
THEY ALL LOOK DIFFERENT. ESPECIALLY THE MUTANTS. THEY DRESS DIFFERENTLY, TALK DIFFERENTLY, DEPENDING ON WHERE THEY'RE FROM. THEY HAVE DIFFERENT CULTURES, EAT DIFFERENT FOODS, LISTEN TO DIFFERENT KINDS OF MUSIC, PRAY TO DIFFERENT GODS.
THOSE DIFFERENCES... OFTENTIMES DIVIDE THEM. THEY HAVE FOUGHT MANY WARS OVER THOSE DIFFERENCES. AND YET...
YET PLACES LIKE THE JEAN GREY SCHOOL, WHERE I WAS A STUDENT...ACTUALLY ENCOURAGE PEOPLE TO BE DIFFERENT.
THEY TEACH THEIR STUDENTS... TO CELEBRATE THEIR DIFFERENCES. THAT ONLY BY DOING SO WILL THEY EVER BE AT PEACE WITH EACH OTHER. AND...AND THEMSELVES.
SO...IT SOUNDS LIKE YOU QUITE ENJOYED YOUR TIME ON EARTH?
ENJOYED?
NO. NO, OF COURSE NOT.
I HATED IT THERE. THE EARTHLINGS, THEY'RE ALL...QUITE...QUITE HIDEOUS COMPARED TO TRUEBORN SHI'AR. NOT ENOUGH FEATHERS. AND THEIR MUSICAL CONCERTS RARELY RESULT IN BLOODSHED. AND...AND...
THAT WILL BE QUITE ENOUGH, CADET.
YES, THEN I GUESS...I GUESS THIS CONCLUDES MY REPORT.
ARE THERE ANY QUESTIONS?

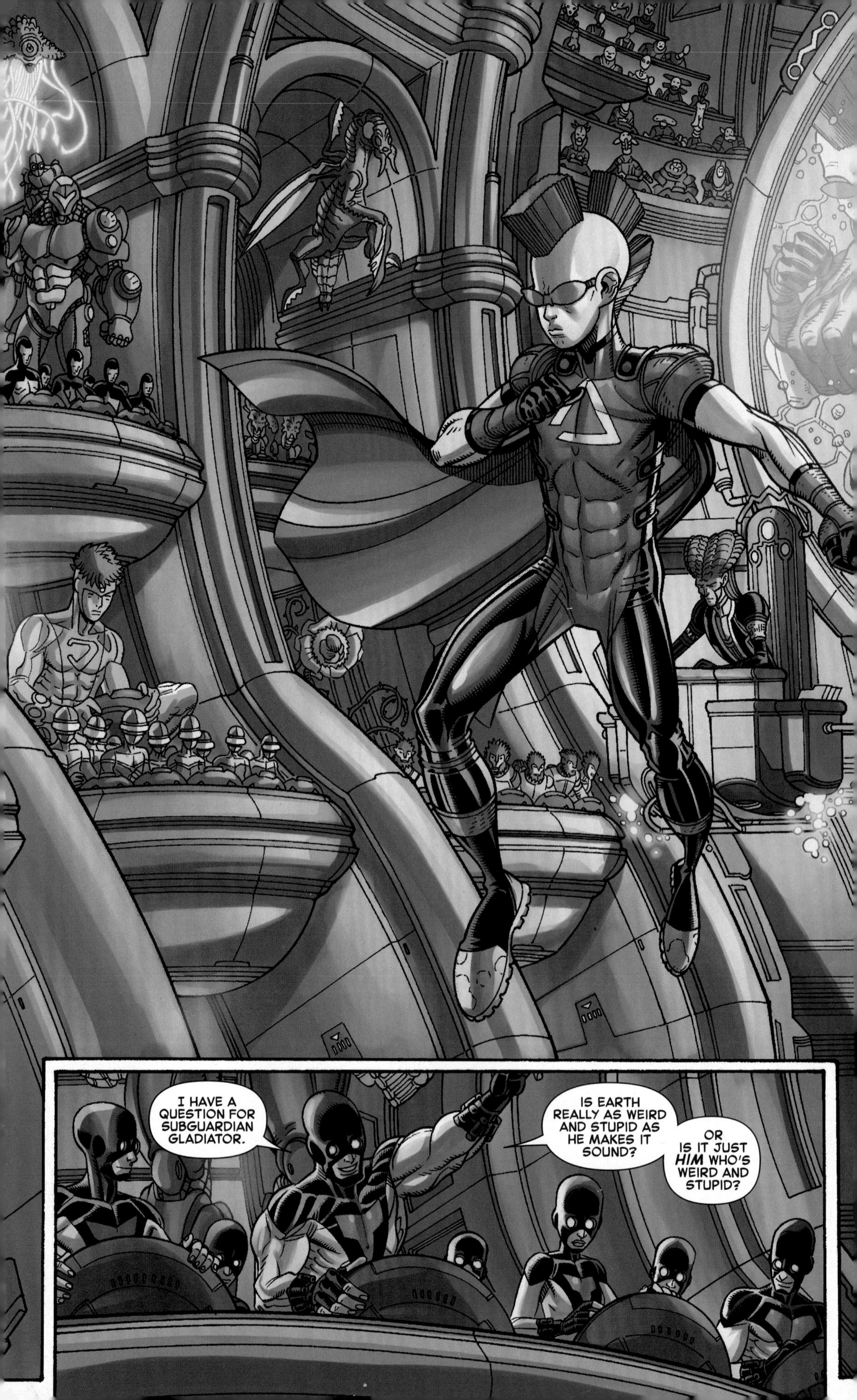
I HAVE A QUESTION FOR SUBGUARDIAN GLADIATOR.
IS EARTH REALLY AS WEIRD AND STUPID AS HE MAKES IT SOUND?
OR IS IT JUST *HIM* WHO'S WEIRD AND STUPID?

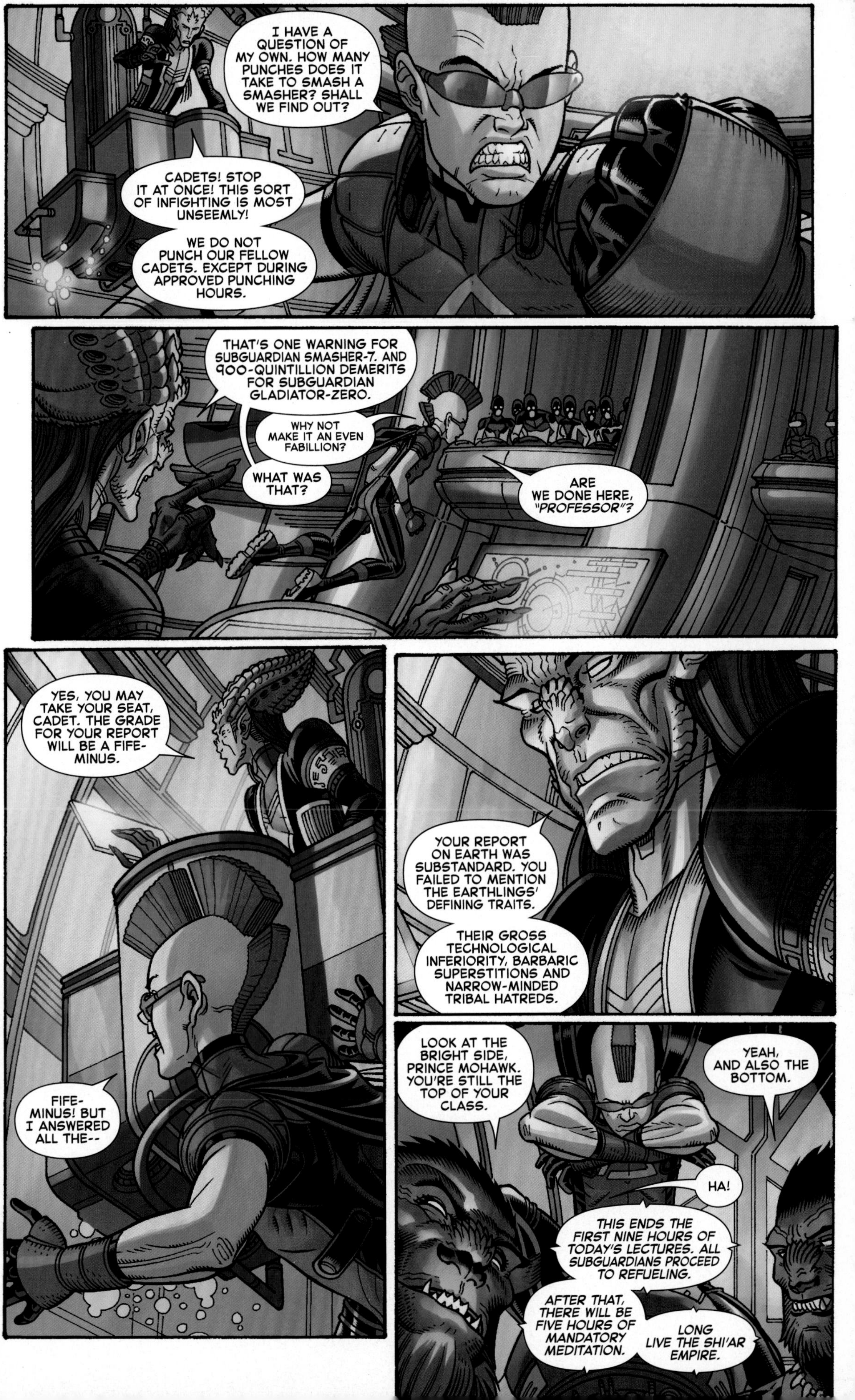
I HAVE A QUESTION OF MY OWN. HOW MANY PUNCHES DOES IT TAKE TO SMASH A SMASHER? SHALL WE FIND OUT?
CADETS! STOP IT AT ONCE! THIS SORT OF INFIGHTING IS MOST UNSEEMLY!
WE DO NOT PUNCH OUR FELLOW CADETS. EXCEPT DURING APPROVED PUNCHING HOURS.
THAT'S ONE WARNING FOR SUBGUARDIAN SMASHER-7. AND 900-QUINTILLION DEMERITS FOR SUBGUARDIAN GLADIATOR-ZERO.
WHY NOT MAKE IT AN EVEN FABILLION?
WHAT WAS THAT?
ARE WE DONE HERE, "PROFESSOR"?
YES, YOU MAY TAKE YOUR SEAT, CADET. THE GRADE FOR YOUR REPORT WILL BE A FIFE-MINUS.
FIFE-MINUS! BUT I ANSWERED ALL THE--
YOUR REPORT ON EARTH WAS SUBSTANDARD. YOU FAILED TO MENTION THE EARTHLINGS' DEFINING TRAITS.
THEIR GROSS TECHNOLOGICAL INFERIORITY, BARBARIC SUPERSTITIONS AND NARROW-MINDED TRIBAL HATREDS.
LOOK AT THE BRIGHT SIDE, PRINCE MOHAWK. YOU'RE STILL THE TOP OF YOUR CLASS.
YEAH, AND ALSO THE BOTTOM.
HA!
THIS ENDS THE FIRST NINE HOURS OF TODAY'S LECTURES. ALL SUBGUARDIANS PROCEED TO REFUELING.
AFTER THAT, THERE WILL BE FIVE HOURS OF MANDATORY MEDITATION.
LONG LIVE THE SHI'AR EMPIRE.

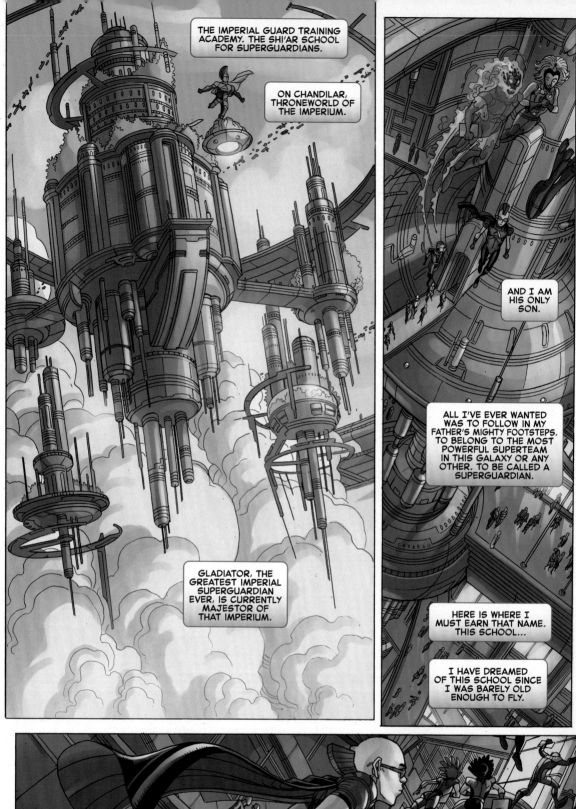

THE IMPERIAL GUARD TRAINING ACADEMY. THE SHI'AR SCHOOL FOR SUPERGUARDIANS.

ON CHANDILAR, THRONEWORLD OF THE IMPERIUM.

AND I AM HIS ONLY SON.

ALL I'VE EVER WANTED WAS TO FOLLOW IN MY FATHER'S MIGHTY FOOTSTEPS. TO BELONG TO THE MOST POWERFUL SUPERTEAM IN THIS GALAXY OR ANY OTHER. TO BE CALLED A SUPERGUARDIAN.

GLADIATOR, THE GREATEST IMPERIAL SUPERGUARDIAN EVER, IS CURRENTLY MAJESTOR OF THAT IMPERIUM.

HERE IS WHERE I MUST EARN THAT NAME. THIS SCHOOL...

I HAVE DREAMED OF THIS SCHOOL SINCE I WAS BARELY OLD ENOUGH TO FLY.

YET SO FAR, I HAVE TO SAY...

IT'S NOT EXACTLY THE WAY I DREAMED IT WOULD BE.

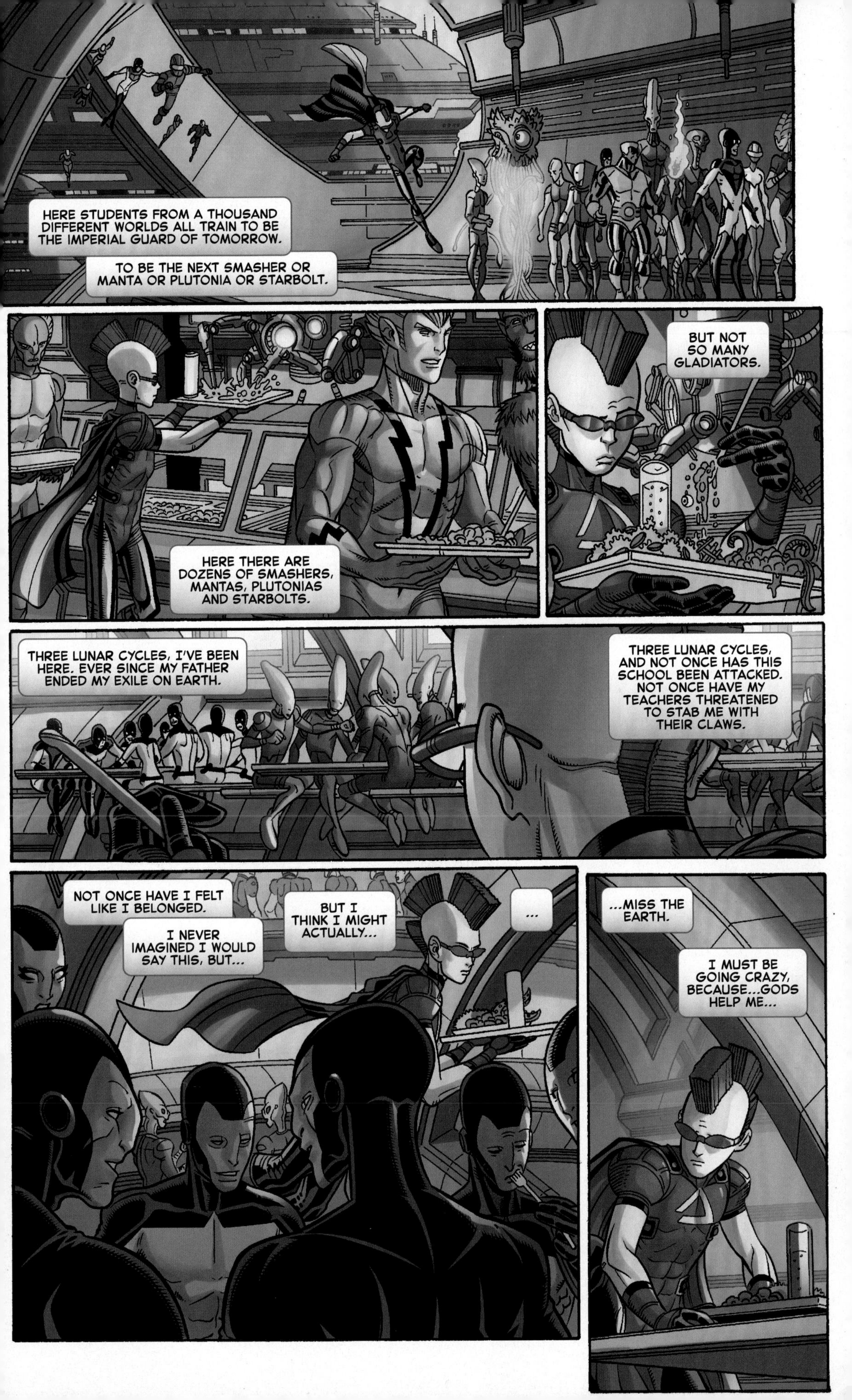
HERE STUDENTS FROM A THOUSAND DIFFERENT WORLDS ALL TRAIN TO BE THE IMPERIAL GUARD OF TOMORROW.
TO BE THE NEXT SMASHER OR MANTA OR PLUTONIA OR STARBOLT.
HERE THERE ARE DOZENS OF SMASHERS, MANTAS, PLUTONIAS AND STARBOLTS.
BUT NOT SO MANY GLADIATORS.
THREE LUNAR CYCLES, I'VE BEEN HERE. EVER SINCE MY FATHER ENDED MY EXILE ON EARTH.
THREE LUNAR CYCLES, AND NOT ONCE HAS THIS SCHOOL BEEN ATTACKED. NOT ONCE HAVE MY TEACHERS THREATENED TO STAB ME WITH THEIR CLAWS.
NOT ONCE HAVE I FELT LIKE I BELONGED.
I NEVER IMAGINED I WOULD SAY THIS, BUT...
BUT I THINK I MIGHT ACTUALLY...
...
...MISS THE EARTH.
I MUST BE GOING CRAZY, BECAUSE...GODS HELP ME...

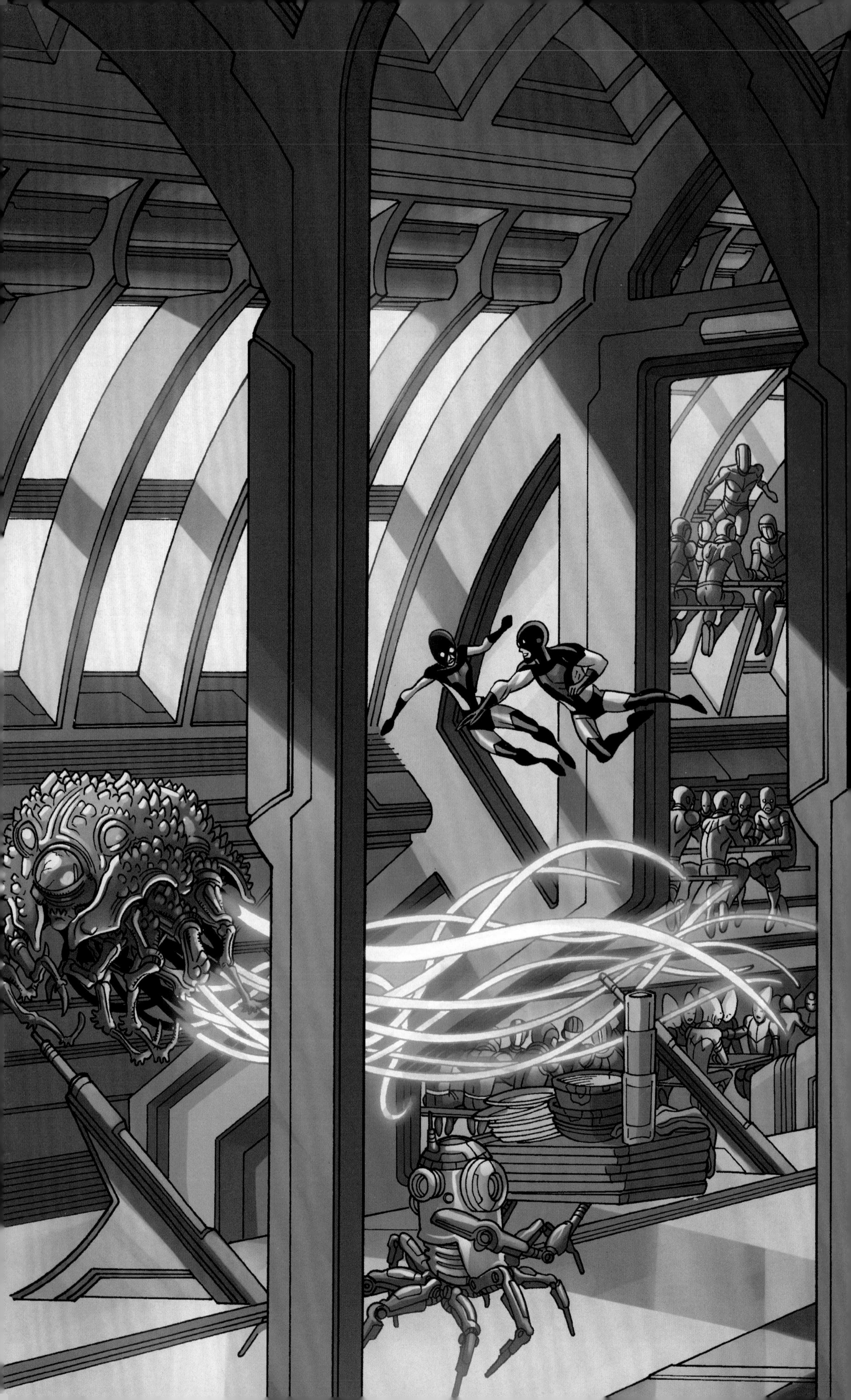

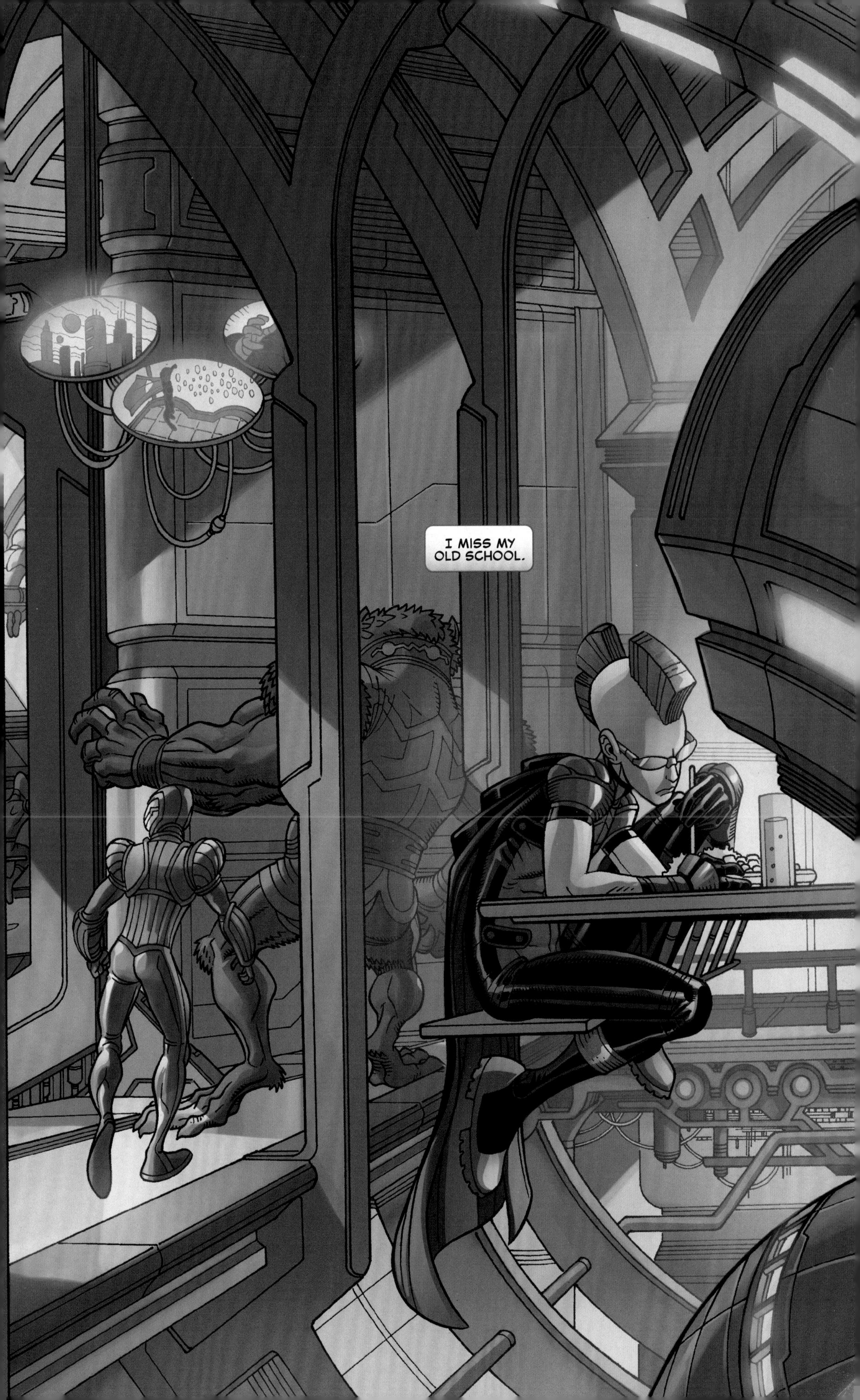
I MISS MY OLD SCHOOL.

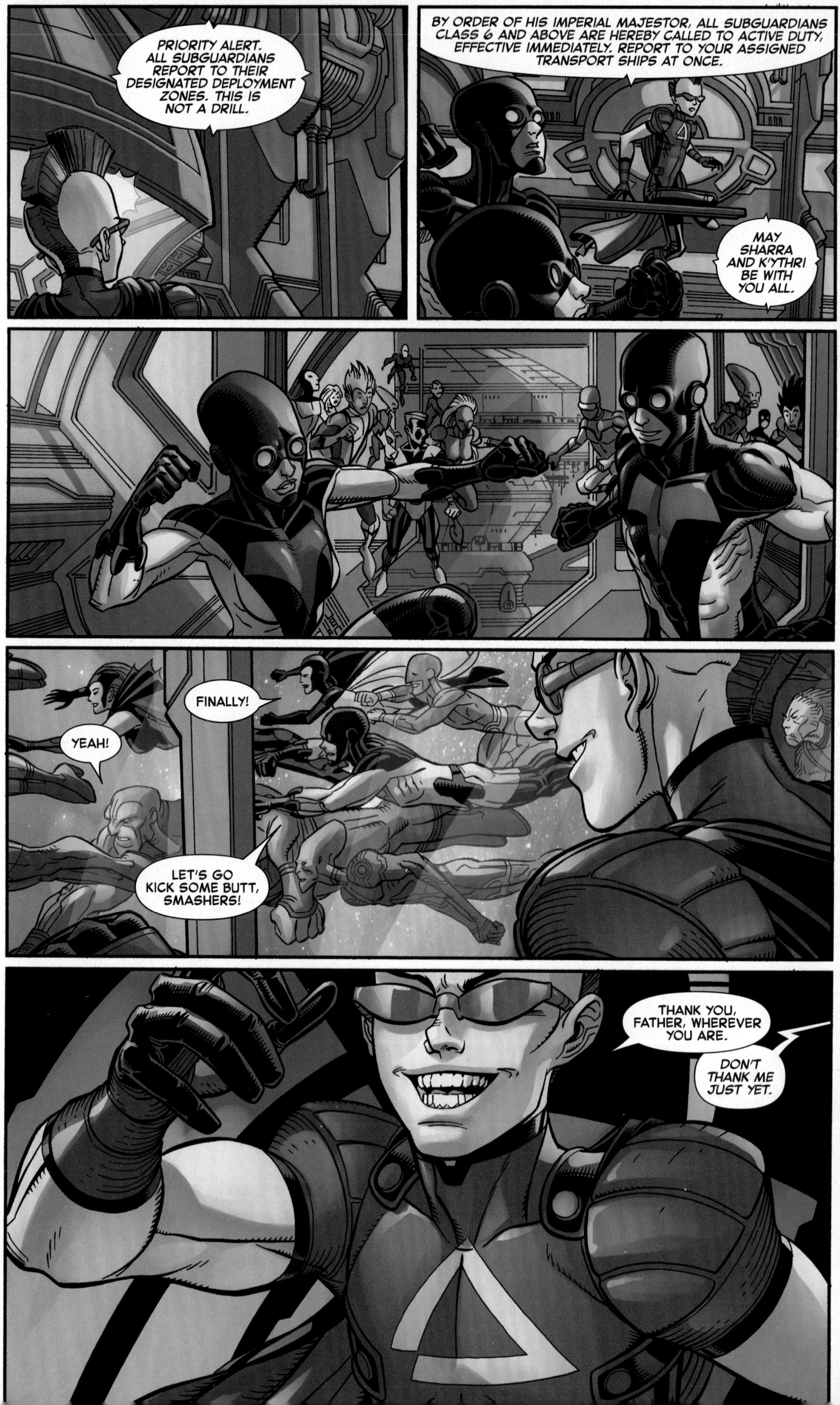
PRIORITY ALERT. ALL SUBGUARDIANS REPORT TO THEIR DESIGNATED DEPLOYMENT ZONES. THIS IS NOT A DRILL.
BY ORDER OF HIS IMPERIAL MAJESTOR, ALL SUBGUARDIANS CLASS 6 AND ABOVE ARE HEREBY CALLED TO ACTIVE DUTY, EFFECTIVE IMMEDIATELY. REPORT TO YOUR ASSIGNED TRANSPORT SHIPS AT ONCE.
MAY SHARRA AND K'YTHRI BE WITH YOU ALL.
FINALLY!
YEAH!
LET'S GO KICK SOME BUTT, SMASHERS!
THANK YOU, FATHER, WHEREVER YOU ARE.
DON'T THANK ME JUST YET.

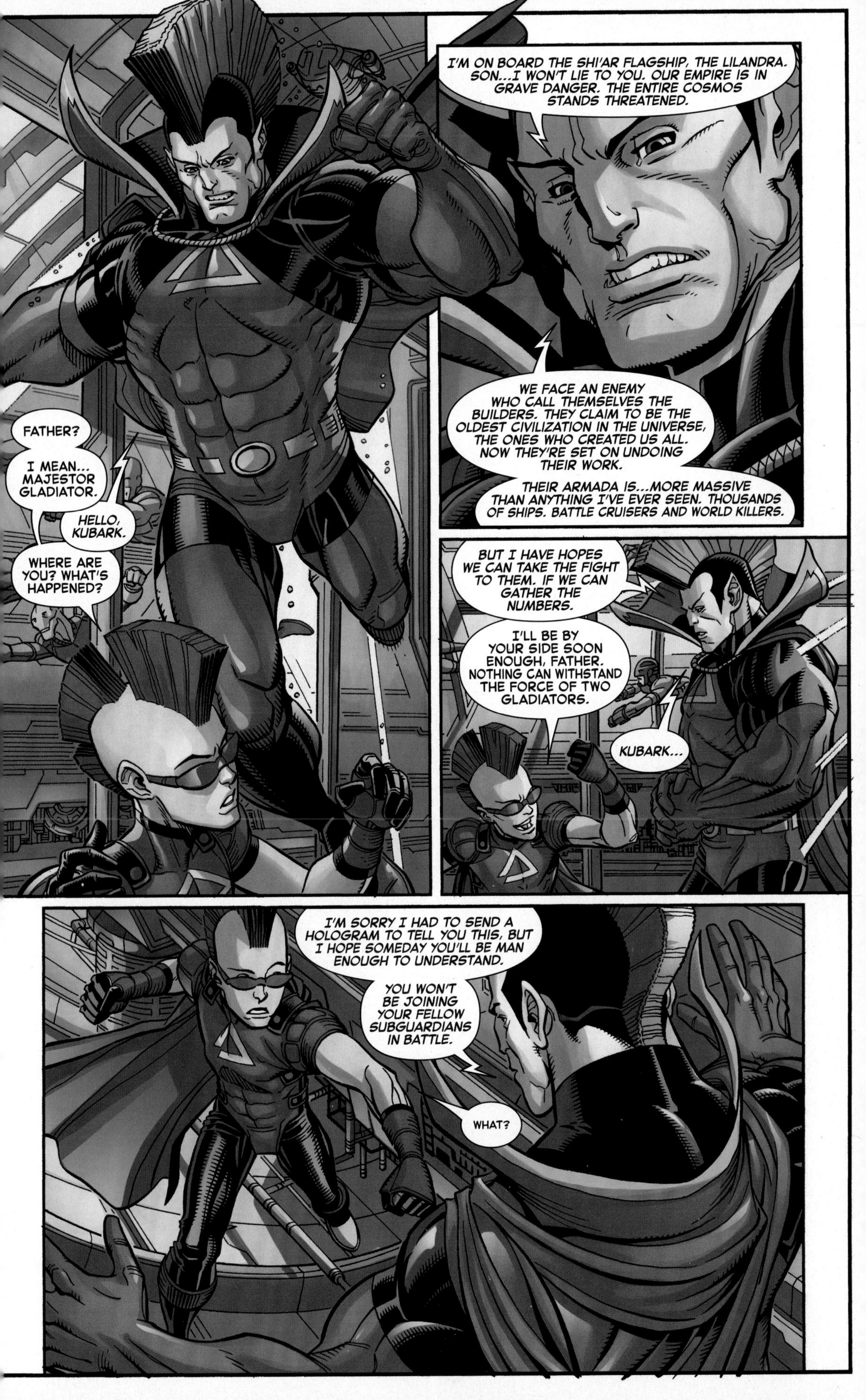
FATHER?
I MEAN... MAJESTOR GLADIATOR.
HELLO, KUBARK.
WHERE ARE YOU? WHAT'S HAPPENED?
I'M ON BOARD THE SHI'AR FLAGSHIP, THE LILANDRA. SON...I WON'T LIE TO YOU. OUR EMPIRE IS IN GRAVE DANGER. THE ENTIRE COSMOS STANDS THREATENED.
WE FACE AN ENEMY WHO CALL THEMSELVES THE BUILDERS. THEY CLAIM TO BE THE OLDEST CIVILIZATION IN THE UNIVERSE, THE ONES WHO CREATED US ALL. NOW THEY'RE SET ON UNDOING THEIR WORK.
THEIR ARMADA IS...MORE MASSIVE THAN ANYTHING I'VE EVER SEEN. THOUSANDS OF SHIPS. BATTLE CRUISERS AND WORLD KILLERS.
BUT I HAVE HOPES WE CAN TAKE THE FIGHT TO THEM. IF WE CAN GATHER THE NUMBERS.
I'LL BE BY YOUR SIDE SOON ENOUGH, FATHER. NOTHING CAN WITHSTAND THE FORCE OF TWO GLADIATORS.
KUBARK...
I'M SORRY I HAD TO SEND A HOLOGRAM TO TELL YOU THIS, BUT I HOPE SOMEDAY YOU'LL BE MAN ENOUGH TO UNDERSTAND.
YOU WON'T BE JOINING YOUR FELLOW SUBGUARDIANS IN BATTLE.
WHAT?

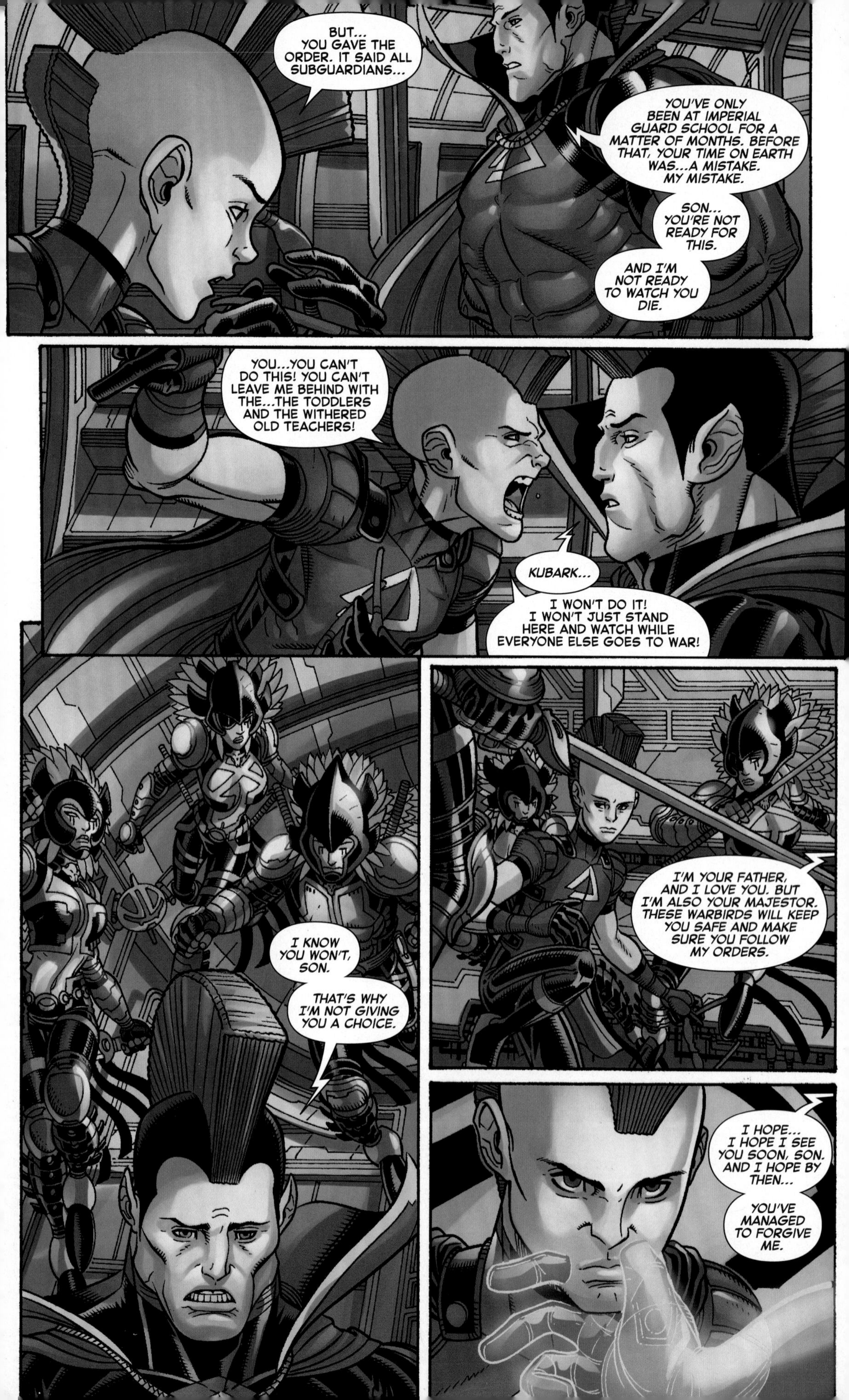
BUT... YOU GAVE THE ORDER. IT SAID ALL SUBGUARDIANS...
YOU'VE ONLY BEEN AT IMPERIAL GUARD SCHOOL FOR A MATTER OF MONTHS. BEFORE THAT, YOUR TIME ON EARTH WAS...A MISTAKE. MY MISTAKE.
SON... YOU'RE NOT READY FOR THIS.
AND I'M NOT READY TO WATCH YOU DIE.
YOU...YOU CAN'T DO THIS! YOU CAN'T LEAVE ME BEHIND WITH THE...THE TODDLERS AND THE WITHERED OLD TEACHERS!
KUBARK...
I WON'T DO IT! I WON'T JUST STAND HERE AND WATCH WHILE EVERYONE ELSE GOES TO WAR!
I KNOW YOU WON'T, SON.
THAT'S WHY I'M NOT GIVING YOU A CHOICE.
I'M YOUR FATHER, AND I LOVE YOU. BUT I'M ALSO YOUR MAJESTOR. THESE WARBIRDS WILL KEEP YOU SAFE AND MAKE SURE YOU FOLLOW MY ORDERS.
I HOPE... I HOPE I SEE YOU SOON, SON. AND I HOPE BY THEN...
YOU'VE MANAGED TO FORGIVE ME.

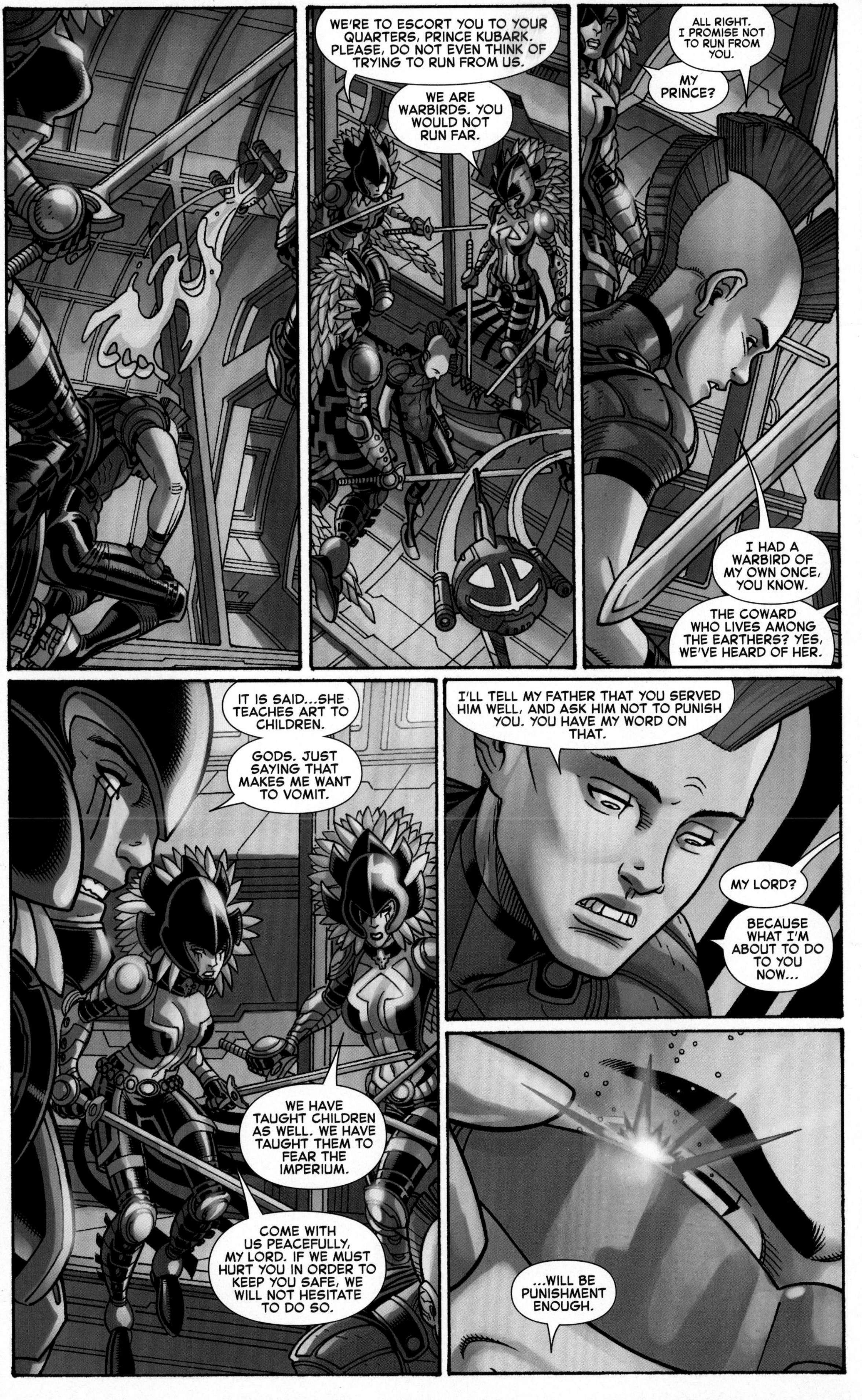
WE'RE TO ESCORT YOU TO YOUR QUARTERS, PRINCE KUBARK. PLEASE, DO NOT EVEN THINK OF TRYING TO RUN FROM US.
WE ARE WARBIRDS. YOU WOULD NOT RUN FAR.
ALL RIGHT. I PROMISE NOT TO RUN FROM YOU.
MY PRINCE?
I HAD A WARBIRD OF MY OWN ONCE, YOU KNOW.
THE COWARD WHO LIVES AMONG THE EARTHERS? YES, WE'VE HEARD OF HER.
IT IS SAID...SHE TEACHES ART TO CHILDREN.
GODS. JUST SAYING THAT MAKES ME WANT TO VOMIT.
WE HAVE TAUGHT CHILDREN AS WELL. WE HAVE TAUGHT THEM TO FEAR THE IMPERIUM.
COME WITH US PEACEFULLY, MY LORD. IF WE MUST HURT YOU IN ORDER TO KEEP YOU SAFE, WE WILL NOT HESITATE TO DO SO.
I'LL TELL MY FATHER THAT YOU SERVED HIM WELL, AND ASK HIM NOT TO PUNISH YOU. YOU HAVE MY WORD ON THAT.
MY LORD?
BECAUSE WHAT I'M ABOUT TO DO TO YOU NOW...
...WILL BE PUNISHMENT ENOUGH.

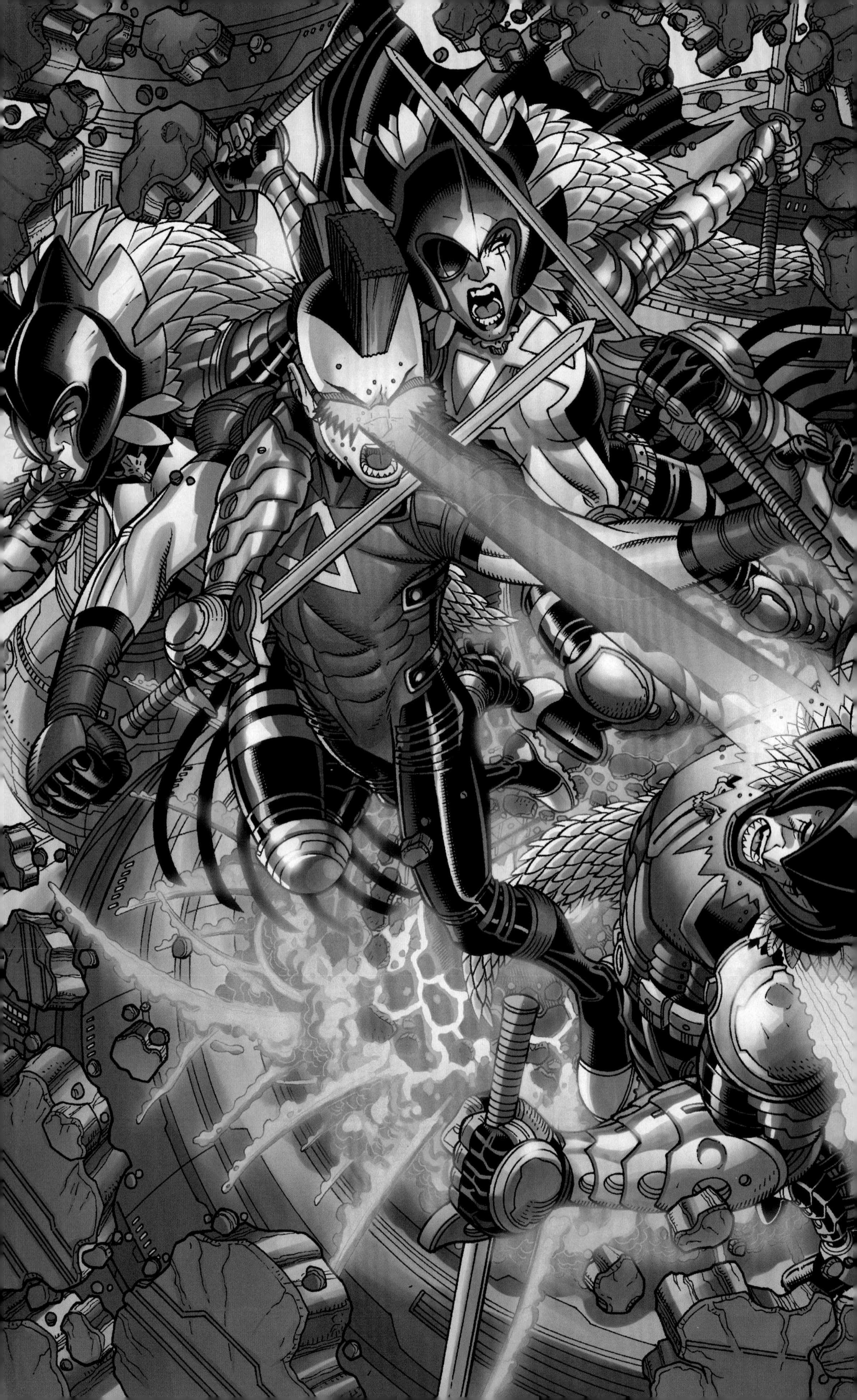

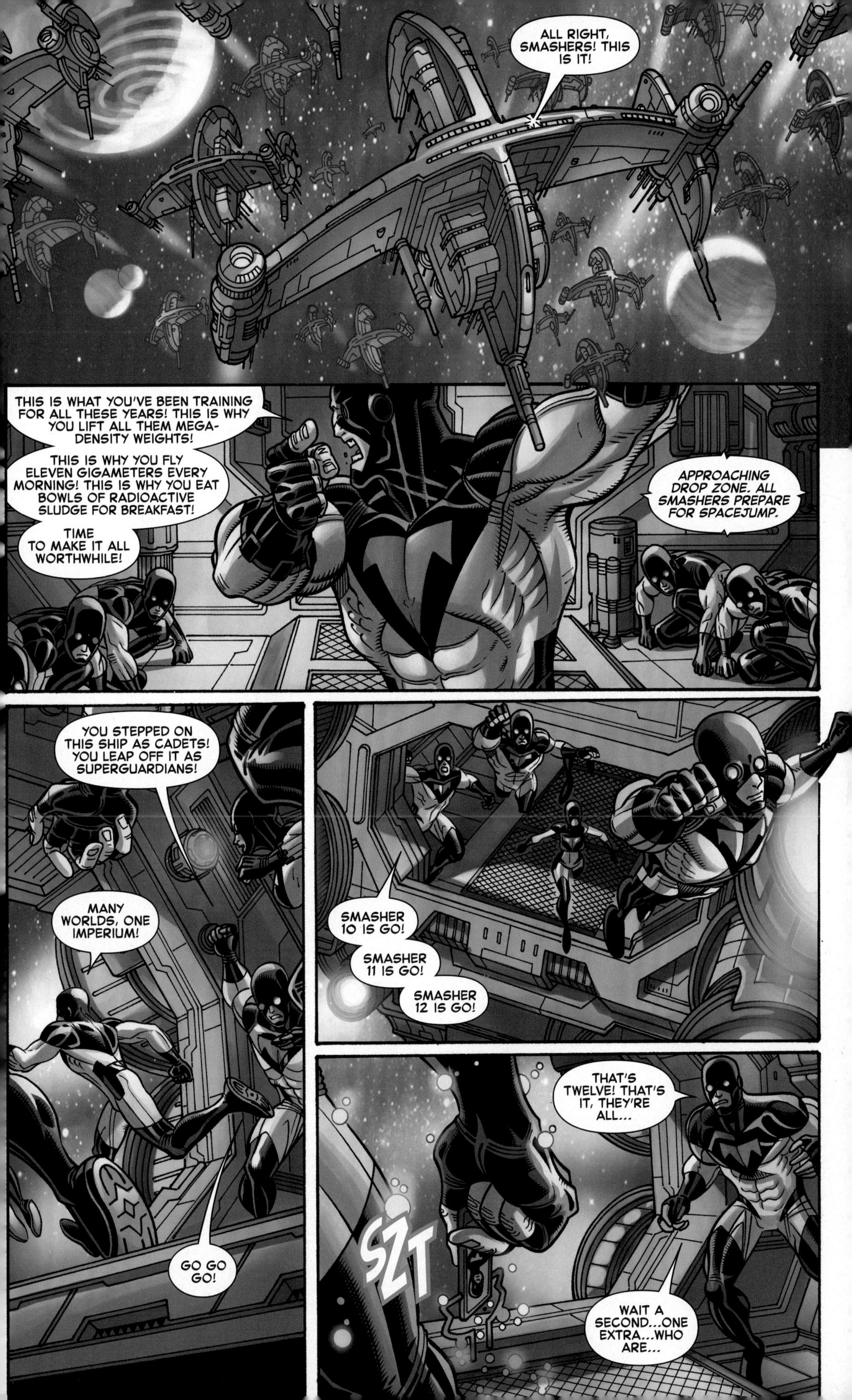
ALL RIGHT, SMASHERS! THIS IS IT!
THIS IS WHAT YOU'VE BEEN TRAINING FOR ALL THESE YEARS! THIS IS WHY YOU LIFT ALL THEM MEGA-DENSITY WEIGHTS!
THIS IS WHY YOU FLY ELEVEN GIGAMETERS EVERY MORNING! THIS IS WHY YOU EAT BOWLS OF RADIOACTIVE SLUDGE FOR BREAKFAST!
TIME TO MAKE IT ALL WORTHWHILE!
APPROACHING DROP ZONE. ALL SMASHERS PREPARE FOR SPACEJUMP.
YOU STEPPED ON THIS SHIP AS CADETS! YOU LEAP OFF IT AS SUPERGUARDIANS!
MANY WORLDS, ONE IMPERIUM!
GO GO GO!
SMASHER 10 IS GO!
SMASHER 11 IS GO!
SMASHER 12 IS GO!
THAT'S TWELVE! THAT'S IT, THEY'RE ALL...
SZT
WAIT A SECOND...ONE EXTRA...WHO ARE...

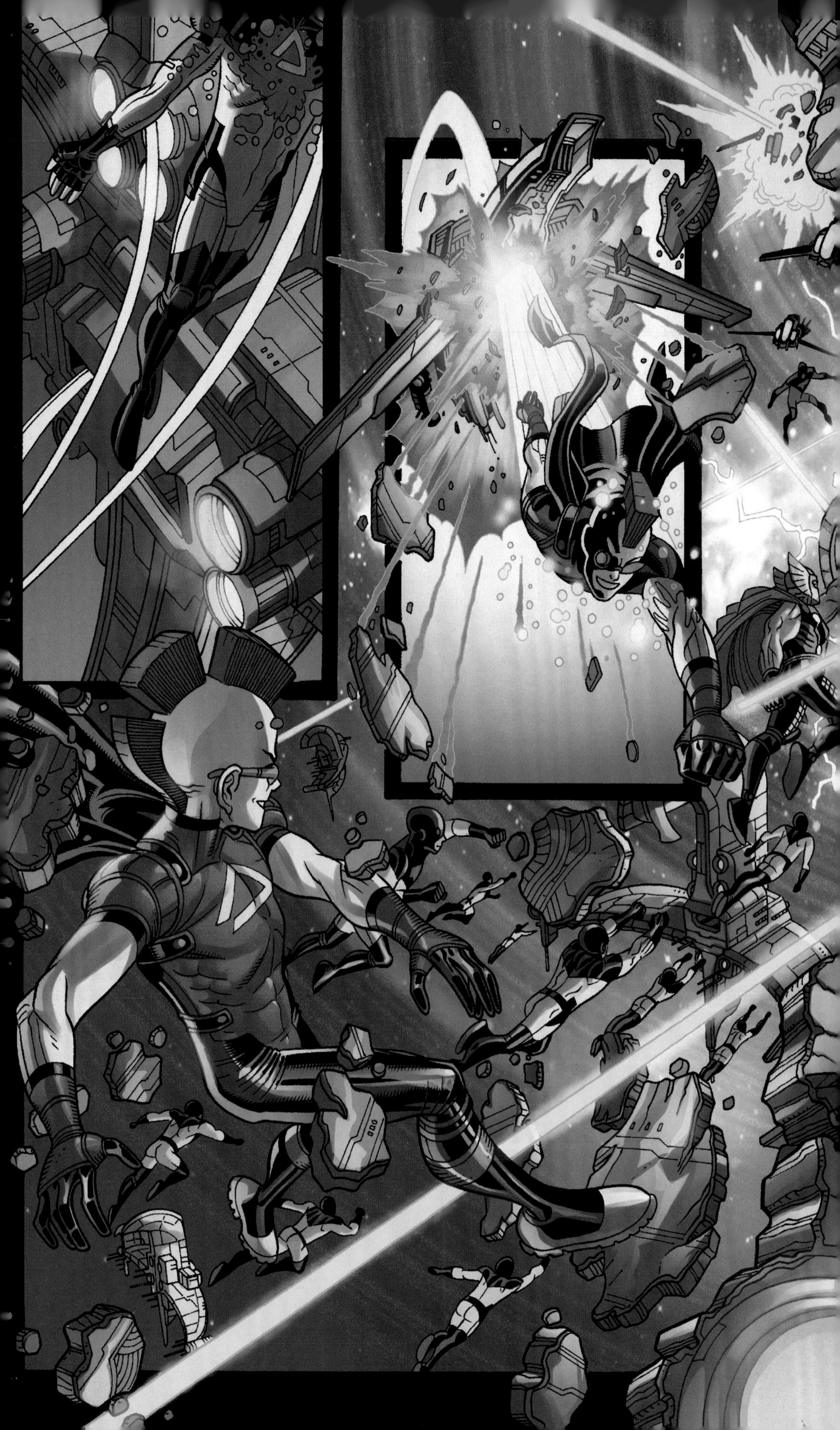

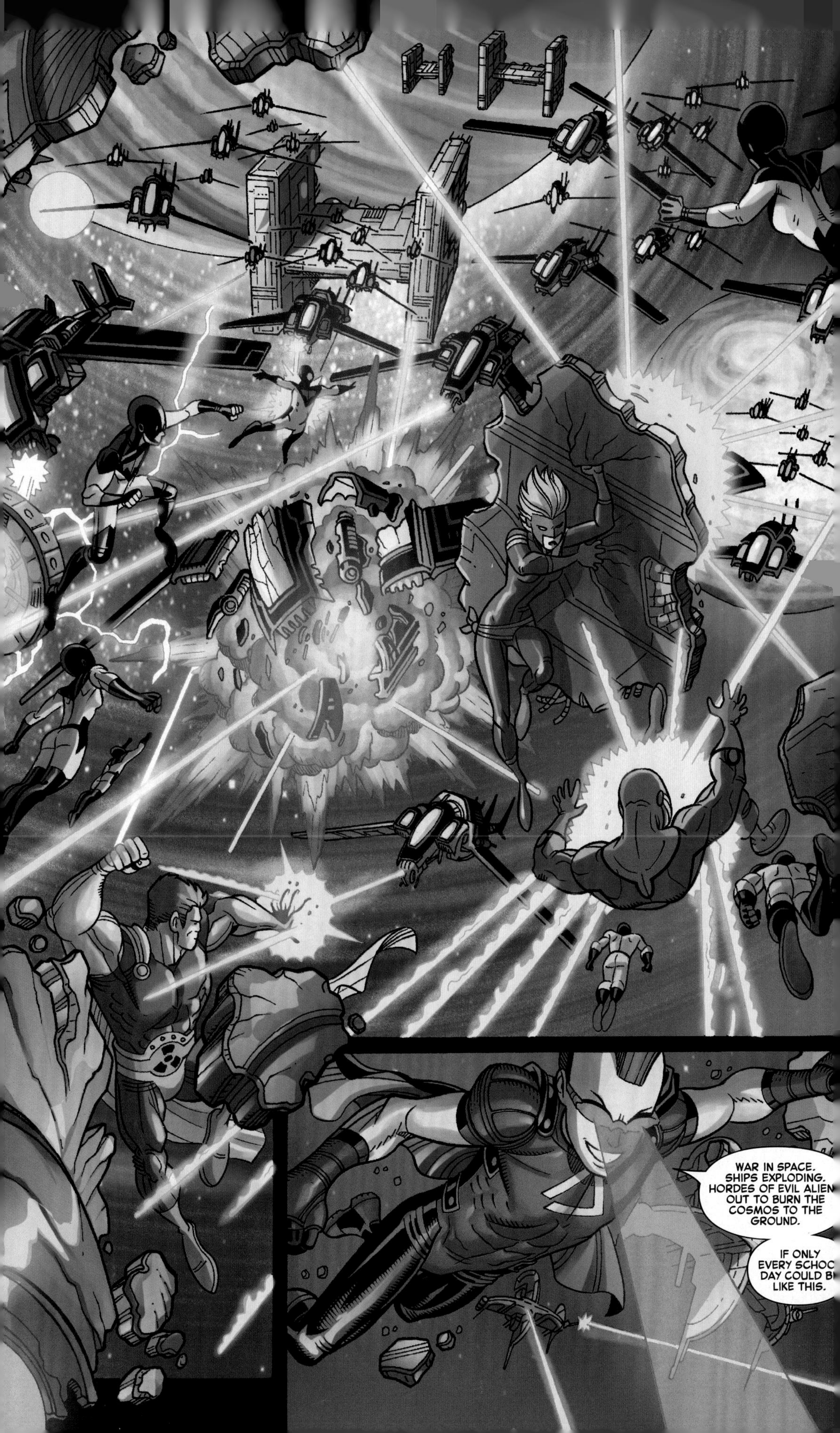
WAR IN SPACE. SHIPS EXPLODING. HORDES OF EVIL ALIEN OUT TO BURN THE COSMOS TO THE GROUND.
IF ONLY EVERY SCHOO DAY COULD B LIKE THIS.

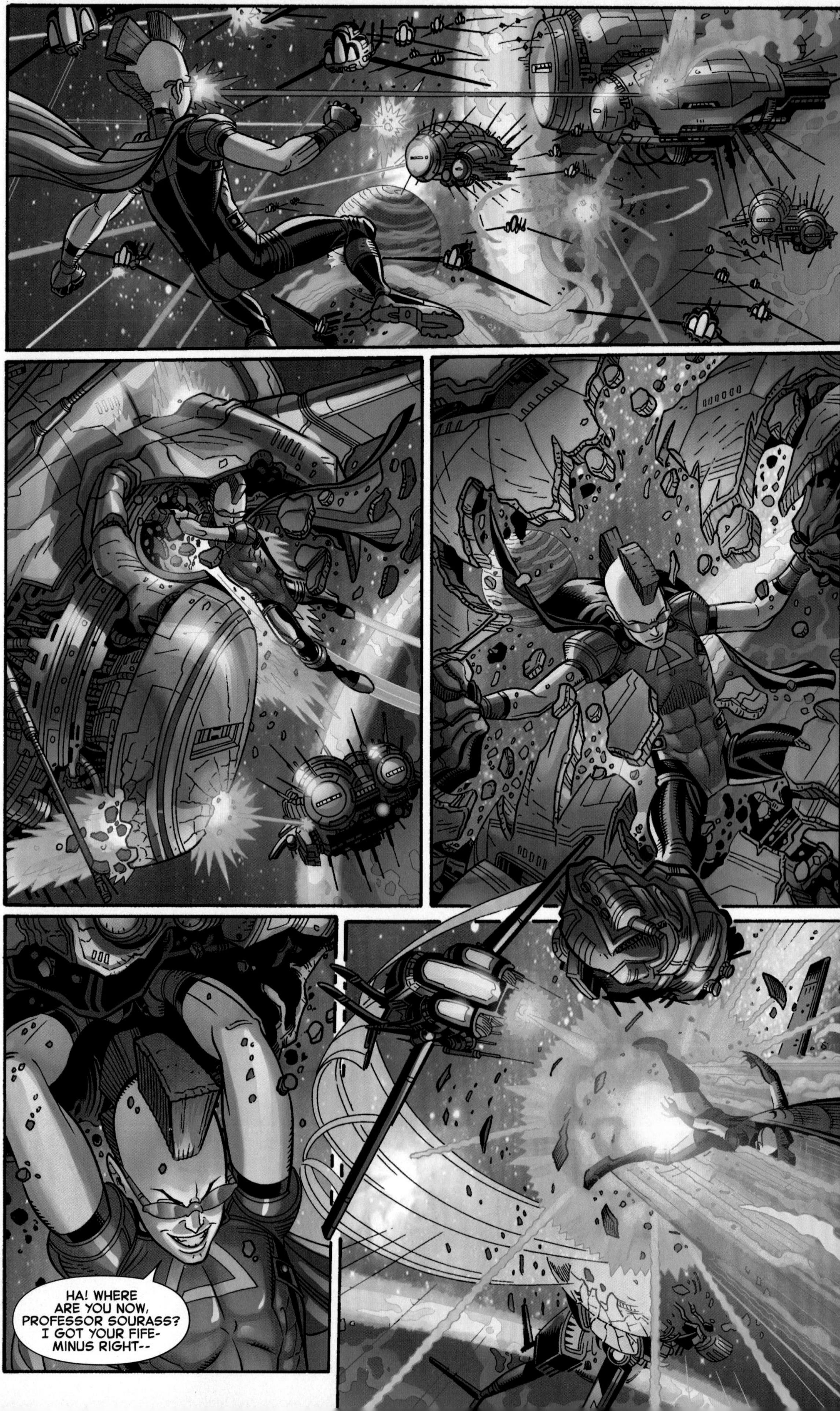
HA! WHERE ARE YOU NOW, PROFESSOR SOURASS? I GOT YOUR FIFE-MINUS RIGHT--

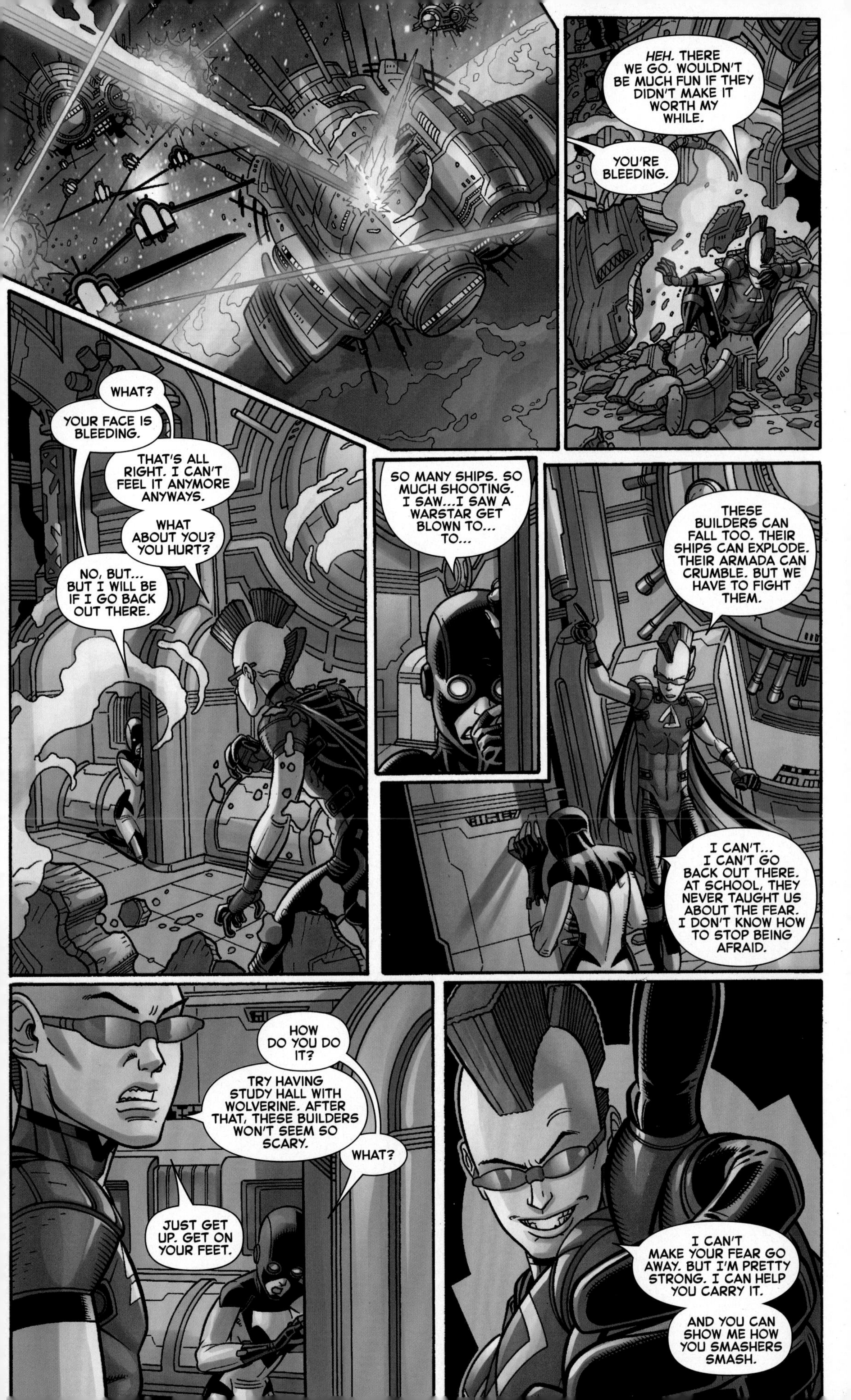
HEH. THERE WE GO. WOULDN'T BE MUCH FUN IF THEY DIDN'T MAKE IT WORTH MY WHILE.
YOU'RE BLEEDING.
WHAT?
YOUR FACE IS BLEEDING.
THAT'S ALL RIGHT. I CAN'T FEEL IT ANYMORE ANYWAYS.
WHAT ABOUT YOU? YOU HURT?
NO, BUT... BUT I WILL BE IF I GO BACK OUT THERE.
SO MANY SHIPS. SO MUCH SHOOTING. I SAW...I SAW A WARSTAR GET BLOWN TO... TO...
THESE BUILDERS CAN FALL TOO. THEIR SHIPS CAN EXPLODE. THEIR ARMADA CAN CRUMBLE. BUT WE HAVE TO FIGHT THEM.
I CAN'T... I CAN'T GO BACK OUT THERE. AT SCHOOL, THEY NEVER TAUGHT US ABOUT THE FEAR. I DON'T KNOW HOW TO STOP BEING AFRAID.
HOW DO YOU DO IT?
TRY HAVING STUDY HALL WITH WOLVERINE. AFTER THAT, THESE BUILDERS WON'T SEEM SO SCARY.
WHAT?
JUST GET UP. GET ON YOUR FEET.
I CAN'T MAKE YOUR FEAR GO AWAY. BUT I'M PRETTY STRONG. I CAN HELP YOU CARRY IT.
AND YOU CAN SHOW ME HOW YOU SMASHERS SMASH.

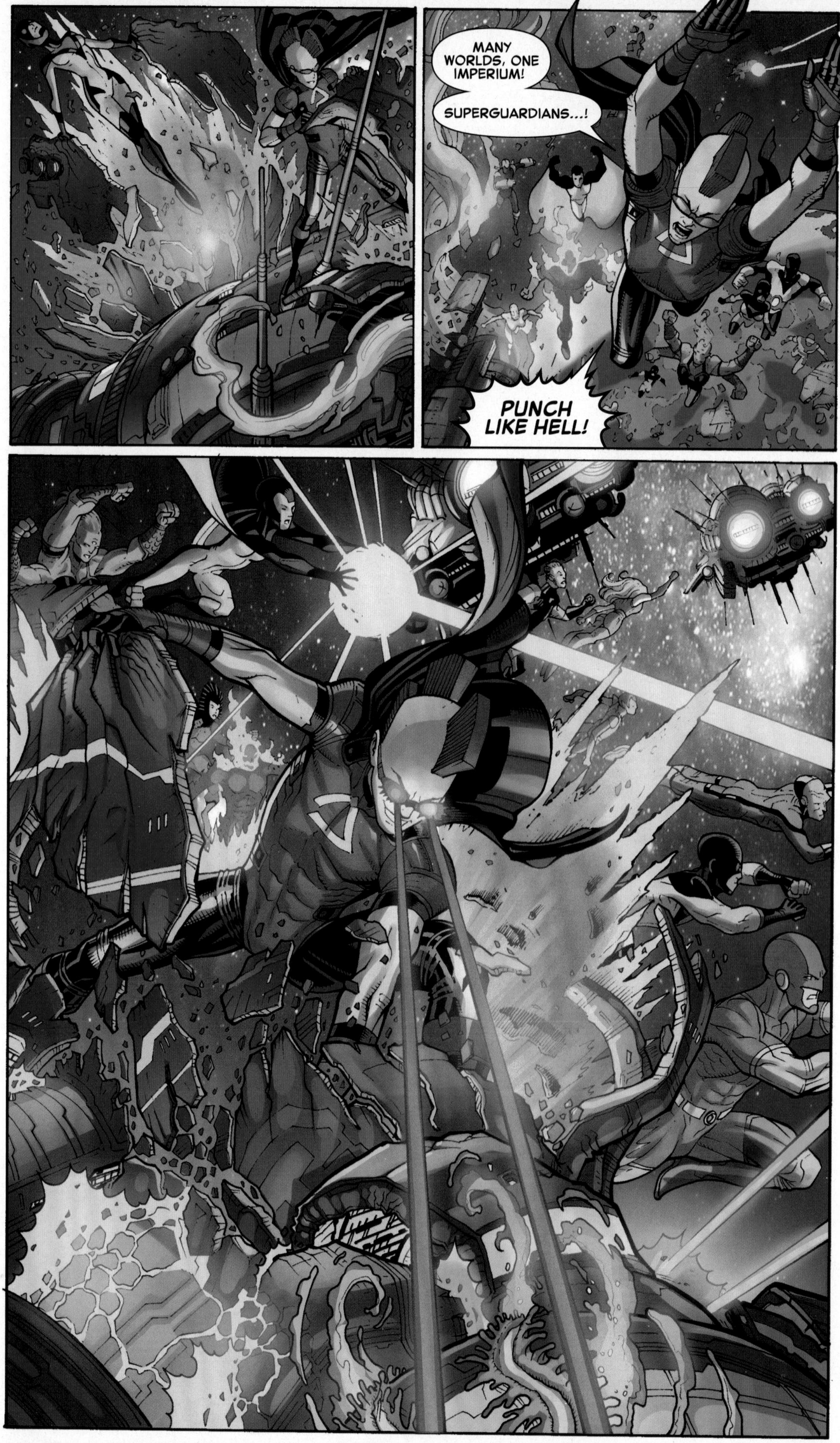
MANY WORLDS, ONE IMPERIUM!
SUPERGUARDIANS...!
PUNCH LIKE HELL!

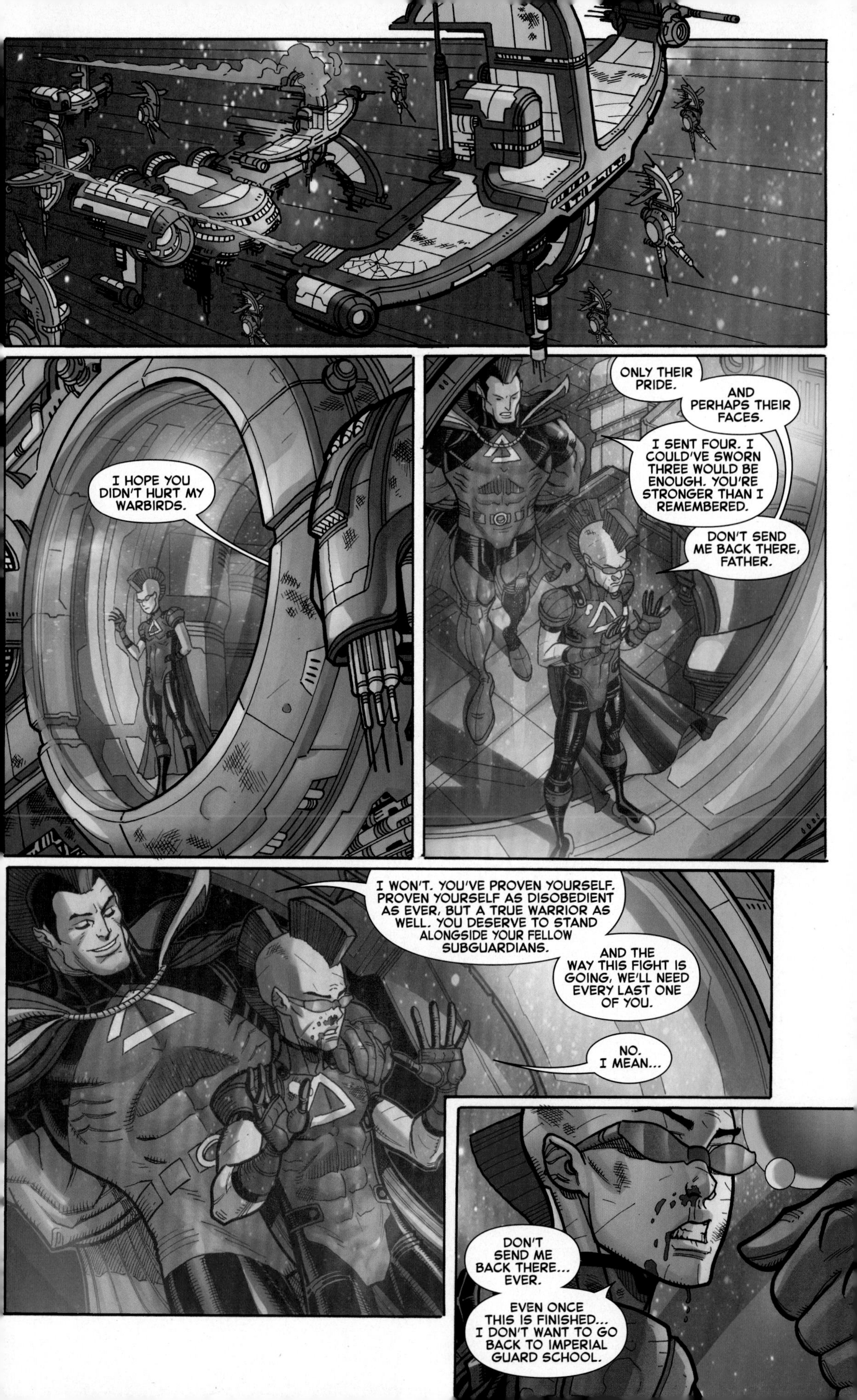
I HOPE YOU DIDN'T HURT MY WARBIRDS.
ONLY THEIR PRIDE.
AND PERHAPS THEIR FACES.
I SENT FOUR. I COULD'VE SWORN THREE WOULD BE ENOUGH. YOU'RE STRONGER THAN I REMEMBERED.
DON'T SEND ME BACK THERE, FATHER.
I WON'T. YOU'VE PROVEN YOURSELF. PROVEN YOURSELF AS DISOBEDIENT AS EVER, BUT A TRUE WARRIOR AS WELL. YOU DESERVE TO STAND ALONGSIDE YOUR FELLOW SUBGUARDIANS.
AND THE WAY THIS FIGHT IS GOING, WE'LL NEED EVERY LAST ONE OF YOU.
NO. I MEAN...
DON'T SEND ME BACK THERE... EVER.
EVEN ONCE THIS IS FINISHED... I DON'T WANT TO GO BACK TO IMPERIAL GUARD SCHOOL.

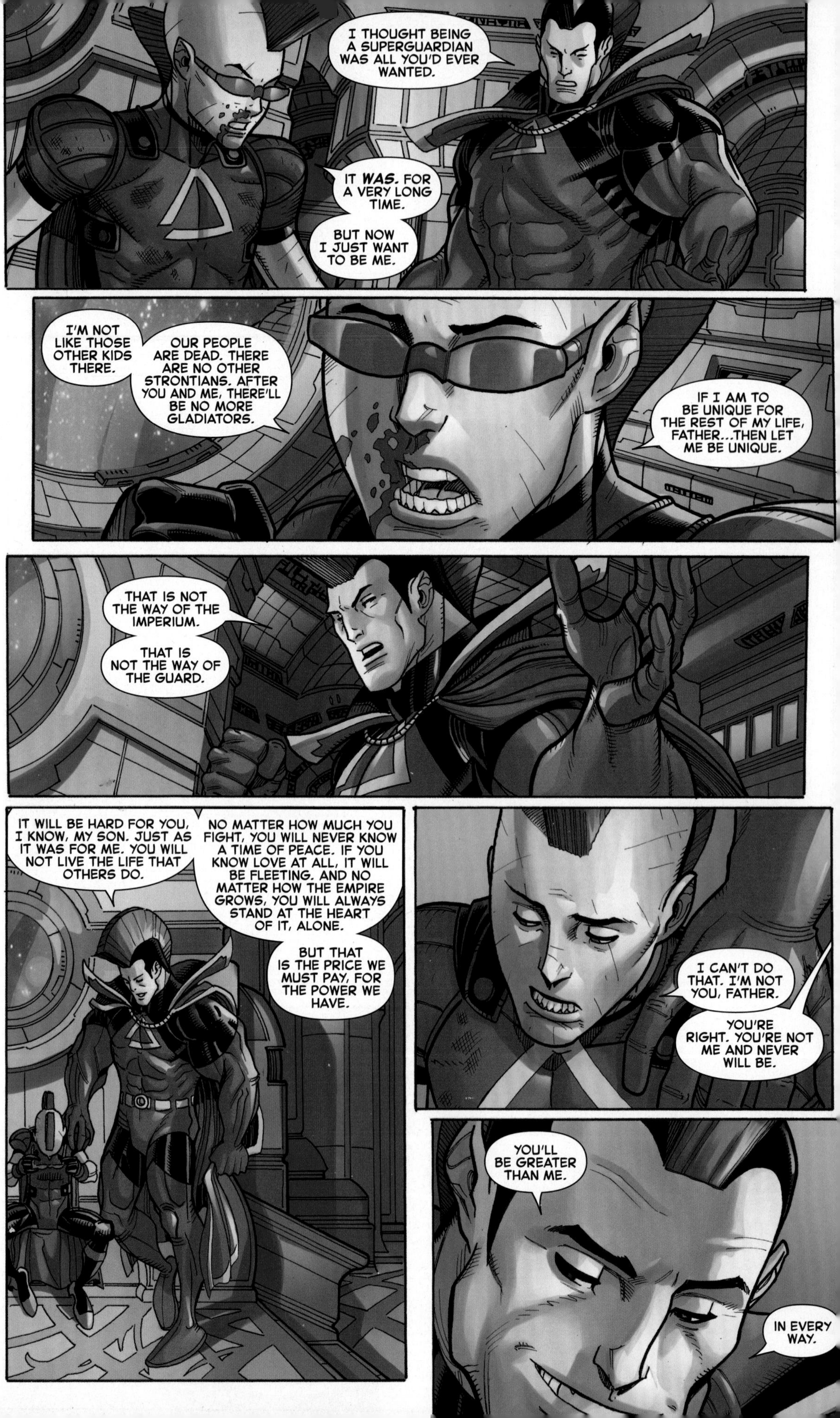
I THOUGHT BEING A SUPERGUARDIAN WAS ALL YOU'D EVER WANTED.
IT WAS. FOR A VERY LONG TIME.
BUT NOW I JUST WANT TO BE ME.
I'M NOT LIKE THOSE OTHER KIDS THERE.
OUR PEOPLE ARE DEAD. THERE ARE NO OTHER STRONTIANS. AFTER YOU AND ME, THERE'LL BE NO MORE GLADIATORS.
IF I AM TO BE UNIQUE FOR THE REST OF MY LIFE, FATHER...THEN LET ME BE UNIQUE.
THAT IS NOT THE WAY OF THE IMPERIUM.
THAT IS NOT THE WAY OF THE GUARD.
IT WILL BE HARD FOR YOU, I KNOW, MY SON. JUST AS IT WAS FOR ME. YOU WILL NOT LIVE THE LIFE THAT OTHERS DO.
NO MATTER HOW MUCH YOU FIGHT, YOU WILL NEVER KNOW A TIME OF PEACE. IF YOU KNOW LOVE AT ALL, IT WILL BE FLEETING. AND NO MATTER HOW THE EMPIRE GROWS, YOU WILL ALWAYS STAND AT THE HEART OF IT, ALONE.
BUT THAT IS THE PRICE WE MUST PAY, FOR THE POWER WE HAVE.
I CAN'T DO THAT. I'M NOT YOU, FATHER.
YOU'RE RIGHT. YOU'RE NOT ME AND NEVER WILL BE.
YOU'LL BE GREATER THAN ME.
IN EVERY WAY.

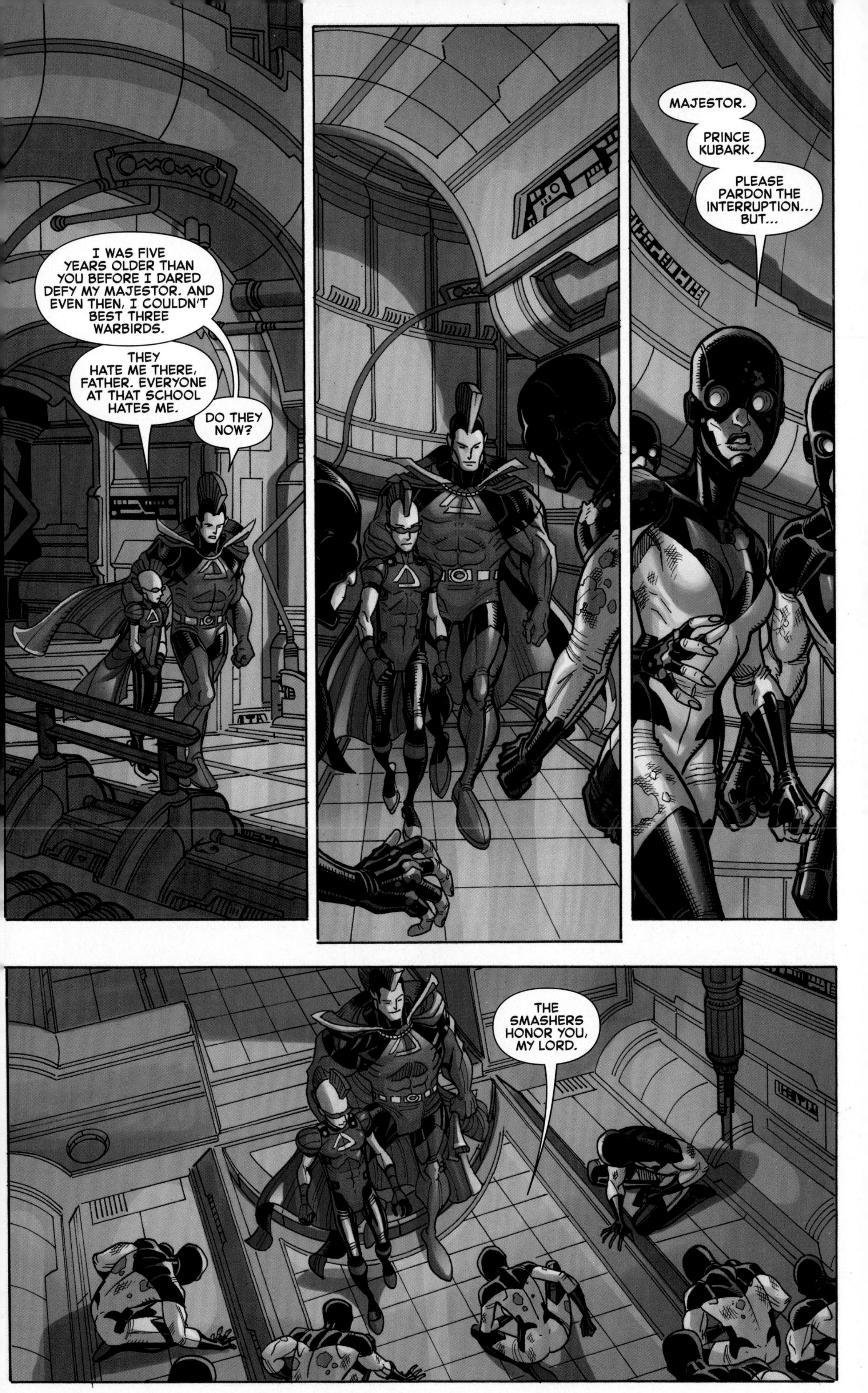
I WAS FIVE YEARS OLDER THAN YOU BEFORE I DARED DEFY MY MAJESTOR. AND EVEN THEN, I COULDN'T BEST THREE WARBIRDS.
THEY HATE ME THERE, FATHER. EVERYONE AT THAT SCHOOL HATES ME.
DO THEY NOW?
MAJESTOR.
PRINCE KUBARK.
PLEASE PARDON THE INTERRUPTION... BUT...
THE SMASHERS HONOR YOU, MY LORD.

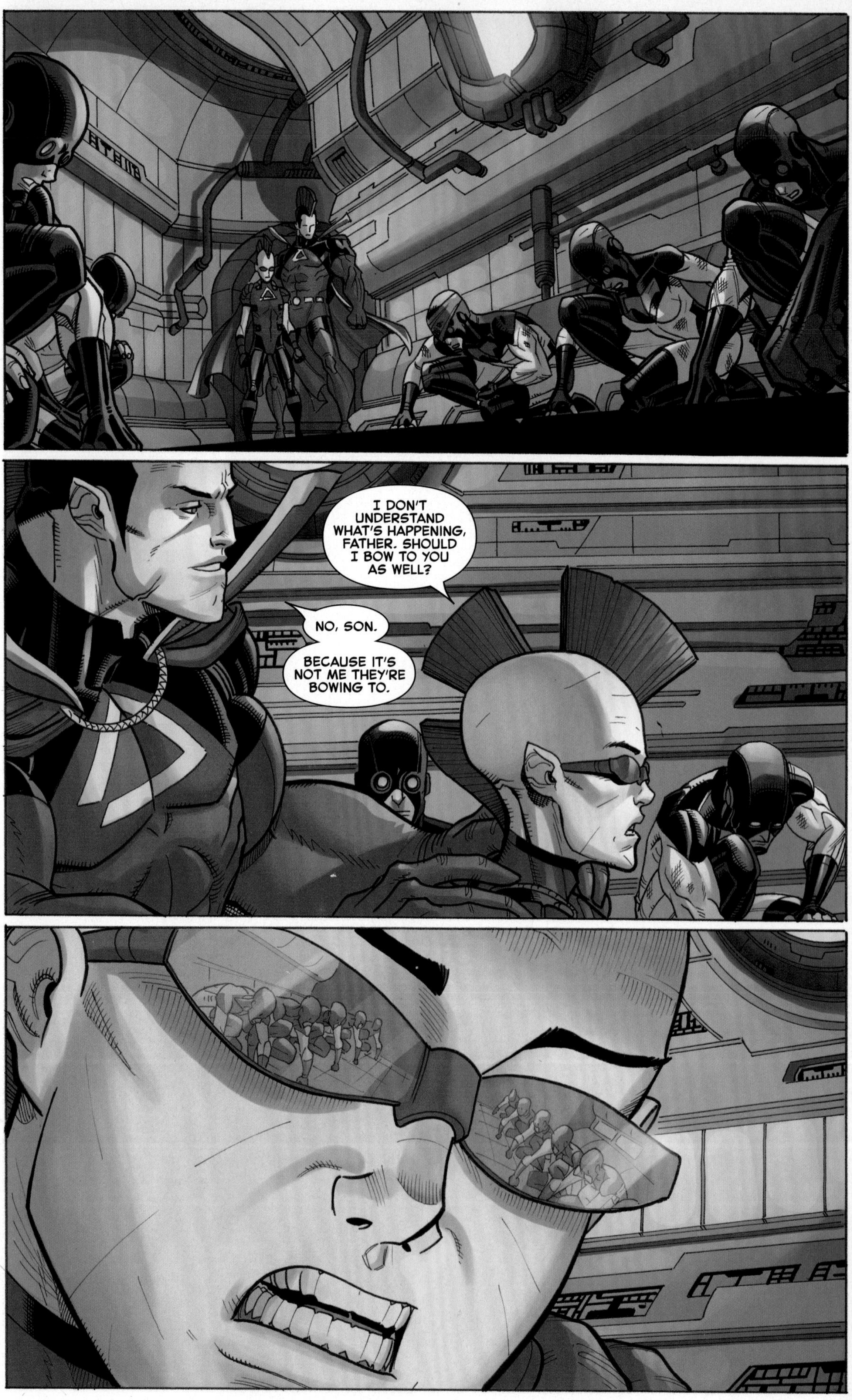
I DON'T UNDERSTAND WHAT'S HAPPENING, FATHER. SHOULD I BOW TO YOU AS WELL?
NO, SON.
BECAUSE IT'S NOT ME THEY'RE BOWING TO.

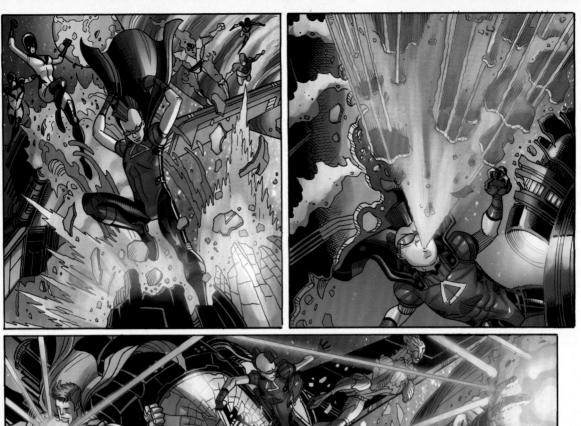

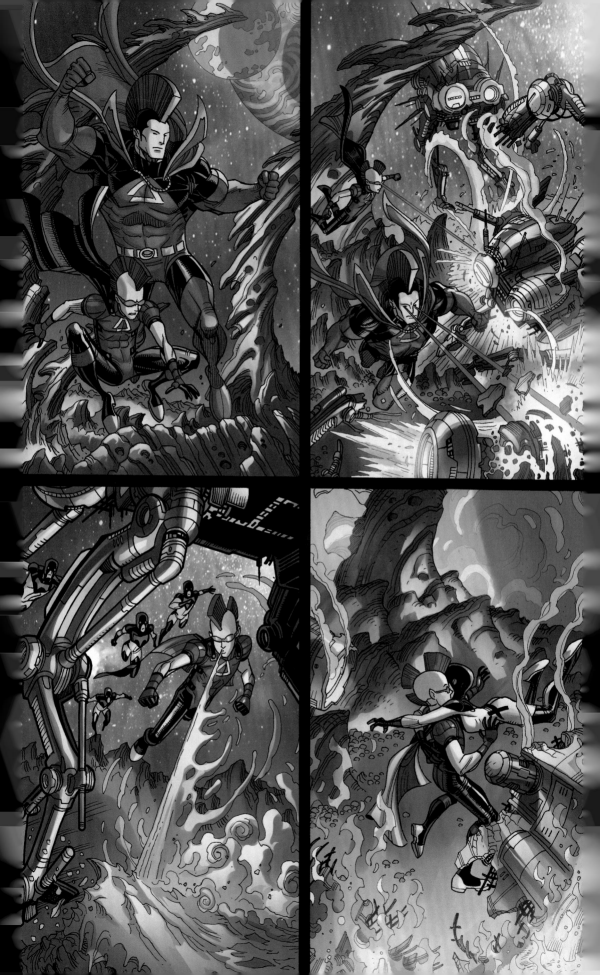

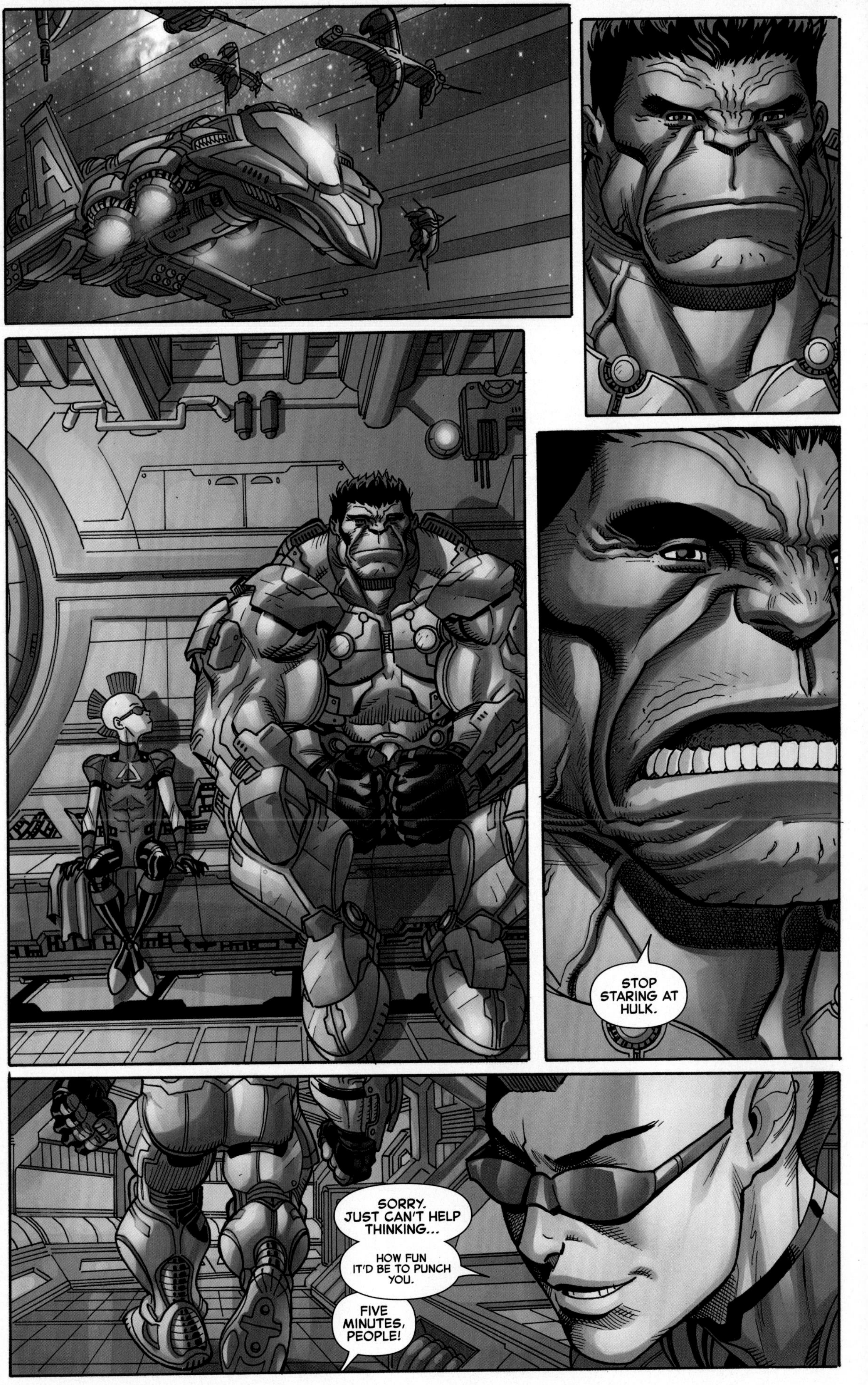
STOP STARING AT HULK.
SORRY. JUST CAN'T HELP THINKING...
HOW FUN IT'D BE TO PUNCH YOU.
FIVE MINUTES, PEOPLE!

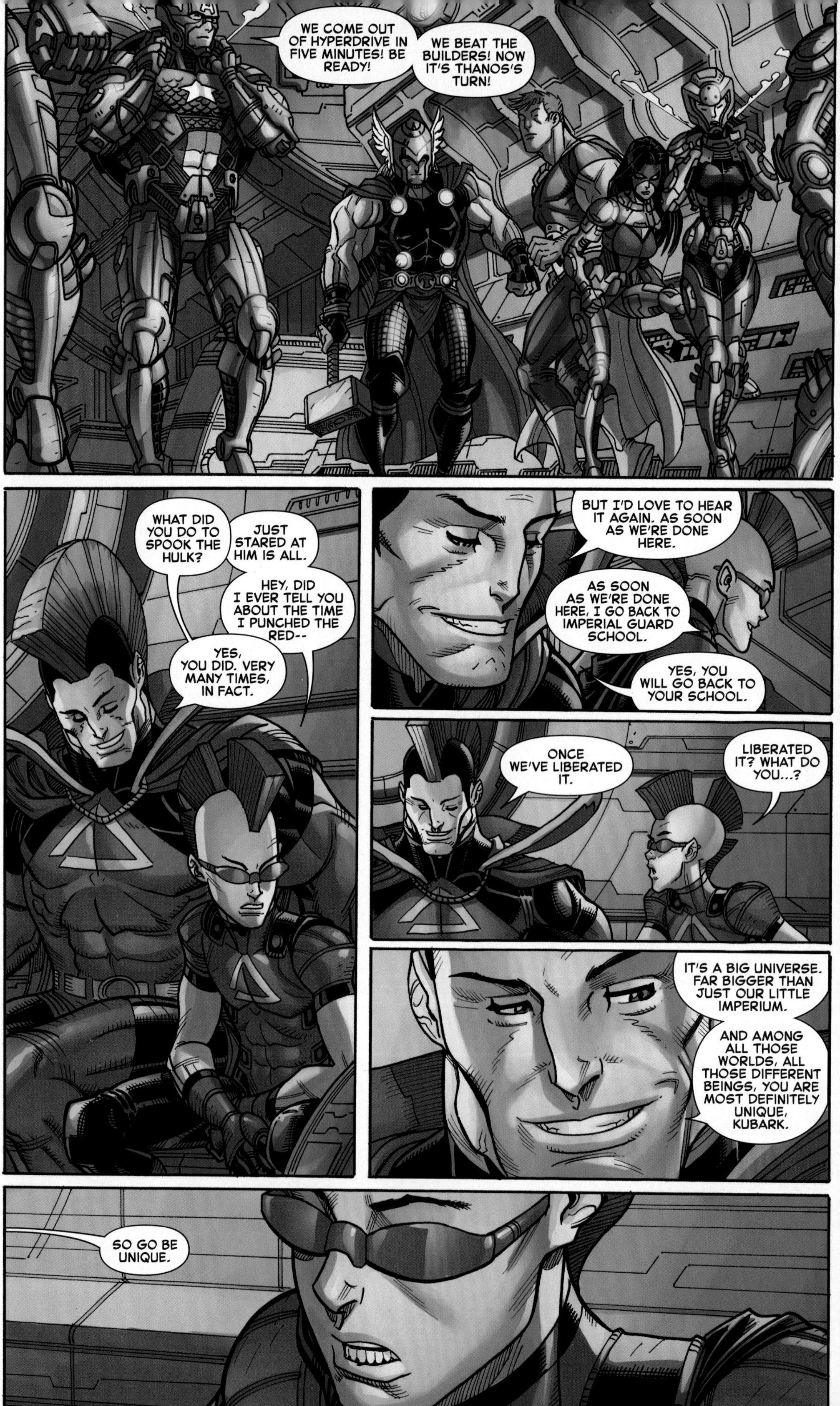
WE COME OUT OF HYPERDRIVE IN FIVE MINUTES! BE READY!
WE BEAT THE BUILDERS! NOW IT'S THANOS'S TURN!
WHAT DID YOU DO TO SPOOK THE HULK?
JUST STARED AT HIM IS ALL.
HEY, DID I EVER TELL YOU ABOUT THE TIME I PUNCHED THE RED--
YES, YOU DID. VERY MANY TIMES, IN FACT.
BUT I'D LOVE TO HEAR IT AGAIN. AS SOON AS WE'RE DONE HERE.
AS SOON AS WE'RE DONE HERE, I GO BACK TO IMPERIAL GUARD SCHOOL.
YES, YOU WILL GO BACK TO YOUR SCHOOL.
ONCE WE'VE LIBERATED IT.
LIBERATED IT? WHAT DO YOU...?
IT'S A BIG UNIVERSE. FAR BIGGER THAN JUST OUR LITTLE IMPERIUM.
AND AMONG ALL THOSE WORLDS, ALL THOSE DIFFERENT BEINGS, YOU ARE MOST DEFINITELY UNIQUE, KUBARK.
SO GO BE UNIQUE.

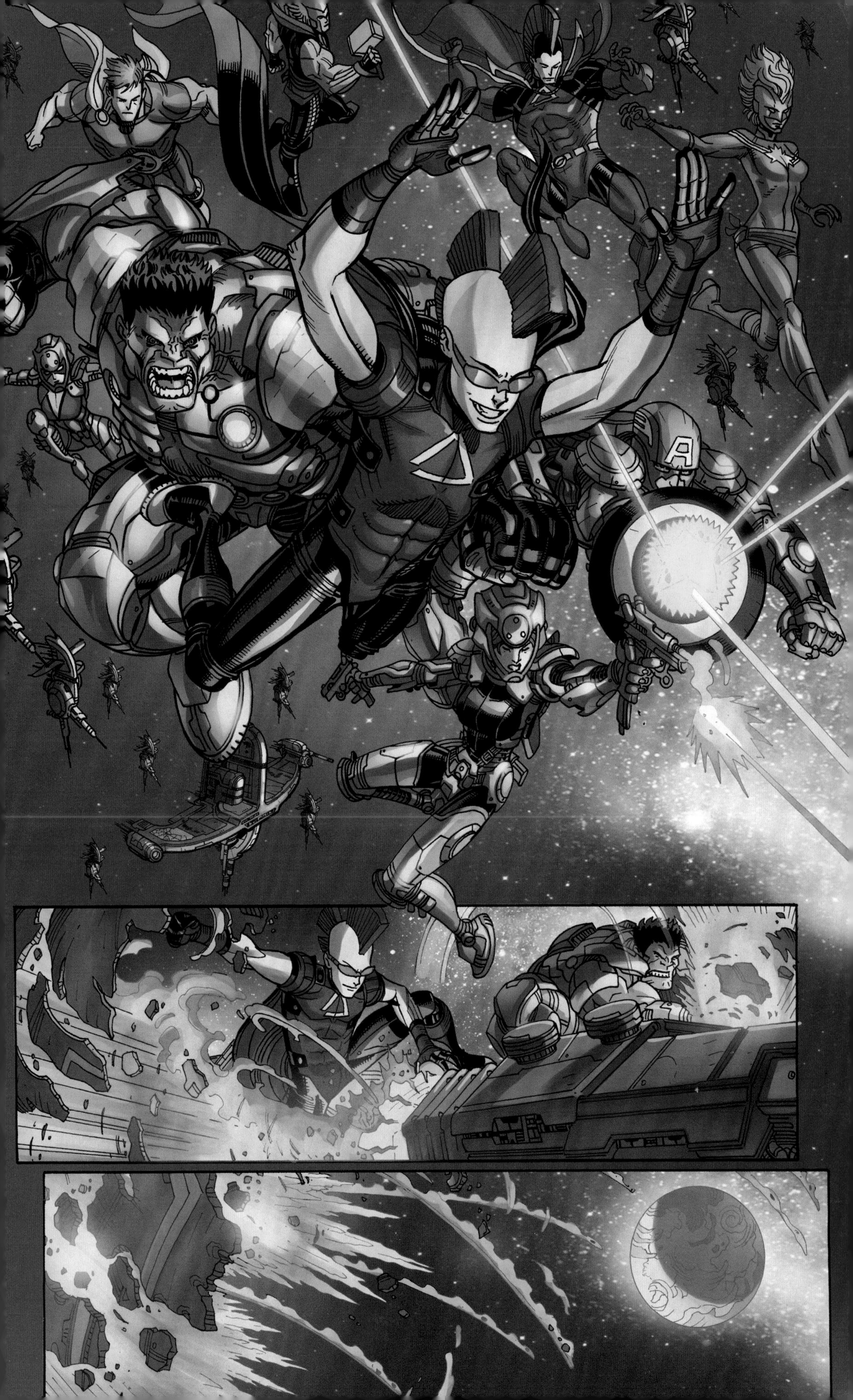

AND THEN WE BEAT THANOS'S FLEET OF SPACE PIRATES AND HELPED THE AVENGERS LIBERATE THE EARTH.

YOU'RE WELCOME.

SOUNDS LIKE QUITE AN ADVENTURE.

ALSO, I KISSED A SMASHER. DID I MENTION THAT PART? AND BEAT THOR AT ARM WRESTLING.

RIGHT. I'M SURE YOU DID. WHAT ABOUT THIS IMPERIAL GUARD SCHOOL? I WOULDN'T MIND HEARING MORE ABOUT THAT.

ASSIGNMENT: ORAL REPO

W DURING T O ION OF EAR

THE SCHOOL? WELL, IT WAS...

IT WAS QUITE AWESOME, OF COURSE. LOTS OF PUNCHING AND... AND NEVER ONCE WERE WE FORCED TO MEDIATE.

I WAS, OF COURSE, THE MOST POPULAR KID THERE.

WOW, YOU'RE RIGHT, SOUNDS PRETTY GREAT. SO TELL ME ONE THING, THEN...

DURING THANOS ON OF EARTH?

WHY'D YOU COME BACK?

TODAYS ASSIGN

WHAT I DI OCCUPA

MY FATHER MADE ME, OF COURSE. I'M BEING...PUNISHED AGAIN FOR...EXCESSIVE PUNCHING.

THIS IS PUNISHMENT, BEING HERE WITH YOU PEOPLE.

TERRIBLE TERRIBLE PUNISHMENT.

WARNING, THIS SCHOOL IS CURRENTLY UNDER ATTACK BY SUBTERRANEAN FORCES LED BY THE MOLE MAN.

ANYBODY LEAVES THIS ROOM, I CUT YOUR LEGS OFF.

SNIKT

WONDERFUL, WONDERFUL PUNISHMENT.

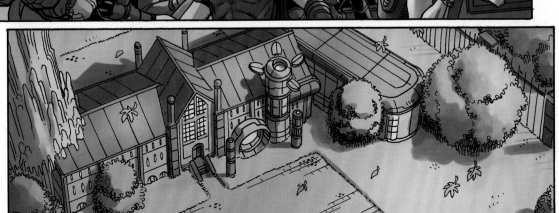

THE WOLVERINE SCHOOL FOR GIFTED YOUNGSTERS

PART ONE: THE DAY S.H.I.E.L.D. SHOWED UP

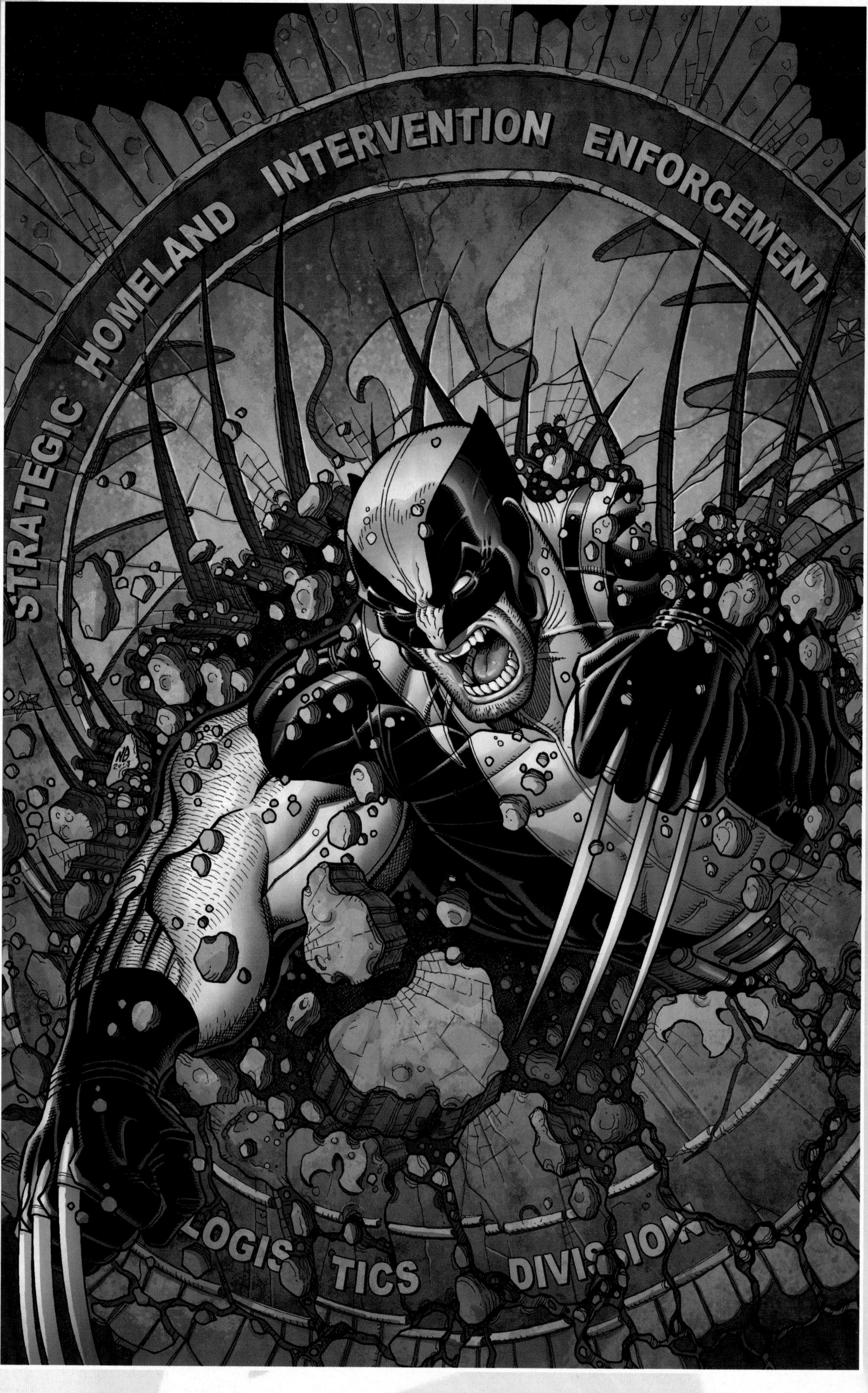
STRATEGIC HOMELAND INTERVENTION ENFORCEMENT
LOGIS TICS DIVISION

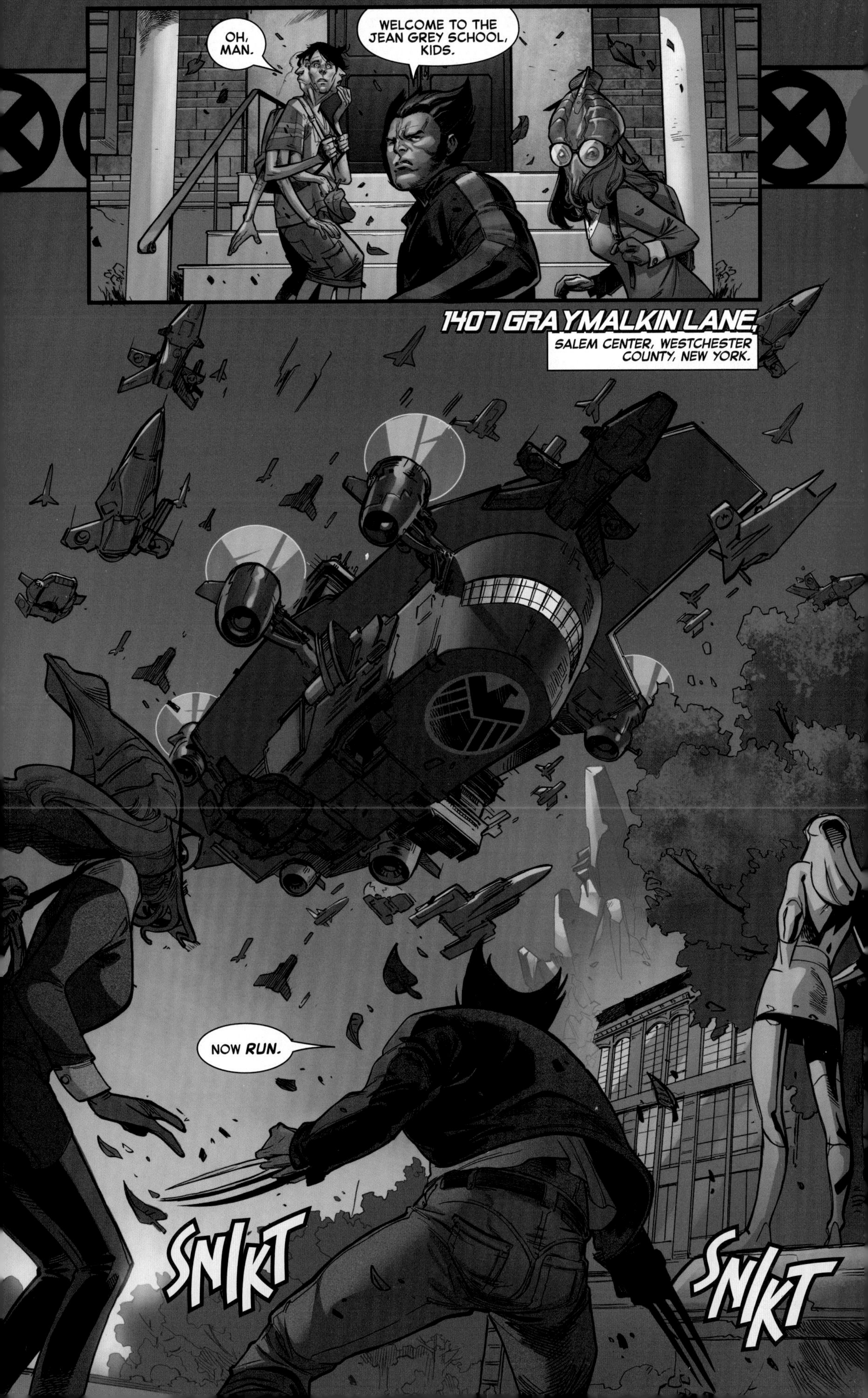

OH, MAN.
WELCOME TO THE JEAN GREY SCHOOL, KIDS.
1407 GRAYMALKIN LANE,
SALEM CENTER, WESTCHESTER COUNTY, NEW YORK.
NOW RUN.
SNIKT
SNIKT

WOLVERINE and the X-MEN

If you were born different with mutant super-powers, the Jean Grey School for Higher Learning is the school for you. Founded by Wolverine and staffed by experienced X-Men, you will learn everything you need to know to survive in a world that hates and fears you.

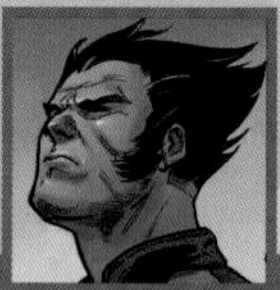

WOLVERINE
Clawed Headmaster

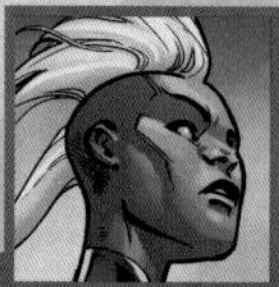

STORM
Weather-controlling educator

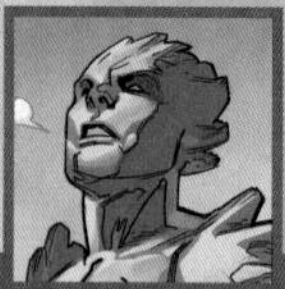

ICEMAN
Arctic educator

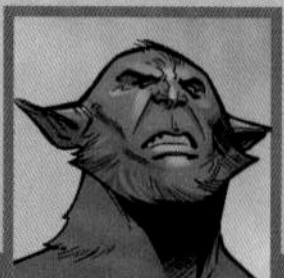

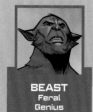

BEAST
Feral Genius

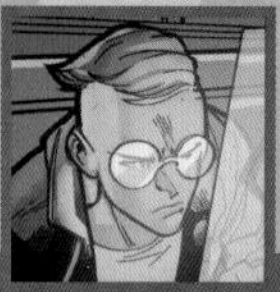

KID OMEGA
Telepathic Student

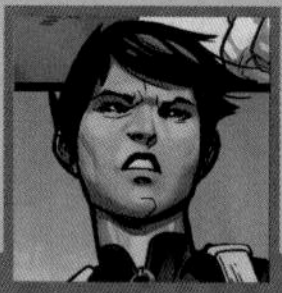

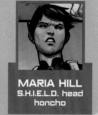

MARIA HILL
S.H.I.E.L.D. head honcho

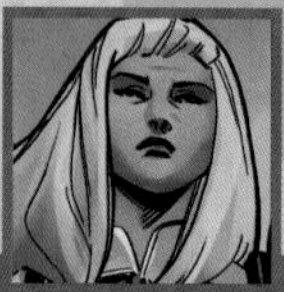

DAZZLER
Makes sound into energy

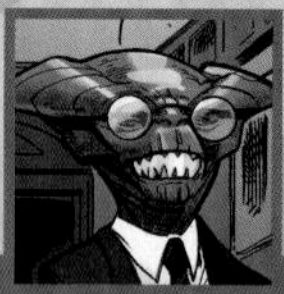

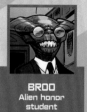

BROO
Alien honor student

PREVIOUSLY

A LOT HAS HAPPENED IN THE WORLD OF THE X-MEN RECENTLY – A GROUP OF TIME TRAVELING MUTANTS CLAIMED TO BE THE X-MEN OF THE FUTURE – BUT WERE IN FACT A VILLAINOUS FUTURE BROTHERHOOD OF MUTANTS. DURING THEIR DESPERATE BATTLE TO DEFEAT THEIR FUTURE ENEMIES (AND PROTECT THE VERY SPACE-TIME CONTINUUM ITSELF), INTERNATIONAL PEACEKEEPING FORCE S.H.I.E.L.D. LAUNCHED THE FULL MIGHT OF THEIR ARSENAL ON THE TEAM – INCLUDING THEIR OWN SENTINELS, ROBOTS ONCE DESIGNED TO EXTERMINATE THE MUTANT RACE. WOLVERINE AND HIS TEAM ARE (FOR THE MOST PART) BACK IN WESTCHESTER – BUT THEY HAVE A TERRIFYING NEW WORLD TO CONFRONT...

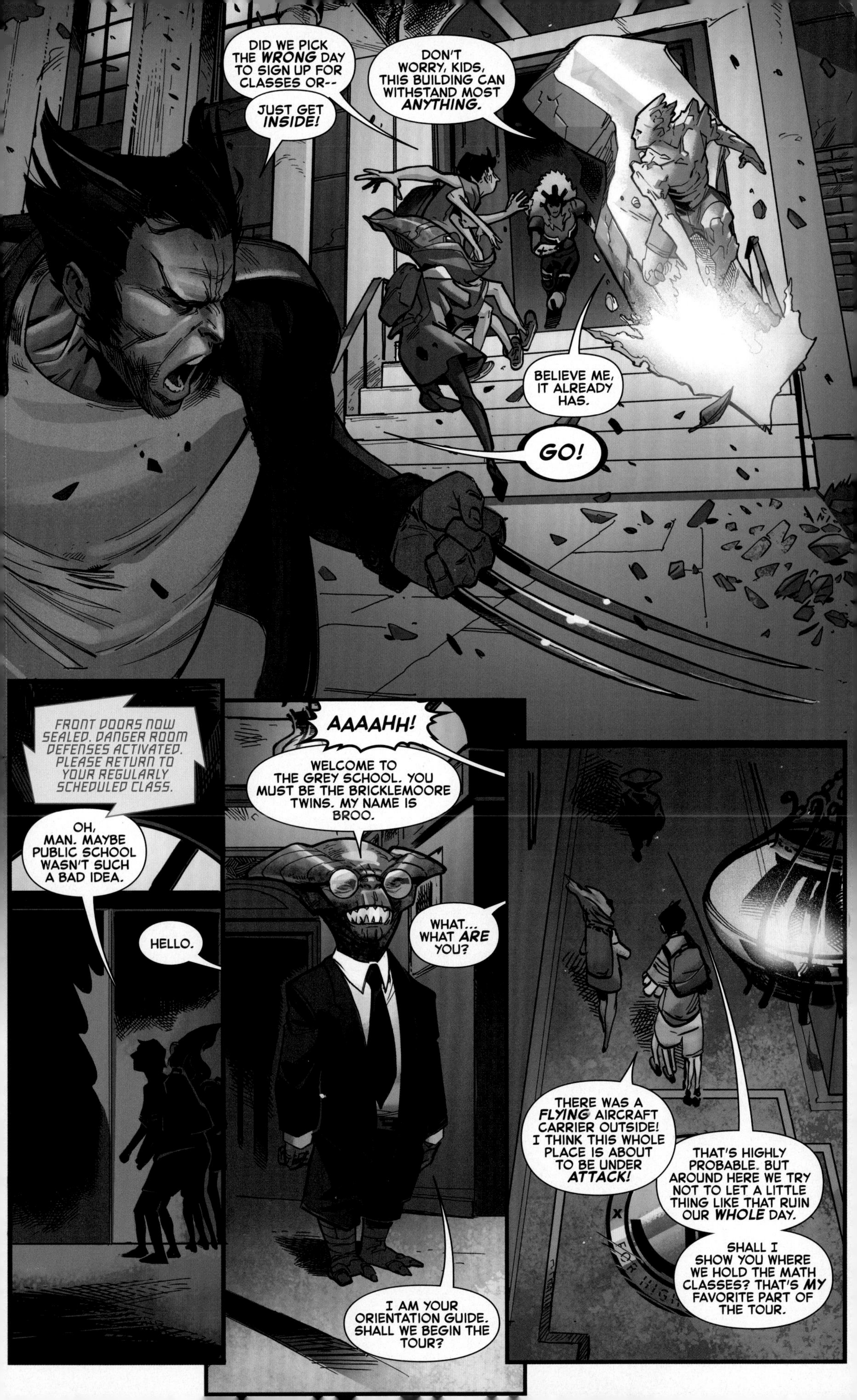
DID WE PICK THE WRONG DAY TO SIGN UP FOR CLASSES OR--
JUST GET INSIDE!
DON'T WORRY, KIDS, THIS BUILDING CAN WITHSTAND MOST ANYTHING.
BELIEVE ME, IT ALREADY HAS.
GO!
FRONT DOORS NOW SEALED. DANGER ROOM DEFENSES ACTIVATED. PLEASE RETURN TO YOUR REGULARLY SCHEDULED CLASS.
OH, MAN. MAYBE PUBLIC SCHOOL WASN'T SUCH A BAD IDEA.
HELLO.
AAAAHH!
WELCOME TO THE GREY SCHOOL. YOU MUST BE THE BRICKLEMOORE TWINS. MY NAME IS BROO.
WHAT... WHAT ARE YOU?
I AM YOUR ORIENTATION GUIDE. SHALL WE BEGIN THE TOUR?
THERE WAS A FLYING AIRCRAFT CARRIER OUTSIDE! I THINK THIS WHOLE PLACE IS ABOUT TO BE UNDER ATTACK!
THAT'S HIGHLY PROBABLE. BUT AROUND HERE WE TRY NOT TO LET A LITTLE THING LIKE THAT RUIN OUR WHOLE DAY.
SHALL I SHOW YOU WHERE WE HOLD THE MATH CLASSES? THAT'S MY FAVORITE PART OF THE TOUR.

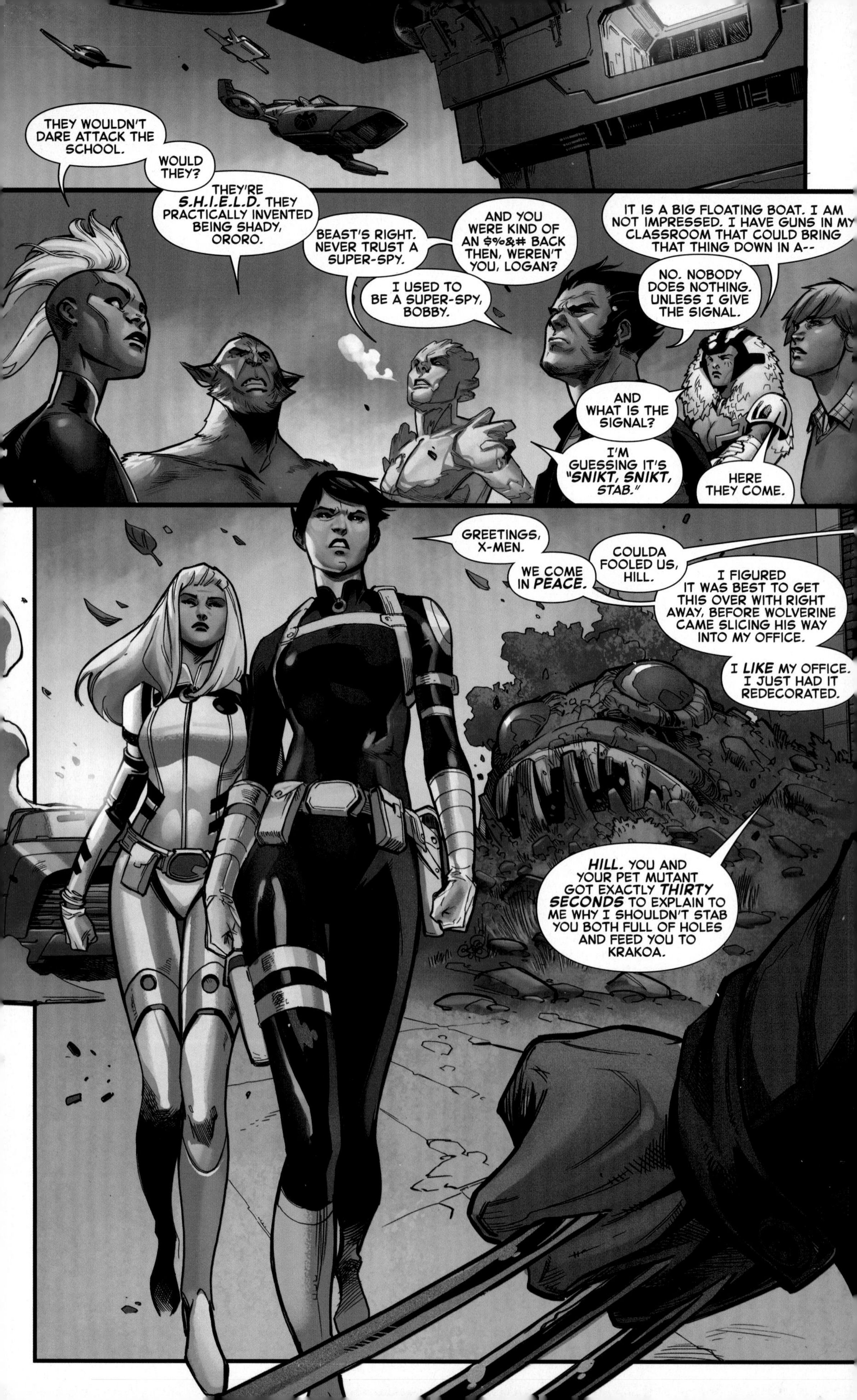
THEY WOULDN'T DARE ATTACK THE SCHOOL.
WOULD THEY?
THEY'RE S.H.I.E.L.D. THEY PRACTICALLY INVENTED BEING SHADY, ORORO.
BEAST'S RIGHT. NEVER TRUST A SUPER-SPY.
AND YOU WERE KIND OF AN $%&# BACK THEN, WEREN'T YOU, LOGAN?
I USED TO BE A SUPER-SPY, BOBBY.
IT IS A BIG FLOATING BOAT. I AM NOT IMPRESSED. I HAVE GUNS IN MY CLASSROOM THAT COULD BRING THAT THING DOWN IN A--
NO. NOBODY DOES NOTHING. UNLESS I GIVE THE SIGNAL.
AND WHAT IS THE SIGNAL?
I'M GUESSING IT'S "SNIKT, SNIKT, STAB."
HERE THEY COME.
GREETINGS, X-MEN.
WE COME IN PEACE.
COULDA FOOLED US, HILL.
I FIGURED IT WAS BEST TO GET THIS OVER WITH RIGHT AWAY, BEFORE WOLVERINE CAME SLICING HIS WAY INTO MY OFFICE.
I LIKE MY OFFICE. I JUST HAD IT REDECORATED.
HILL. YOU AND YOUR PET MUTANT GOT EXACTLY THIRTY SECONDS TO EXPLAIN TO ME WHY I SHOULDN'T STAB YOU BOTH FULL OF HOLES AND FEED YOU TO KRAKOA.

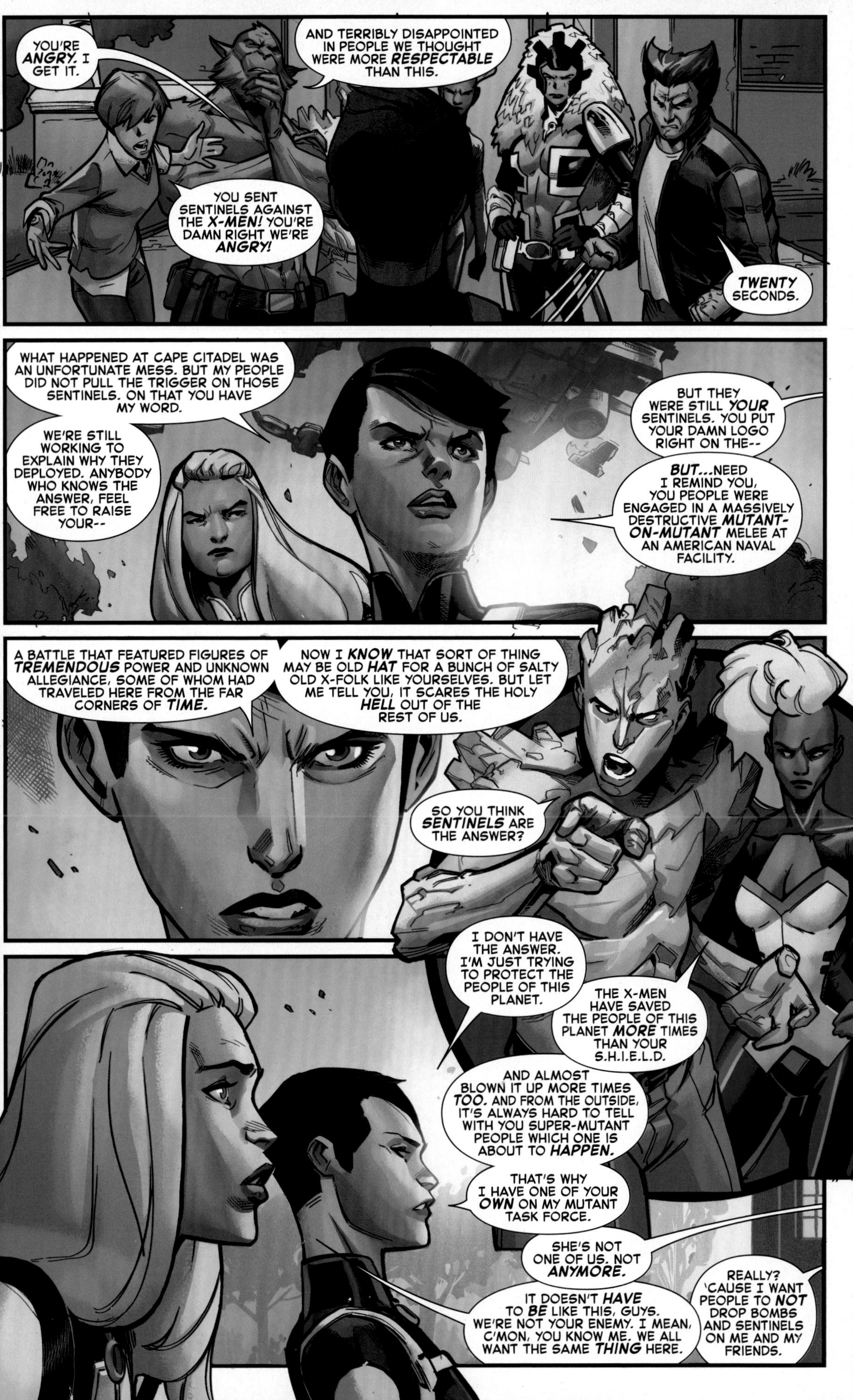
YOU'RE ANGRY. I GET IT.
AND TERRIBLY DISAPPOINTED IN PEOPLE WE THOUGHT WERE MORE RESPECTABLE THAN THIS.
YOU SENT SENTINELS AGAINST THE X-MEN! YOU'RE DAMN RIGHT WE'RE ANGRY!
TWENTY SECONDS.
WHAT HAPPENED AT CAPE CITADEL WAS AN UNFORTUNATE MESS. BUT MY PEOPLE DID NOT PULL THE TRIGGER ON THOSE SENTINELS. ON THAT YOU HAVE MY WORD.
WE'RE STILL WORKING TO EXPLAIN WHY THEY DEPLOYED. ANYBODY WHO KNOWS THE ANSWER, FEEL FREE TO RAISE YOUR--
BUT THEY WERE STILL YOUR SENTINELS. YOU PUT YOUR DAMN LOGO RIGHT ON THE--
BUT...NEED I REMIND YOU, YOU PEOPLE WERE ENGAGED IN A MASSIVELY DESTRUCTIVE MUTANT-ON-MUTANT MELEE AT AN AMERICAN NAVAL FACILITY.
A BATTLE THAT FEATURED FIGURES OF TREMENDOUS POWER AND UNKNOWN ALLEGIANCE, SOME OF WHOM HAD TRAVELED HERE FROM THE FAR CORNERS OF TIME.
NOW I KNOW THAT SORT OF THING MAY BE OLD HAT FOR A BUNCH OF SALTY OLD X-FOLK LIKE YOURSELVES. BUT LET ME TELL YOU, IT SCARES THE HOLY HELL OUT OF THE REST OF US.
SO YOU THINK SENTINELS ARE THE ANSWER?
I DON'T HAVE THE ANSWER. I'M JUST TRYING TO PROTECT THE PEOPLE OF THIS PLANET.
THE X-MEN HAVE SAVED THE PEOPLE OF THIS PLANET MORE TIMES THAN YOUR S.H.I.E.L.D.
AND ALMOST BLOWN IT UP MORE TIMES TOO. AND FROM THE OUTSIDE, IT'S ALWAYS HARD TO TELL WITH YOU SUPER-MUTANT PEOPLE WHICH ONE IS ABOUT TO HAPPEN.
THAT'S WHY I HAVE ONE OF YOUR OWN ON MY MUTANT TASK FORCE.
SHE'S NOT ONE OF US. NOT ANYMORE.
IT DOESN'T HAVE TO BE LIKE THIS, GUYS. WE'RE NOT YOUR ENEMY. I MEAN, C'MON, YOU KNOW ME. WE ALL WANT THE SAME THING HERE.
REALLY? 'CAUSE I WANT PEOPLE TO NOT DROP BOMBS AND SENTINELS ON ME AND MY FRIENDS.

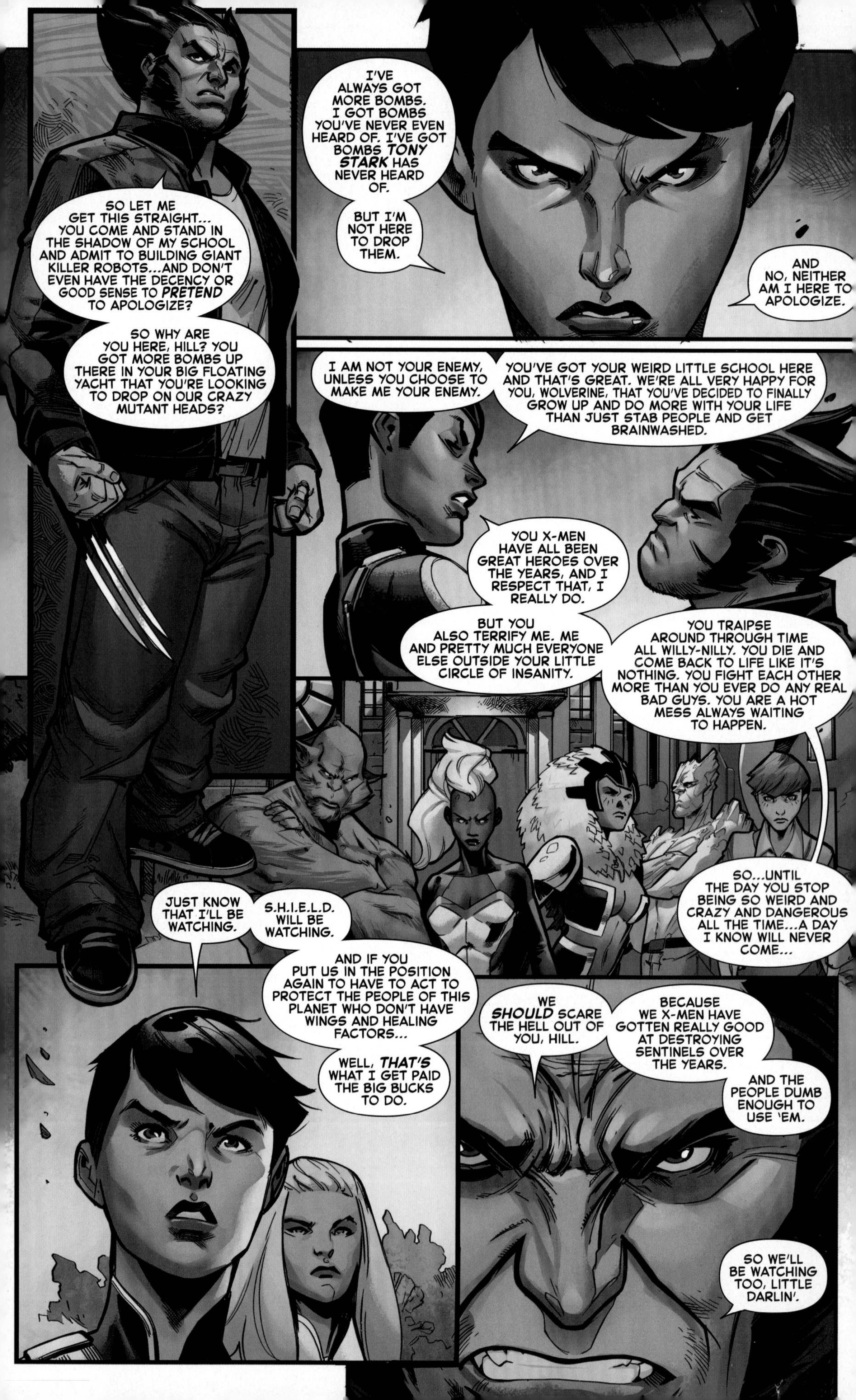
SO LET ME GET THIS STRAIGHT... YOU COME AND STAND IN THE SHADOW OF MY SCHOOL AND ADMIT TO BUILDING GIANT KILLER ROBOTS...AND DON'T EVEN HAVE THE DECENCY OR GOOD SENSE TO PRETEND TO APOLOGIZE?
SO WHY ARE YOU HERE, HILL? YOU GOT MORE BOMBS UP THERE IN YOUR BIG FLOATING YACHT THAT YOU'RE LOOKING TO DROP ON OUR CRAZY MUTANT HEADS?
I'VE ALWAYS GOT MORE BOMBS. I GOT BOMBS YOU'VE NEVER EVEN HEARD OF. I'VE GOT BOMBS TONY STARK HAS NEVER HEARD OF.
BUT I'M NOT HERE TO DROP THEM.
AND NO, NEITHER AM I HERE TO APOLOGIZE.
I AM NOT YOUR ENEMY, UNLESS YOU CHOOSE TO MAKE ME YOUR ENEMY.
YOU'VE GOT YOUR WEIRD LITTLE SCHOOL HERE AND THAT'S GREAT. WE'RE ALL VERY HAPPY FOR YOU, WOLVERINE, THAT YOU'VE DECIDED TO FINALLY GROW UP AND DO MORE WITH YOUR LIFE THAN JUST STAB PEOPLE AND GET BRAINWASHED.
YOU X-MEN HAVE ALL BEEN GREAT HEROES OVER THE YEARS, AND I RESPECT THAT, I REALLY DO.
BUT YOU ALSO TERRIFY ME. ME AND PRETTY MUCH EVERYONE ELSE OUTSIDE YOUR LITTLE CIRCLE OF INSANITY.
YOU TRAIPSE AROUND THROUGH TIME ALL WILLY-NILLY. YOU DIE AND COME BACK TO LIFE LIKE IT'S NOTHING. YOU FIGHT EACH OTHER MORE THAN YOU EVER DO ANY REAL BAD GUYS. YOU ARE A HOT MESS ALWAYS WAITING TO HAPPEN.
SO...UNTIL THE DAY YOU STOP BEING SO WEIRD AND CRAZY AND DANGEROUS ALL THE TIME...A DAY I KNOW WILL NEVER COME...
JUST KNOW THAT I'LL BE WATCHING.
S.H.I.E.L.D. WILL BE WATCHING.
AND IF YOU PUT US IN THE POSITION AGAIN TO HAVE TO ACT TO PROTECT THE PEOPLE OF THIS PLANET WHO DON'T HAVE WINGS AND HEALING FACTORS...
WELL, THAT'S WHAT I GET PAID THE BIG BUCKS TO DO.
WE SHOULD SCARE THE HELL OUT OF YOU, HILL.
BECAUSE WE X-MEN HAVE GOTTEN REALLY GOOD AT DESTROYING SENTINELS OVER THE YEARS.
AND THE PEOPLE DUMB ENOUGH TO USE 'EM.
SO WE'LL BE WATCHING TOO, LITTLE DARLIN'.

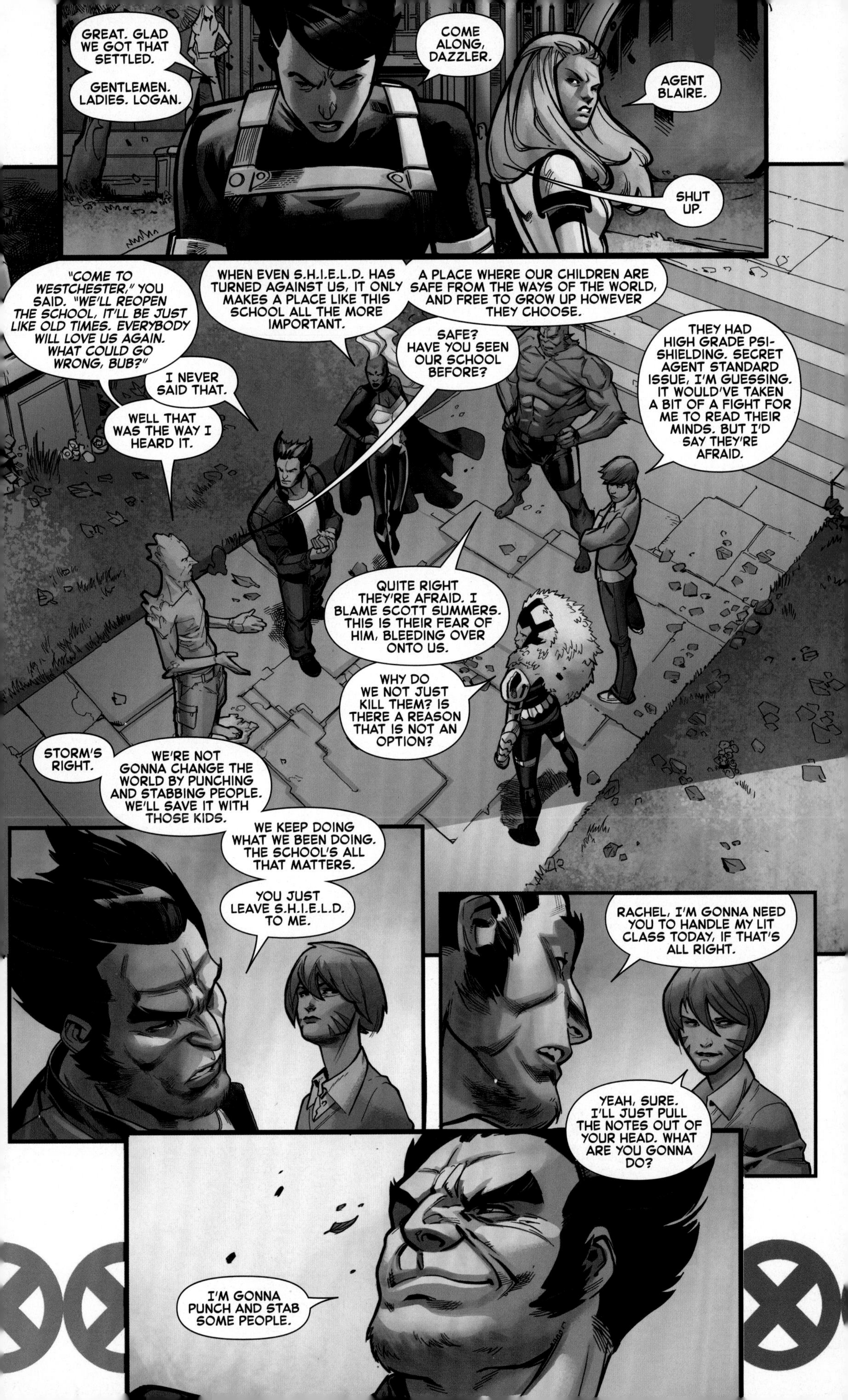
GREAT. GLAD WE GOT THAT SETTLED.
GENTLEMEN. LADIES. LOGAN.
COME ALONG, DAZZLER.
AGENT BLAIRE.
SHUT UP.
"COME TO WESTCHESTER," YOU SAID. "WE'LL REOPEN THE SCHOOL, IT'LL BE JUST LIKE OLD TIMES. EVERYBODY WILL LOVE US AGAIN. WHAT COULD GO WRONG, BUB?"
I NEVER SAID THAT.
WELL THAT WAS THE WAY I HEARD IT.
WHEN EVEN S.H.I.E.L.D. HAS TURNED AGAINST US, IT ONLY MAKES A PLACE LIKE THIS SCHOOL ALL THE MORE IMPORTANT.
A PLACE WHERE OUR CHILDREN ARE SAFE FROM THE WAYS OF THE WORLD, AND FREE TO GROW UP HOWEVER THEY CHOOSE.
SAFE? HAVE YOU SEEN OUR SCHOOL BEFORE?
THEY HAD HIGH GRADE PSI-SHIELDING. SECRET AGENT STANDARD ISSUE, I'M GUESSING. IT WOULD'VE TAKEN A BIT OF A FIGHT FOR ME TO READ THEIR MINDS. BUT I'D SAY THEY'RE AFRAID.
QUITE RIGHT THEY'RE AFRAID. I BLAME SCOTT SUMMERS. THIS IS THEIR FEAR OF HIM, BLEEDING OVER ONTO US.
WHY DO WE NOT JUST KILL THEM? IS THERE A REASON THAT IS NOT AN OPTION?
STORM'S RIGHT.
WE'RE NOT GONNA CHANGE THE WORLD BY PUNCHING AND STABBING PEOPLE. WE'LL SAVE IT WITH THOSE KIDS.
WE KEEP DOING WHAT WE BEEN DOING. THE SCHOOL'S ALL THAT MATTERS.
YOU JUST LEAVE S.H.I.E.L.D. TO ME.
RACHEL, I'M GONNA NEED YOU TO HANDLE MY LIT CLASS TODAY, IF THAT'S ALL RIGHT.
YEAH, SURE. I'LL JUST PULL THE NOTES OUT OF YOUR HEAD. WHAT ARE YOU GONNA DO?
I'M GONNA PUNCH AND STAB SOME PEOPLE.

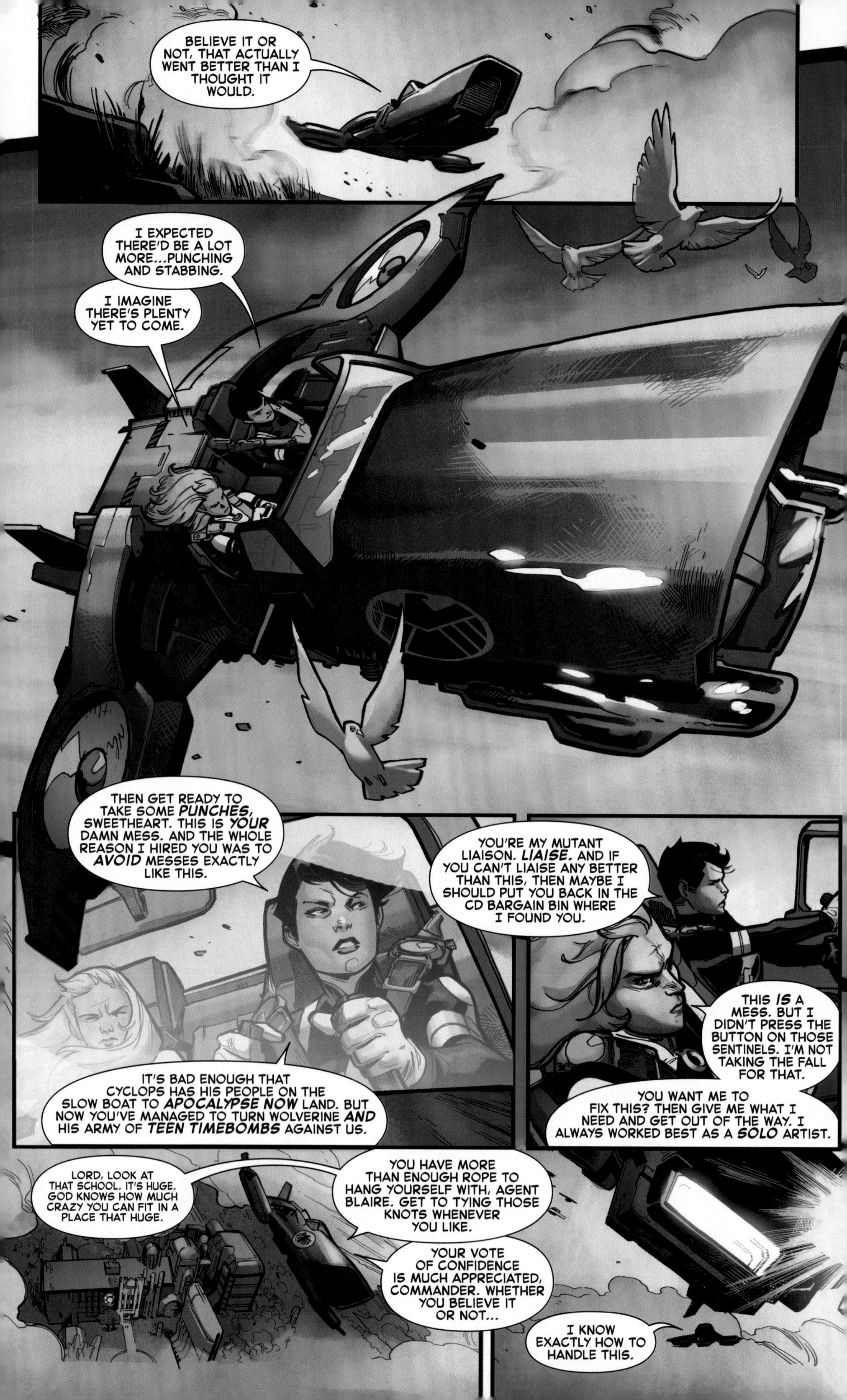
BELIEVE IT OR NOT, THAT ACTUALLY WENT BETTER THAN I THOUGHT IT WOULD.
I EXPECTED THERE'D BE A LOT MORE...PUNCHING AND STABBING.
I IMAGINE THERE'S PLENTY YET TO COME.
THEN GET READY TO TAKE SOME PUNCHES, SWEETHEART. THIS IS YOUR DAMN MESS. AND THE WHOLE REASON I HIRED YOU WAS TO AVOID MESSES EXACTLY LIKE THIS.
IT'S BAD ENOUGH THAT CYCLOPS HAS HIS PEOPLE ON THE SLOW BOAT TO APOCALYPSE NOW LAND. BUT NOW YOU'VE MANAGED TO TURN WOLVERINE AND HIS ARMY OF TEEN TIMEBOMBS AGAINST US.
YOU'RE MY MUTANT LIAISON. LIAISE. AND IF YOU CAN'T LIAISE ANY BETTER THAN THIS, THEN MAYBE I SHOULD PUT YOU BACK IN THE CD BARGAIN BIN WHERE I FOUND YOU.
THIS IS A MESS. BUT I DIDN'T PRESS THE BUTTON ON THOSE SENTINELS. I'M NOT TAKING THE FALL FOR THAT.
YOU WANT ME TO FIX THIS? THEN GIVE ME WHAT I NEED AND GET OUT OF THE WAY. I ALWAYS WORKED BEST AS A SOLO ARTIST.
LORD, LOOK AT THAT SCHOOL. IT'S HUGE. GOD KNOWS HOW MUCH CRAZY YOU CAN FIT IN A PLACE THAT HUGE.
YOU HAVE MORE THAN ENOUGH ROPE TO HANG YOURSELF WITH, AGENT BLAIRE. GET TO TYING THOSE KNOTS WHENEVER YOU LIKE.
YOUR VOTE OF CONFIDENCE IS MUCH APPRECIATED, COMMANDER. WHETHER YOU BELIEVE IT OR NOT...
I KNOW EXACTLY HOW TO HANDLE THIS.

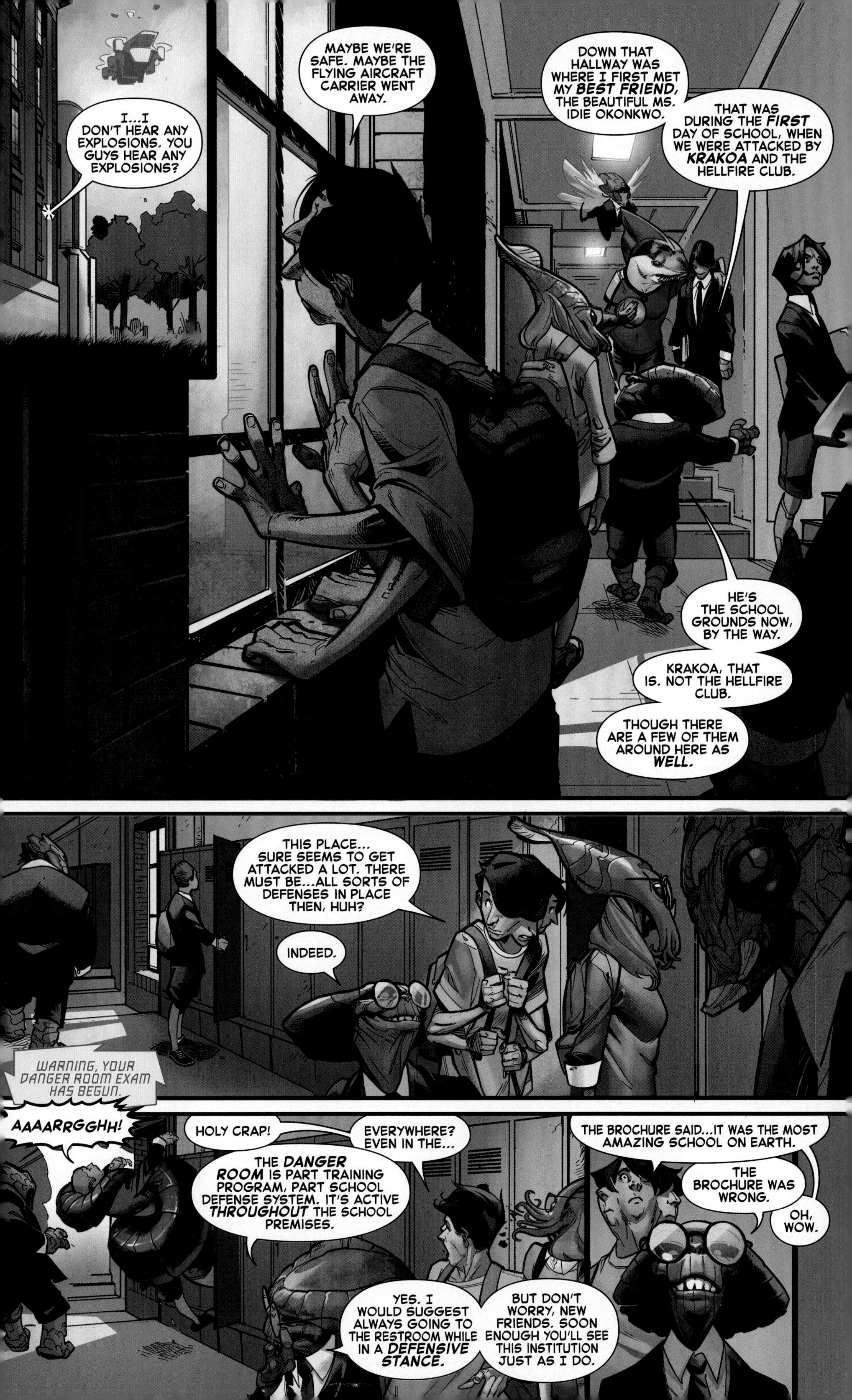
I...I DON'T HEAR ANY EXPLOSIONS. YOU GUYS HEAR ANY EXPLOSIONS?
MAYBE WE'RE SAFE. MAYBE THE FLYING AIRCRAFT CARRIER WENT AWAY.
DOWN THAT HALLWAY WAS WHERE I FIRST MET MY BEST FRIEND, THE BEAUTIFUL MS. IDIE OKONKWO.
THAT WAS DURING THE FIRST DAY OF SCHOOL, WHEN WE WERE ATTACKED BY KRAKOA AND THE HELLFIRE CLUB.
HE'S THE SCHOOL GROUNDS NOW, BY THE WAY.
KRAKOA, THAT IS. NOT THE HELLFIRE CLUB.
THOUGH THERE ARE A FEW OF THEM AROUND HERE AS WELL.
THIS PLACE... SURE SEEMS TO GET ATTACKED A LOT. THERE MUST BE...ALL SORTS OF DEFENSES IN PLACE THEN, HUH?
INDEED.
WARNING, YOUR DANGER ROOM EXAM HAS BEGUN.
AAAARRGGHH!
HOLY CRAP!
THE DANGER ROOM IS PART TRAINING PROGRAM, PART SCHOOL DEFENSE SYSTEM. IT'S ACTIVE THROUGHOUT THE SCHOOL PREMISES.
EVERYWHERE? EVEN IN THE...
YES. I WOULD SUGGEST ALWAYS GOING TO THE RESTROOM WHILE IN A DEFENSIVE STANCE.
BUT DON'T WORRY, NEW FRIENDS. SOON ENOUGH YOU'LL SEE THIS INSTITUTION JUST AS I DO.
THE BROCHURE SAID...IT WAS THE MOST AMAZING SCHOOL ON EARTH.
THE BROCHURE WAS WRONG.
OH, WOW.

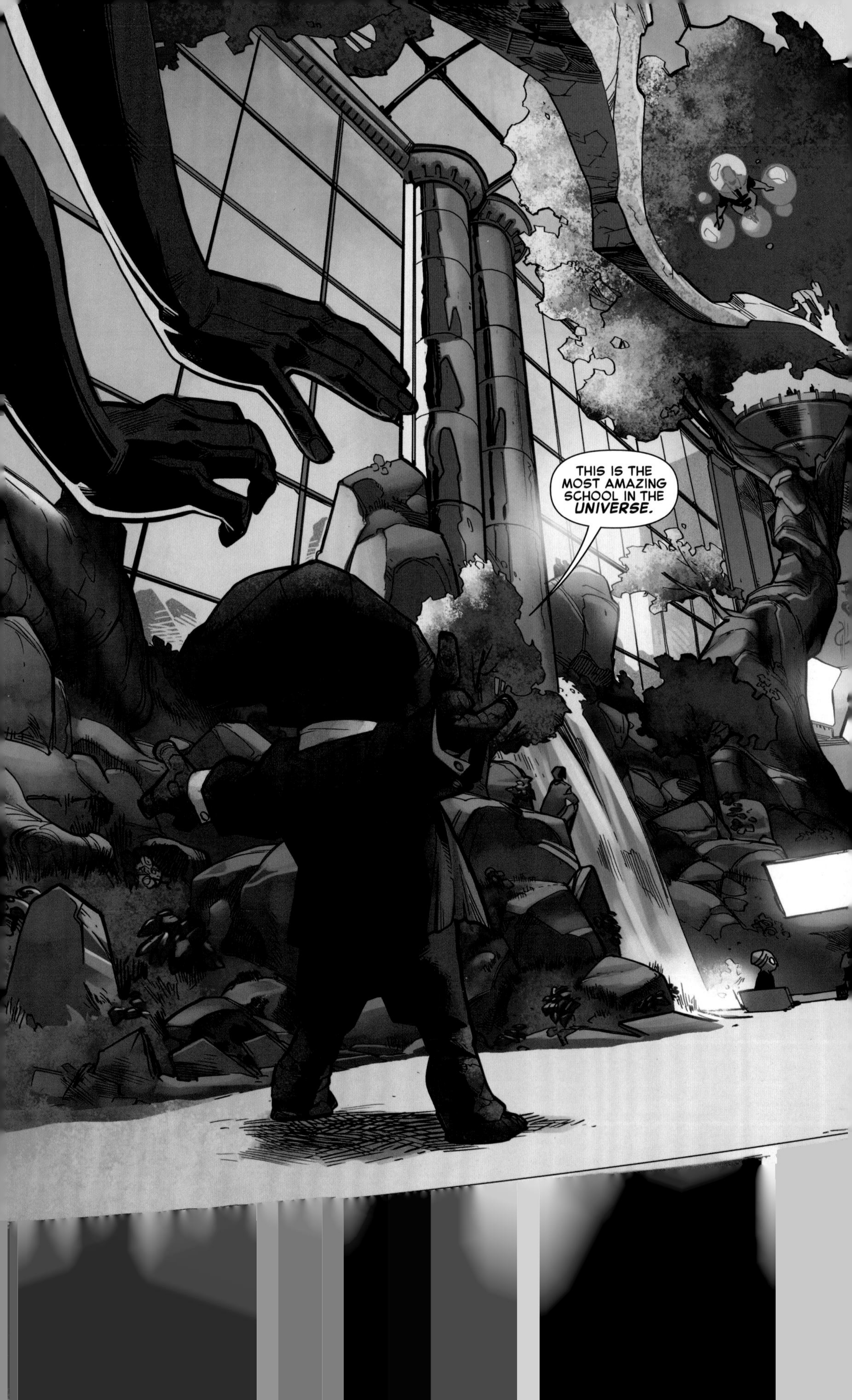
THIS IS THE MOST AMAZING SCHOOL IN THE *UNIVERSE.*

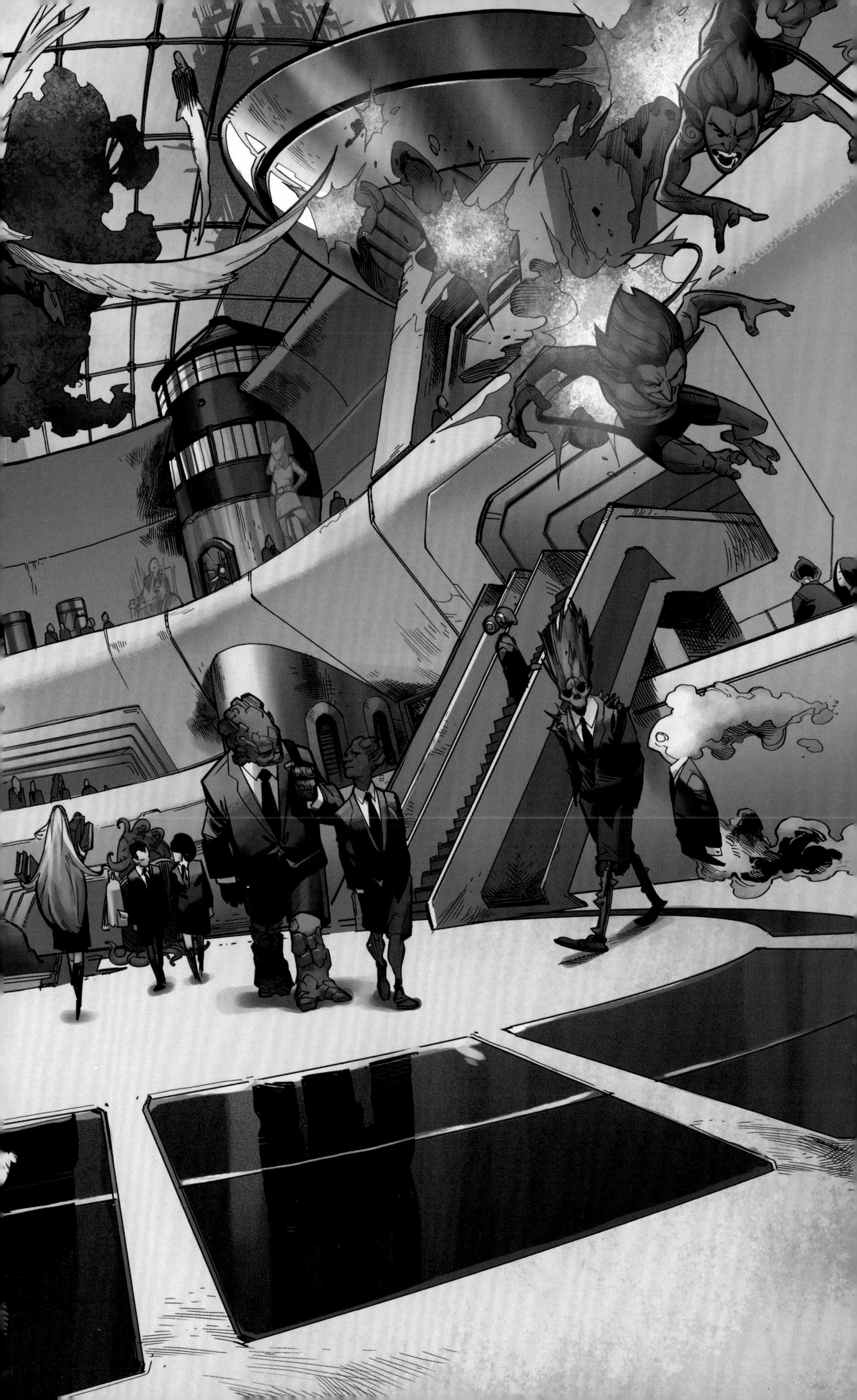

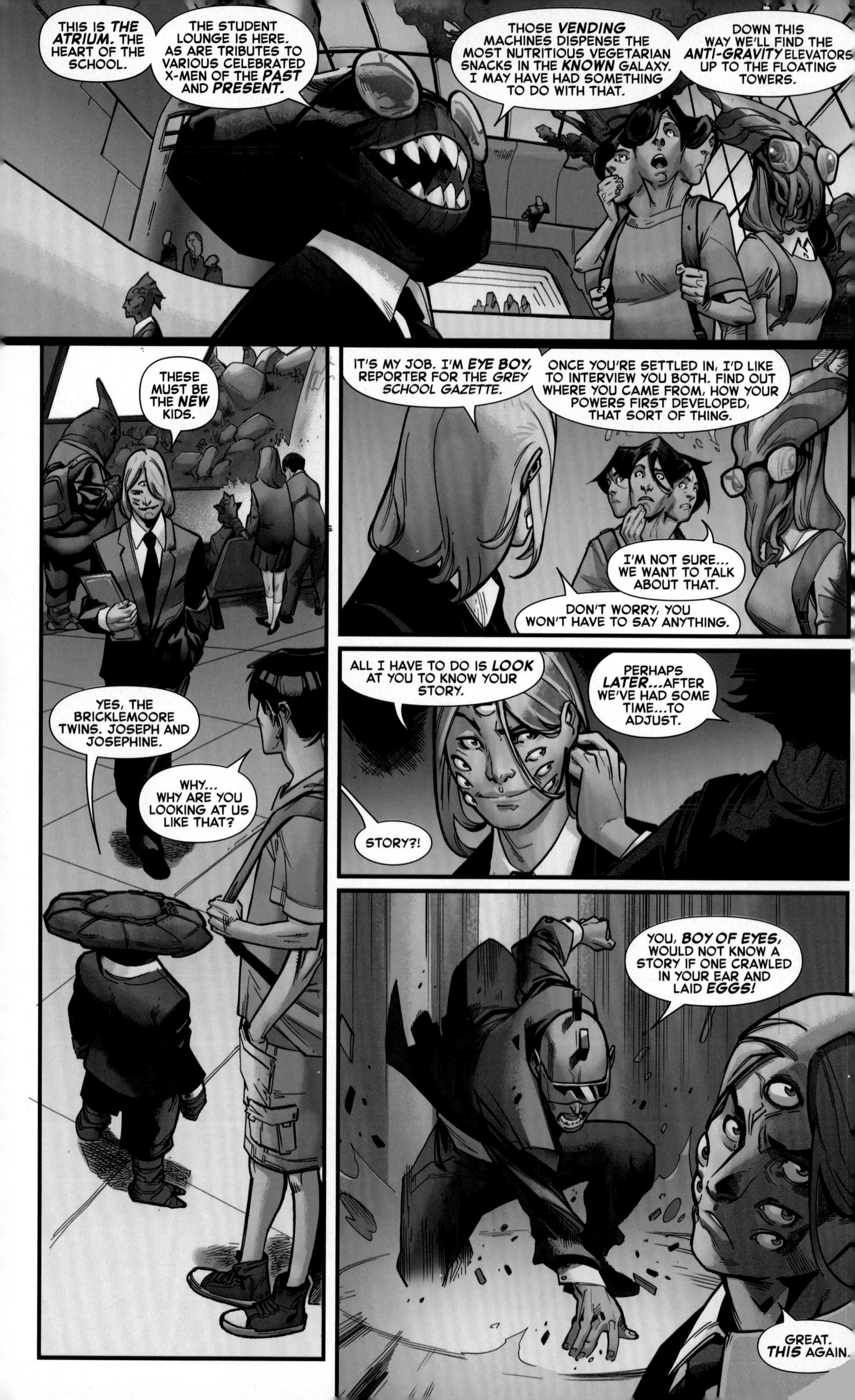
THIS IS THE ATRIUM. THE HEART OF THE SCHOOL.
THE STUDENT LOUNGE IS HERE. AS ARE TRIBUTES TO VARIOUS CELEBRATED X-MEN OF THE PAST AND PRESENT.
THOSE VENDING MACHINES DISPENSE THE MOST NUTRITIOUS VEGETARIAN SNACKS IN THE KNOWN GALAXY. I MAY HAVE HAD SOMETHING TO DO WITH THAT.
DOWN THIS WAY WE'LL FIND THE ANTI-GRAVITY ELEVATORS UP TO THE FLOATING TOWERS.
THESE MUST BE THE NEW KIDS.
YES, THE BRICKLEMOORE TWINS. JOSEPH AND JOSEPHINE.
WHY... WHY ARE YOU LOOKING AT US LIKE THAT?
IT'S MY JOB. I'M EYE BOY, REPORTER FOR THE GREY SCHOOL GAZETTE.
ONCE YOU'RE SETTLED IN, I'D LIKE TO INTERVIEW YOU BOTH. FIND OUT WHERE YOU CAME FROM, HOW YOUR POWERS FIRST DEVELOPED, THAT SORT OF THING.
I'M NOT SURE... WE WANT TO TALK ABOUT THAT.
DON'T WORRY, YOU WON'T HAVE TO SAY ANYTHING.
ALL I HAVE TO DO IS LOOK AT YOU TO KNOW YOUR STORY.
PERHAPS LATER...AFTER WE'VE HAD SOME TIME...TO ADJUST.
STORY?!
YOU, BOY OF EYES, WOULD NOT KNOW A STORY IF ONE CRAWLED IN YOUR EAR AND LAID EGGS!
GREAT. THIS AGAIN.

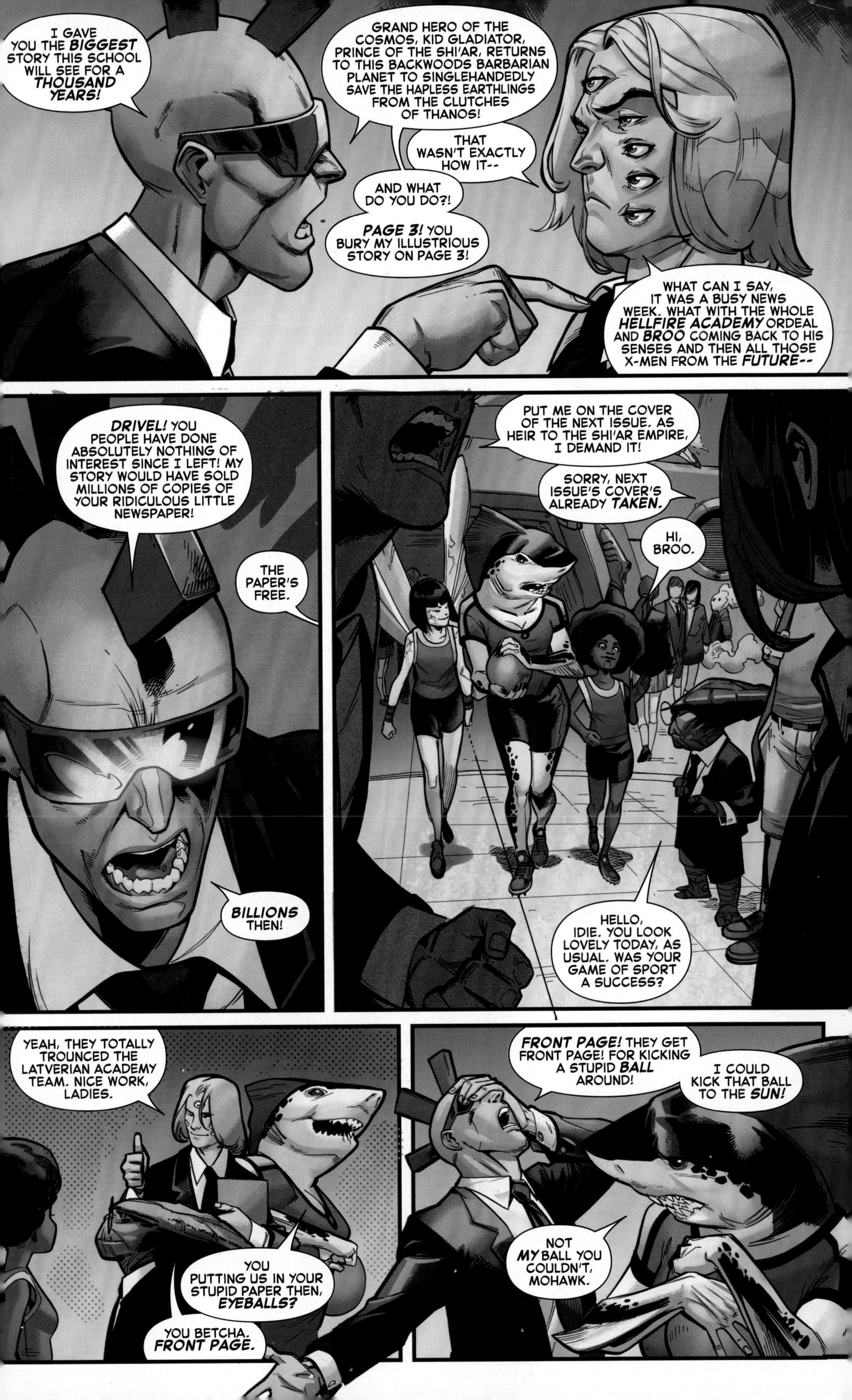

I GAVE YOU THE BIGGEST STORY THIS SCHOOL WILL SEE FOR A THOUSAND YEARS!
GRAND HERO OF THE COSMOS, KID GLADIATOR, PRINCE OF THE SHI'AR, RETURNS TO THIS BACKWOODS BARBARIAN PLANET TO SINGLEHANDEDLY SAVE THE HAPLESS EARTHLINGS FROM THE CLUTCHES OF THANOS!
THAT WASN'T EXACTLY HOW IT--
AND WHAT DO YOU DO?!
PAGE 3! YOU BURY MY ILLUSTRIOUS STORY ON PAGE 3!
WHAT CAN I SAY, IT WAS A BUSY NEWS WEEK. WHAT WITH THE WHOLE HELLFIRE ACADEMY ORDEAL AND BROO COMING BACK TO HIS SENSES AND THEN ALL THOSE X-MEN FROM THE FUTURE--
DRIVEL! YOU PEOPLE HAVE DONE ABSOLUTELY NOTHING OF INTEREST SINCE I LEFT! MY STORY WOULD HAVE SOLD MILLIONS OF COPIES OF YOUR RIDICULOUS LITTLE NEWSPAPER!
THE PAPER'S FREE.
BILLIONS THEN!
PUT ME ON THE COVER OF THE NEXT ISSUE. AS HEIR TO THE SHI'AR EMPIRE, I DEMAND IT!
SORRY, NEXT ISSUE'S COVER'S ALREADY TAKEN.
HI, BROO.
HELLO, IDIE. YOU LOOK LOVELY TODAY, AS USUAL. WAS YOUR GAME OF SPORT A SUCCESS?
YEAH, THEY TOTALLY TROUNCED THE LATVERIAN ACADEMY TEAM. NICE WORK, LADIES.
YOU PUTTING US IN YOUR STUPID PAPER THEN, EYEBALLS?
YOU BETCHA. FRONT PAGE.
FRONT PAGE! THEY GET FRONT PAGE! FOR KICKING A STUPID BALL AROUND!
I COULD KICK THAT BALL TO THE SUN!
NOT MY BALL YOU COULDN'T, MOHAWK.

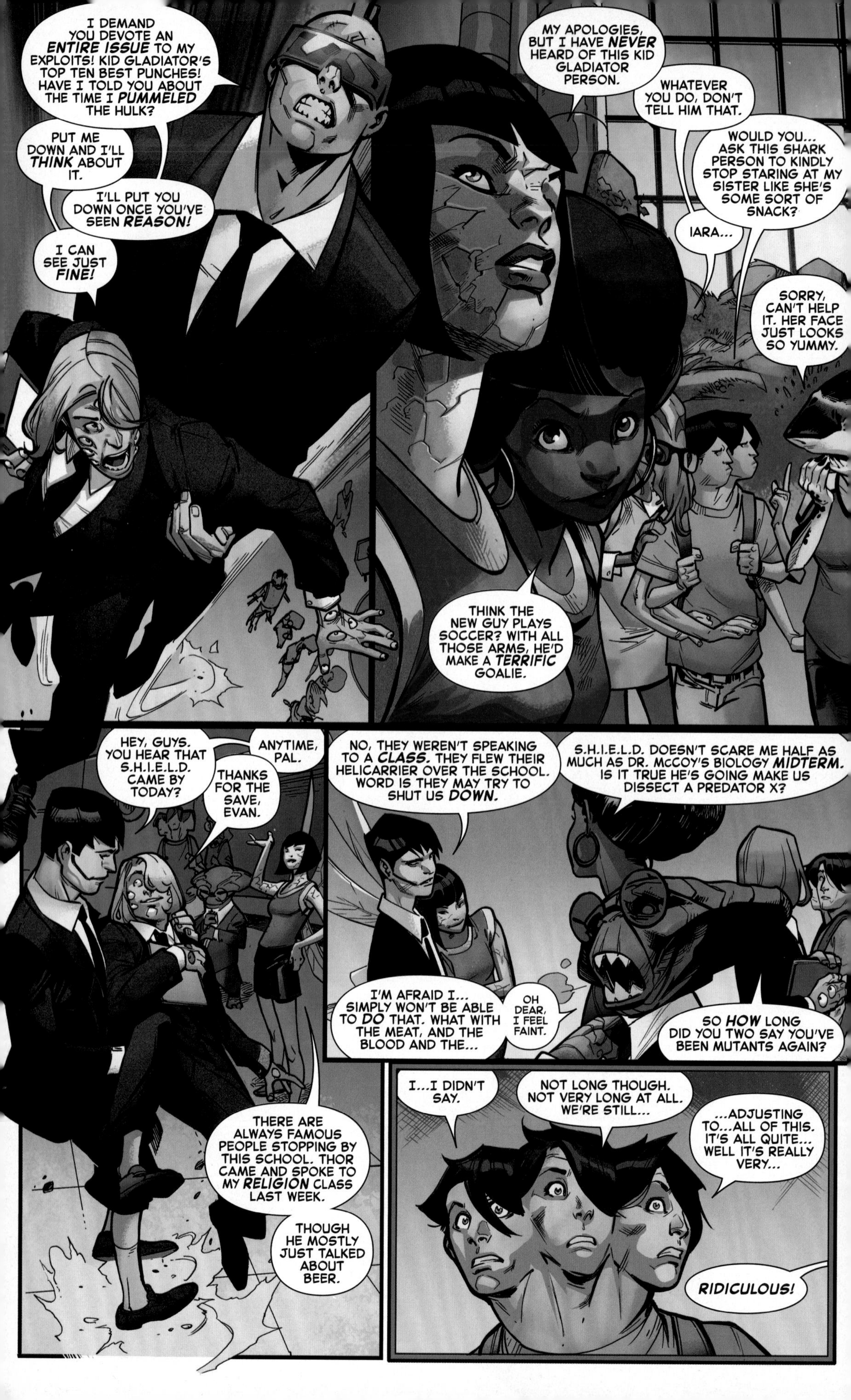
I DEMAND YOU DEVOTE AN ENTIRE ISSUE TO MY EXPLOITS! KID GLADIATOR'S TOP TEN BEST PUNCHES! HAVE I TOLD YOU ABOUT THE TIME I PUMMELED THE HULK?
PUT ME DOWN AND I'LL THINK ABOUT IT.
I'LL PUT YOU DOWN ONCE YOU'VE SEEN REASON!
I CAN SEE JUST FINE!
MY APOLOGIES, BUT I HAVE NEVER HEARD OF THIS KID GLADIATOR PERSON.
WHATEVER YOU DO, DON'T TELL HIM THAT.
IARA...
WOULD YOU... ASK THIS SHARK PERSON TO KINDLY STOP STARING AT MY SISTER LIKE SHE'S SOME SORT OF SNACK?
SORRY, CAN'T HELP IT. HER FACE JUST LOOKS SO YUMMY.
THINK THE NEW GUY PLAYS SOCCER? WITH ALL THOSE ARMS, HE'D MAKE A TERRIFIC GOALIE.
HEY, GUYS. YOU HEAR THAT S.H.I.E.L.D. CAME BY TODAY?
ANYTIME, PAL.
THANKS FOR THE SAVE, EVAN.
THERE ARE ALWAYS FAMOUS PEOPLE STOPPING BY THIS SCHOOL. THOR CAME AND SPOKE TO MY RELIGION CLASS LAST WEEK.
THOUGH HE MOSTLY JUST TALKED ABOUT BEER.
NO, THEY WEREN'T SPEAKING TO A CLASS. THEY FLEW THEIR HELICARRIER OVER THE SCHOOL. WORD IS THEY MAY TRY TO SHUT US DOWN.
S.H.I.E.L.D. DOESN'T SCARE ME HALF AS MUCH AS DR. McCOY'S BIOLOGY MIDTERM. IS IT TRUE HE'S GOING MAKE US DISSECT A PREDATOR X?
I'M AFRAID I... SIMPLY WON'T BE ABLE TO DO THAT. WHAT WITH THE MEAT, AND THE BLOOD AND THE...
OH DEAR, I FEEL FAINT.
SO HOW LONG DID YOU TWO SAY YOU'VE BEEN MUTANTS AGAIN?
I...I DIDN'T SAY.
NOT LONG THOUGH. NOT VERY LONG AT ALL. WE'RE STILL...
...ADJUSTING TO...ALL OF THIS. IT'S ALL QUITE... WELL IT'S REALLY VERY...
RIDICULOUS!

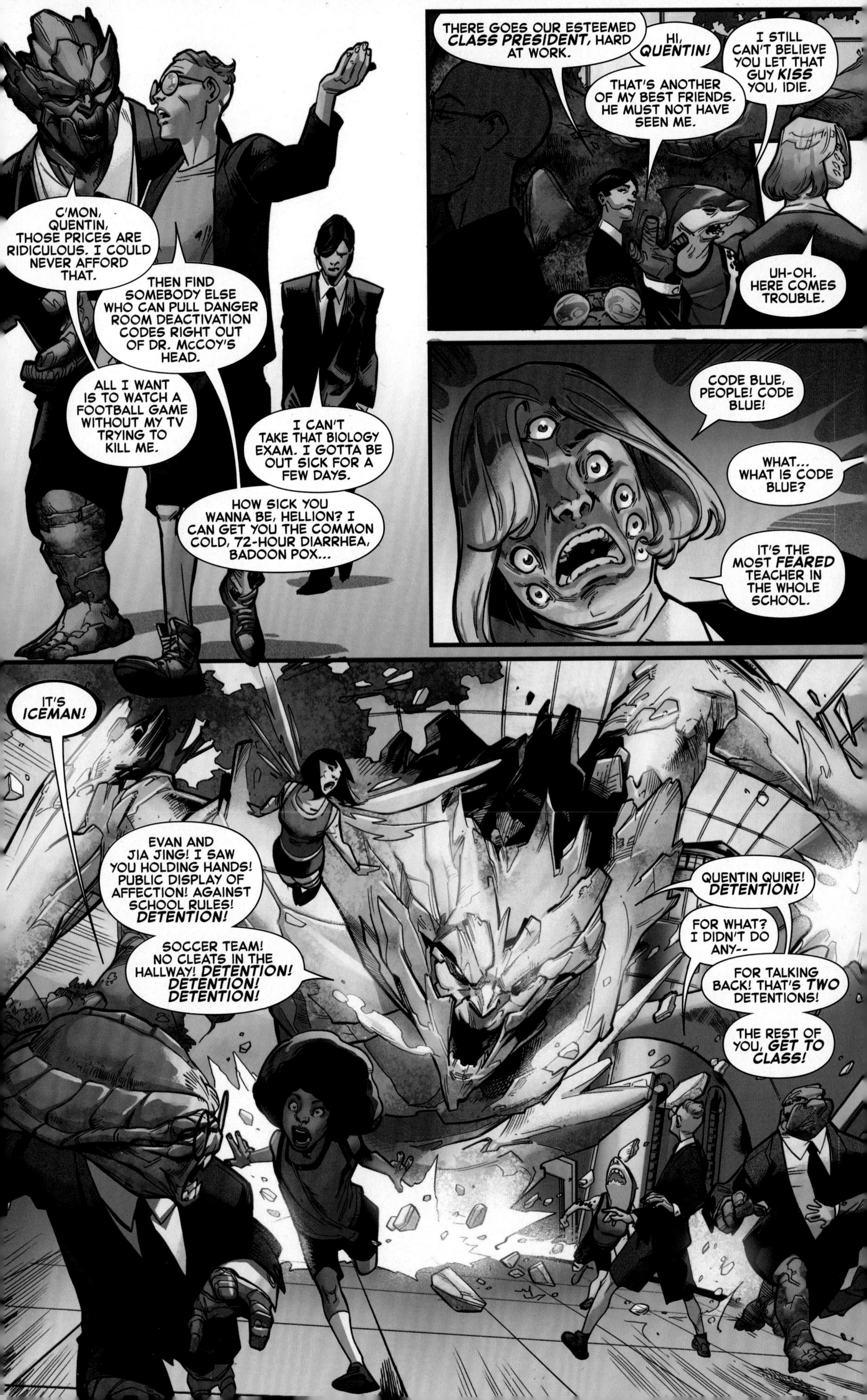
C'MON, QUENTIN, THOSE PRICES ARE RIDICULOUS. I COULD NEVER AFFORD THAT.
THEN FIND SOMEBODY ELSE WHO CAN PULL DANGER ROOM DEACTIVATION CODES RIGHT OUT OF DR. McCOY'S HEAD.
ALL I WANT IS TO WATCH A FOOTBALL GAME WITHOUT MY TV TRYING TO KILL ME.
I CAN'T TAKE THAT BIOLOGY EXAM. I GOTTA BE OUT SICK FOR A FEW DAYS.
HOW SICK YOU WANNA BE, HELLION? I CAN GET YOU THE COMMON COLD, 72-HOUR DIARRHEA, BADOON POX...
THERE GOES OUR ESTEEMED *CLASS PRESIDENT*, HARD AT WORK.
HI, *QUENTIN!*
THAT'S ANOTHER OF MY BEST FRIENDS. HE MUST NOT HAVE SEEN ME.
I STILL CAN'T BELIEVE YOU LET THAT GUY *KISS* YOU, IDIE.
UH-OH. HERE COMES TROUBLE.
CODE BLUE, PEOPLE! CODE BLUE!
WHAT... WHAT IS CODE BLUE?
IT'S THE MOST *FEARED* TEACHER IN THE WHOLE SCHOOL.
IT'S *ICEMAN!*
EVAN AND JIA JING! I SAW YOU HOLDING HANDS! PUBLIC DISPLAY OF AFFECTION! AGAINST SCHOOL RULES! *DETENTION!*
SOCCER TEAM! NO CLEATS IN THE HALLWAY! *DETENTION! DETENTION! DETENTION!*
QUENTIN QUIRE! *DETENTION!*
FOR WHAT? I DIDN'T DO ANY--
FOR TALKING BACK! THAT'S *TWO* DETENTIONS!
THE REST OF YOU, *GET TO CLASS!*

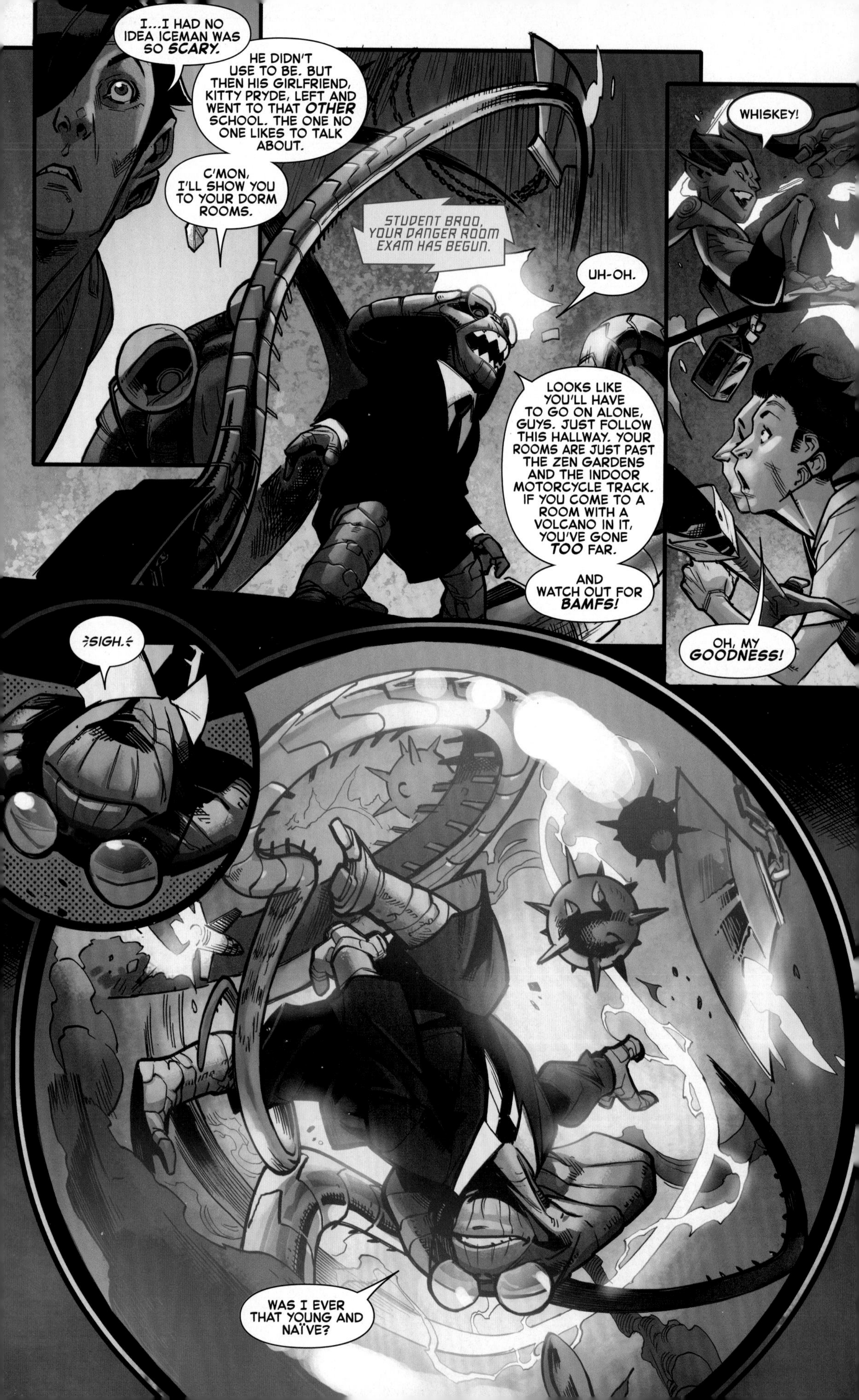
I...I HAD NO IDEA ICEMAN WAS SO SCARY.
HE DIDN'T USE TO BE. BUT THEN HIS GIRLFRIEND, KITTY PRYDE, LEFT AND WENT TO THAT OTHER SCHOOL. THE ONE NO ONE LIKES TO TALK ABOUT.
C'MON, I'LL SHOW YOU TO YOUR DORM ROOMS.
STUDENT BROO, YOUR DANGER ROOM EXAM HAS BEGUN.
UH-OH.
LOOKS LIKE YOU'LL HAVE TO GO ON ALONE, GUYS. JUST FOLLOW THIS HALLWAY. YOUR ROOMS ARE JUST PAST THE ZEN GARDENS AND THE INDOOR MOTORCYCLE TRACK. IF YOU COME TO A ROOM WITH A VOLCANO IN IT, YOU'VE GONE TOO FAR.
AND WATCH OUT FOR BAMFS!
WHISKEY!
OH, MY GOODNESS!
SIGH.
WAS I EVER THAT YOUNG AND NAÏVE?

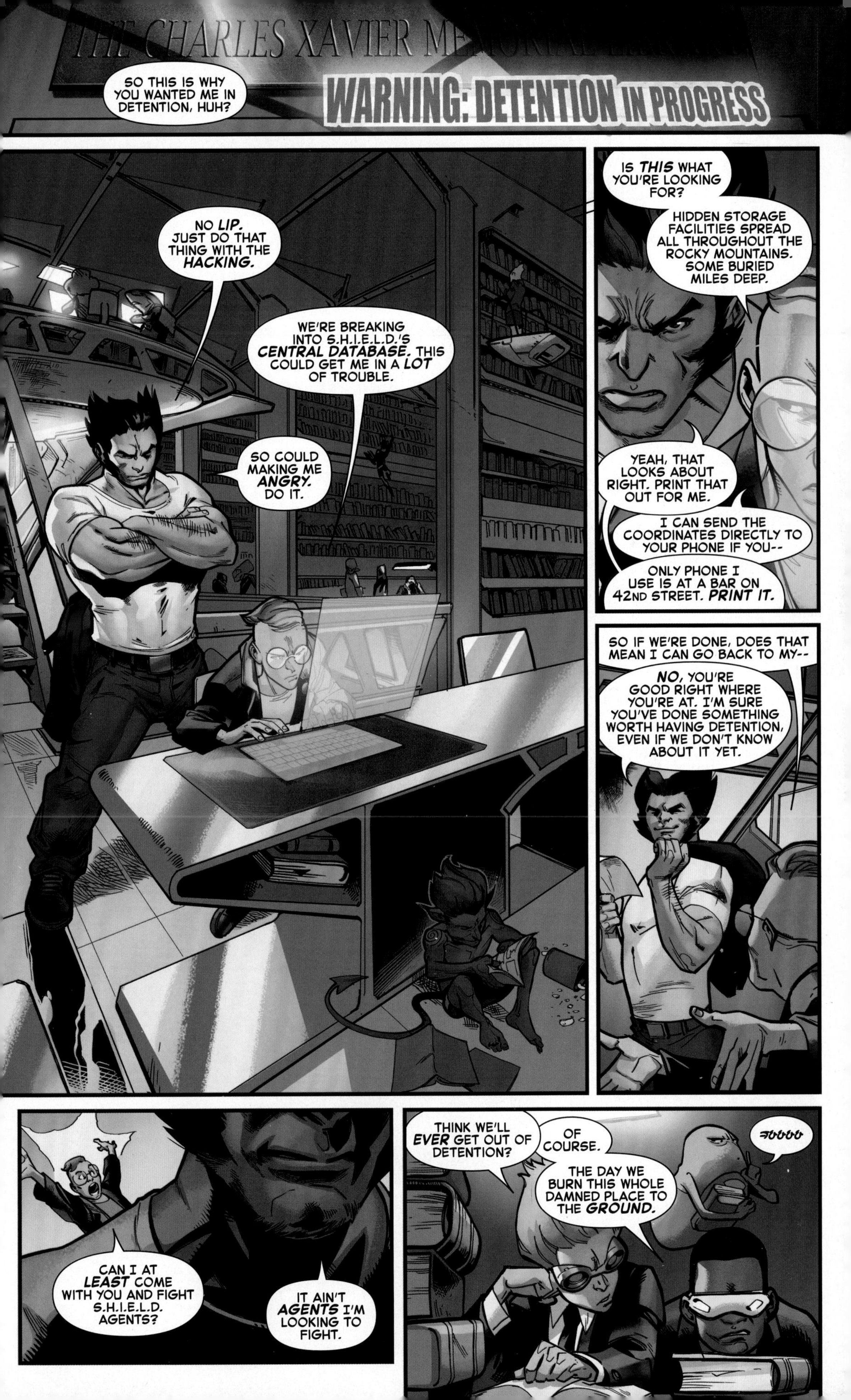
THE CHARLES XAVIER ME...
SO THIS IS WHY YOU WANTED ME IN DETENTION, HUH?
WARNING: DETENTION IN PROGRESS
NO LIP. JUST DO THAT THING WITH THE HACKING.
WE'RE BREAKING INTO S.H.I.E.L.D.'S CENTRAL DATABASE. THIS COULD GET ME IN A LOT OF TROUBLE.
SO COULD MAKING ME ANGRY. DO IT.
IS THIS WHAT YOU'RE LOOKING FOR?
HIDDEN STORAGE FACILITIES SPREAD ALL THROUGHOUT THE ROCKY MOUNTAINS. SOME BURIED MILES DEEP.
YEAH, THAT LOOKS ABOUT RIGHT. PRINT THAT OUT FOR ME.
I CAN SEND THE COORDINATES DIRECTLY TO YOUR PHONE IF YOU--
ONLY PHONE I USE IS AT A BAR ON 42ND STREET. PRINT IT.
SO IF WE'RE DONE, DOES THAT MEAN I CAN GO BACK TO MY--
NO, YOU'RE GOOD RIGHT WHERE YOU'RE AT. I'M SURE YOU'VE DONE SOMETHING WORTH HAVING DETENTION, EVEN IF WE DON'T KNOW ABOUT IT YET.
CAN I AT LEAST COME WITH YOU AND FIGHT S.H.I.E.L.D. AGENTS?
IT AIN'T AGENTS I'M LOOKING TO FIGHT.
THINK WE'LL EVER GET OUT OF DETENTION?
OF COURSE.
THE DAY WE BURN THIS WHOLE DAMNED PLACE TO THE GROUND.
FOOOO

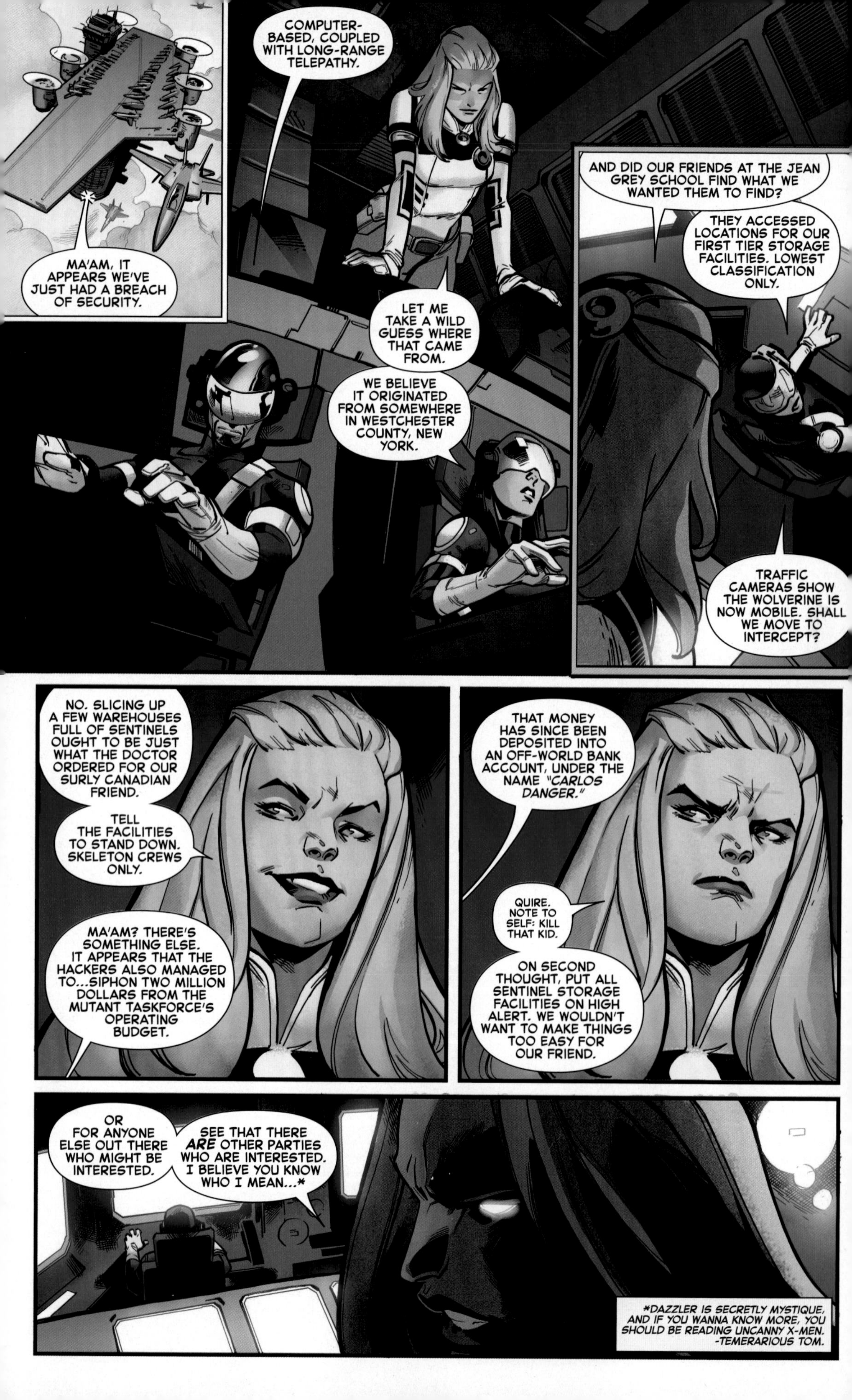
MA'AM, IT APPEARS WE'VE JUST HAD A BREACH OF SECURITY.
COMPUTER-BASED, COUPLED WITH LONG-RANGE TELEPATHY.
LET ME TAKE A WILD GUESS WHERE THAT CAME FROM.
WE BELIEVE IT ORIGINATED FROM SOMEWHERE IN WESTCHESTER COUNTY, NEW YORK.
AND DID OUR FRIENDS AT THE JEAN GREY SCHOOL FIND WHAT WE WANTED THEM TO FIND?
THEY ACCESSED LOCATIONS FOR OUR FIRST TIER STORAGE FACILITIES. LOWEST CLASSIFICATION ONLY.
TRAFFIC CAMERAS SHOW THE WOLVERINE IS NOW MOBILE. SHALL WE MOVE TO INTERCEPT?
NO. SLICING UP A FEW WAREHOUSES FULL OF SENTINELS OUGHT TO BE JUST WHAT THE DOCTOR ORDERED FOR OUR SURLY CANADIAN FRIEND.
TELL THE FACILITIES TO STAND DOWN. SKELETON CREWS ONLY.
MA'AM? THERE'S SOMETHING ELSE. IT APPEARS THAT THE HACKERS ALSO MANAGED TO...SIPHON TWO MILLION DOLLARS FROM THE MUTANT TASKFORCE'S OPERATING BUDGET.
THAT MONEY HAS SINCE BEEN DEPOSITED INTO AN OFF-WORLD BANK ACCOUNT, UNDER THE NAME "CARLOS DANGER."
QUIRE. NOTE TO SELF: KILL THAT KID.
ON SECOND THOUGHT, PUT ALL SENTINEL STORAGE FACILITIES ON HIGH ALERT. WE WOULDN'T WANT TO MAKE THINGS TOO EASY FOR OUR FRIEND.
OR FOR ANYONE ELSE OUT THERE WHO MIGHT BE INTERESTED.
SEE THAT THERE ARE OTHER PARTIES WHO ARE INTERESTED. I BELIEVE YOU KNOW WHO I MEAN...*
*DAZZLER IS SECRETLY MYSTIQUE, AND IF YOU WANNA KNOW MORE, YOU SHOULD BE READING UNCANNY X-MEN. -TEMERARIOUS TOM.

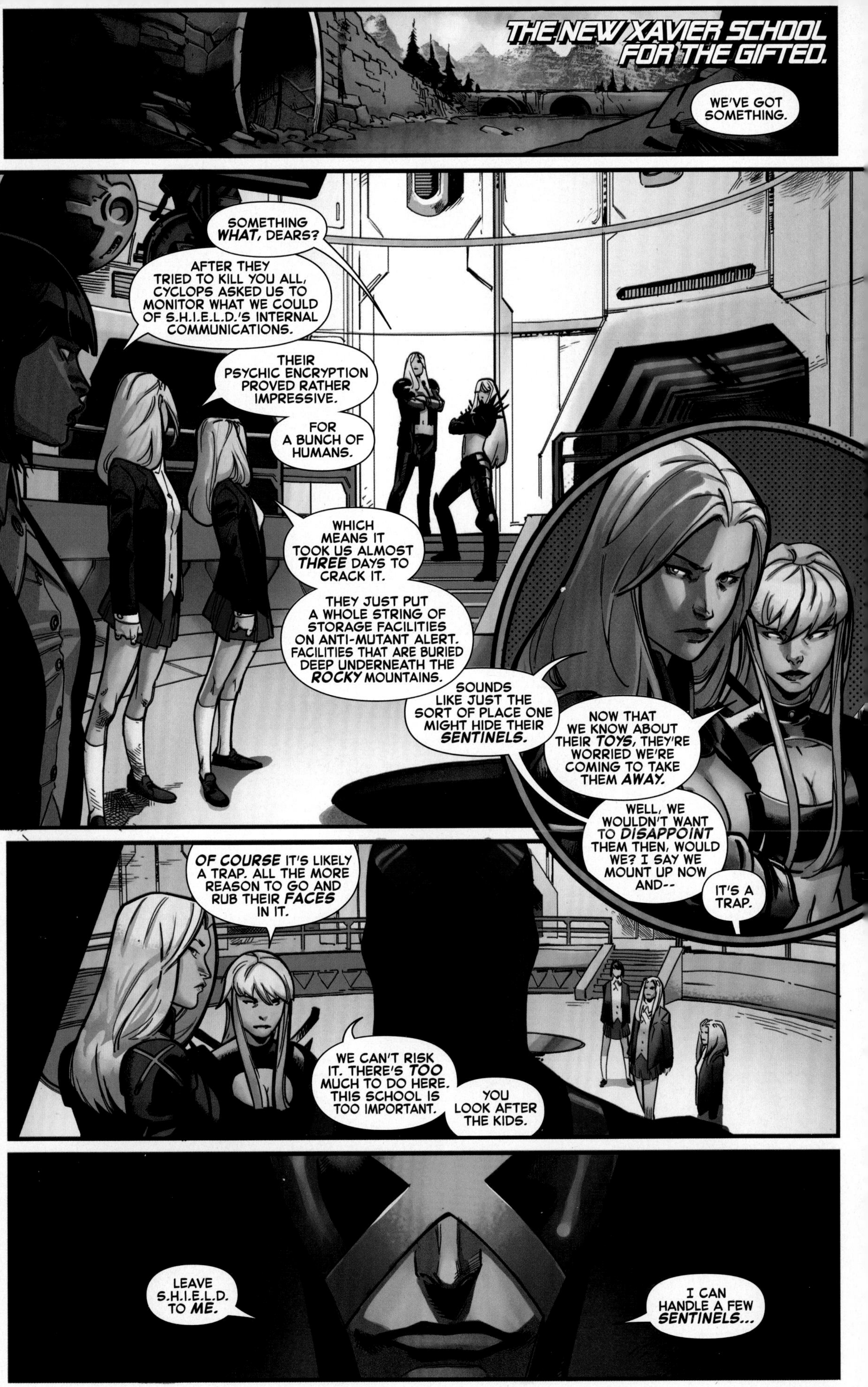
THE NEW XAVIER SCHOOL FOR THE GIFTED.
WE'VE GOT SOMETHING.
SOMETHING WHAT, DEARS?
AFTER THEY TRIED TO KILL YOU ALL, CYCLOPS ASKED US TO MONITOR WHAT WE COULD OF S.H.I.E.L.D.'S INTERNAL COMMUNICATIONS.
THEIR PSYCHIC ENCRYPTION PROVED RATHER IMPRESSIVE.
FOR A BUNCH OF HUMANS.
WHICH MEANS IT TOOK US ALMOST THREE DAYS TO CRACK IT.
THEY JUST PUT A WHOLE STRING OF STORAGE FACILITIES ON ANTI-MUTANT ALERT. FACILITIES THAT ARE BURIED DEEP UNDERNEATH THE ROCKY MOUNTAINS.
SOUNDS LIKE JUST THE SORT OF PLACE ONE MIGHT HIDE THEIR SENTINELS.
NOW THAT WE KNOW ABOUT THEIR TOYS, THEY'RE WORRIED WE'RE COMING TO TAKE THEM AWAY.
WELL, WE WOULDN'T WANT TO DISAPPOINT THEM THEN, WOULD WE? I SAY WE MOUNT UP NOW AND--
IT'S A TRAP.
OF COURSE IT'S LIKELY A TRAP. ALL THE MORE REASON TO GO AND RUB THEIR FACES IN IT.
WE CAN'T RISK IT. THERE'S TOO MUCH TO DO HERE. THIS SCHOOL IS TOO IMPORTANT.
YOU LOOK AFTER THE KIDS.
LEAVE S.H.I.E.L.D. TO ME.
I CAN HANDLE A FEW SENTINELS...

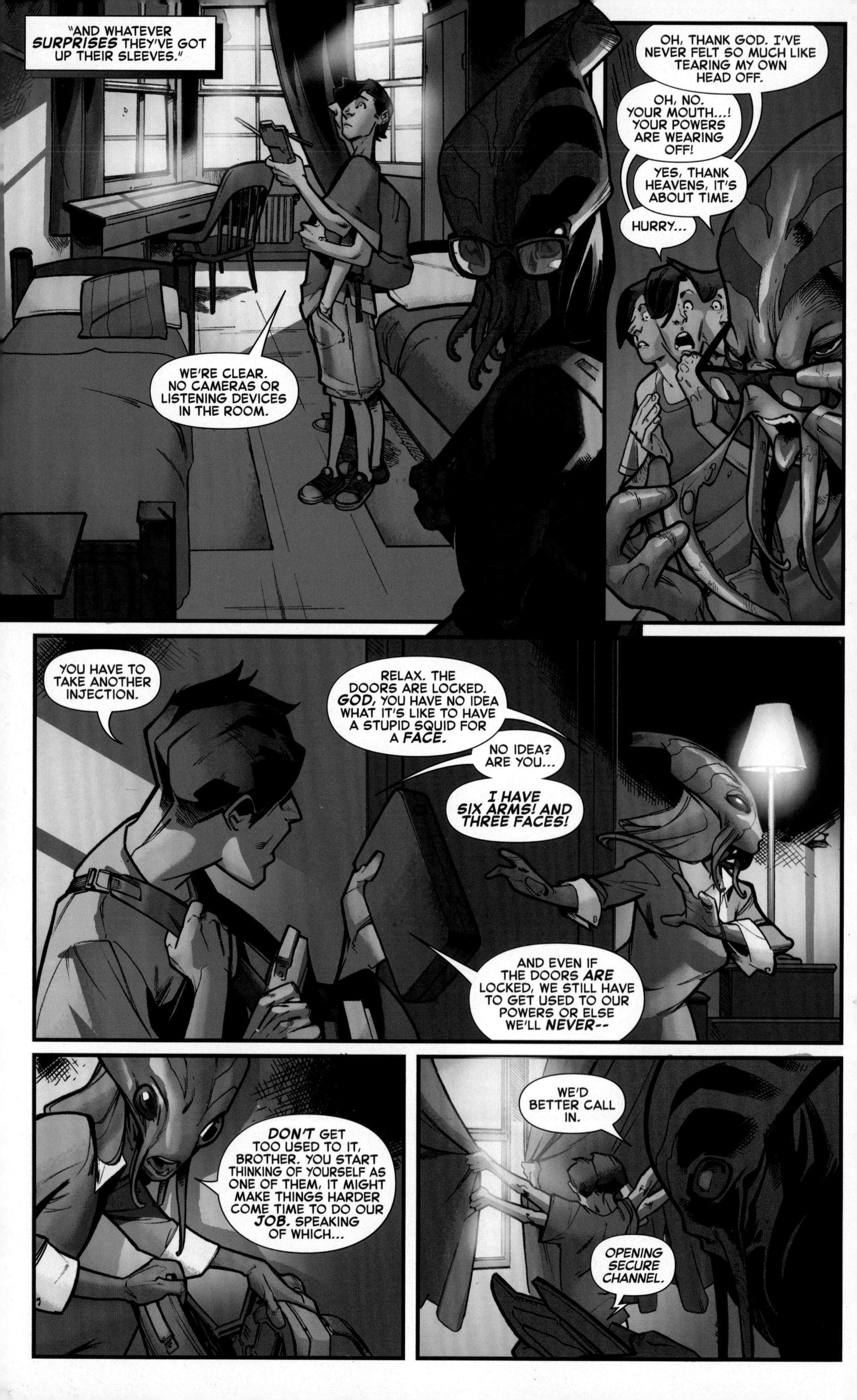
"AND WHATEVER SURPRISES THEY'VE GOT UP THEIR SLEEVES."
WE'RE CLEAR. NO CAMERAS OR LISTENING DEVICES IN THE ROOM.
OH, THANK GOD. I'VE NEVER FELT SO MUCH LIKE TEARING MY OWN HEAD OFF.
OH, NO. YOUR MOUTH...! YOUR POWERS ARE WEARING OFF!
YES, THANK HEAVENS, IT'S ABOUT TIME.
HURRY...
YOU HAVE TO TAKE ANOTHER INJECTION.
RELAX. THE DOORS ARE LOCKED. GOD, YOU HAVE NO IDEA WHAT IT'S LIKE TO HAVE A STUPID SQUID FOR A FACE.
NO IDEA? ARE YOU...
I HAVE SIX ARMS! AND THREE FACES!
AND EVEN IF THE DOORS ARE LOCKED, WE STILL HAVE TO GET USED TO OUR POWERS OR ELSE WE'LL NEVER--
DON'T GET TOO USED TO IT, BROTHER. YOU START THINKING OF YOURSELF AS ONE OF THEM, IT MIGHT MAKE THINGS HARDER COME TIME TO DO OUR JOB. SPEAKING OF WHICH...
WE'D BETTER CALL IN.
OPENING SECURE CHANNEL.

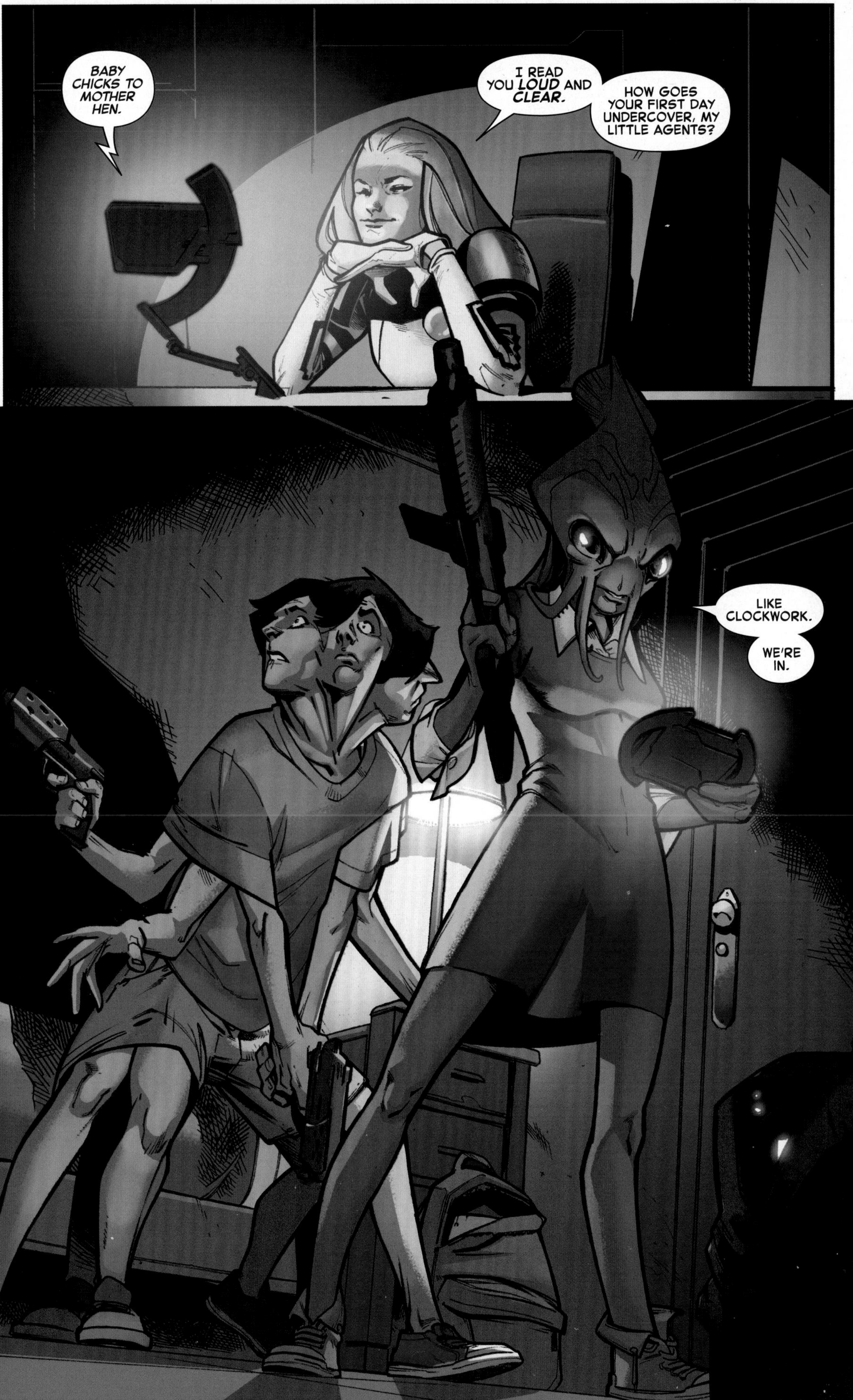
BABY CHICKS TO MOTHER HEN.
I READ YOU LOUD AND CLEAR.
HOW GOES YOUR FIRST DAY UNDERCOVER, MY LITTLE AGENTS?
LIKE CLOCKWORK.
WE'RE IN.

THE WOLVERINE SCHOOL FOR GIFTED YOUNGSTERS 39

PART TWO: OLD FRIENDS AND NEW ENEMIES

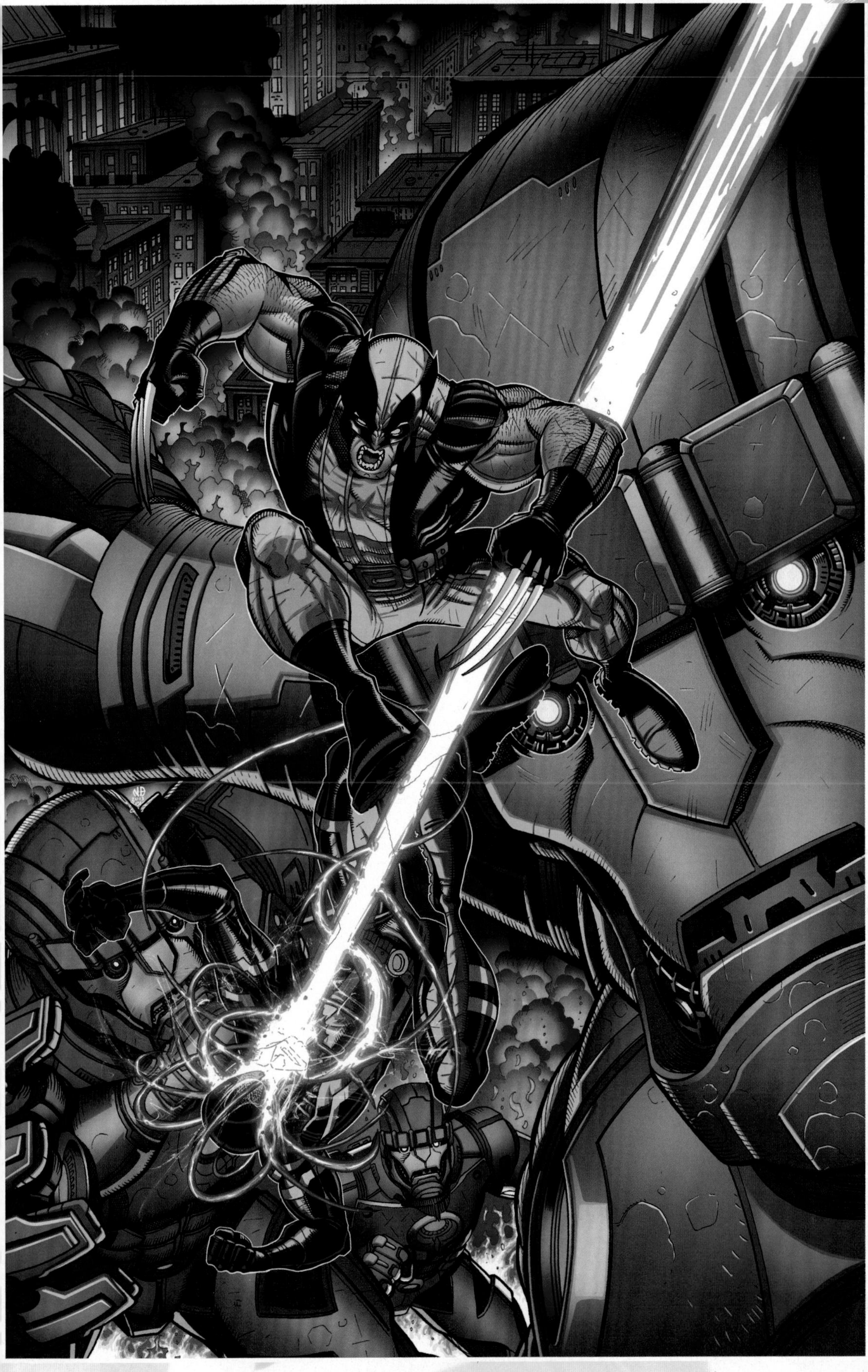

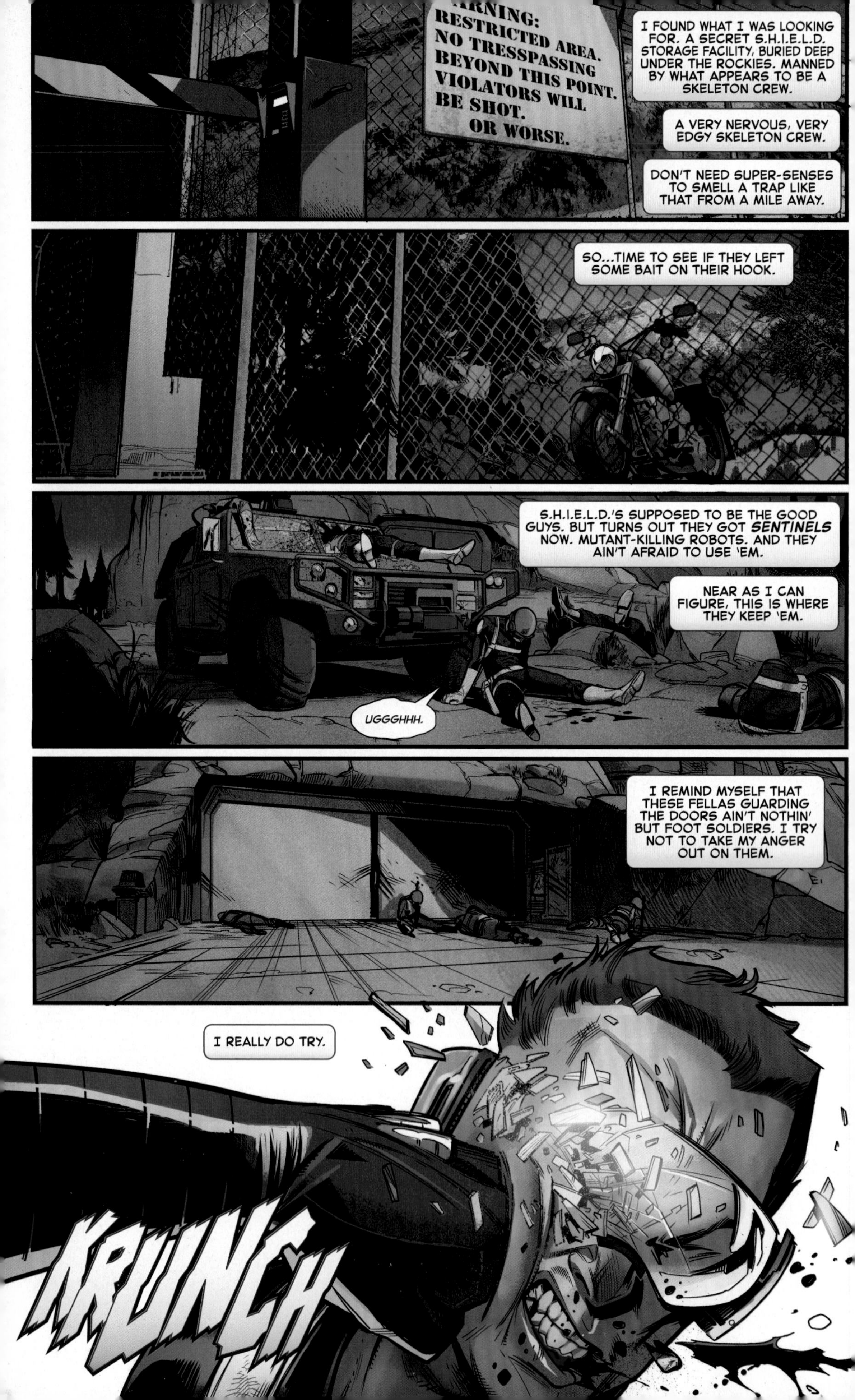

ARNING:
RESTRICTED AREA.
NO TRESSPASSING
BEYOND THIS POINT.
VIOLATORS WILL
BE SHOT.
OR WORSE.
I FOUND WHAT I WAS LOOKING FOR. A SECRET S.H.I.E.L.D. STORAGE FACILITY, BURIED DEEP UNDER THE ROCKIES. MANNED BY WHAT APPEARS TO BE A SKELETON CREW.
A VERY NERVOUS, VERY EDGY SKELETON CREW.
DON'T NEED SUPER-SENSES TO SMELL A TRAP LIKE THAT FROM A MILE AWAY.
SO...TIME TO SEE IF THEY LEFT SOME BAIT ON THEIR HOOK.
S.H.I.E.L.D.'S SUPPOSED TO BE THE GOOD GUYS. BUT TURNS OUT THEY GOT *SENTINELS* NOW. MUTANT-KILLING ROBOTS. AND THEY AIN'T AFRAID TO USE 'EM.
NEAR AS I CAN FIGURE, THIS IS WHERE THEY KEEP 'EM.
UGGGHHH.
I REMIND MYSELF THAT THESE FELLAS GUARDING THE DOORS AIN'T NOTHIN' BUT FOOT SOLDIERS. I TRY NOT TO TAKE MY ANGER OUT ON THEM.
I REALLY DO TRY.
KRUNCH

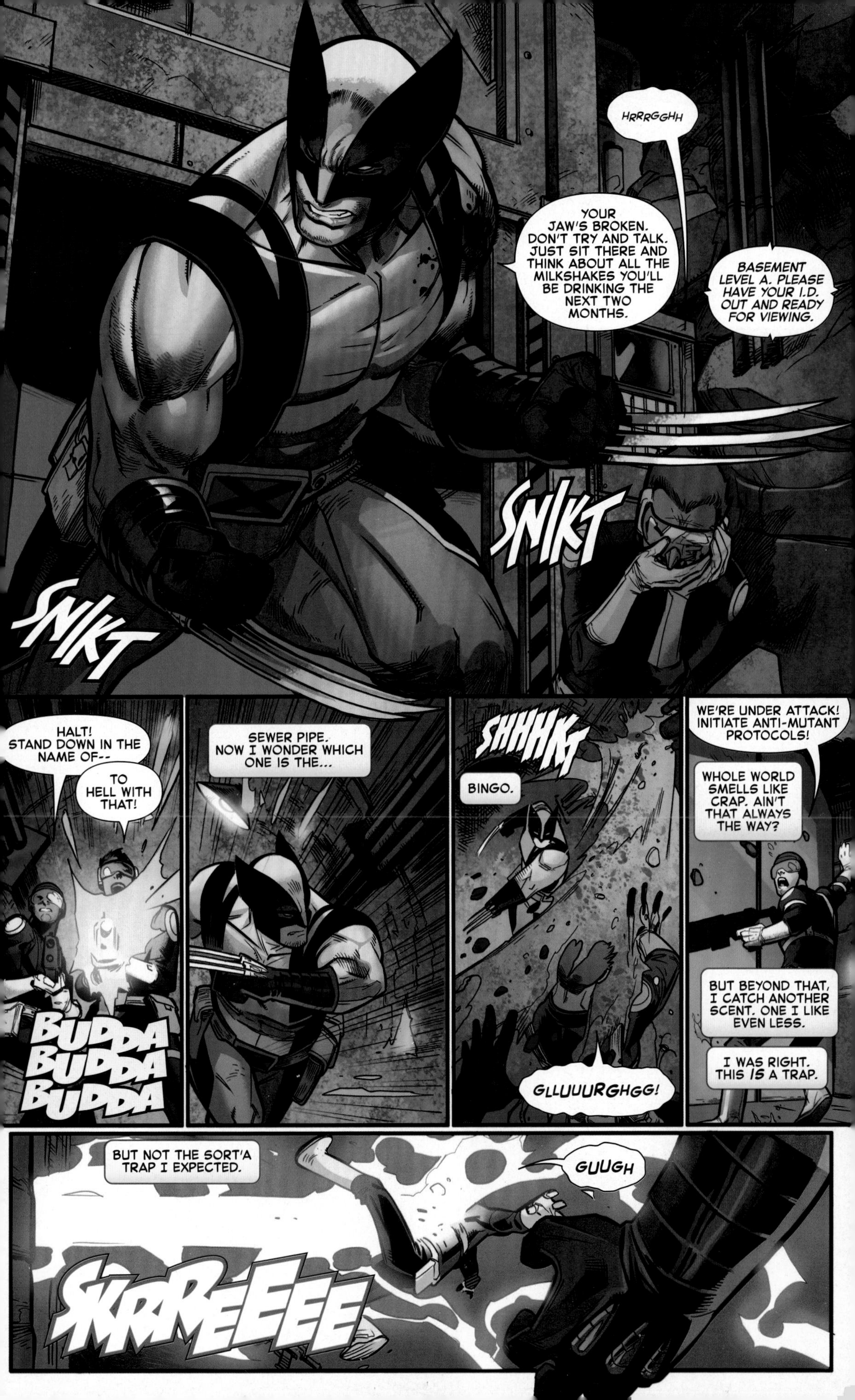
HRRRGGHH
YOUR JAW'S BROKEN. DON'T TRY AND TALK. JUST SIT THERE AND THINK ABOUT ALL THE MILKSHAKES YOU'LL BE DRINKING THE NEXT TWO MONTHS.
BASEMENT LEVEL A. PLEASE HAVE YOUR I.D. OUT AND READY FOR VIEWING.
SNIKT
SNIKT
HALT! STAND DOWN IN THE NAME OF--
TO HELL WITH THAT!
BUDDA BUDDA BUDDA
SEWER PIPE. NOW I WONDER WHICH ONE IS THE...
SHHHKT
BINGO.
GLLUUURGHGG!
WE'RE UNDER ATTACK! INITIATE ANTI-MUTANT PROTOCOLS!
WHOLE WORLD SMELLS LIKE CRAP. AIN'T THAT ALWAYS THE WAY?
BUT BEYOND THAT, I CATCH ANOTHER SCENT. ONE I LIKE EVEN LESS.
I WAS RIGHT. THIS *IS* A TRAP.
BUT NOT THE SORT'A TRAP I EXPECTED.
GUUGH
SKRREEEE

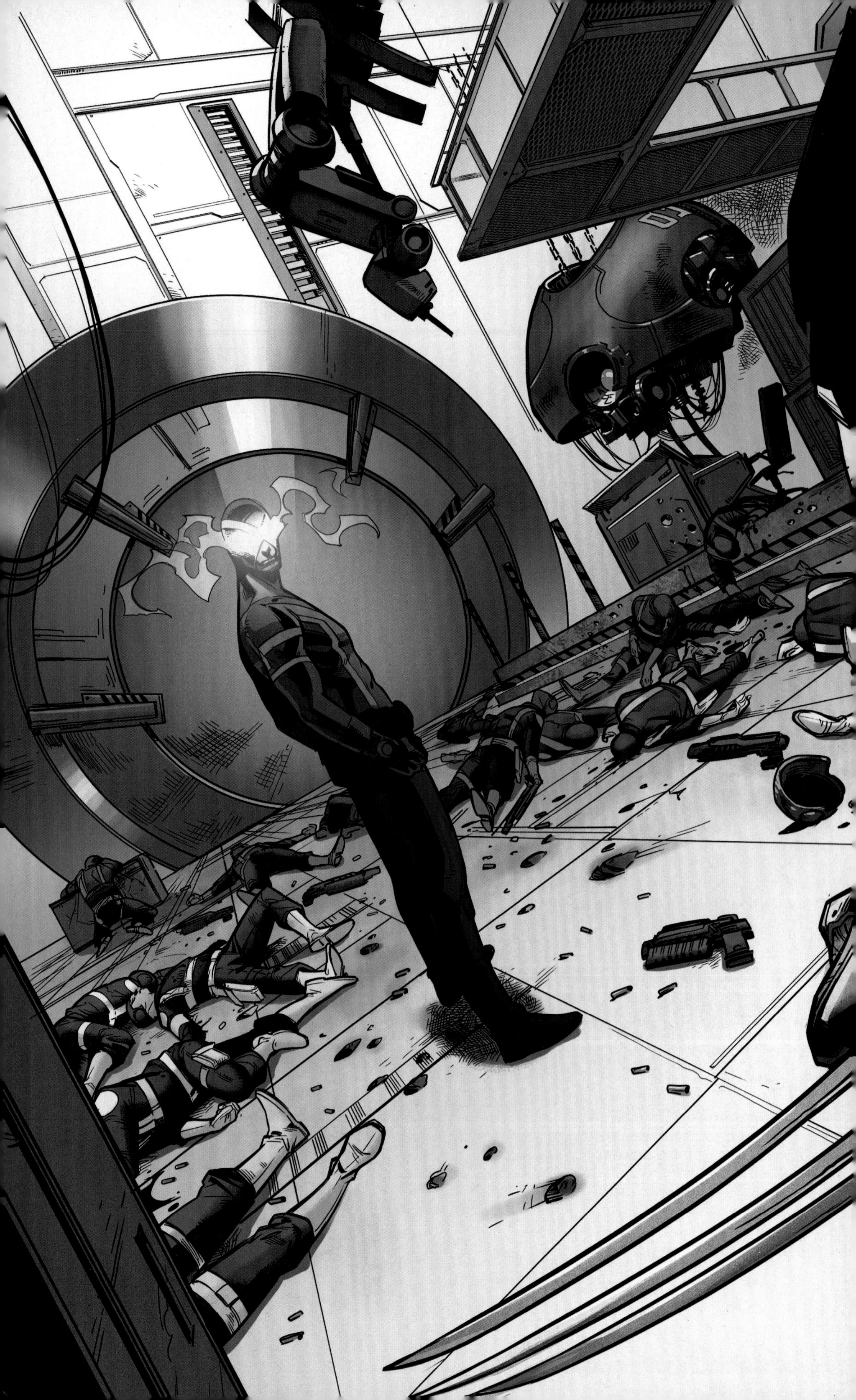

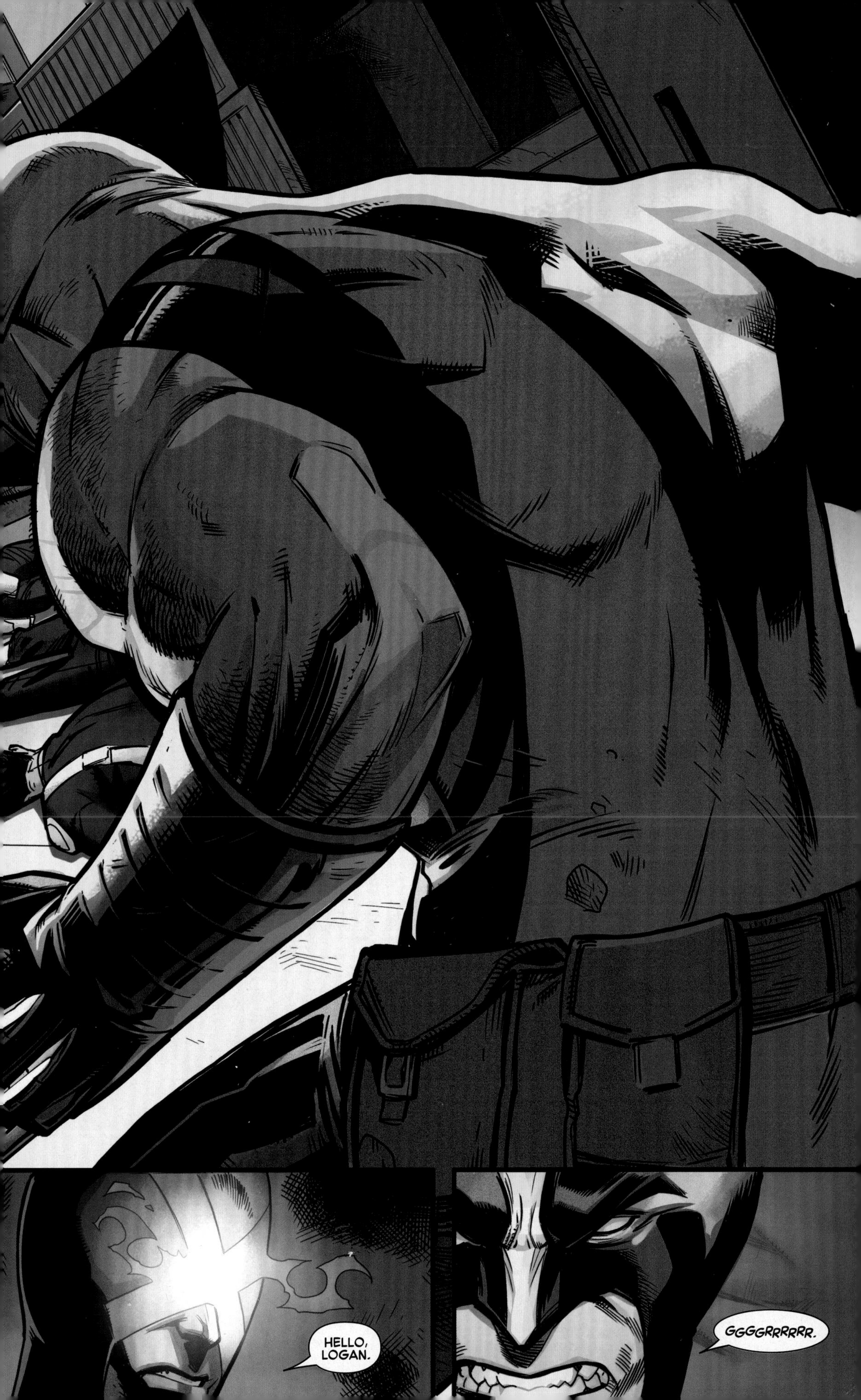
HELLO, LOGAN.
GGGGRRRRRR.

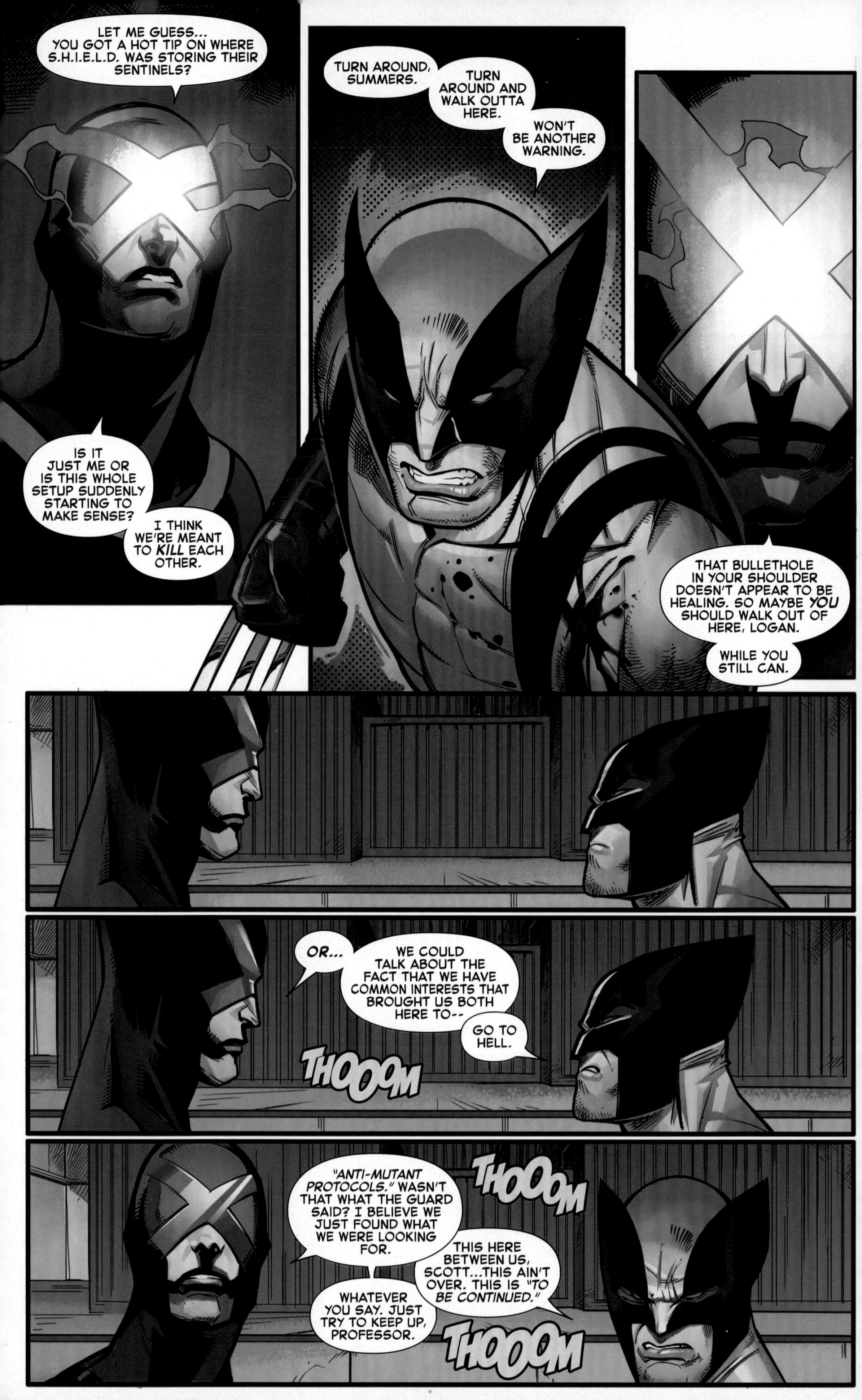
LET ME GUESS... YOU GOT A HOT TIP ON WHERE S.H.I.E.L.D. WAS STORING THEIR SENTINELS?
IS IT JUST ME OR IS THIS WHOLE SETUP SUDDENLY STARTING TO MAKE SENSE?
I THINK WE'RE MEANT TO *KILL* EACH OTHER.
TURN AROUND, SUMMERS.
TURN AROUND AND WALK OUTTA HERE.
WON'T BE ANOTHER WARNING.
THAT BULLETHOLE IN YOUR SHOULDER DOESN'T APPEAR TO BE HEALING. SO MAYBE *YOU* SHOULD WALK OUT OF HERE, LOGAN.
WHILE YOU STILL CAN.
OR...
WE COULD TALK ABOUT THE FACT THAT WE HAVE COMMON INTERESTS THAT BROUGHT US BOTH HERE TO--
GO TO HELL.
THOOOM
"ANTI-MUTANT PROTOCOLS." WASN'T THAT WHAT THE GUARD SAID? I BELIEVE WE JUST FOUND WHAT WE WERE LOOKING FOR.
THOOOM
THIS HERE BETWEEN US, SCOTT...THIS AIN'T OVER. THIS IS *"TO BE CONTINUED."*
WHATEVER YOU SAY. JUST TRY TO KEEP UP, PROFESSOR.
THOOOM

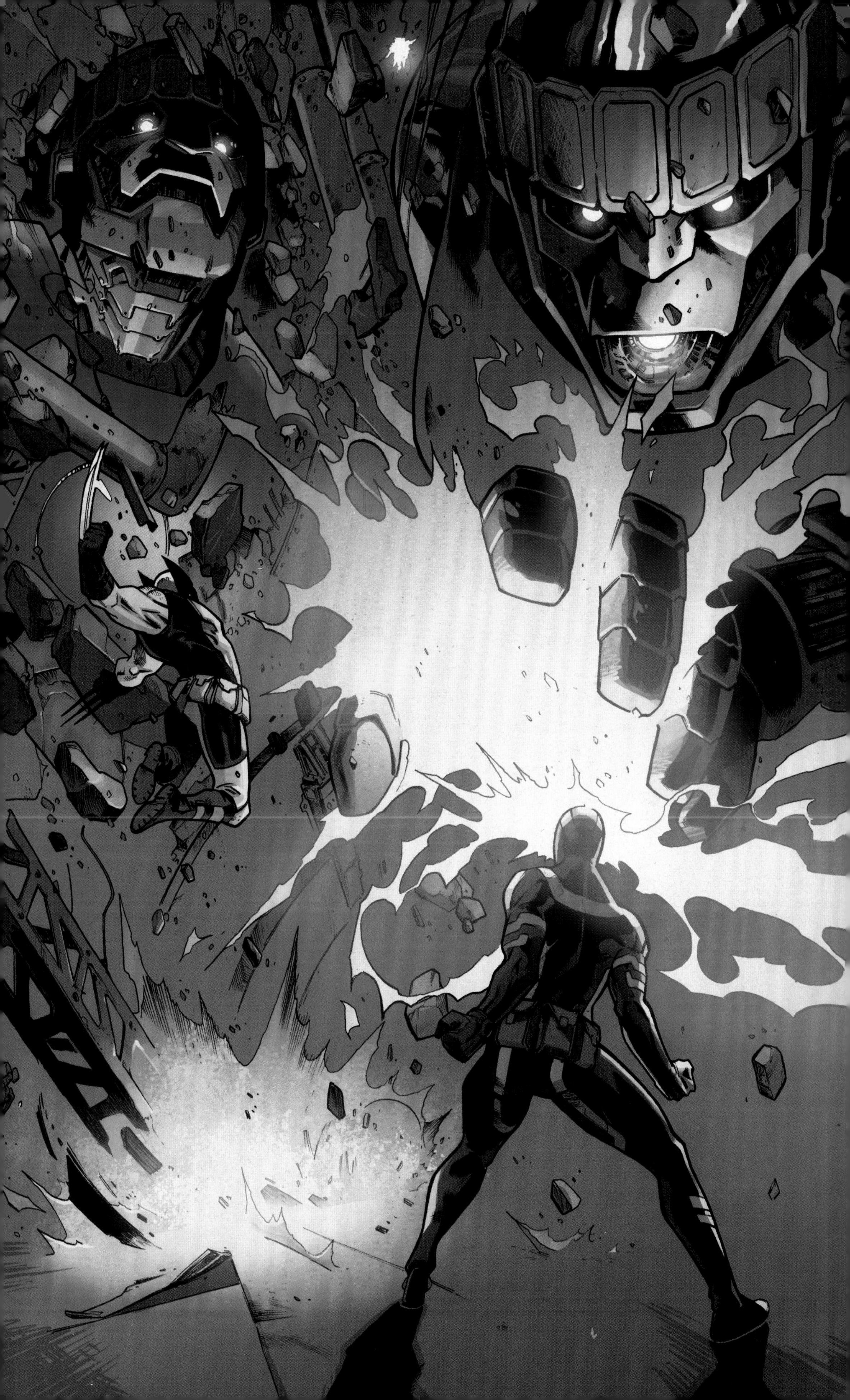

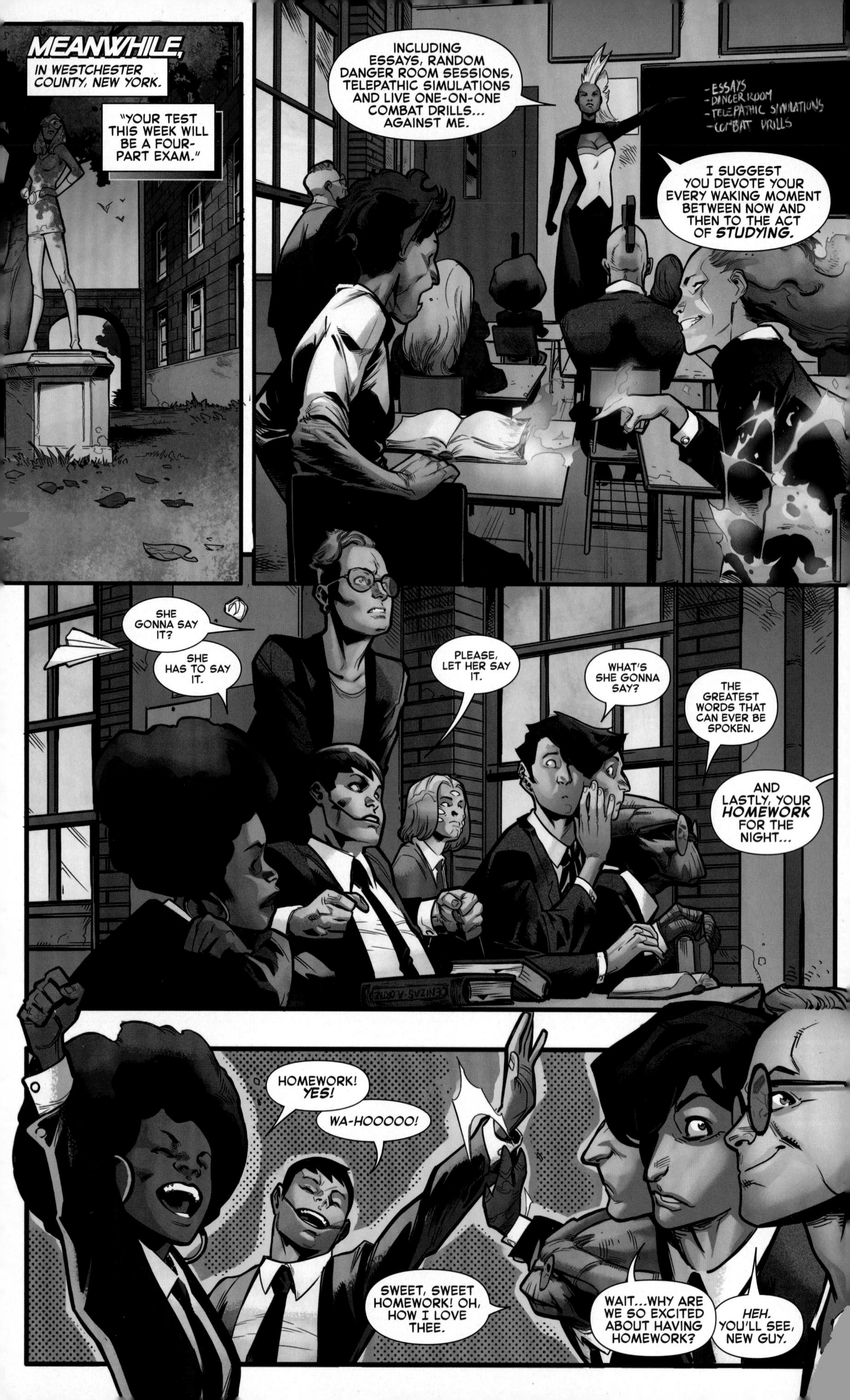
MEANWHILE,
IN WESTCHESTER COUNTY, NEW YORK.
"YOUR TEST THIS WEEK WILL BE A FOUR-PART EXAM."
INCLUDING ESSAYS, RANDOM DANGER ROOM SESSIONS, TELEPATHIC SIMULATIONS AND LIVE ONE-ON-ONE COMBAT DRILLS... AGAINST ME.
-ESSAYS
-DANGER ROOM
-TELEPATHIC SIMULATIONS
-COMBAT DRILLS
I SUGGEST YOU DEVOTE YOUR EVERY WAKING MOMENT BETWEEN NOW AND THEN TO THE ACT OF STUDYING.
SHE GONNA SAY IT?
SHE HAS TO SAY IT.
PLEASE, LET HER SAY IT.
WHAT'S SHE GONNA SAY?
THE GREATEST WORDS THAT CAN EVER BE SPOKEN.
AND LASTLY, YOUR HOMEWORK FOR THE NIGHT...
HOMEWORK! YES!
WA-HOOOOO!
SWEET, SWEET HOMEWORK! OH, HOW I LOVE THEE.
WAIT...WHY ARE WE SO EXCITED ABOUT HAVING HOMEWORK?
HEH. YOU'LL SEE, NEW GUY.

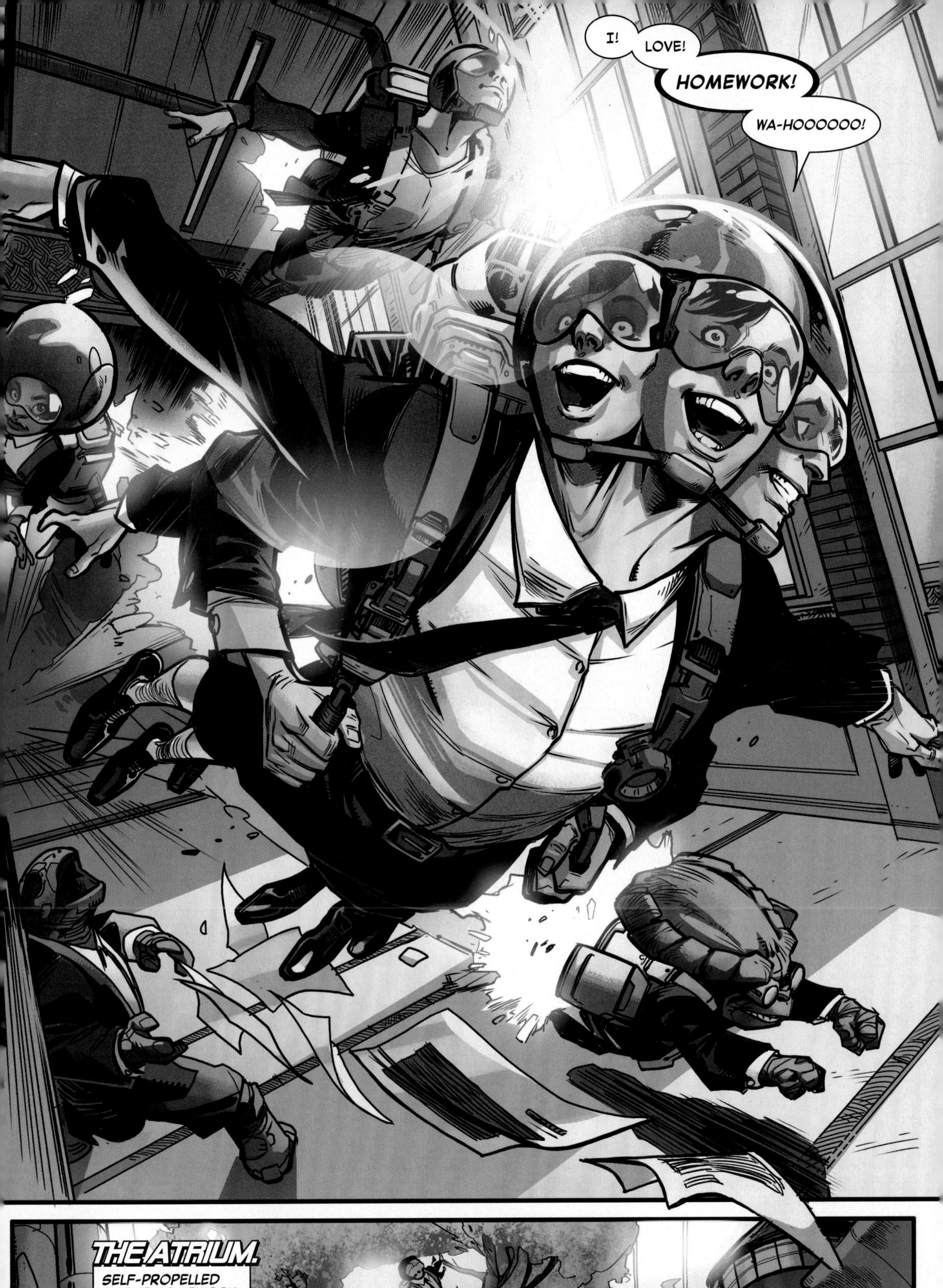
I!
LOVE!
HOMEWORK!
WA-HOOOOOO!

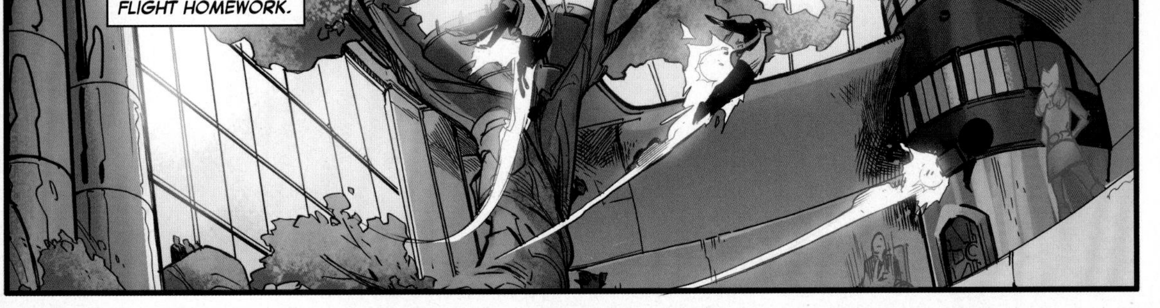
THE ATRIUM.
SELF-PROPELLED FLIGHT HOMEWORK.

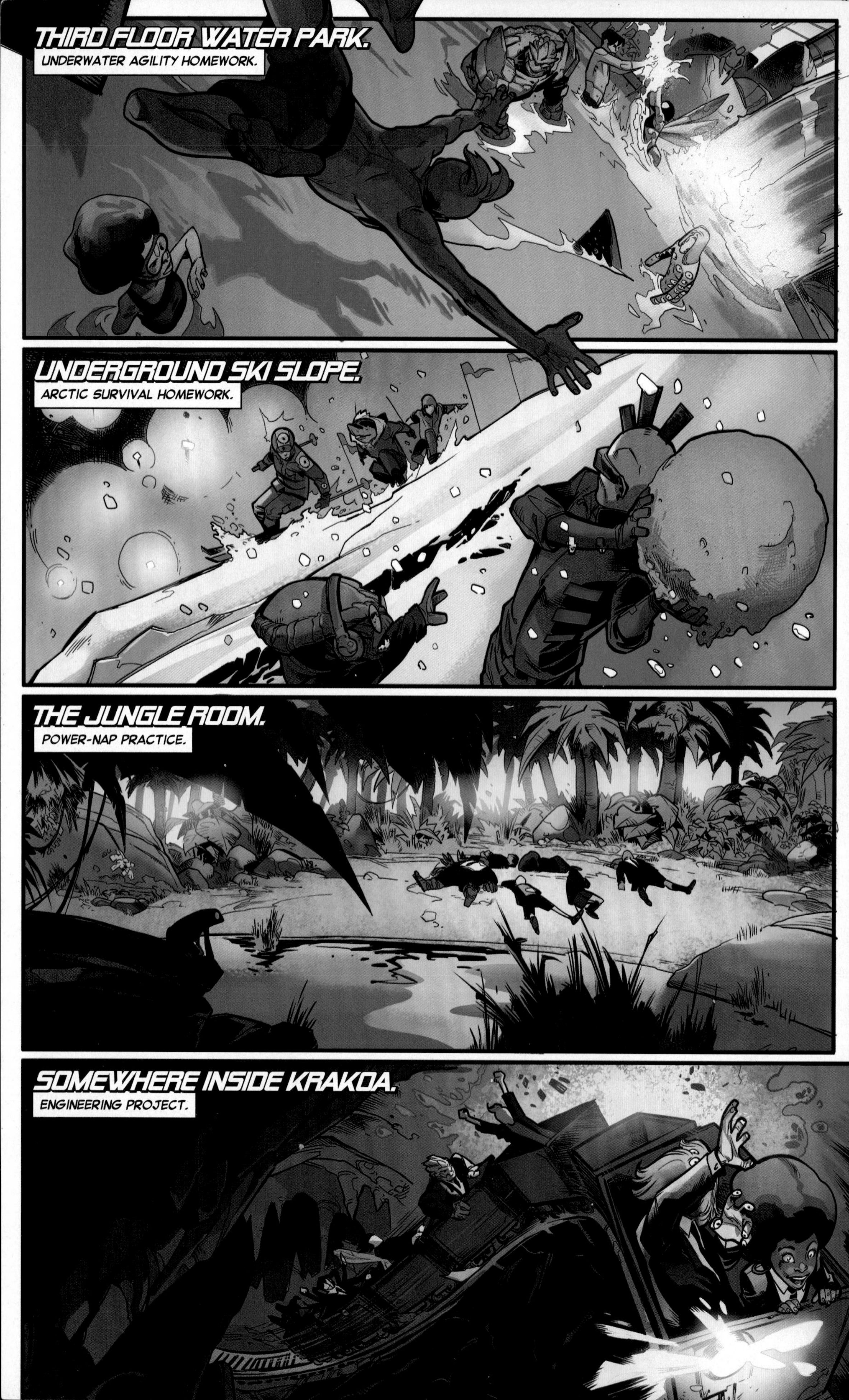
THIRD FLOOR WATER PARK.
UNDERWATER AGILITY HOMEWORK.
UNDERGROUND SKI SLOPE.
ARCTIC SURVIVAL HOMEWORK.
THE JUNGLE ROOM.
POWER-NAP PRACTICE.
SOMEWHERE INSIDE KRAKOA.
ENGINEERING PROJECT.

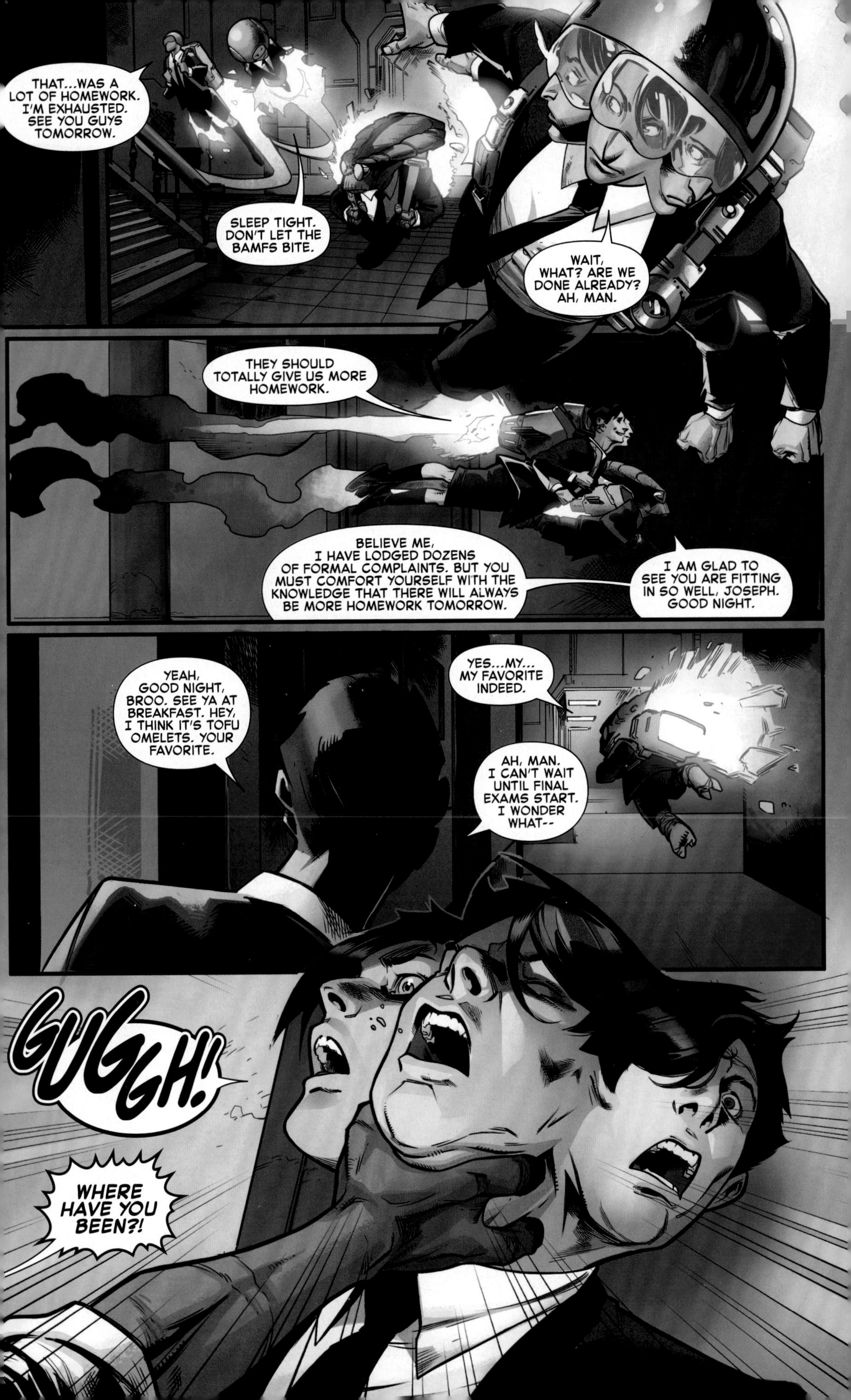
THAT...WAS A LOT OF HOMEWORK. I'M EXHAUSTED. SEE YOU GUYS TOMORROW.
SLEEP TIGHT. DON'T LET THE BAMFS BITE.
WAIT, WHAT? ARE WE DONE ALREADY? AH, MAN.
THEY SHOULD TOTALLY GIVE US MORE HOMEWORK.
BELIEVE ME, I HAVE LODGED DOZENS OF FORMAL COMPLAINTS. BUT YOU MUST COMFORT YOURSELF WITH THE KNOWLEDGE THAT THERE WILL ALWAYS BE MORE HOMEWORK TOMORROW.
I AM GLAD TO SEE YOU ARE FITTING IN SO WELL, JOSEPH. GOOD NIGHT.
YEAH, GOOD NIGHT, BROO. SEE YA AT BREAKFAST. HEY, I THINK IT'S TOFU OMELETS. YOUR FAVORITE.
YES...MY... MY FAVORITE INDEED.
AH, MAN. I CAN'T WAIT UNTIL FINAL EXAMS START. I WONDER WHAT--
GUGGH!
WHERE HAVE YOU BEEN?!

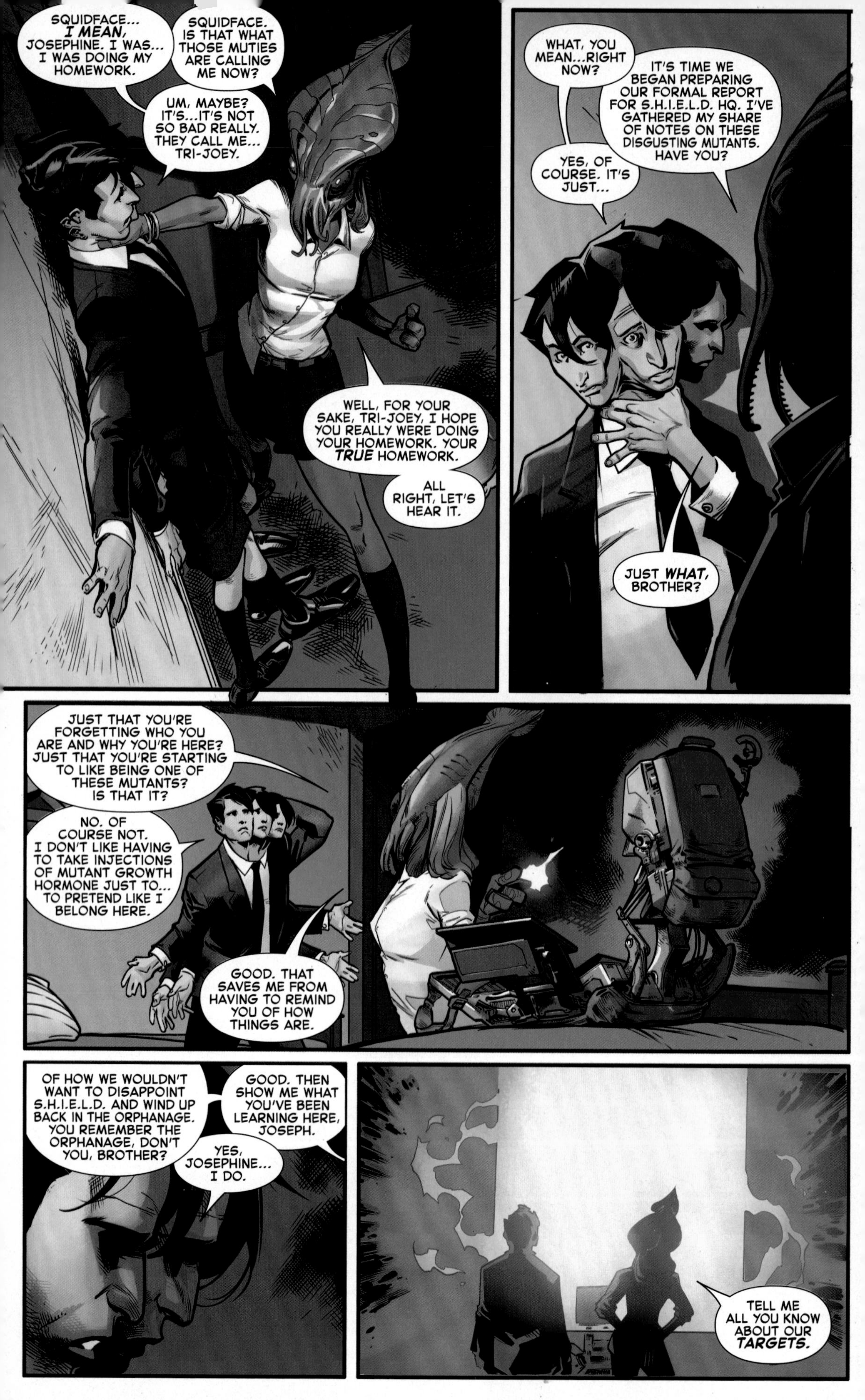
SQUIDFACE... I MEAN, JOSEPHINE. I WAS... I WAS DOING MY HOMEWORK.
SQUIDFACE. IS THAT WHAT THOSE MUTIES ARE CALLING ME NOW?
UM, MAYBE? IT'S...IT'S NOT SO BAD REALLY. THEY CALL ME... TRI-JOEY.
WELL, FOR YOUR SAKE, TRI-JOEY, I HOPE YOU REALLY WERE DOING YOUR HOMEWORK. YOUR TRUE HOMEWORK.
ALL RIGHT, LET'S HEAR IT.
WHAT, YOU MEAN...RIGHT NOW?
IT'S TIME WE BEGAN PREPARING OUR FORMAL REPORT FOR S.H.I.E.L.D. HQ. I'VE GATHERED MY SHARE OF NOTES ON THESE DISGUSTING MUTANTS. HAVE YOU?
YES, OF COURSE. IT'S JUST...
JUST WHAT, BROTHER?
JUST THAT YOU'RE FORGETTING WHO YOU ARE AND WHY YOU'RE HERE? JUST THAT YOU'RE STARTING TO LIKE BEING ONE OF THESE MUTANTS? IS THAT IT?
NO. OF COURSE NOT. I DON'T LIKE HAVING TO TAKE INJECTIONS OF MUTANT GROWTH HORMONE JUST TO... TO PRETEND LIKE I BELONG HERE.
GOOD. THAT SAVES ME FROM HAVING TO REMIND YOU OF HOW THINGS ARE.
OF HOW WE WOULDN'T WANT TO DISAPPOINT S.H.I.E.L.D. AND WIND UP BACK IN THE ORPHANAGE. YOU REMEMBER THE ORPHANAGE, DON'T YOU, BROTHER?
YES, JOSEPHINE... I DO.
GOOD. THEN SHOW ME WHAT YOU'VE BEEN LEARNING HERE, JOSEPH.
TELL ME ALL YOU KNOW ABOUT OUR TARGETS.

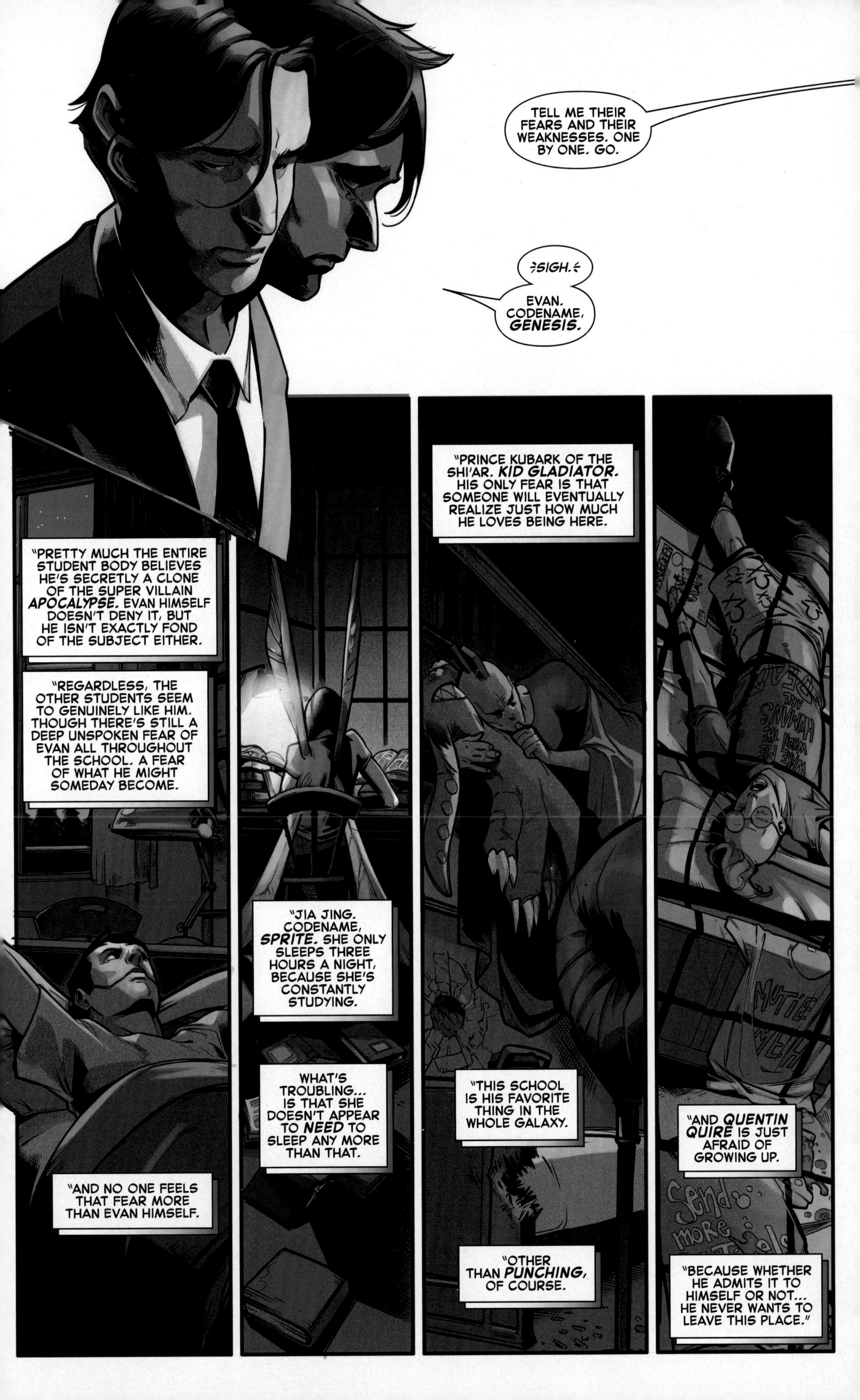

TELL ME THEIR FEARS AND THEIR WEAKNESSES. ONE BY ONE. GO.
SIGH.
EVAN. CODENAME, GENESIS.
"PRETTY MUCH THE ENTIRE STUDENT BODY BELIEVES HE'S SECRETLY A CLONE OF THE SUPER VILLAIN APOCALYPSE. EVAN HIMSELF DOESN'T DENY IT, BUT HE ISN'T EXACTLY FOND OF THE SUBJECT EITHER.
"REGARDLESS, THE OTHER STUDENTS SEEM TO GENUINELY LIKE HIM. THOUGH THERE'S STILL A DEEP UNSPOKEN FEAR OF EVAN ALL THROUGHOUT THE SCHOOL. A FEAR OF WHAT HE MIGHT SOMEDAY BECOME.
"AND NO ONE FEELS THAT FEAR MORE THAN EVAN HIMSELF.
"JIA JING. CODENAME, SPRITE. SHE ONLY SLEEPS THREE HOURS A NIGHT, BECAUSE SHE'S CONSTANTLY STUDYING.
WHAT'S TROUBLING... IS THAT SHE DOESN'T APPEAR TO NEED TO SLEEP ANY MORE THAN THAT.
"PRINCE KUBARK OF THE SHI'AR. KID GLADIATOR. HIS ONLY FEAR IS THAT SOMEONE WILL EVENTUALLY REALIZE JUST HOW MUCH HE LOVES BEING HERE.
"THIS SCHOOL IS HIS FAVORITE THING IN THE WHOLE GALAXY.
"OTHER THAN PUNCHING, OF COURSE.
"AND QUENTIN QUIRE IS JUST AFRAID OF GROWING UP.
"BECAUSE WHETHER HE ADMITS IT TO HIMSELF OR NOT... HE NEVER WANTS TO LEAVE THIS PLACE."

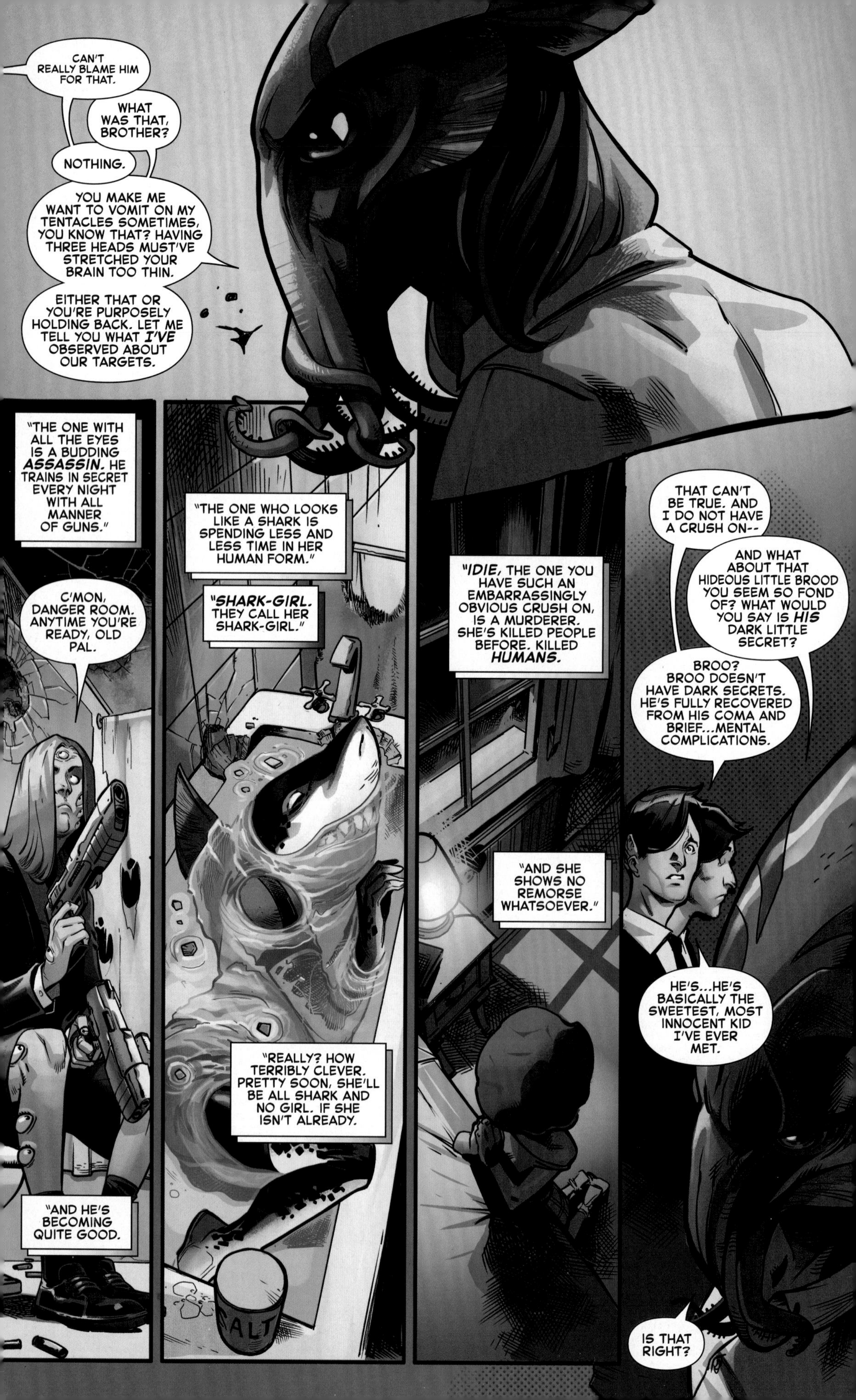
CAN'T REALLY BLAME HIM FOR THAT.
WHAT WAS THAT, BROTHER?
NOTHING.
YOU MAKE ME WANT TO VOMIT ON MY TENTACLES SOMETIMES, YOU KNOW THAT? HAVING THREE HEADS MUST'VE STRETCHED YOUR BRAIN TOO THIN.
EITHER THAT OR YOU'RE PURPOSELY HOLDING BACK. LET ME TELL YOU WHAT I'VE OBSERVED ABOUT OUR TARGETS.
"THE ONE WITH ALL THE EYES IS A BUDDING ASSASSIN. HE TRAINS IN SECRET EVERY NIGHT WITH ALL MANNER OF GUNS."
C'MON, DANGER ROOM. ANYTIME YOU'RE READY, OLD PAL.
"AND HE'S BECOMING QUITE GOOD.
"THE ONE WHO LOOKS LIKE A SHARK IS SPENDING LESS AND LESS TIME IN HER HUMAN FORM."
"SHARK-GIRL. THEY CALL HER SHARK-GIRL."
"REALLY? HOW TERRIBLY CLEVER. PRETTY SOON, SHE'LL BE ALL SHARK AND NO GIRL. IF SHE ISN'T ALREADY.
SALT
"IDIE, THE ONE YOU HAVE SUCH AN EMBARRASSINGLY OBVIOUS CRUSH ON, IS A MURDERER. SHE'S KILLED PEOPLE BEFORE. KILLED HUMANS.
"AND SHE SHOWS NO REMORSE WHATSOEVER."
THAT CAN'T BE TRUE. AND I DO NOT HAVE A CRUSH ON--
AND WHAT ABOUT THAT HIDEOUS LITTLE BROOD YOU SEEM SO FOND OF? WHAT WOULD YOU SAY IS HIS DARK LITTLE SECRET?
BROO? BROO DOESN'T HAVE DARK SECRETS. HE'S FULLY RECOVERED FROM HIS COMA AND BRIEF...MENTAL COMPLICATIONS.
HE'S...HE'S BASICALLY THE SWEETEST, MOST INNOCENT KID I'VE EVER MET.
IS THAT RIGHT?

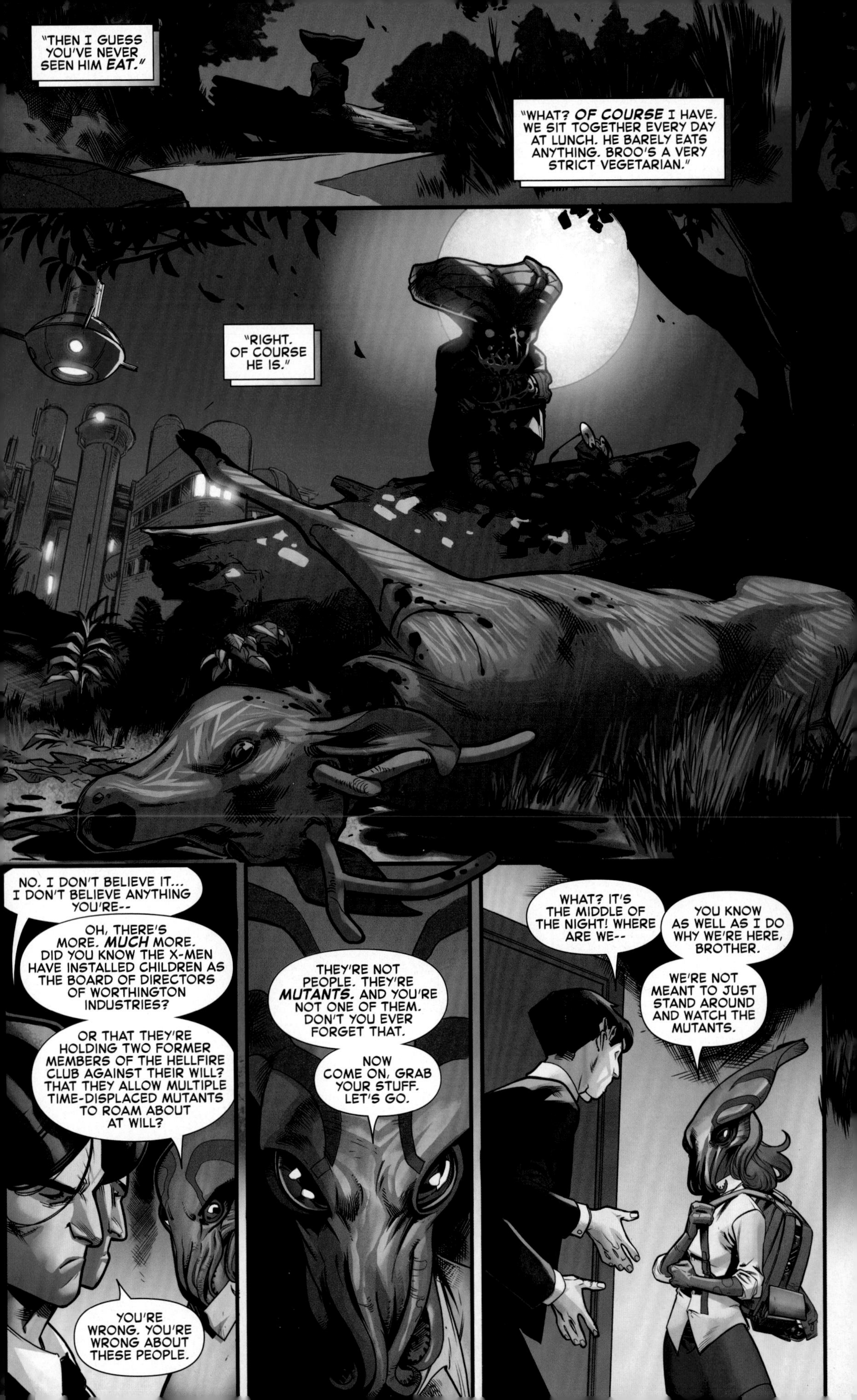
"THEN I GUESS YOU'VE NEVER SEEN HIM *EAT.*"
"WHAT? *OF COURSE* I HAVE. WE SIT TOGETHER EVERY DAY AT LUNCH. HE BARELY EATS ANYTHING. BROO'S A VERY STRICT VEGETARIAN."
"RIGHT. OF COURSE HE IS."
NO. I DON'T BELIEVE IT... I DON'T BELIEVE ANYTHING YOU'RE--
OH, THERE'S MORE. *MUCH* MORE. DID YOU KNOW THE X-MEN HAVE INSTALLED CHILDREN AS THE BOARD OF DIRECTORS OF WORTHINGTON INDUSTRIES?
OR THAT THEY'RE HOLDING TWO FORMER MEMBERS OF THE HELLFIRE CLUB AGAINST THEIR WILL? THAT THEY ALLOW MULTIPLE TIME-DISPLACED MUTANTS TO ROAM ABOUT AT WILL?
YOU'RE WRONG. YOU'RE WRONG ABOUT THESE PEOPLE.
THEY'RE NOT PEOPLE. THEY'RE *MUTANTS.* AND YOU'RE NOT ONE OF THEM. DON'T YOU EVER FORGET THAT.
NOW COME ON, GRAB YOUR STUFF. LET'S GO.
WHAT? IT'S THE MIDDLE OF THE NIGHT! WHERE ARE WE--
YOU KNOW AS WELL AS I DO WHY WE'RE HERE, BROTHER.
WE'RE NOT MEANT TO JUST STAND AROUND AND WATCH THE MUTANTS.

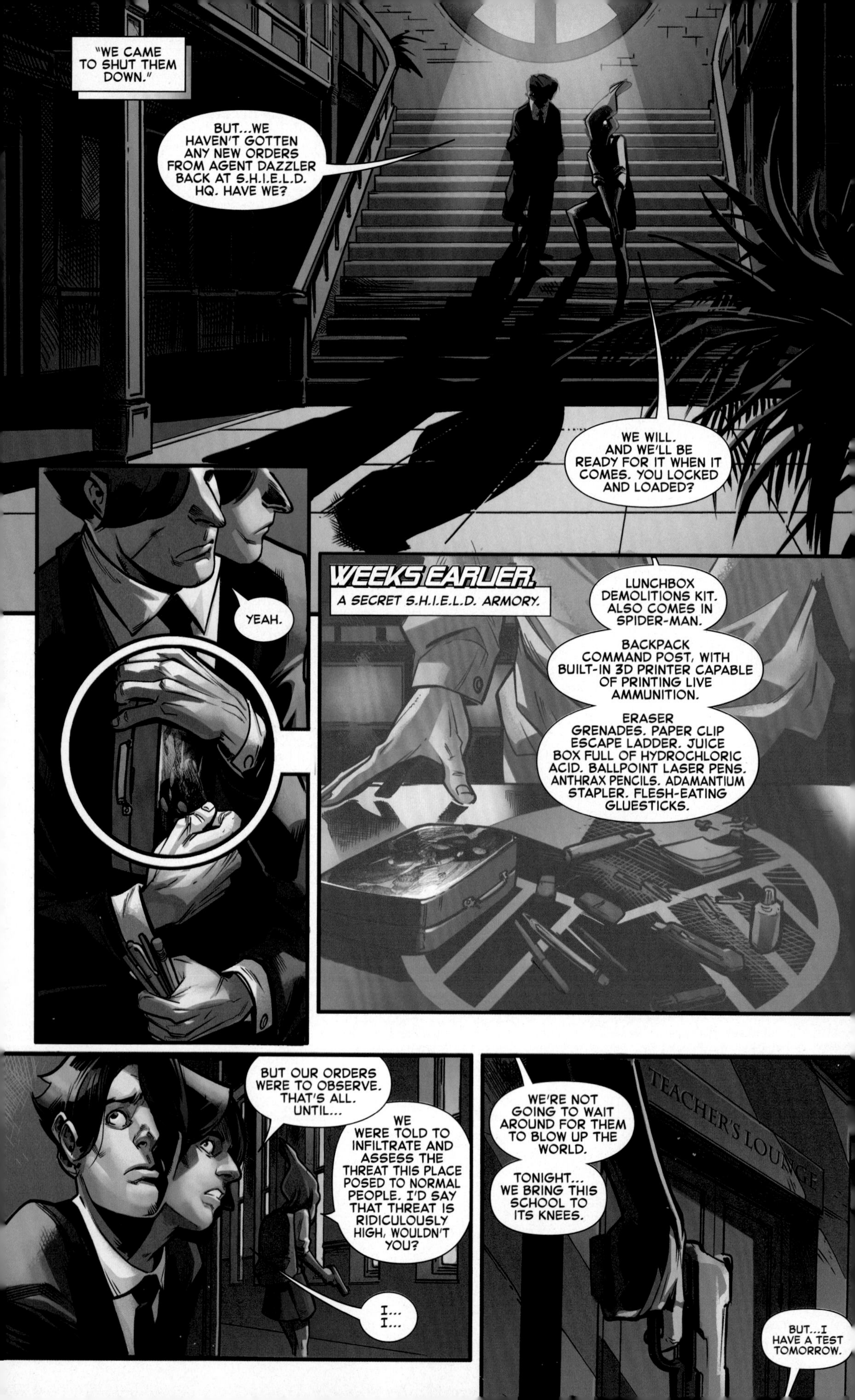
"WE CAME TO SHUT THEM DOWN."
BUT...WE HAVEN'T GOTTEN ANY NEW ORDERS FROM AGENT DAZZLER BACK AT S.H.I.E.L.D. HQ. HAVE WE?
WE WILL. AND WE'LL BE READY FOR IT WHEN IT COMES. YOU LOCKED AND LOADED?
YEAH.
WEEKS EARLIER.
A SECRET S.H.I.E.L.D. ARMORY.
LUNCHBOX DEMOLITIONS KIT. ALSO COMES IN SPIDER-MAN.
BACKPACK COMMAND POST, WITH BUILT-IN 3D PRINTER CAPABLE OF PRINTING LIVE AMMUNITION.
ERASER GRENADES. PAPER CLIP ESCAPE LADDER. JUICE BOX FULL OF HYDROCHLORIC ACID. BALLPOINT LASER PENS. ANTHRAX PENCILS. ADAMANTIUM STAPLER. FLESH-EATING GLUESTICKS.
BUT OUR ORDERS WERE TO OBSERVE. THAT'S ALL. UNTIL...
WE WERE TOLD TO INFILTRATE AND ASSESS THE THREAT THIS PLACE POSED TO NORMAL PEOPLE. I'D SAY THAT THREAT IS RIDICULOUSLY HIGH, WOULDN'T YOU?
I... I...
TEACHER'S LOUNGE
WE'RE NOT GOING TO WAIT AROUND FOR THEM TO BLOW UP THE WORLD.
TONIGHT... WE BRING THIS SCHOOL TO ITS KNEES.
BUT...I HAVE A TEST TOMORROW.

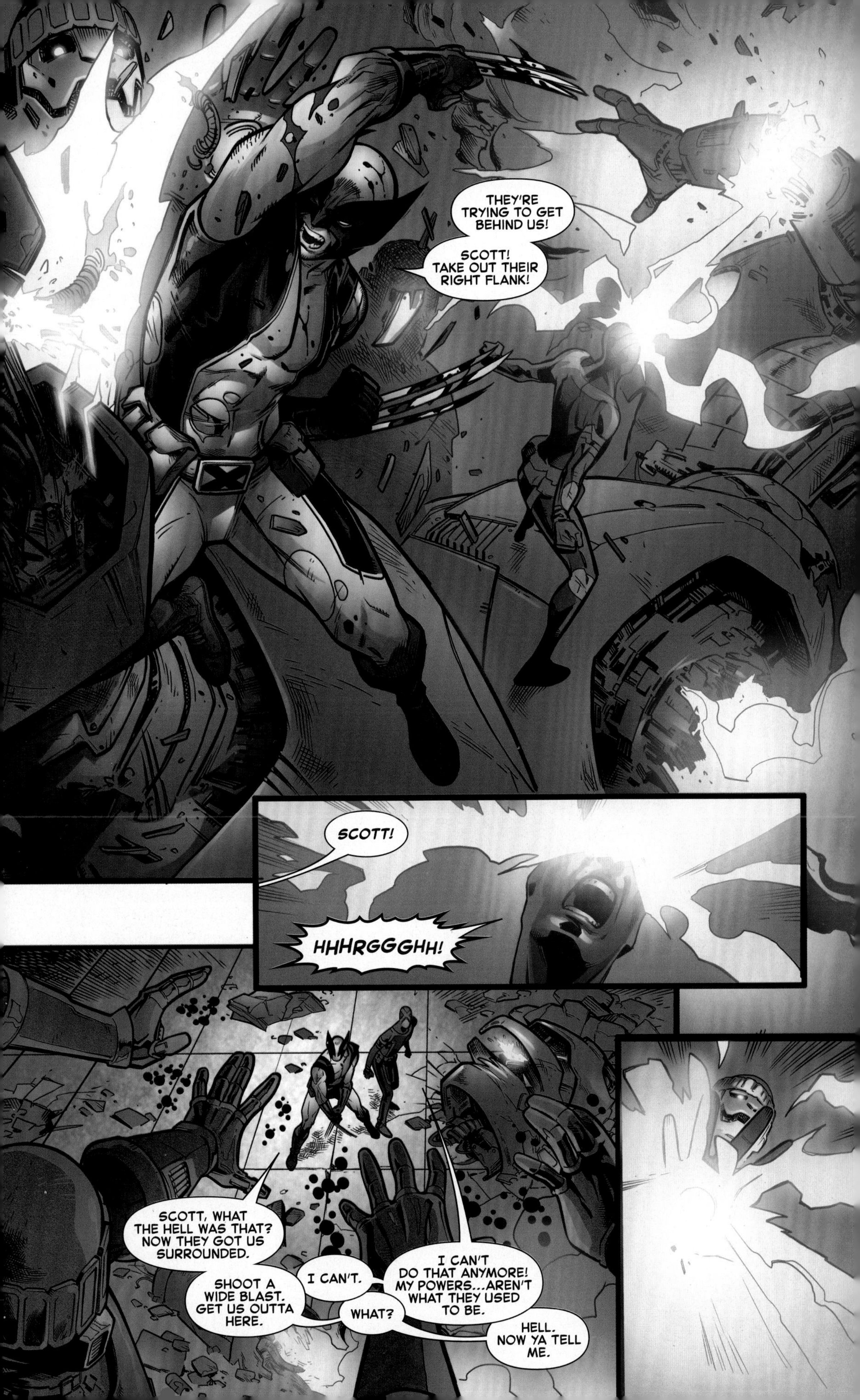
THEY'RE TRYING TO GET BEHIND US!
SCOTT! TAKE OUT THEIR RIGHT FLANK!
SCOTT!
HHHRGGGHH!
SCOTT, WHAT THE HELL WAS THAT? NOW THEY GOT US SURROUNDED.
SHOOT A WIDE BLAST. GET US OUTTA HERE.
I CAN'T.
I CAN'T DO THAT ANYMORE! MY POWERS...AREN'T WHAT THEY USED TO BE.
WHAT?
HELL. NOW YA TELL ME.

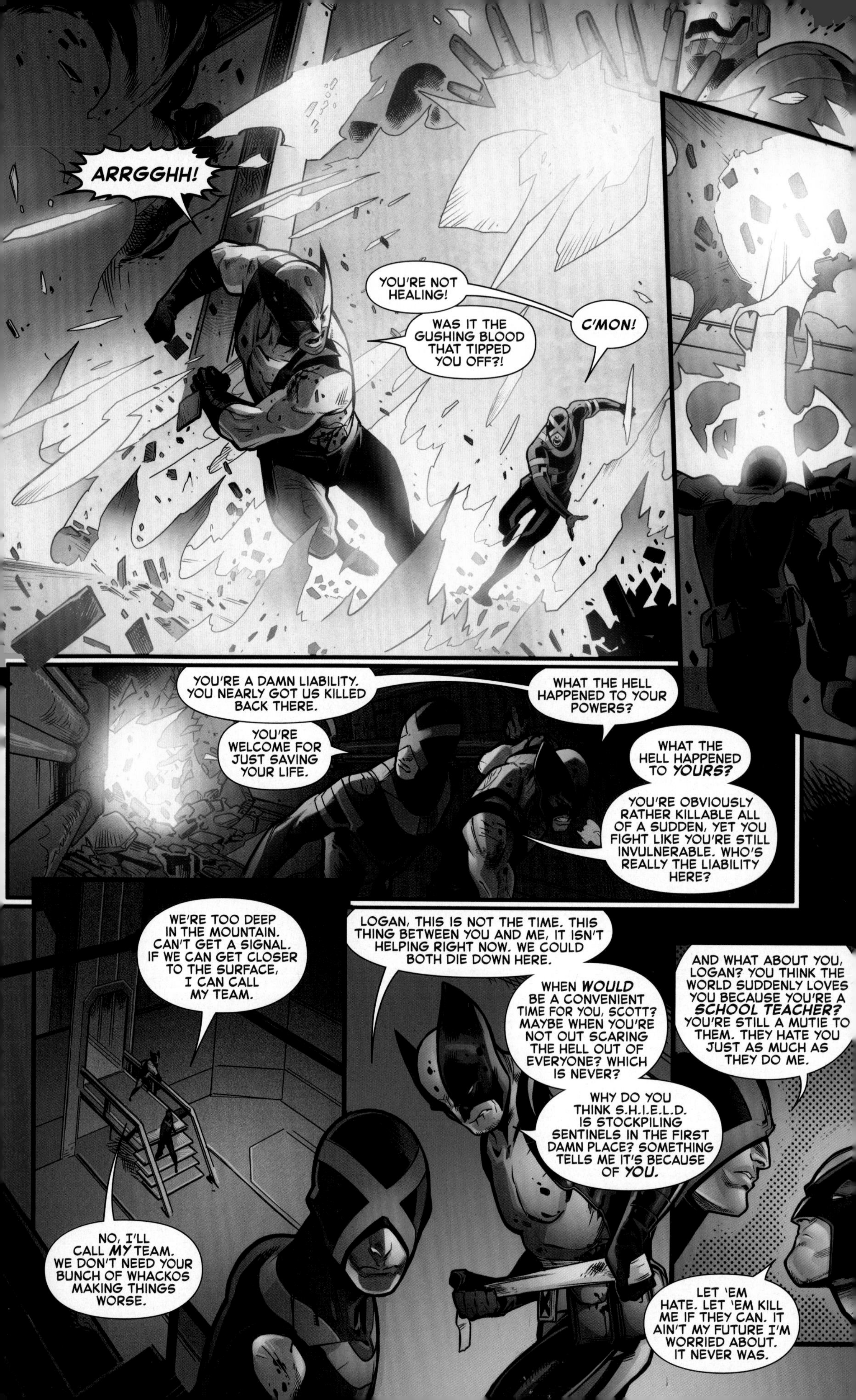
ARRGGHH!
YOU'RE NOT HEALING!
WAS IT THE GUSHING BLOOD THAT TIPPED YOU OFF?!
C'MON!
YOU'RE A DAMN LIABILITY. YOU NEARLY GOT US KILLED BACK THERE.
YOU'RE WELCOME FOR JUST SAVING YOUR LIFE.
WHAT THE HELL HAPPENED TO YOUR POWERS?
WHAT THE HELL HAPPENED TO YOURS?
YOU'RE OBVIOUSLY RATHER KILLABLE ALL OF A SUDDEN, YET YOU FIGHT LIKE YOU'RE STILL INVULNERABLE. WHO'S REALLY THE LIABILITY HERE?
WE'RE TOO DEEP IN THE MOUNTAIN. CAN'T GET A SIGNAL. IF WE CAN GET CLOSER TO THE SURFACE, I CAN CALL MY TEAM.
NO, I'LL CALL MY TEAM. WE DON'T NEED YOUR BUNCH OF WHACKOS MAKING THINGS WORSE.
LOGAN, THIS IS NOT THE TIME. THIS THING BETWEEN YOU AND ME, IT ISN'T HELPING RIGHT NOW. WE COULD BOTH DIE DOWN HERE.
WHEN WOULD BE A CONVENIENT TIME FOR YOU, SCOTT? MAYBE WHEN YOU'RE NOT OUT SCARING THE HELL OUT OF EVERYONE? WHICH IS NEVER?
WHY DO YOU THINK S.H.I.E.L.D. IS STOCKPILING SENTINELS IN THE FIRST DAMN PLACE? SOMETHING TELLS ME IT'S BECAUSE OF YOU.
AND WHAT ABOUT YOU, LOGAN? YOU THINK THE WORLD SUDDENLY LOVES YOU BECAUSE YOU'RE A SCHOOL TEACHER? YOU'RE STILL A MUTIE TO THEM. THEY HATE YOU JUST AS MUCH AS THEY DO ME.
LET 'EM HATE. LET 'EM KILL ME IF THEY CAN. IT AIN'T MY FUTURE I'M WORRIED ABOUT. IT NEVER WAS.

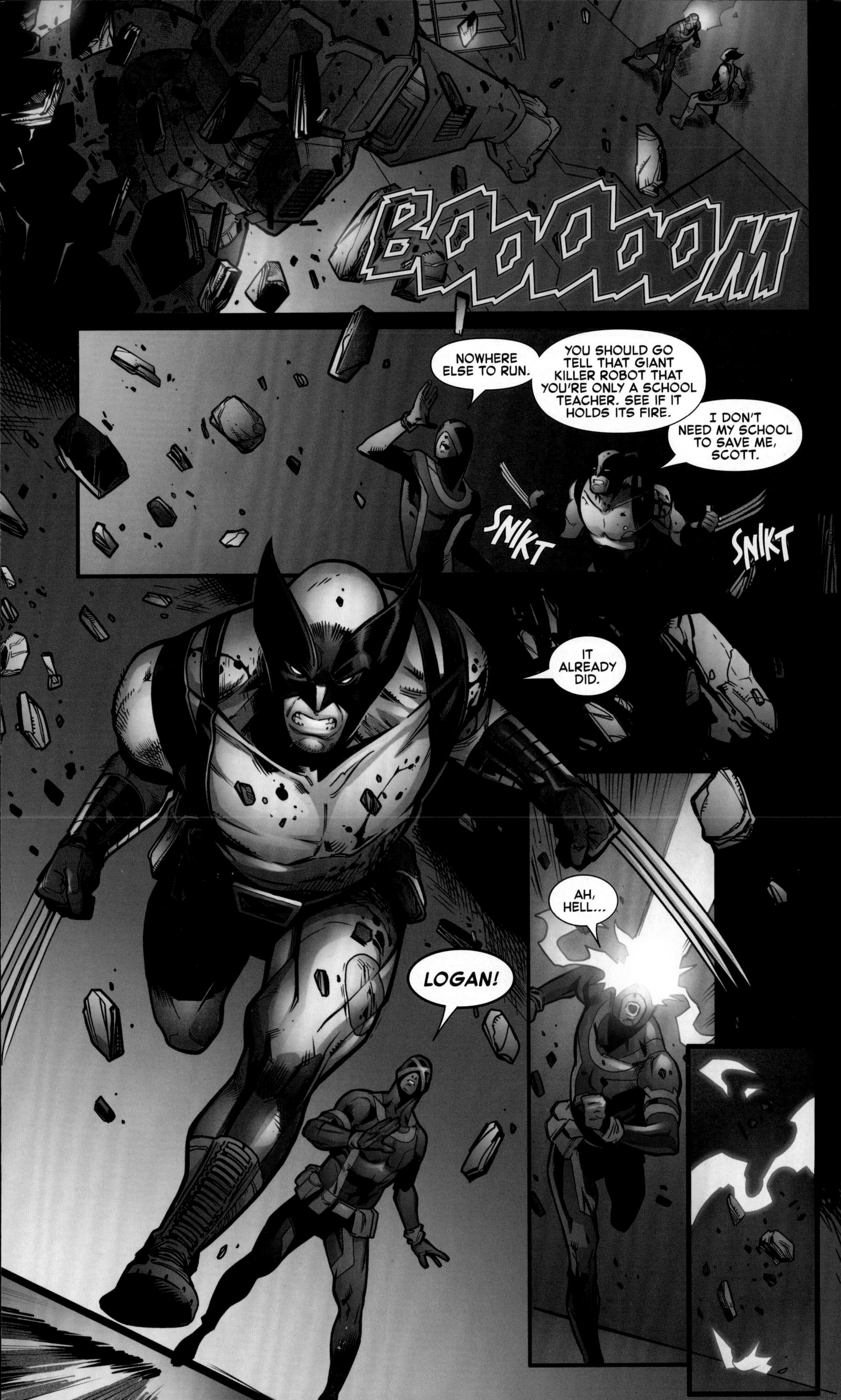

BOOOOOM
NOWHERE ELSE TO RUN.
YOU SHOULD GO TELL THAT GIANT KILLER ROBOT THAT YOU'RE ONLY A SCHOOL TEACHER. SEE IF IT HOLDS ITS FIRE.
I DON'T NEED MY SCHOOL TO SAVE ME, SCOTT.
SNIKT
SNIKT
IT ALREADY DID.
AH, HELL...
LOGAN!

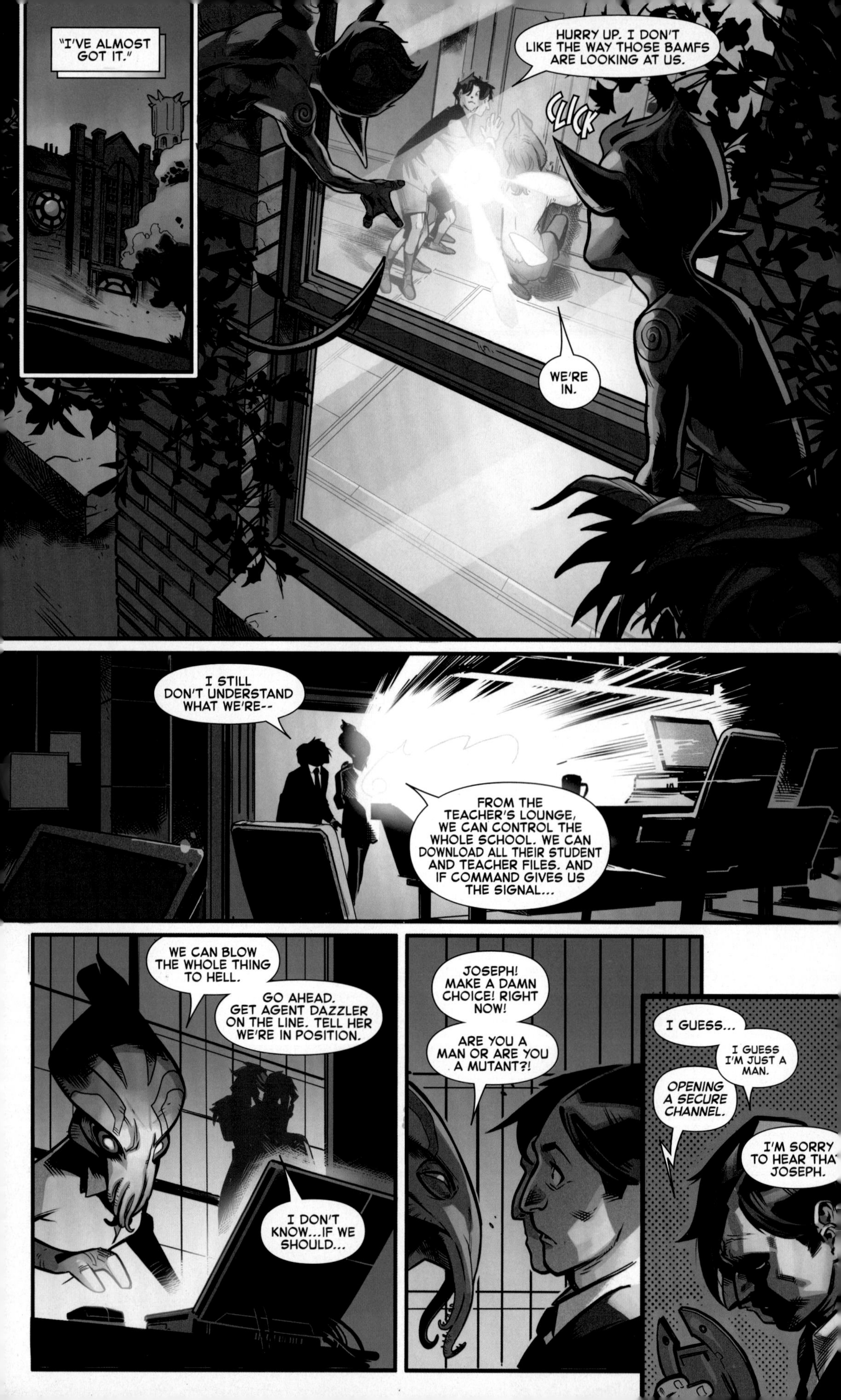
"I'VE ALMOST GOT IT."
HURRY UP. I DON'T LIKE THE WAY THOSE BAMFS ARE LOOKING AT US.
CLICK
WE'RE IN.
I STILL DON'T UNDERSTAND WHAT WE'RE--
FROM THE TEACHER'S LOUNGE, WE CAN CONTROL THE WHOLE SCHOOL. WE CAN DOWNLOAD ALL THEIR STUDENT AND TEACHER FILES. AND IF COMMAND GIVES US THE SIGNAL...
WE CAN BLOW THE WHOLE THING TO HELL.
GO AHEAD. GET AGENT DAZZLER ON THE LINE. TELL HER WE'RE IN POSITION.
I DON'T KNOW...IF WE SHOULD...
JOSEPH! MAKE A DAMN CHOICE! RIGHT NOW!
ARE YOU A MAN OR ARE YOU A MUTANT?!
I GUESS...
I GUESS I'M JUST A MAN.
OPENING A SECURE CHANNEL.
I'M SORRY TO HEAR THA JOSEPH.

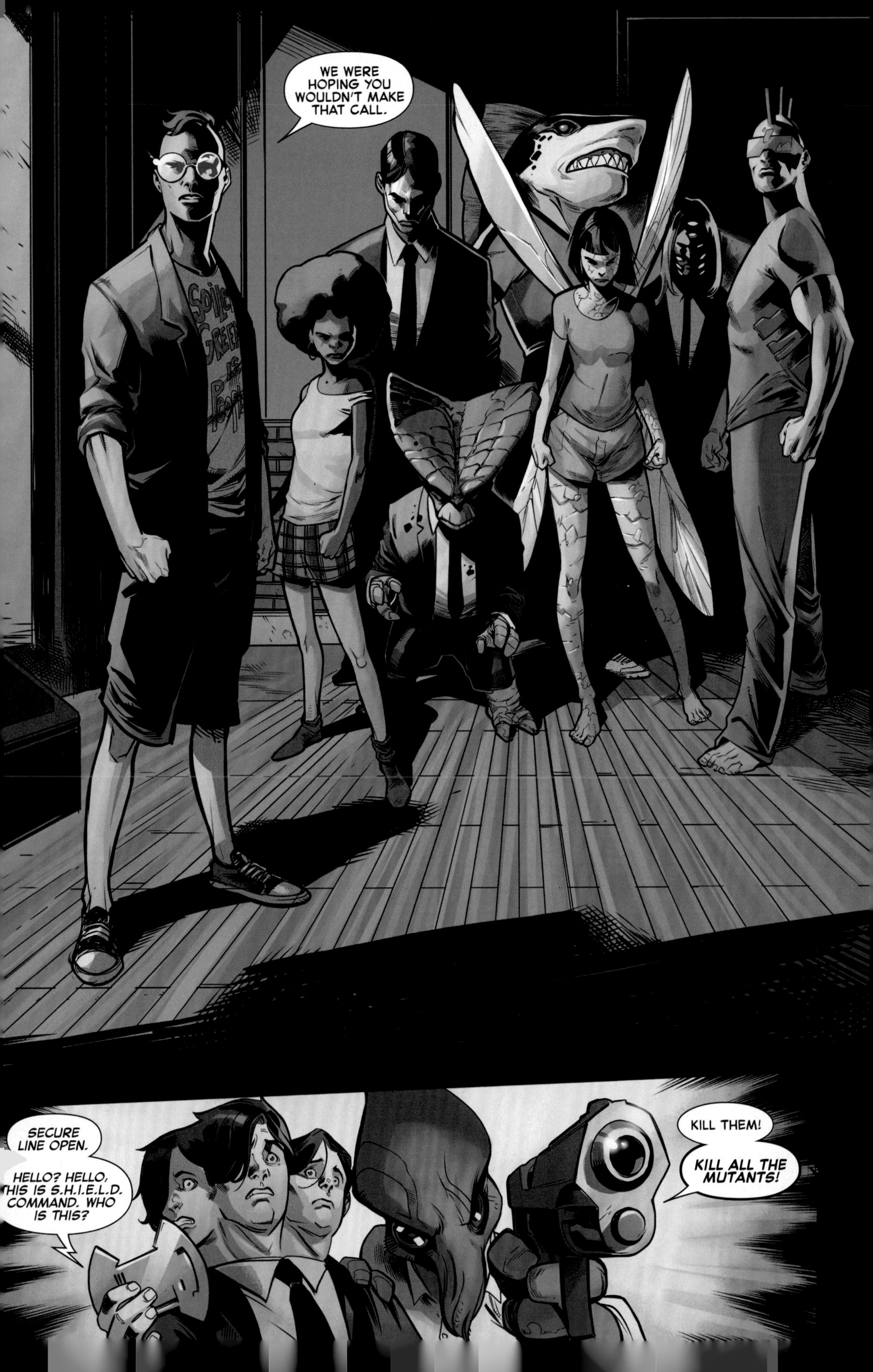
WE WERE HOPING YOU WOULDN'T MAKE THAT CALL.
SECURE LINE OPEN.
HELLO? HELLO, THIS IS S.H.I.E.L.D. COMMAND. WHO IS THIS?
KILL THEM!
KILL ALL THE MUTANTS!

40 THE WOLVERINE SCHOOL FOR GIFTED YOUNGSTERS
CONCLUSION: JGS FOREVER

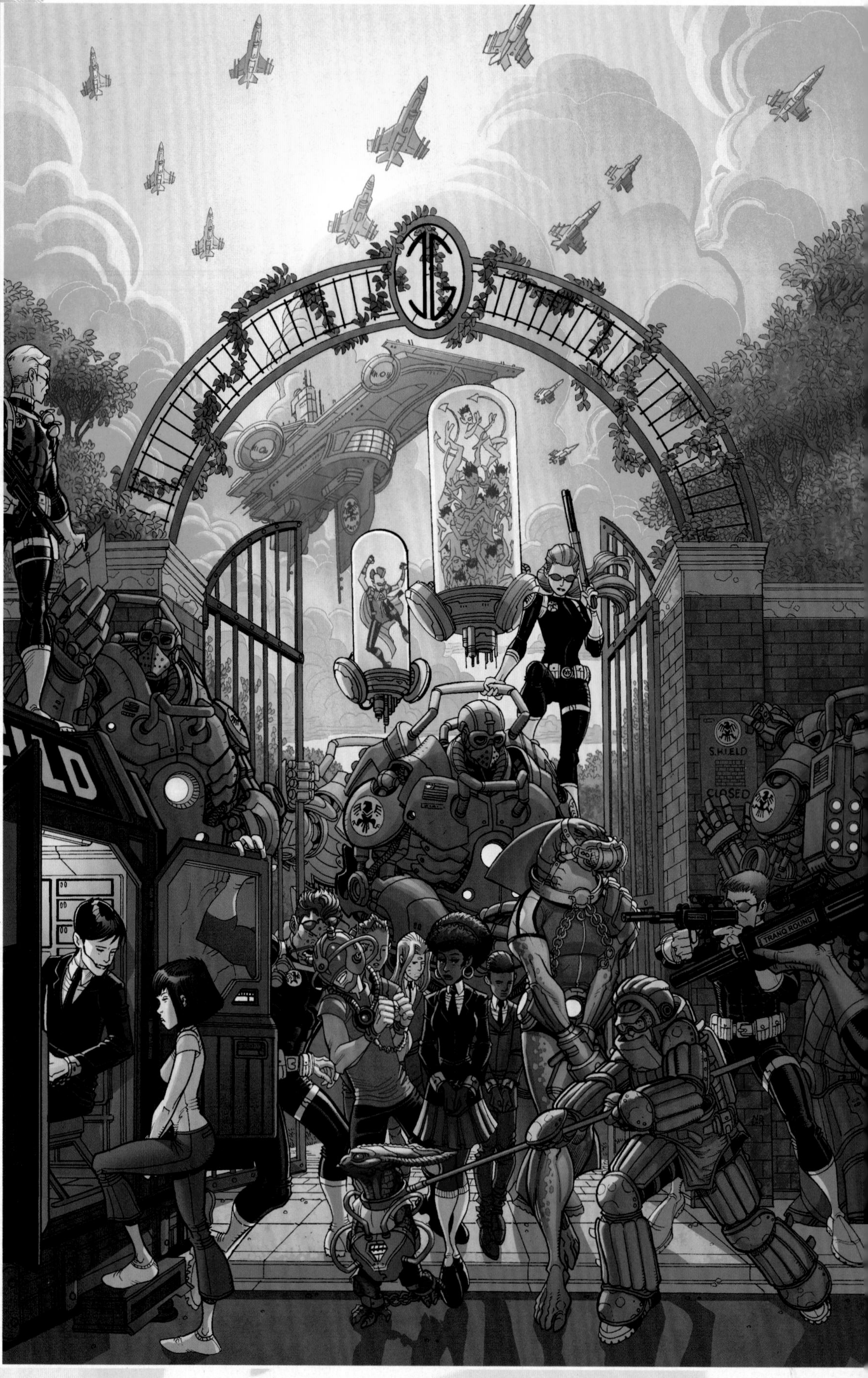
S.H.I.E.LD
CLOSED
TRANQ ROUND

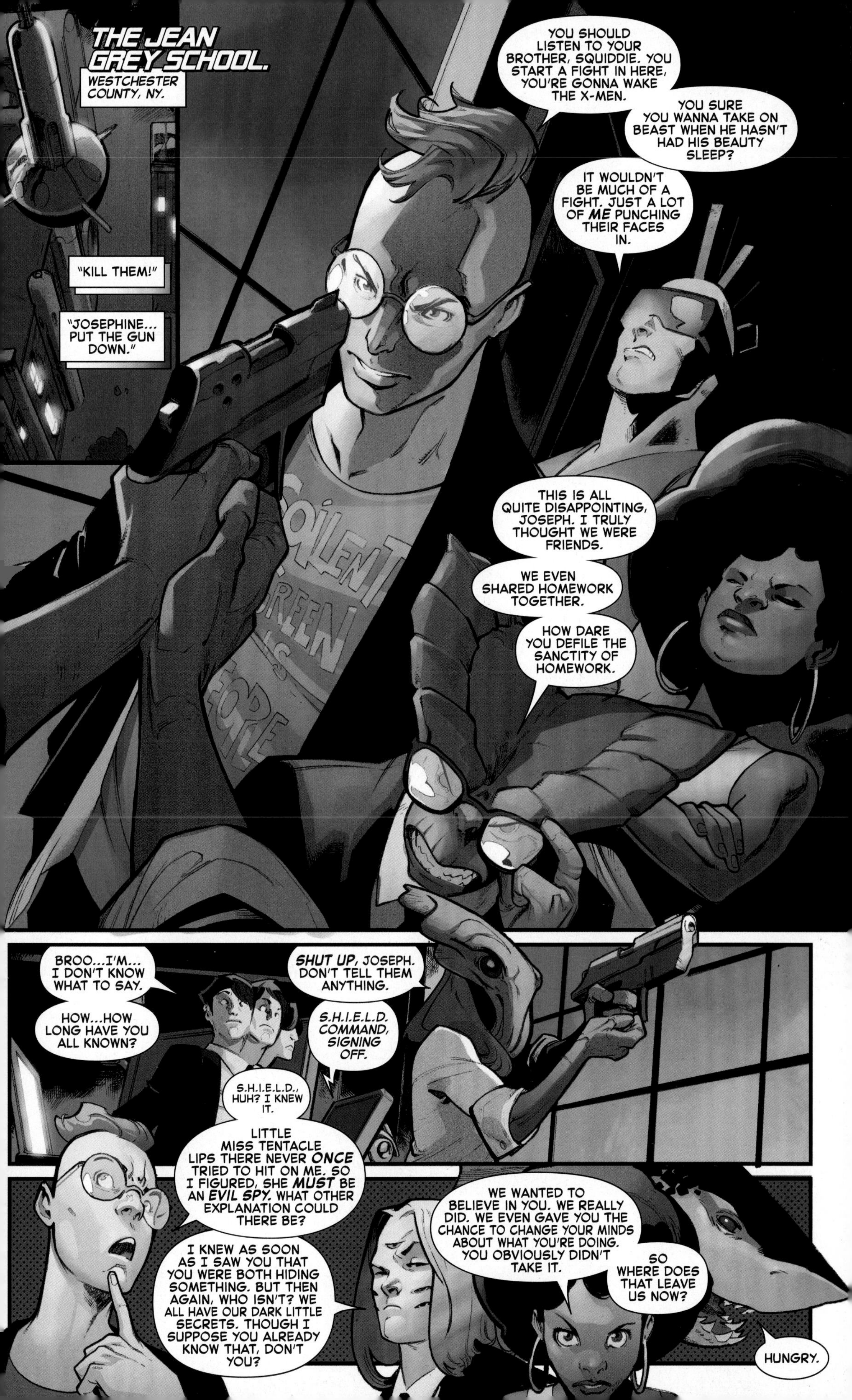
THE JEAN GREY SCHOOL.
WESTCHESTER COUNTY, NY.
YOU SHOULD LISTEN TO YOUR BROTHER, SQUIDDIE. YOU START A FIGHT IN HERE, YOU'RE GONNA WAKE THE X-MEN.
YOU SURE YOU WANNA TAKE ON BEAST WHEN HE HASN'T HAD HIS BEAUTY SLEEP?
IT WOULDN'T BE MUCH OF A FIGHT. JUST A LOT OF ***ME*** PUNCHING THEIR FACES IN.
"KILL THEM!"
"JOSEPHINE... PUT THE GUN DOWN."
SOILENT GREEN IS FORCE
THIS IS ALL QUITE DISAPPOINTING, JOSEPH. I TRULY THOUGHT WE WERE FRIENDS.
WE EVEN SHARED HOMEWORK TOGETHER.
HOW DARE YOU DEFILE THE SANCTITY OF HOMEWORK.
BROO...I'M... I DON'T KNOW WHAT TO SAY.
HOW...HOW LONG HAVE YOU ALL KNOWN?
SHUT UP, JOSEPH. DON'T TELL THEM ANYTHING.
S.H.I.E.L.D. COMMAND, SIGNING OFF.
S.H.I.E.L.D., HUH? I KNEW IT.
LITTLE MISS TENTACLE LIPS THERE NEVER ***ONCE*** TRIED TO HIT ON ME. SO I FIGURED, SHE ***MUST*** BE AN ***EVIL SPY.*** WHAT OTHER EXPLANATION COULD THERE BE?
I KNEW AS SOON AS I SAW YOU THAT YOU WERE BOTH HIDING SOMETHING. BUT THEN AGAIN, WHO ISN'T? WE ALL HAVE OUR DARK LITTLE SECRETS. THOUGH I SUPPOSE YOU ALREADY KNOW THAT, DON'T YOU?
WE WANTED TO BELIEVE IN YOU. WE REALLY DID. WE EVEN GAVE YOU THE CHANCE TO CHANGE YOUR MINDS ABOUT WHAT YOU'RE DOING. YOU OBVIOUSLY DIDN'T TAKE IT.
SO WHERE DOES THAT LEAVE US NOW?
HUNGRY.

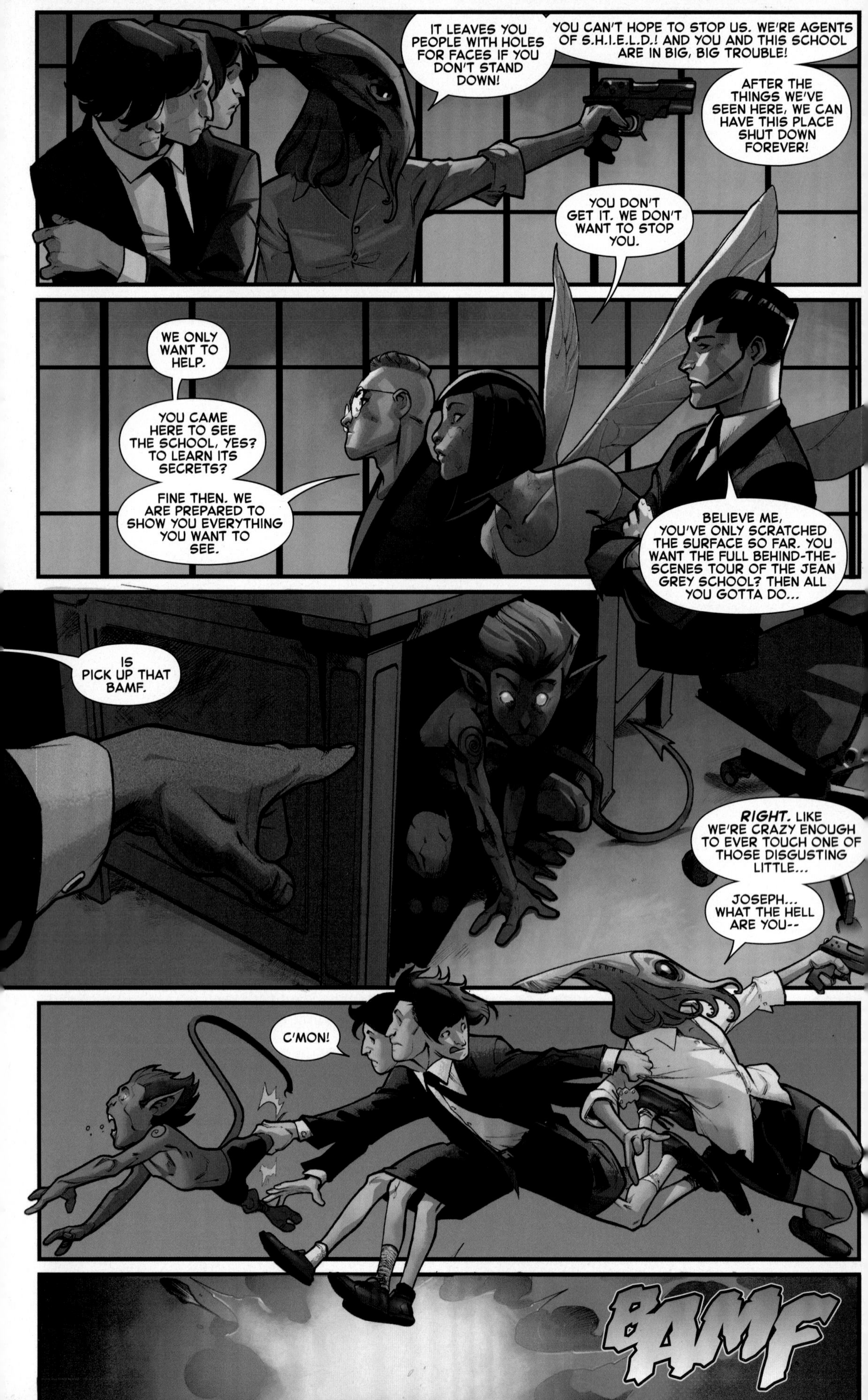
IT LEAVES YOU PEOPLE WITH HOLES FOR FACES IF YOU DON'T STAND DOWN!
YOU CAN'T HOPE TO STOP US. WE'RE AGENTS OF S.H.I.E.L.D.! AND YOU AND THIS SCHOOL ARE IN BIG, BIG TROUBLE!
AFTER THE THINGS WE'VE SEEN HERE, WE CAN HAVE THIS PLACE SHUT DOWN FOREVER!
YOU DON'T GET IT. WE DON'T WANT TO STOP YOU.
WE ONLY WANT TO HELP.
YOU CAME HERE TO SEE THE SCHOOL, YES? TO LEARN ITS SECRETS?
FINE THEN. WE ARE PREPARED TO SHOW YOU EVERYTHING YOU WANT TO SEE.
BELIEVE ME, YOU'VE ONLY SCRATCHED THE SURFACE SO FAR. YOU WANT THE FULL BEHIND-THE-SCENES TOUR OF THE JEAN GREY SCHOOL? THEN ALL YOU GOTTA DO...
IS PICK UP THAT BAMF.
RIGHT. LIKE WE'RE CRAZY ENOUGH TO EVER TOUCH ONE OF THOSE DISGUSTING LITTLE...
JOSEPH... WHAT THE HELL ARE YOU--
C'MON!
BAMF

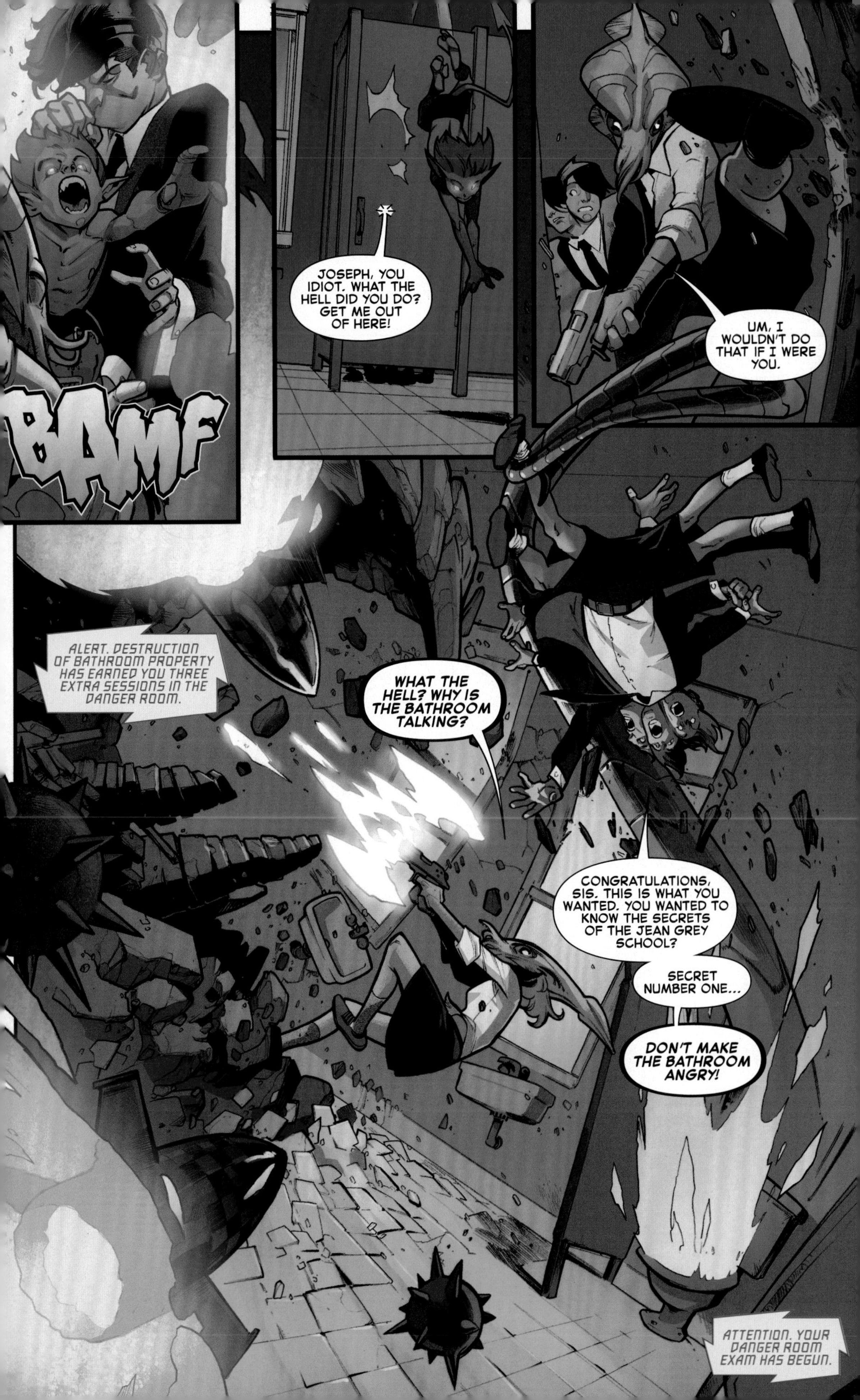
BAMF
JOSEPH, YOU IDIOT. WHAT THE HELL DID YOU DO? GET ME OUT OF HERE!
UM, I WOULDN'T DO THAT IF I WERE YOU.
ALERT. DESTRUCTION OF BATHROOM PROPERTY HAS EARNED YOU THREE EXTRA SESSIONS IN THE DANGER ROOM.
WHAT THE HELL? WHY IS THE BATHROOM TALKING?
CONGRATULATIONS, SIS. THIS IS WHAT YOU WANTED. YOU WANTED TO KNOW THE SECRETS OF THE JEAN GREY SCHOOL?
SECRET NUMBER ONE...
DON'T MAKE THE BATHROOM ANGRY!
ATTENTION. YOUR DANGER ROOM EXAM HAS BEGUN.

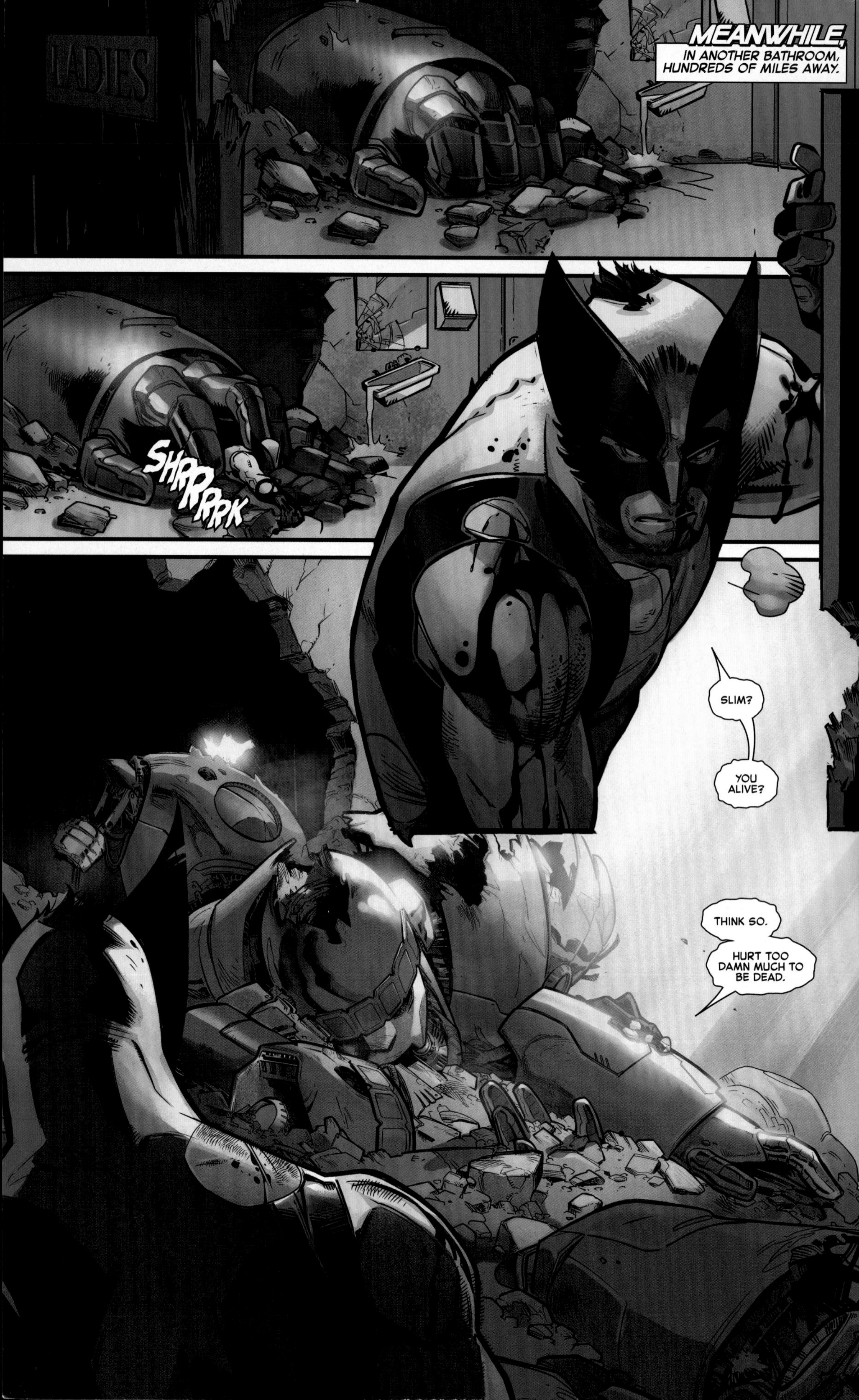
LADIES
MEANWHILE,
IN ANOTHER BATHROOM, HUNDREDS OF MILES AWAY.
SHRRRRK
SLIM?
YOU ALIVE?
THINK SO.
HURT TOO DAMN MUCH TO BE DEAD.

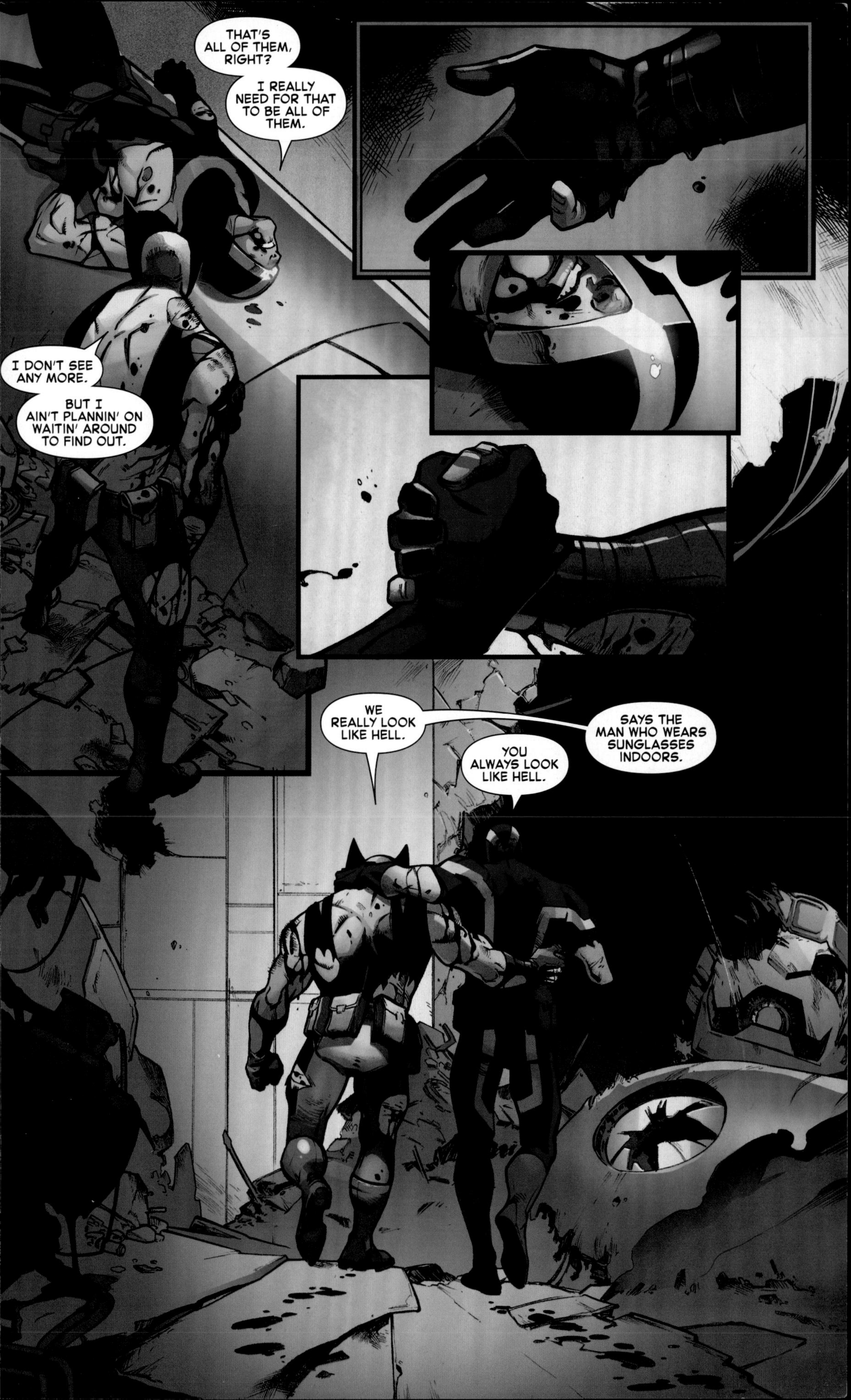
THAT'S ALL OF THEM, RIGHT?
I REALLY NEED FOR THAT TO BE ALL OF THEM.
I DON'T SEE ANY MORE.
BUT I AIN'T PLANNIN' ON WAITIN' AROUND TO FIND OUT.
WE REALLY LOOK LIKE HELL.
YOU ALWAYS LOOK LIKE HELL.
SAYS THE MAN WHO WEARS SUNGLASSES INDOORS.

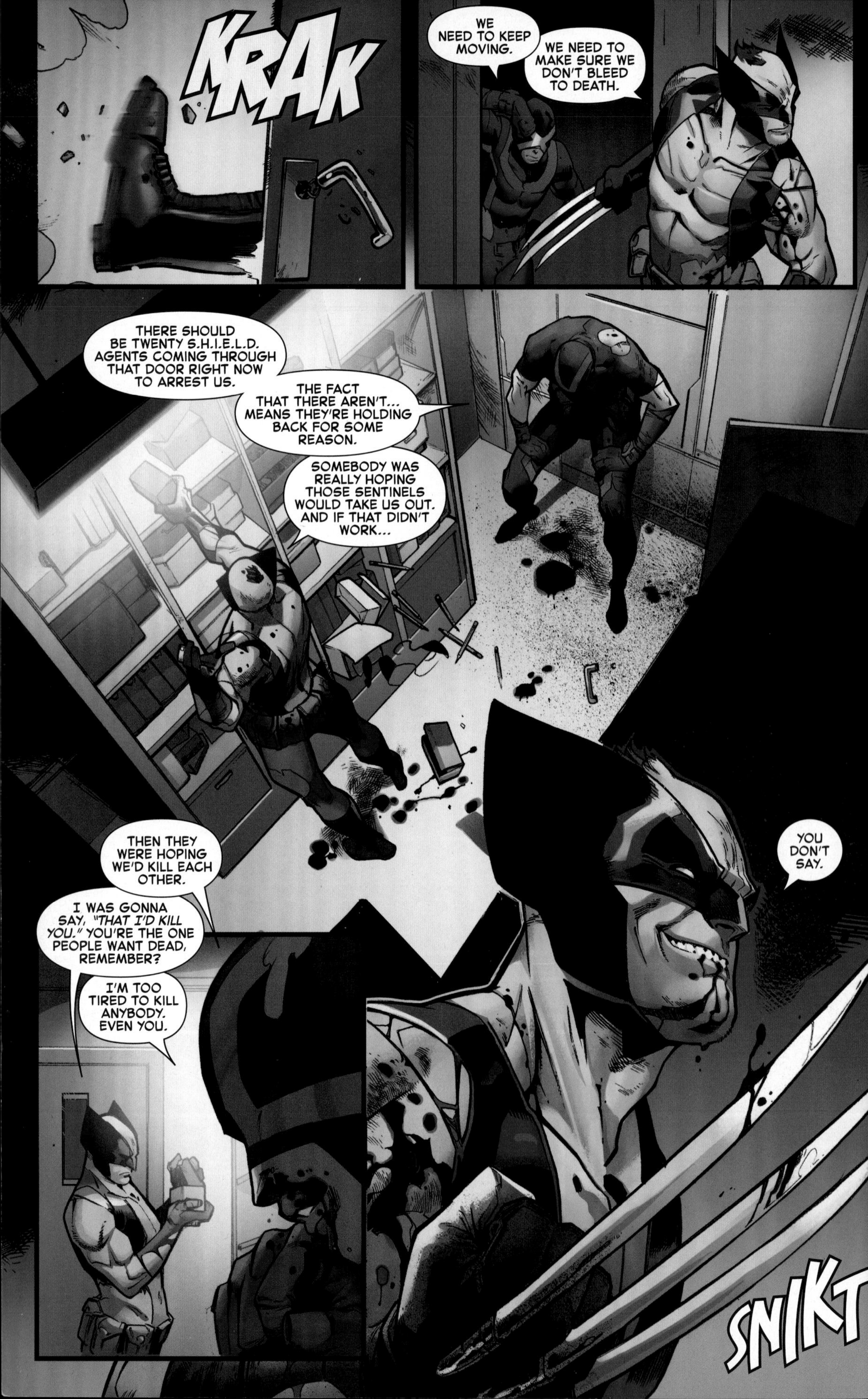
KRAK
WE NEED TO KEEP MOVING.
WE NEED TO MAKE SURE WE DON'T BLEED TO DEATH.
THERE SHOULD BE TWENTY S.H.I.E.L.D. AGENTS COMING THROUGH THAT DOOR RIGHT NOW TO ARREST US.
THE FACT THAT THERE AREN'T... MEANS THEY'RE HOLDING BACK FOR SOME REASON.
SOMEBODY WAS REALLY HOPING THOSE SENTINELS WOULD TAKE US OUT. AND IF THAT DIDN'T WORK...
THEN THEY WERE HOPING WE'D KILL EACH OTHER.
YOU DON'T SAY.
I WAS GONNA SAY, *"THAT I'D KILL YOU."* YOU'RE THE ONE PEOPLE WANT DEAD, REMEMBER?
I'M TOO TIRED TO KILL ANYBODY. EVEN YOU.
SNIKT

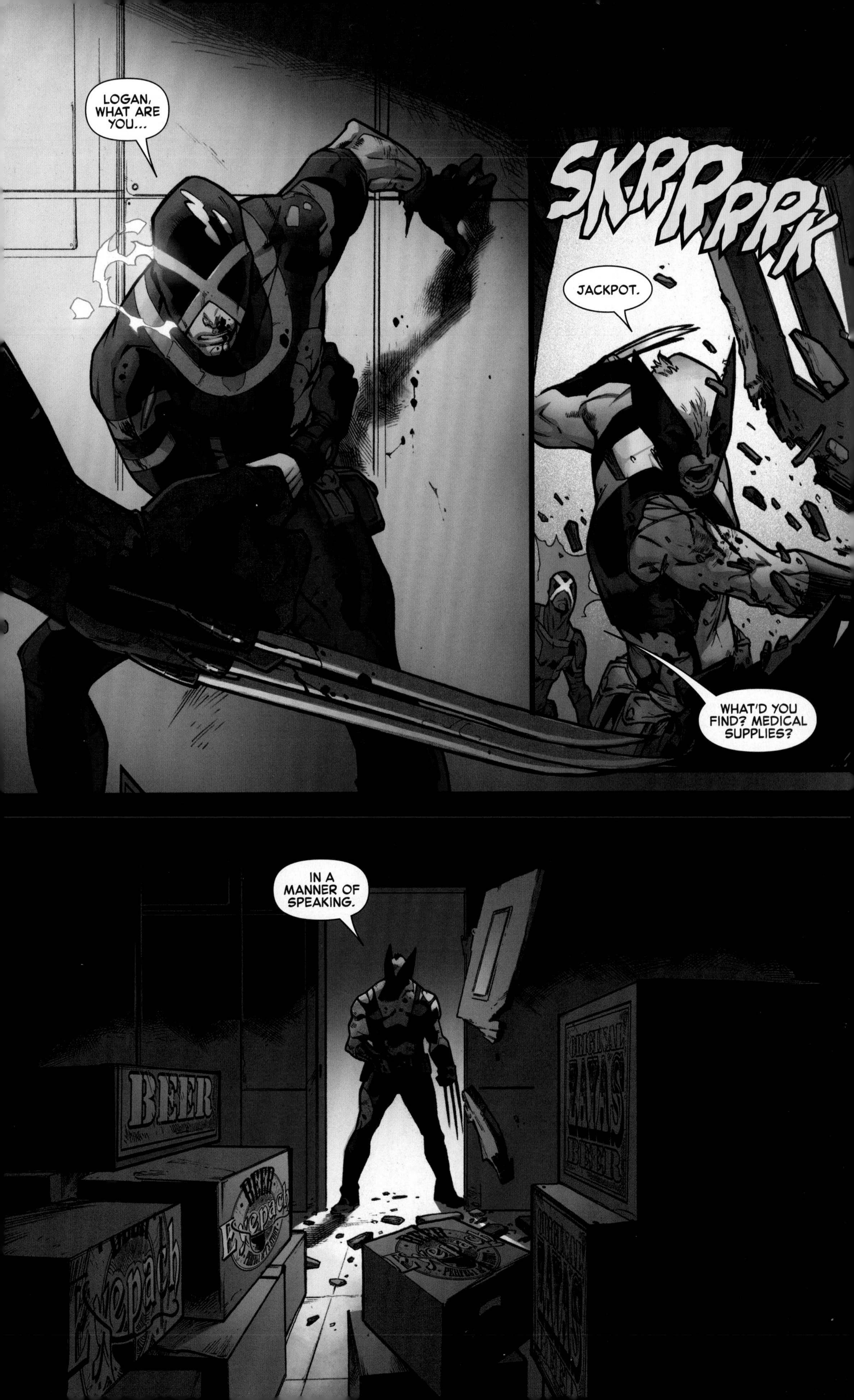
LOGAN, WHAT ARE YOU...
SKRRRRK
JACKPOT.
WHAT'D YOU FIND? MEDICAL SUPPLIES?
IN A MANNER OF SPEAKING.
BEER
ORIGINAL ZAYAS BEER

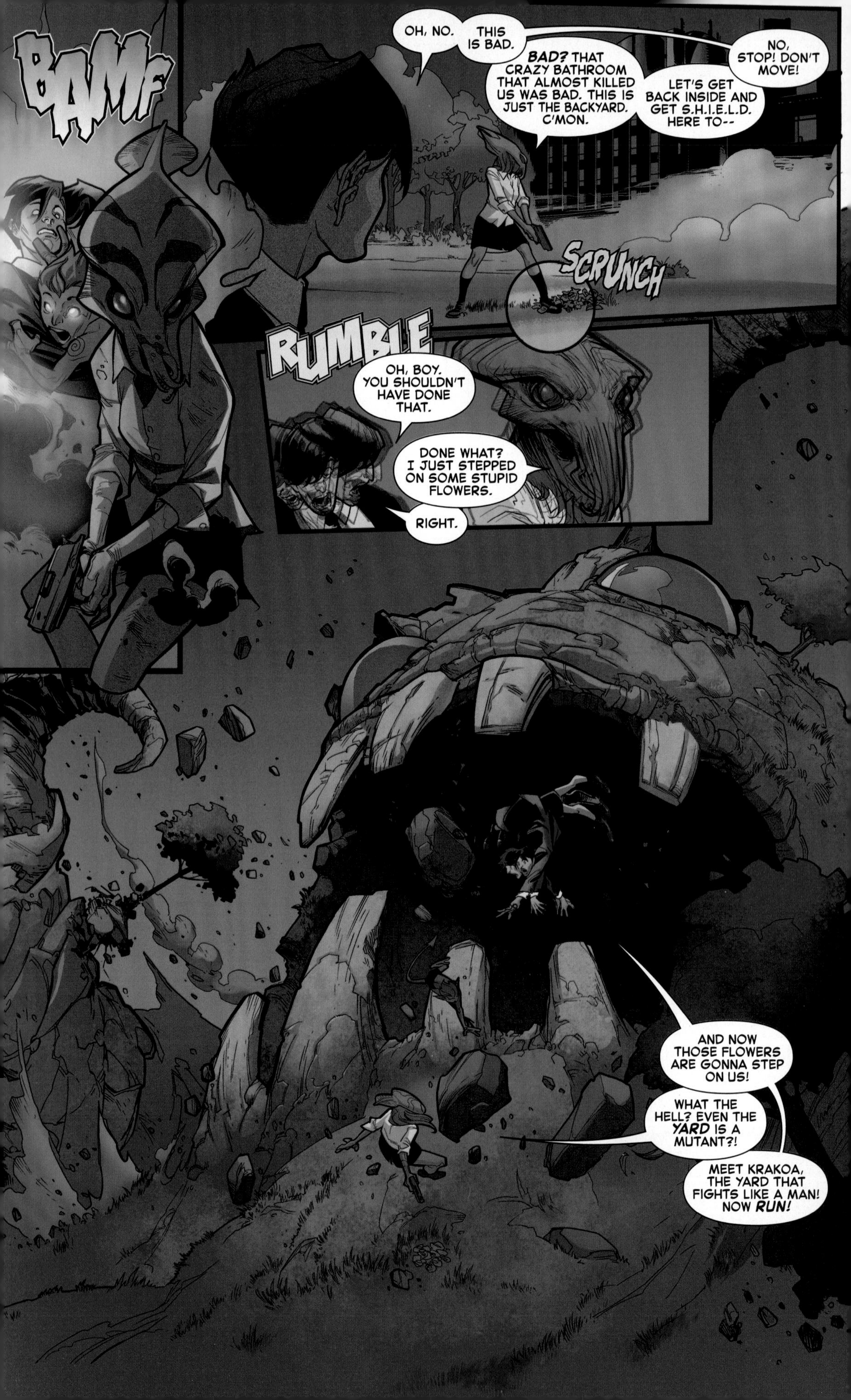
BAMF
OH, NO.
THIS IS BAD.
BAD? THAT CRAZY BATHROOM THAT ALMOST KILLED US WAS BAD. THIS IS JUST THE BACKYARD. C'MON.
NO, STOP! DON'T MOVE!
LET'S GET BACK INSIDE AND GET S.H.I.E.L.D. HERE TO--
SCRUNCH
RUMBLE
OH, BOY. YOU SHOULDN'T HAVE DONE THAT.
DONE WHAT? I JUST STEPPED ON SOME STUPID FLOWERS.
RIGHT.
AND NOW THOSE FLOWERS ARE GONNA STEP ON US!
WHAT THE HELL? EVEN THE YARD IS A MUTANT?!
MEET KRAKOA, THE YARD THAT FIGHTS LIKE A MAN! NOW RUN!

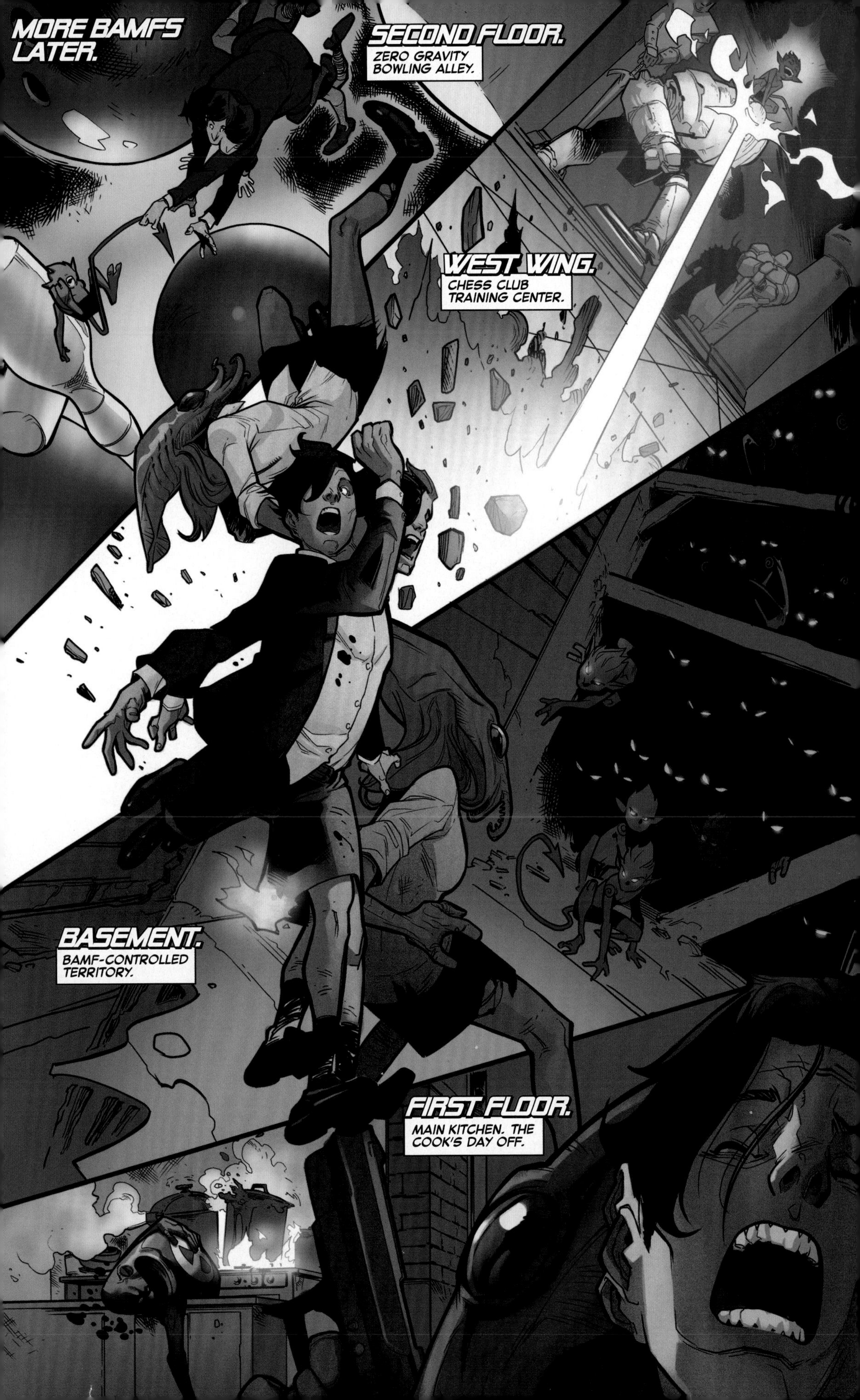
MORE BAMFS LATER.
SECOND FLOOR.
ZERO GRAVITY BOWLING ALLEY.
WEST WING.
CHESS CLUB TRAINING CENTER.
BASEMENT.
BAMF-CONTROLLED TERRITORY.
FIRST FLOOR.
MAIN KITCHEN. THE COOK'S DAY OFF.

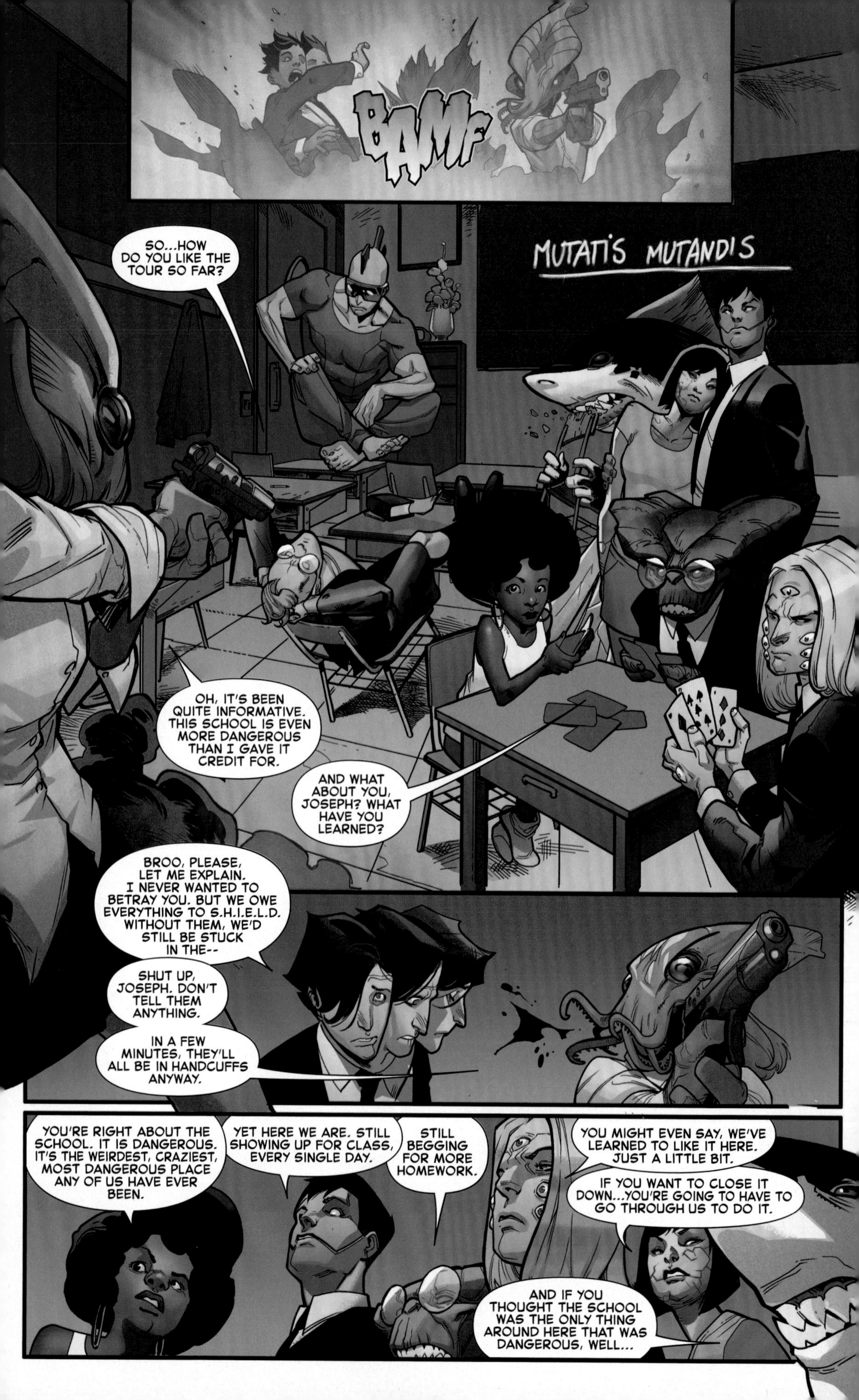
BAMF
MUTATIS MUTANDIS
SO...HOW DO YOU LIKE THE TOUR SO FAR?
OH, IT'S BEEN QUITE INFORMATIVE. THIS SCHOOL IS EVEN MORE DANGEROUS THAN I GAVE IT CREDIT FOR.
AND WHAT ABOUT YOU, JOSEPH? WHAT HAVE YOU LEARNED?
BROO, PLEASE, LET ME EXPLAIN. I NEVER WANTED TO BETRAY YOU. BUT WE OWE EVERYTHING TO S.H.I.E.L.D. WITHOUT THEM, WE'D STILL BE STUCK IN THE--
SHUT UP, JOSEPH. DON'T TELL THEM ANYTHING.
IN A FEW MINUTES, THEY'LL ALL BE IN HANDCUFFS ANYWAY.
YOU'RE RIGHT ABOUT THE SCHOOL. IT IS DANGEROUS. IT'S THE WEIRDEST, CRAZIEST, MOST DANGEROUS PLACE ANY OF US HAVE EVER BEEN.
YET HERE WE ARE. STILL SHOWING UP FOR CLASS, EVERY SINGLE DAY.
STILL BEGGING FOR MORE HOMEWORK.
YOU MIGHT EVEN SAY, WE'VE LEARNED TO LIKE IT HERE. JUST A LITTLE BIT.
IF YOU WANT TO CLOSE IT DOWN...YOU'RE GOING TO HAVE TO GO THROUGH US TO DO IT.
AND IF YOU THOUGHT THE SCHOOL WAS THE ONLY THING AROUND HERE THAT WAS DANGEROUS, WELL...

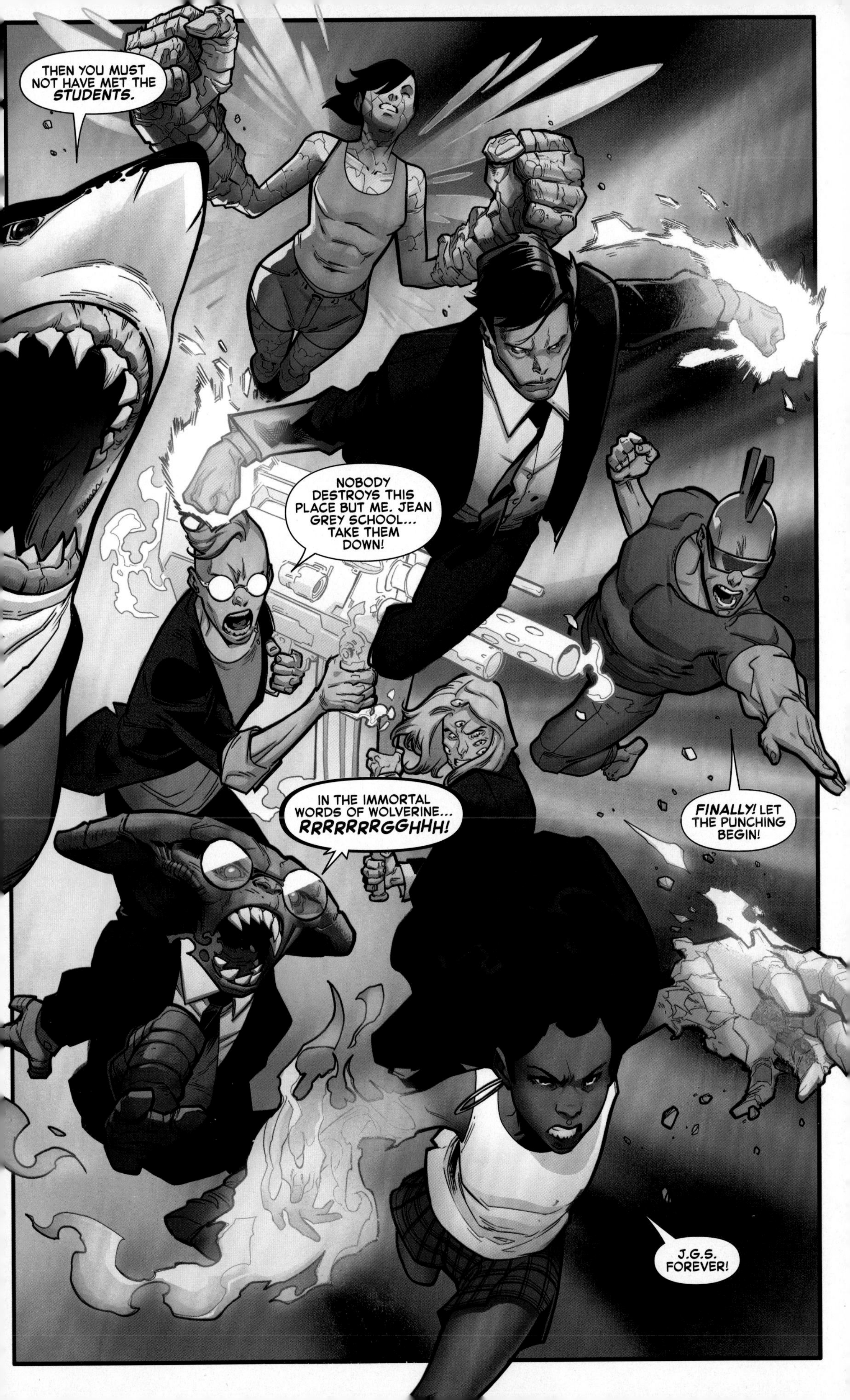
THEN YOU MUST NOT HAVE MET THE STUDENTS.
NOBODY DESTROYS THIS PLACE BUT ME. JEAN GREY SCHOOL... TAKE THEM DOWN!
FINALLY! LET THE PUNCHING BEGIN!
IN THE IMMORTAL WORDS OF WOLVERINE... RRRRRRRGGHHH!
J.G.S. FOREVER!

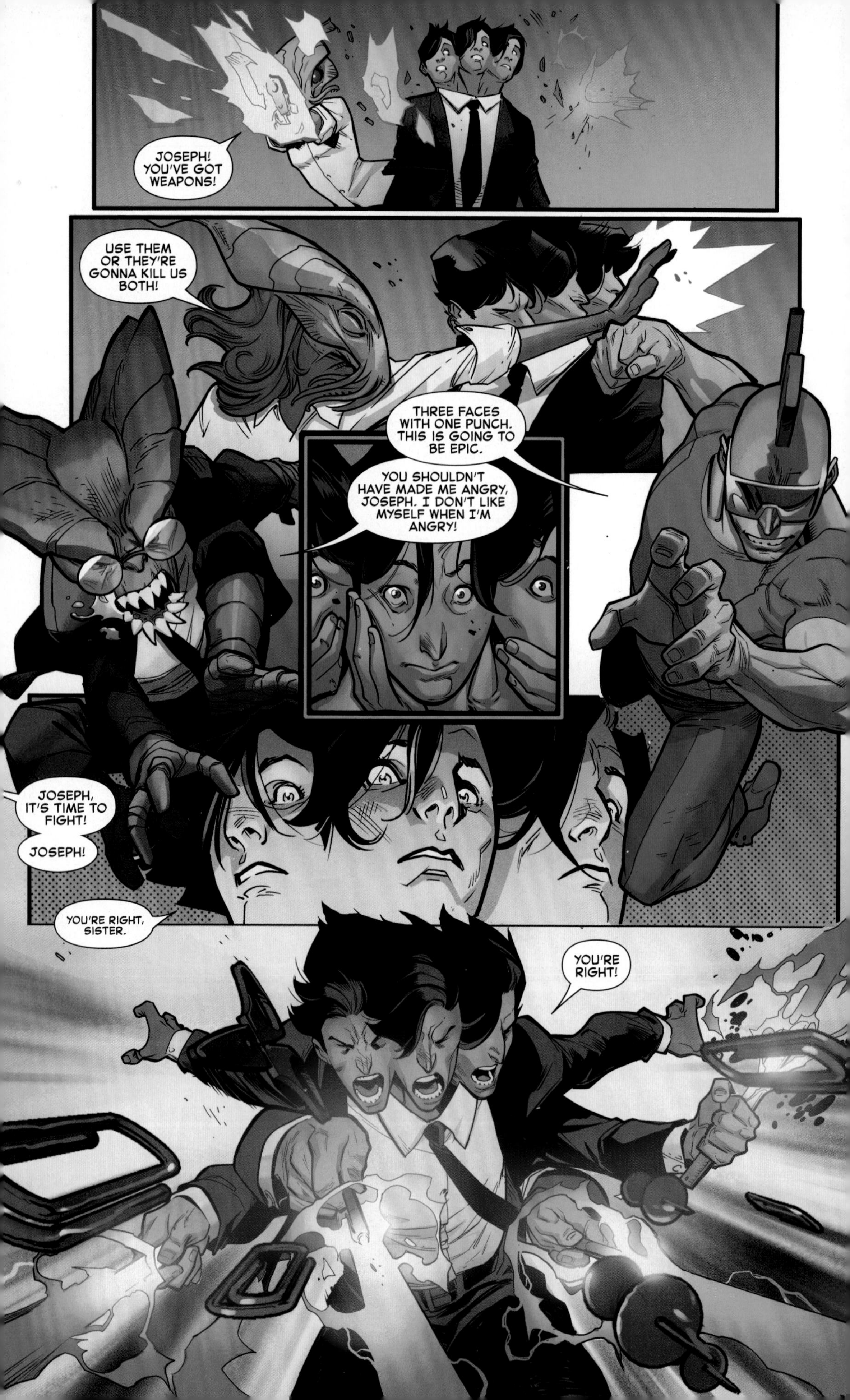
JOSEPH! YOU'VE GOT WEAPONS!
USE THEM OR THEY'RE GONNA KILL US BOTH!
THREE FACES WITH ONE PUNCH. THIS IS GOING TO BE EPIC.
YOU SHOULDN'T HAVE MADE ME ANGRY, JOSEPH. I DON'T LIKE MYSELF WHEN I'M ANGRY!
JOSEPH, IT'S TIME TO FIGHT!
JOSEPH!
YOU'RE RIGHT, SISTER.
YOU'RE RIGHT!

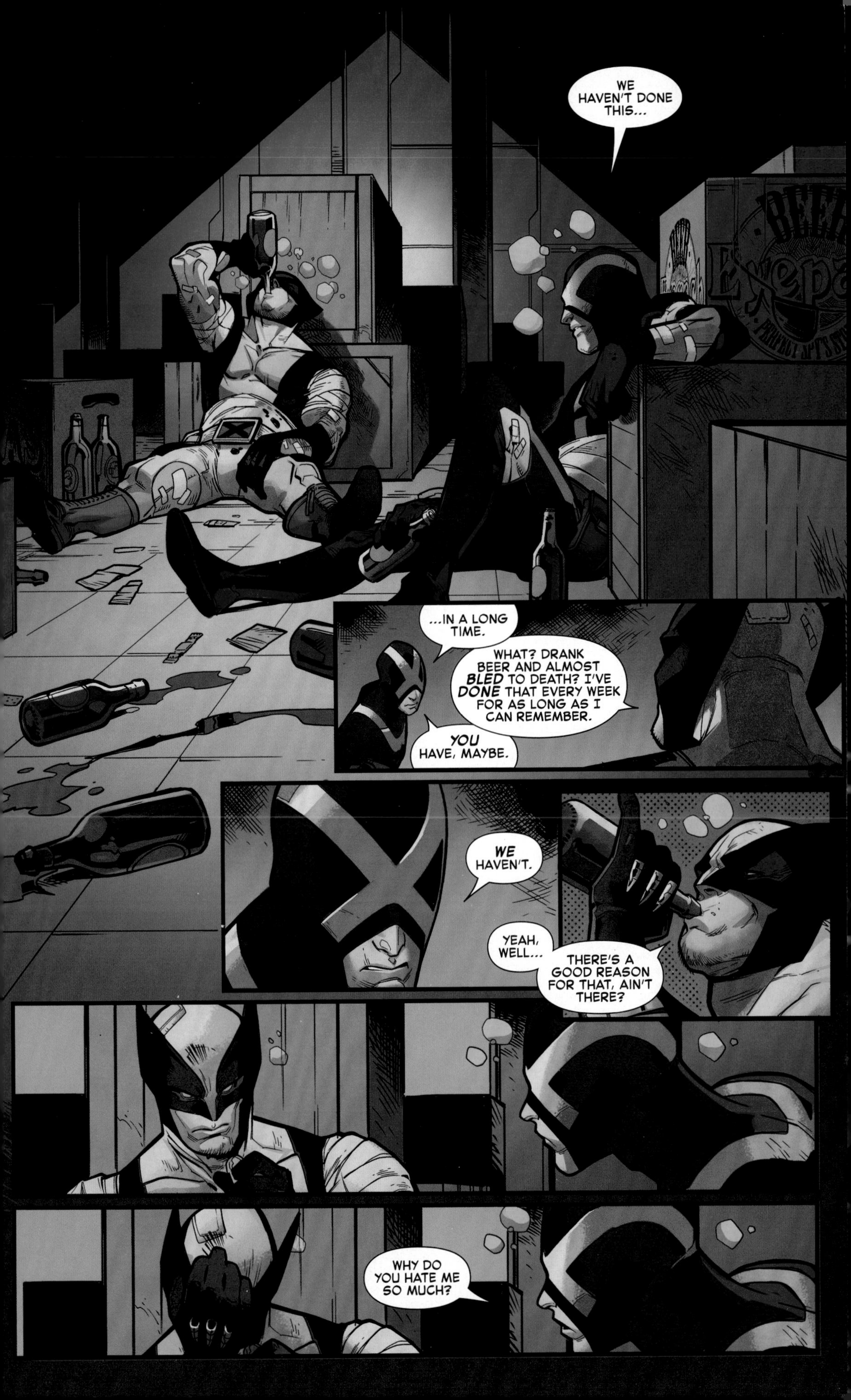
WE HAVEN'T DONE THIS...
...IN A LONG TIME.
WHAT? DRANK BEER AND ALMOST BLED TO DEATH? I'VE DONE THAT EVERY WEEK FOR AS LONG AS I CAN REMEMBER.
YOU HAVE, MAYBE.
WE HAVEN'T.
YEAH, WELL...
THERE'S A GOOD REASON FOR THAT, AIN'T THERE?
WHY DO YOU HATE ME SO MUCH?

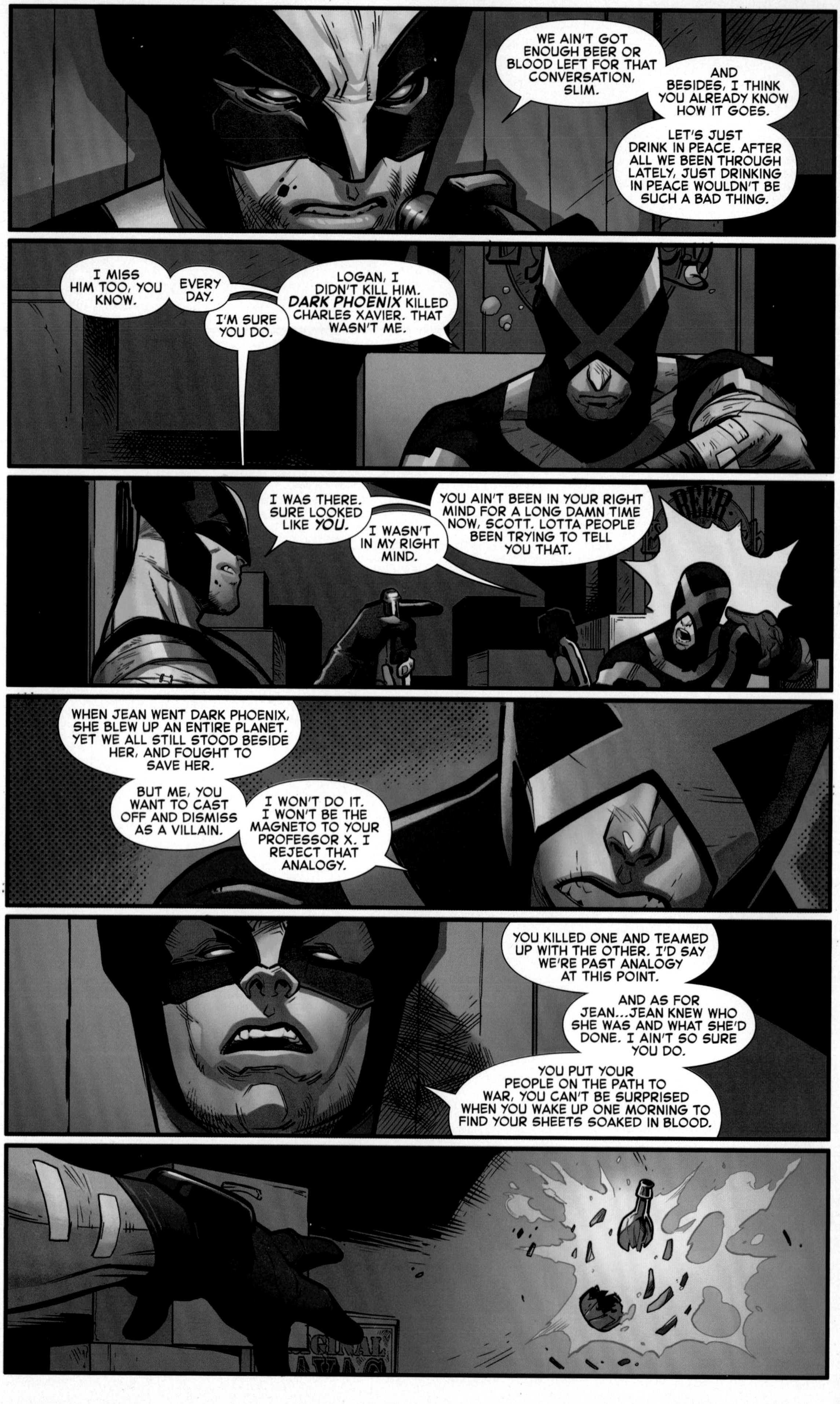

WE AIN'T GOT ENOUGH BEER OR BLOOD LEFT FOR THAT CONVERSATION, SLIM.
AND BESIDES, I THINK YOU ALREADY KNOW HOW IT GOES.
LET'S JUST DRINK IN PEACE. AFTER ALL WE BEEN THROUGH LATELY, JUST DRINKING IN PEACE WOULDN'T BE SUCH A BAD THING.
LOGAN, I DIDN'T KILL HIM. DARK PHOENIX KILLED CHARLES XAVIER. THAT WASN'T ME.
I'M SURE YOU DO.
I MISS HIM TOO, YOU KNOW.
EVERY DAY.
I WAS THERE. SURE LOOKED LIKE YOU.
I WASN'T IN MY RIGHT MIND.
YOU AIN'T BEEN IN YOUR RIGHT MIND FOR A LONG DAMN TIME NOW, SCOTT. LOTTA PEOPLE BEEN TRYING TO TELL YOU THAT.
WHEN JEAN WENT DARK PHOENIX, SHE BLEW UP AN ENTIRE PLANET. YET WE ALL STILL STOOD BESIDE HER, AND FOUGHT TO SAVE HER.
BUT ME, YOU WANT TO CAST OFF AND DISMISS AS A VILLAIN.
I WON'T DO IT. I WON'T BE THE MAGNETO TO YOUR PROFESSOR X. I REJECT THAT ANALOGY.
YOU KILLED ONE AND TEAMED UP WITH THE OTHER. I'D SAY WE'RE PAST ANALOGY AT THIS POINT.
AND AS FOR JEAN...JEAN KNEW WHO SHE WAS AND WHAT SHE'D DONE. I AIN'T SO SURE YOU DO.
YOU PUT YOUR PEOPLE ON THE PATH TO WAR, YOU CAN'T BE SURPRISED WHEN YOU WAKE UP ONE MORNING TO FIND YOUR SHEETS SOAKED IN BLOOD.

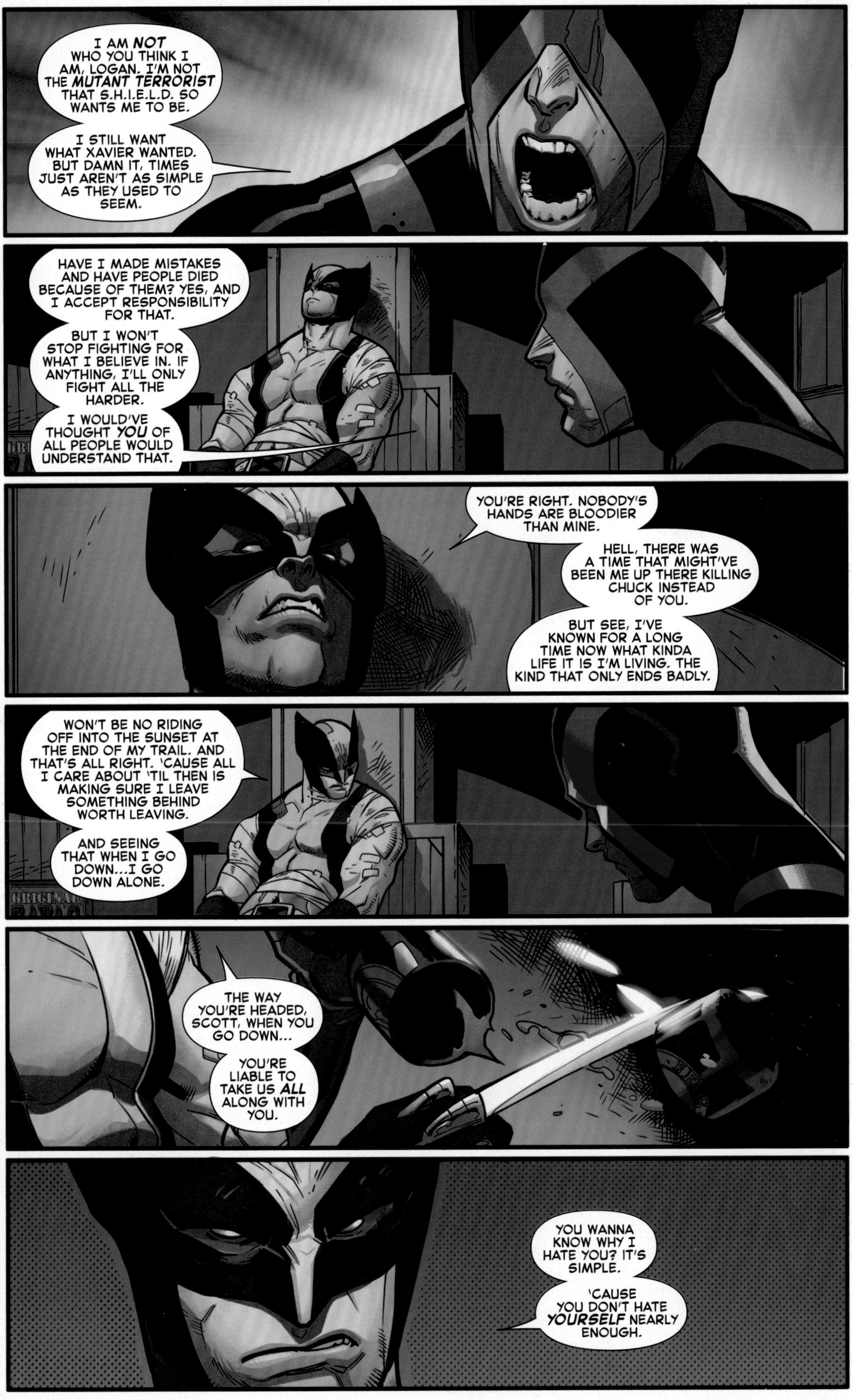
I AM NOT WHO YOU THINK I AM, LOGAN. I'M NOT THE MUTANT TERRORIST THAT S.H.I.E.L.D. SO WANTS ME TO BE.
I STILL WANT WHAT XAVIER WANTED. BUT DAMN IT, TIMES JUST AREN'T AS SIMPLE AS THEY USED TO SEEM.
HAVE I MADE MISTAKES AND HAVE PEOPLE DIED BECAUSE OF THEM? YES, AND I ACCEPT RESPONSIBILITY FOR THAT.
BUT I WON'T STOP FIGHTING FOR WHAT I BELIEVE IN. IF ANYTHING, I'LL ONLY FIGHT ALL THE HARDER.
I WOULD'VE THOUGHT YOU OF ALL PEOPLE WOULD UNDERSTAND THAT.
YOU'RE RIGHT. NOBODY'S HANDS ARE BLOODIER THAN MINE.
HELL, THERE WAS A TIME THAT MIGHT'VE BEEN ME UP THERE KILLING CHUCK INSTEAD OF YOU.
BUT SEE, I'VE KNOWN FOR A LONG TIME NOW WHAT KINDA LIFE IT IS I'M LIVING. THE KIND THAT ONLY ENDS BADLY.
WON'T BE NO RIDING OFF INTO THE SUNSET AT THE END OF MY TRAIL. AND THAT'S ALL RIGHT. 'CAUSE ALL I CARE ABOUT 'TIL THEN IS MAKING SURE I LEAVE SOMETHING BEHIND WORTH LEAVING.
AND SEEING THAT WHEN I GO DOWN...I GO DOWN ALONE.
THE WAY YOU'RE HEADED, SCOTT, WHEN YOU GO DOWN...
YOU'RE LIABLE TO TAKE US ALL ALONG WITH YOU.
YOU WANNA KNOW WHY I HATE YOU? IT'S SIMPLE.
'CAUSE YOU DON'T HATE YOURSELF NEARLY ENOUGH.

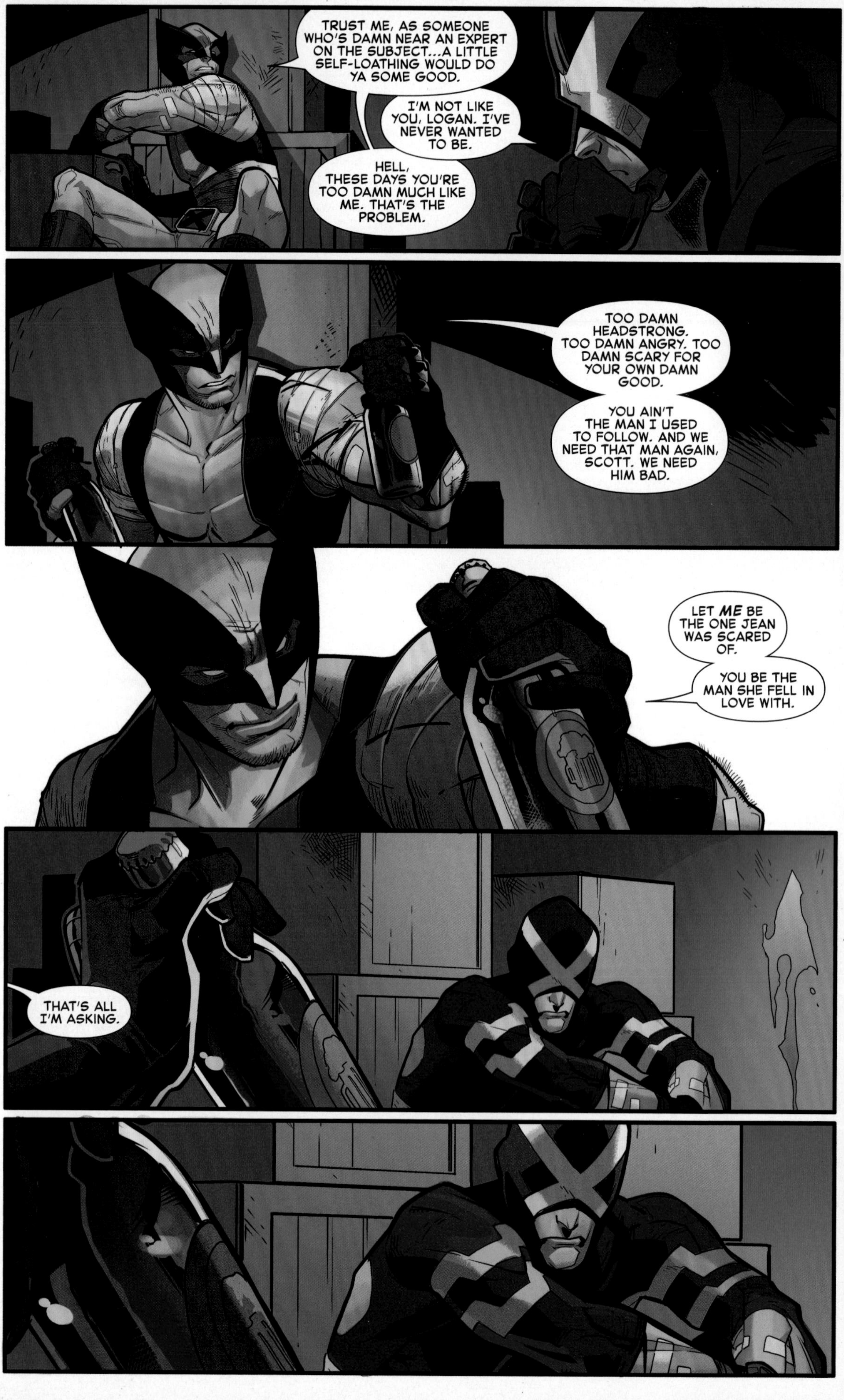
TRUST ME, AS SOMEONE WHO'S DAMN NEAR AN EXPERT ON THE SUBJECT...A LITTLE SELF-LOATHING WOULD DO YA SOME GOOD.
I'M NOT LIKE YOU, LOGAN. I'VE NEVER WANTED TO BE.
HELL, THESE DAYS YOU'RE TOO DAMN MUCH LIKE ME. THAT'S THE PROBLEM.
TOO DAMN HEADSTRONG. TOO DAMN ANGRY. TOO DAMN SCARY FOR YOUR OWN DAMN GOOD.
YOU AIN'T THE MAN I USED TO FOLLOW. AND WE NEED THAT MAN AGAIN, SCOTT. WE NEED HIM BAD.
LET *ME* BE THE ONE JEAN WAS SCARED OF.
YOU BE THE MAN SHE FELL IN LOVE WITH.
THAT'S ALL I'M ASKING.

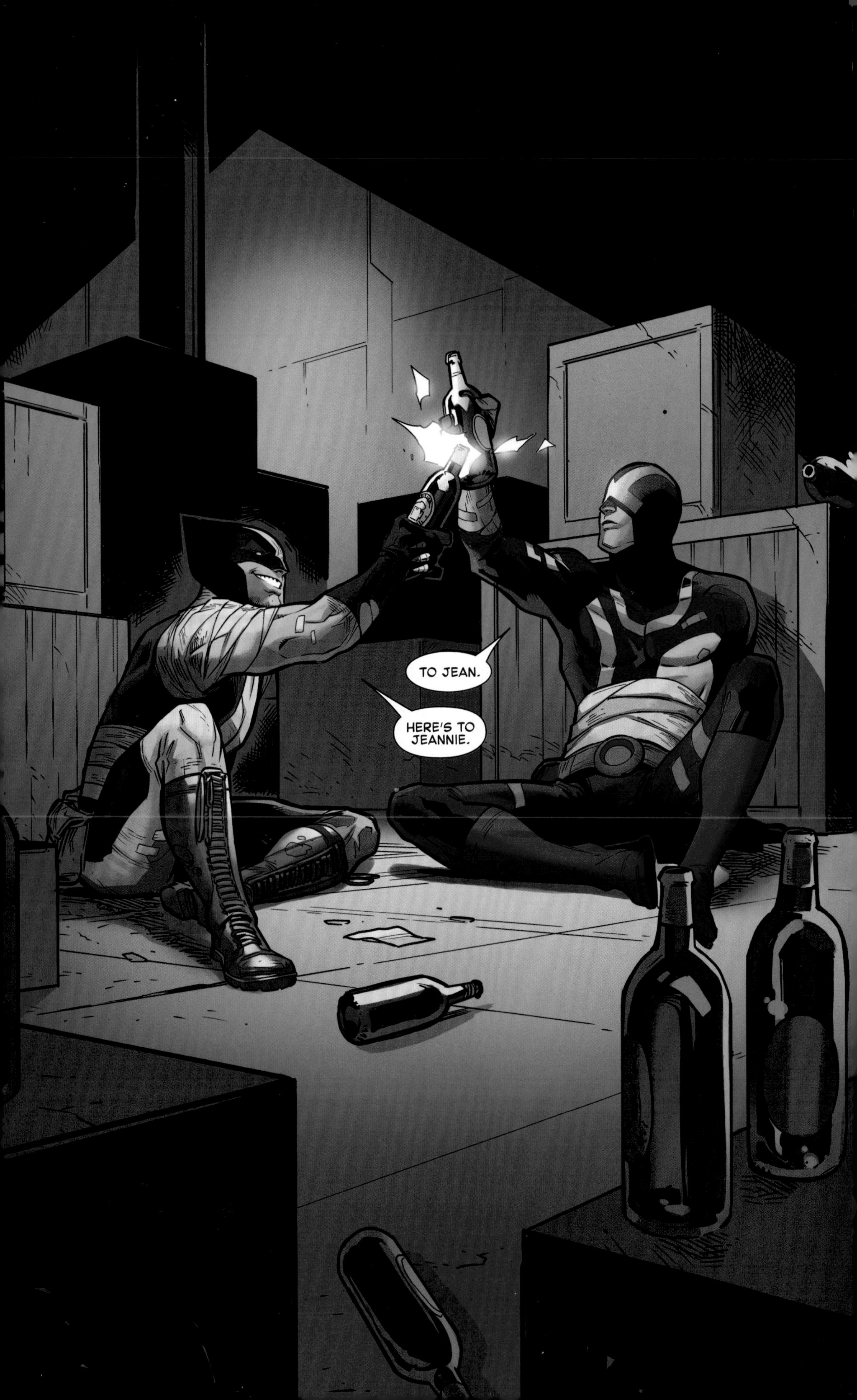
TO JEAN.
HERE'S TO JEANNIE.

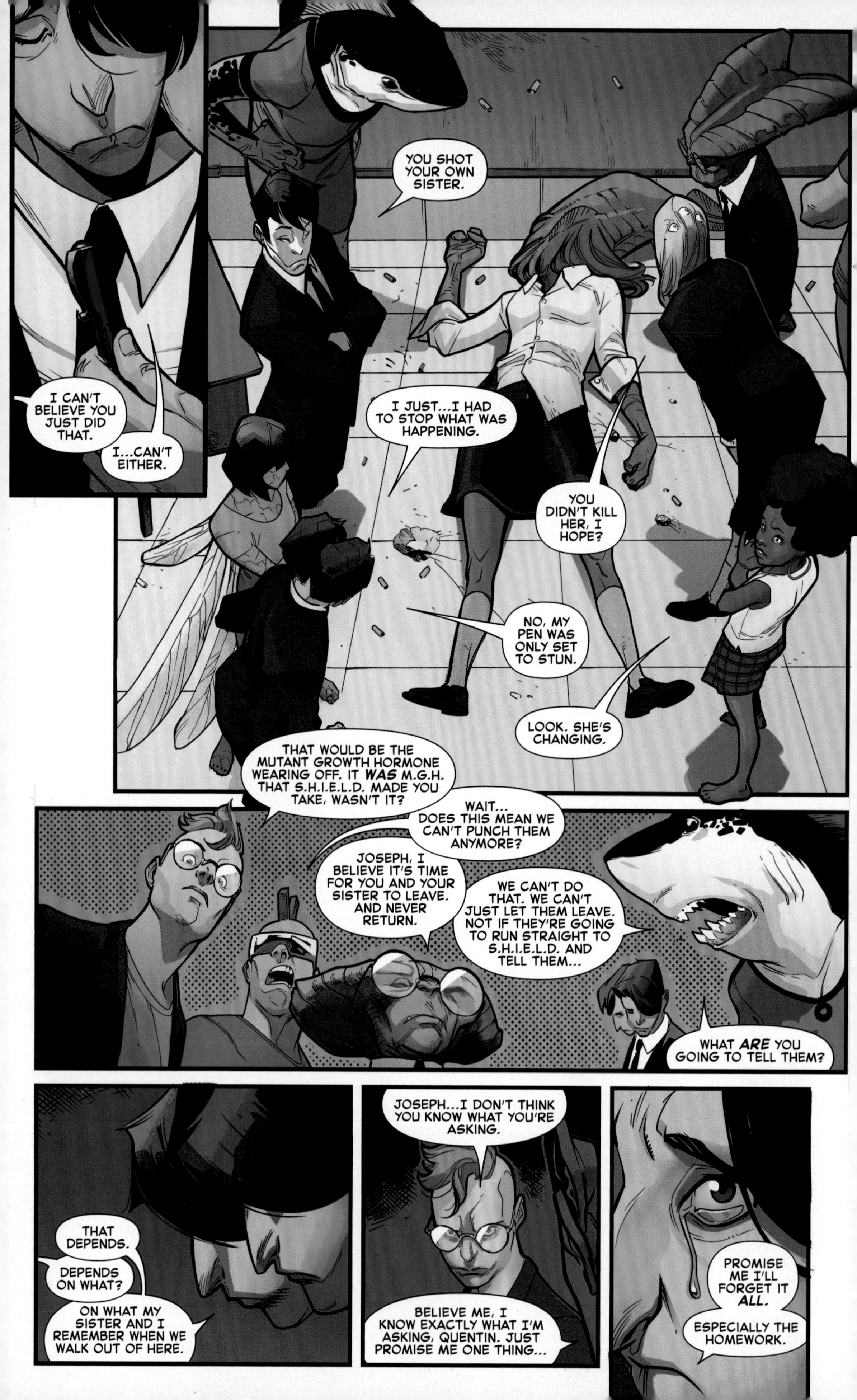
I CAN'T BELIEVE YOU JUST DID THAT.
I...CAN'T EITHER.
YOU SHOT YOUR OWN SISTER.
I JUST...I HAD TO STOP WHAT WAS HAPPENING.
YOU DIDN'T KILL HER, I HOPE?
NO, MY PEN WAS ONLY SET TO STUN.
LOOK. SHE'S CHANGING.
THAT WOULD BE THE MUTANT GROWTH HORMONE WEARING OFF. IT WAS M.G.H. THAT S.H.I.E.L.D. MADE YOU TAKE, WASN'T IT?
WAIT... DOES THIS MEAN WE CAN'T PUNCH THEM ANYMORE?
JOSEPH, I BELIEVE IT'S TIME FOR YOU AND YOUR SISTER TO LEAVE. AND NEVER RETURN.
WE CAN'T DO THAT. WE CAN'T JUST LET THEM LEAVE. NOT IF THEY'RE GOING TO RUN STRAIGHT TO S.H.I.E.L.D. AND TELL THEM...
WHAT ARE YOU GOING TO TELL THEM?
THAT DEPENDS.
DEPENDS ON WHAT?
ON WHAT MY SISTER AND I REMEMBER WHEN WE WALK OUT OF HERE.
JOSEPH...I DON'T THINK YOU KNOW WHAT YOU'RE ASKING.
BELIEVE ME, I KNOW EXACTLY WHAT I'M ASKING, QUENTIN. JUST PROMISE ME ONE THING...
PROMISE ME I'LL FORGET IT ALL.
ESPECIALLY THE HOMEWORK.

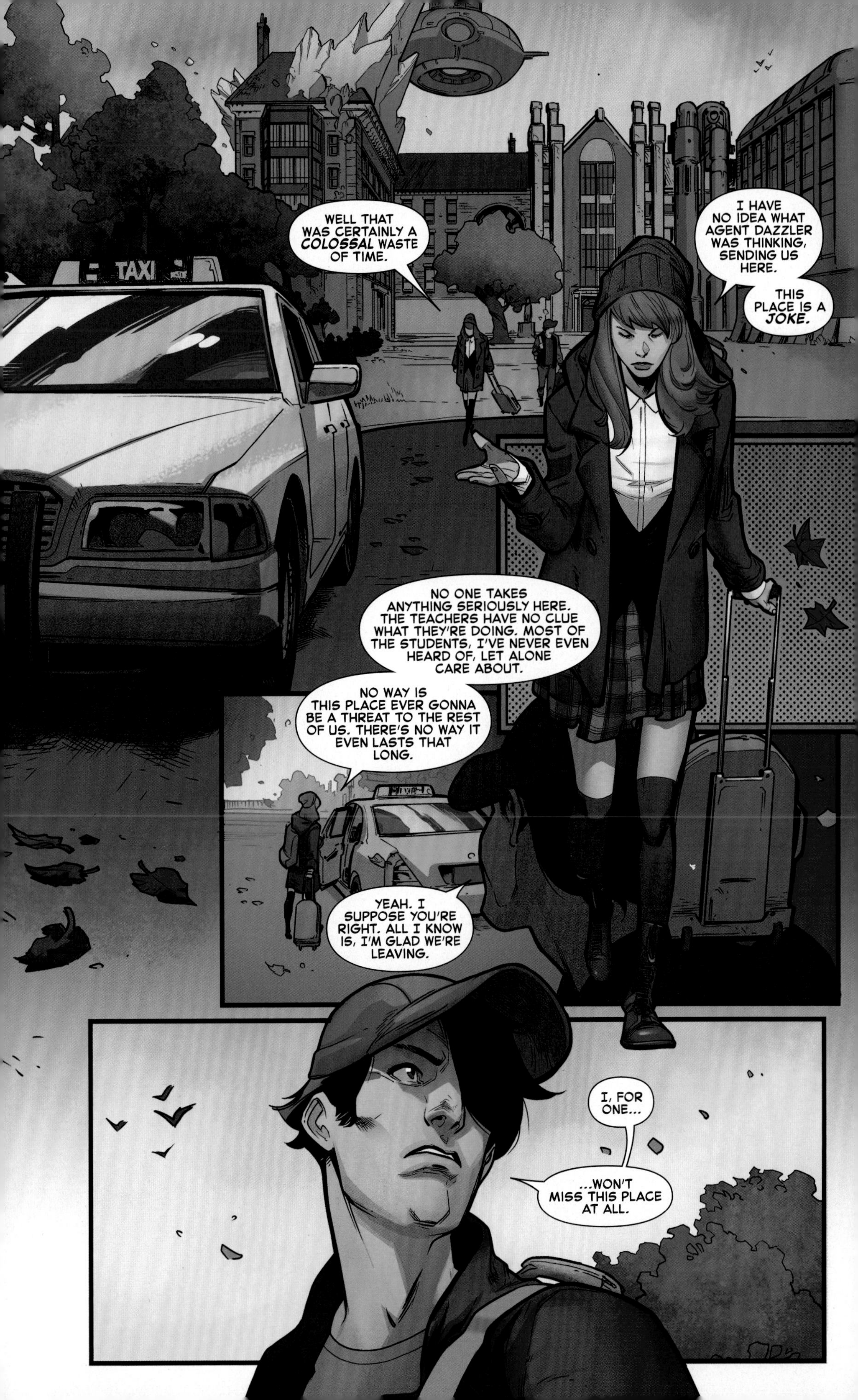
TAXI
WELL THAT WAS CERTAINLY A COLOSSAL WASTE OF TIME.
I HAVE NO IDEA WHAT AGENT DAZZLER WAS THINKING, SENDING US HERE.
THIS PLACE IS A JOKE.
NO ONE TAKES ANYTHING SERIOUSLY HERE. THE TEACHERS HAVE NO CLUE WHAT THEY'RE DOING. MOST OF THE STUDENTS, I'VE NEVER EVEN HEARD OF, LET ALONE CARE ABOUT.
NO WAY IS THIS PLACE EVER GONNA BE A THREAT TO THE REST OF US. THERE'S NO WAY IT EVEN LASTS THAT LONG.
YEAH. I SUPPOSE YOU'RE RIGHT. ALL I KNOW IS, I'M GLAD WE'RE LEAVING.
I, FOR ONE...
...WON'T MISS THIS PLACE AT ALL.

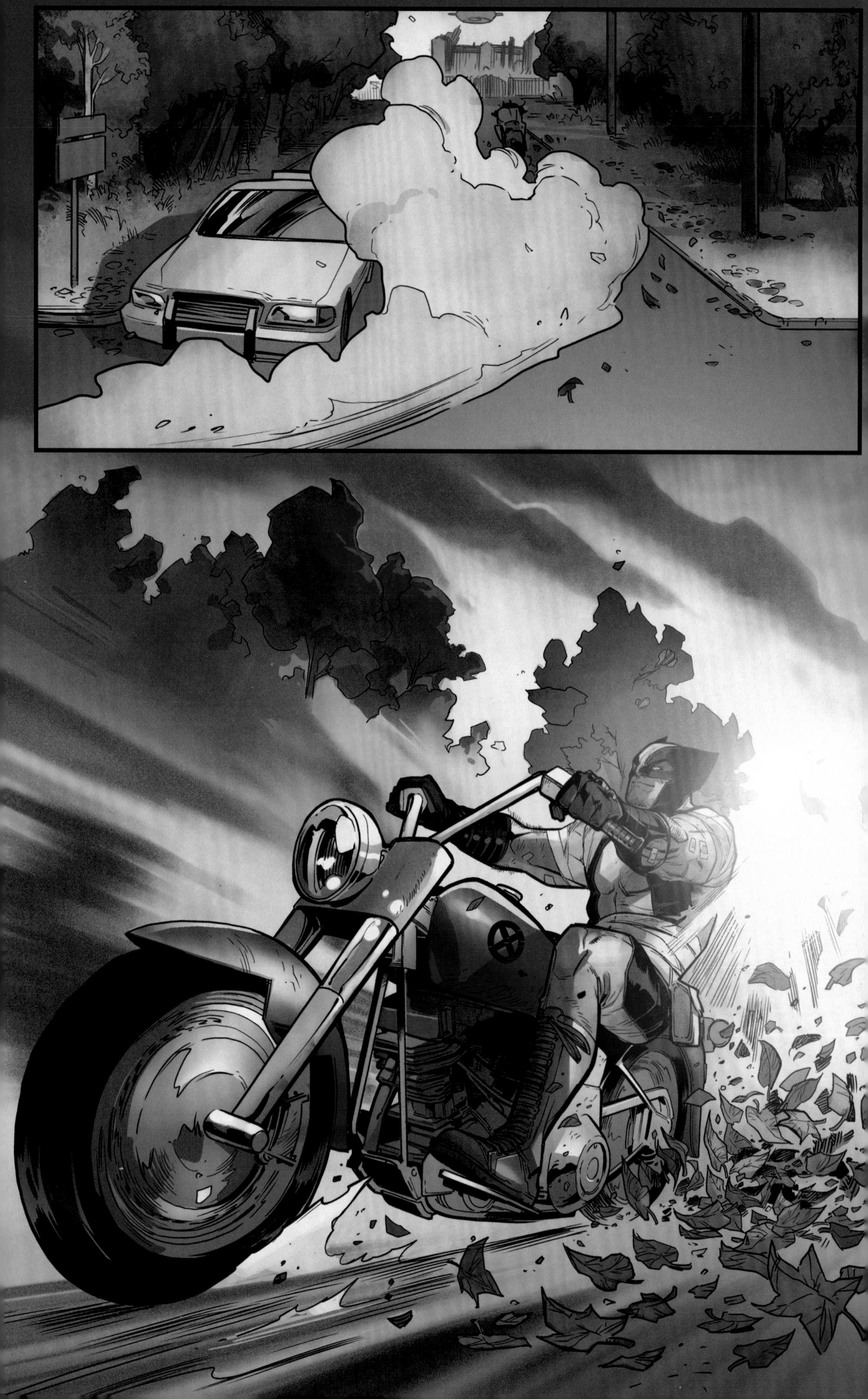

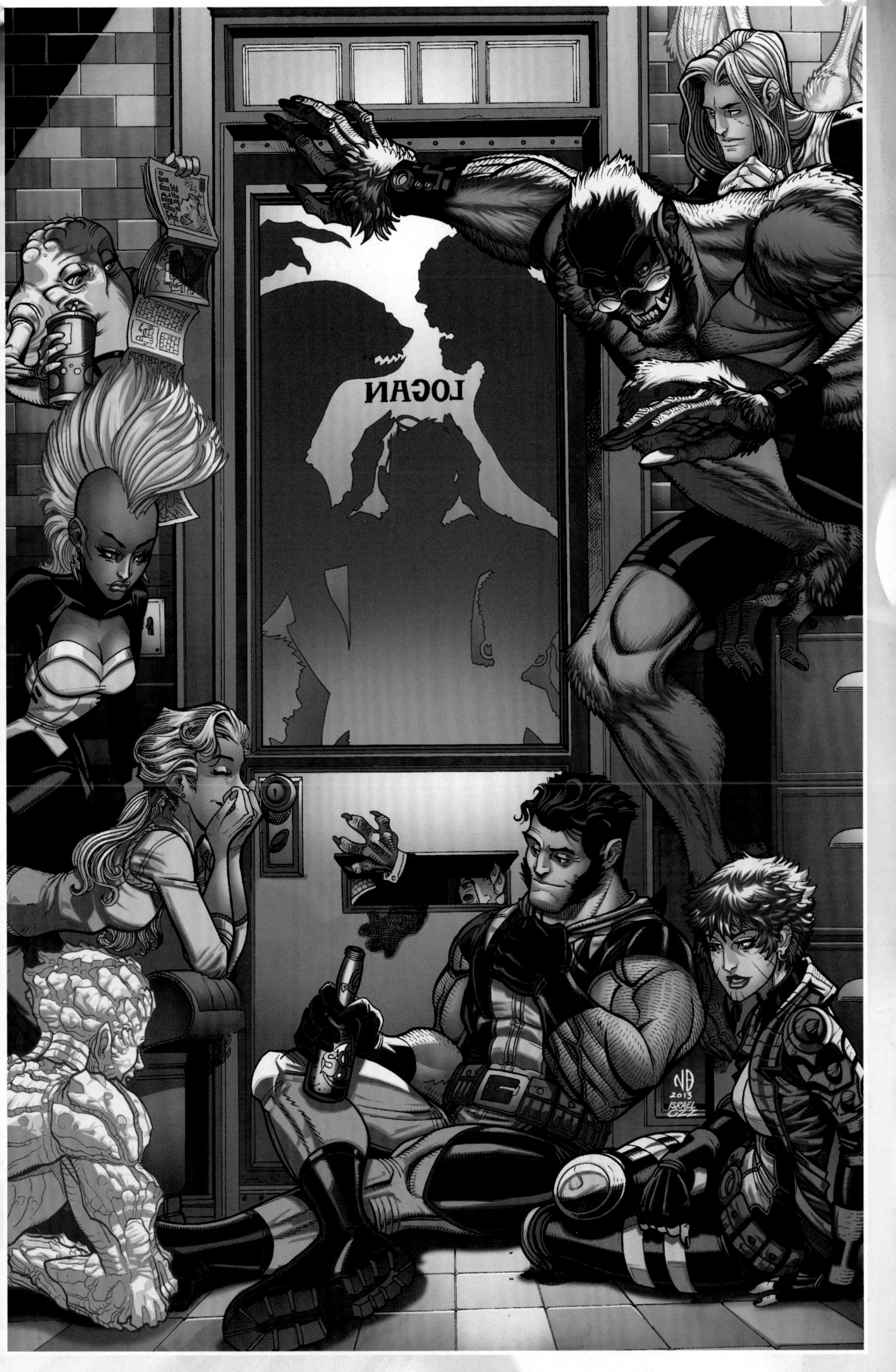
LOGAN

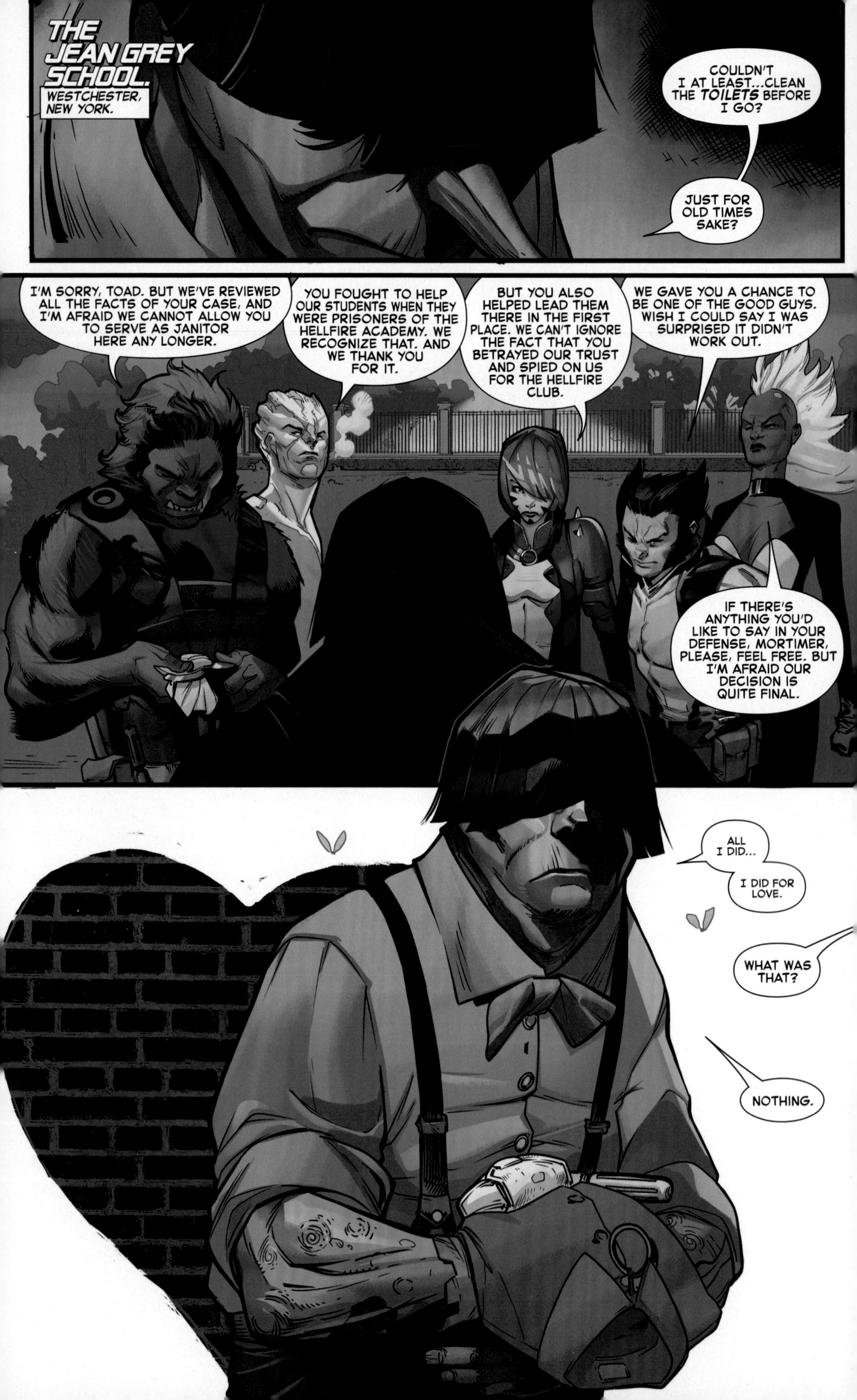
THE JEAN GREY SCHOOL.
WESTCHESTER, NEW YORK.
COULDN'T I AT LEAST...CLEAN THE TOILETS BEFORE I GO?
JUST FOR OLD TIMES SAKE?
I'M SORRY, TOAD. BUT WE'VE REVIEWED ALL THE FACTS OF YOUR CASE, AND I'M AFRAID WE CANNOT ALLOW YOU TO SERVE AS JANITOR HERE ANY LONGER.
YOU FOUGHT TO HELP OUR STUDENTS WHEN THEY WERE PRISONERS OF THE HELLFIRE ACADEMY. WE RECOGNIZE THAT. AND WE THANK YOU FOR IT.
BUT YOU ALSO HELPED LEAD THEM THERE IN THE FIRST PLACE. WE CAN'T IGNORE THE FACT THAT YOU BETRAYED OUR TRUST AND SPIED ON US FOR THE HELLFIRE CLUB.
WE GAVE YOU A CHANCE TO BE ONE OF THE GOOD GUYS. WISH I COULD SAY I WAS SURPRISED IT DIDN'T WORK OUT.
IF THERE'S ANYTHING YOU'D LIKE TO SAY IN YOUR DEFENSE, MORTIMER, PLEASE, FEEL FREE. BUT I'M AFRAID OUR DECISION IS QUITE FINAL.
ALL I DID...
I DID FOR LOVE.
WHAT WAS THAT?
NOTHING.

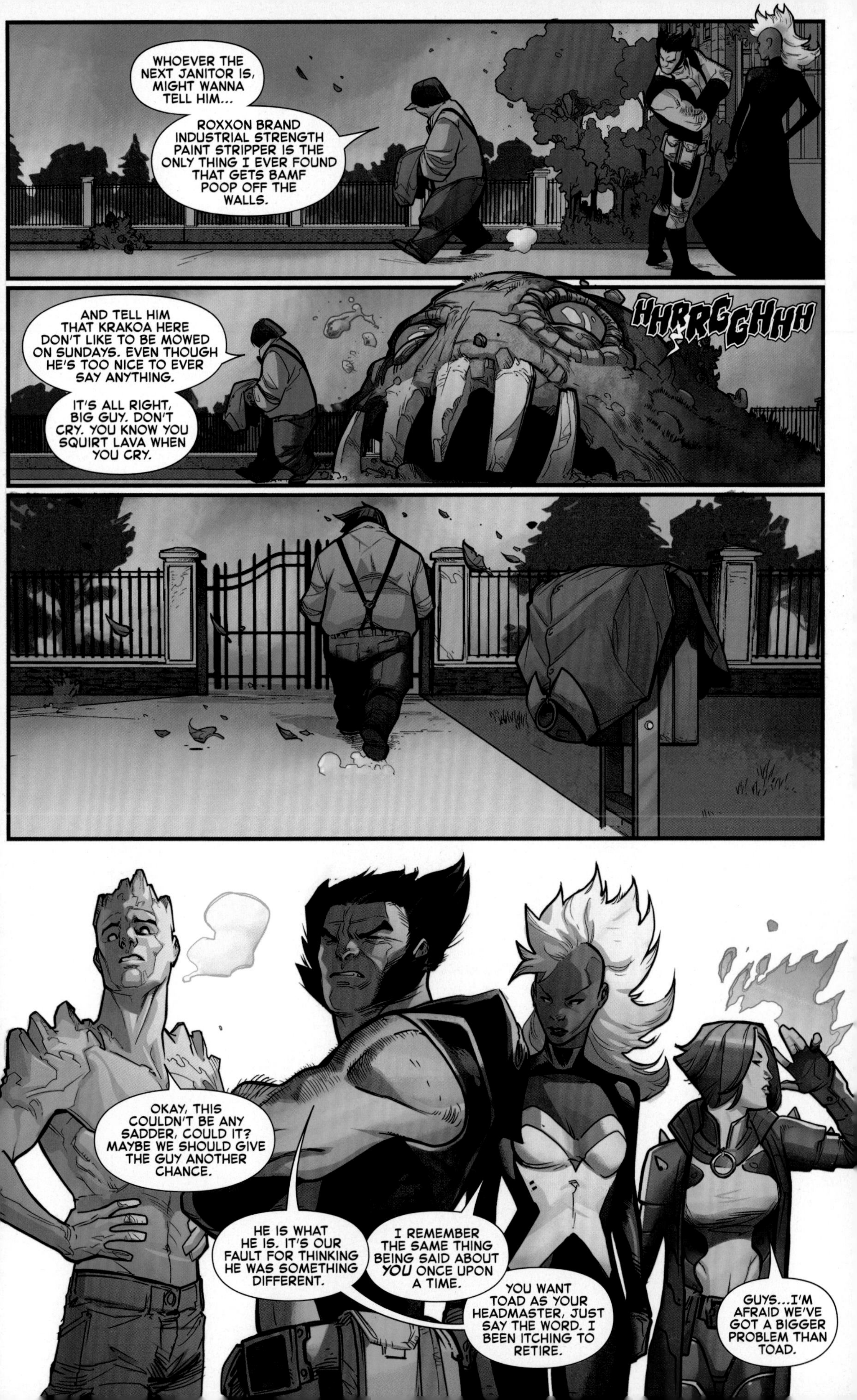

WHOEVER THE NEXT JANITOR IS, MIGHT WANNA TELL HIM...
ROXXON BRAND INDUSTRIAL STRENGTH PAINT STRIPPER IS THE ONLY THING I EVER FOUND THAT GETS BAMF POOP OFF THE WALLS.
AND TELL HIM THAT KRAKOA HERE DON'T LIKE TO BE MOWED ON SUNDAYS. EVEN THOUGH HE'S TOO NICE TO EVER SAY ANYTHING.
IT'S ALL RIGHT, BIG GUY. DON'T CRY. YOU KNOW YOU SQUIRT LAVA WHEN YOU CRY.
HHRRGGHHH
OKAY, THIS COULDN'T BE ANY SADDER, COULD IT? MAYBE WE SHOULD GIVE THE GUY ANOTHER CHANCE.
HE IS WHAT HE IS. IT'S OUR FAULT FOR THINKING HE WAS SOMETHING DIFFERENT.
I REMEMBER THE SAME THING BEING SAID ABOUT YOU ONCE UPON A TIME.
YOU WANT TOAD AS YOUR HEADMASTER, JUST SAY THE WORD. I BEEN ITCHING TO RETIRE.
GUYS...I'M AFRAID WE'VE GOT A BIGGER PROBLEM THAN TOAD.

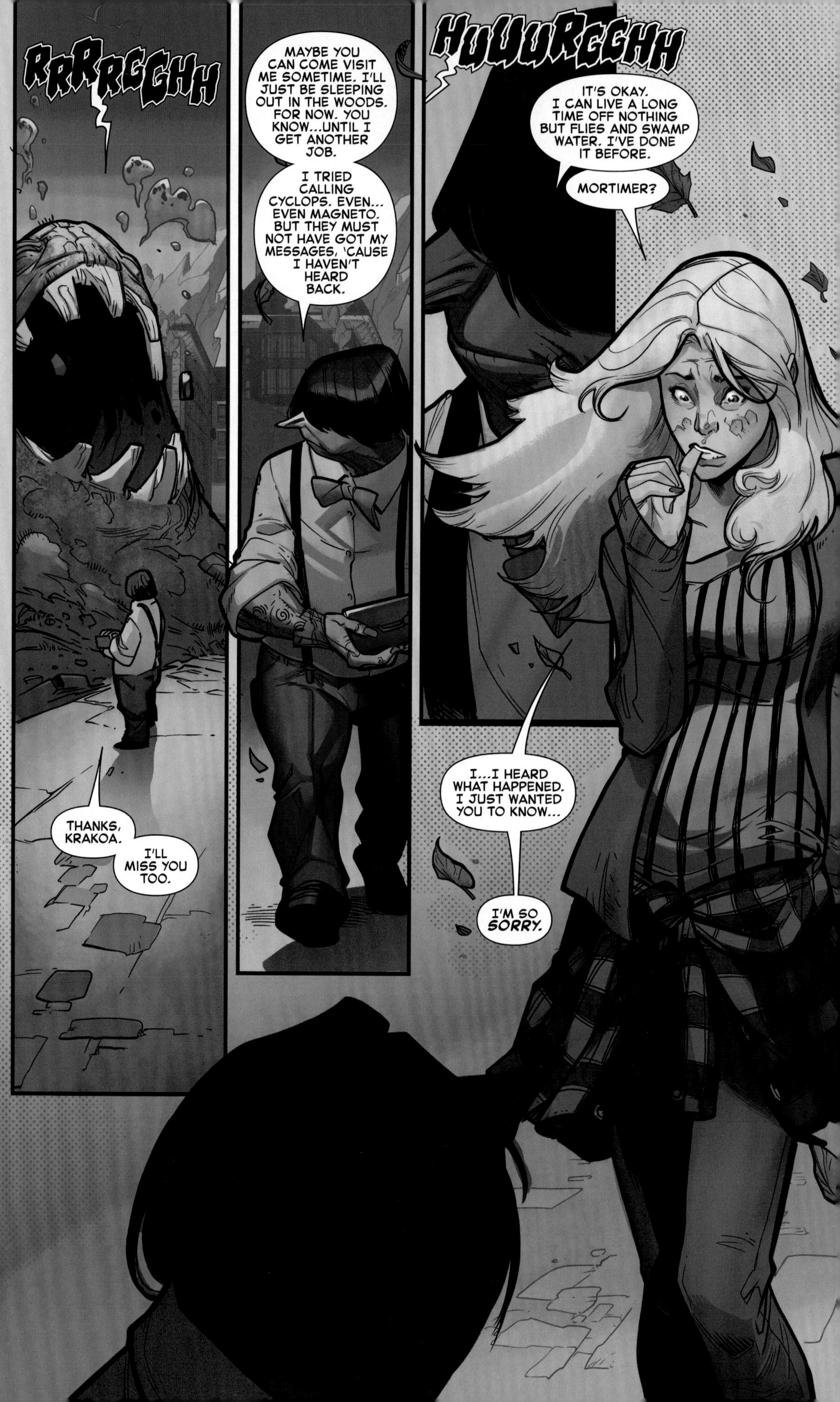
RRRRGGHH
THANKS, KRAKOA.
I'LL MISS YOU TOO.
MAYBE YOU CAN COME VISIT ME SOMETIME. I'LL JUST BE SLEEPING OUT IN THE WOODS. FOR NOW. YOU KNOW...UNTIL I GET ANOTHER JOB.
I TRIED CALLING CYCLOPS. EVEN... EVEN MAGNETO. BUT THEY MUST NOT HAVE GOT MY MESSAGES, 'CAUSE I HAVEN'T HEARD BACK.
HUUURGGHH
IT'S OKAY. I CAN LIVE A LONG TIME OFF NOTHING BUT FLIES AND SWAMP WATER. I'VE DONE IT BEFORE.
MORTIMER?
I...I HEARD WHAT HAPPENED. I JUST WANTED YOU TO KNOW...
I'M SO *SORRY.*

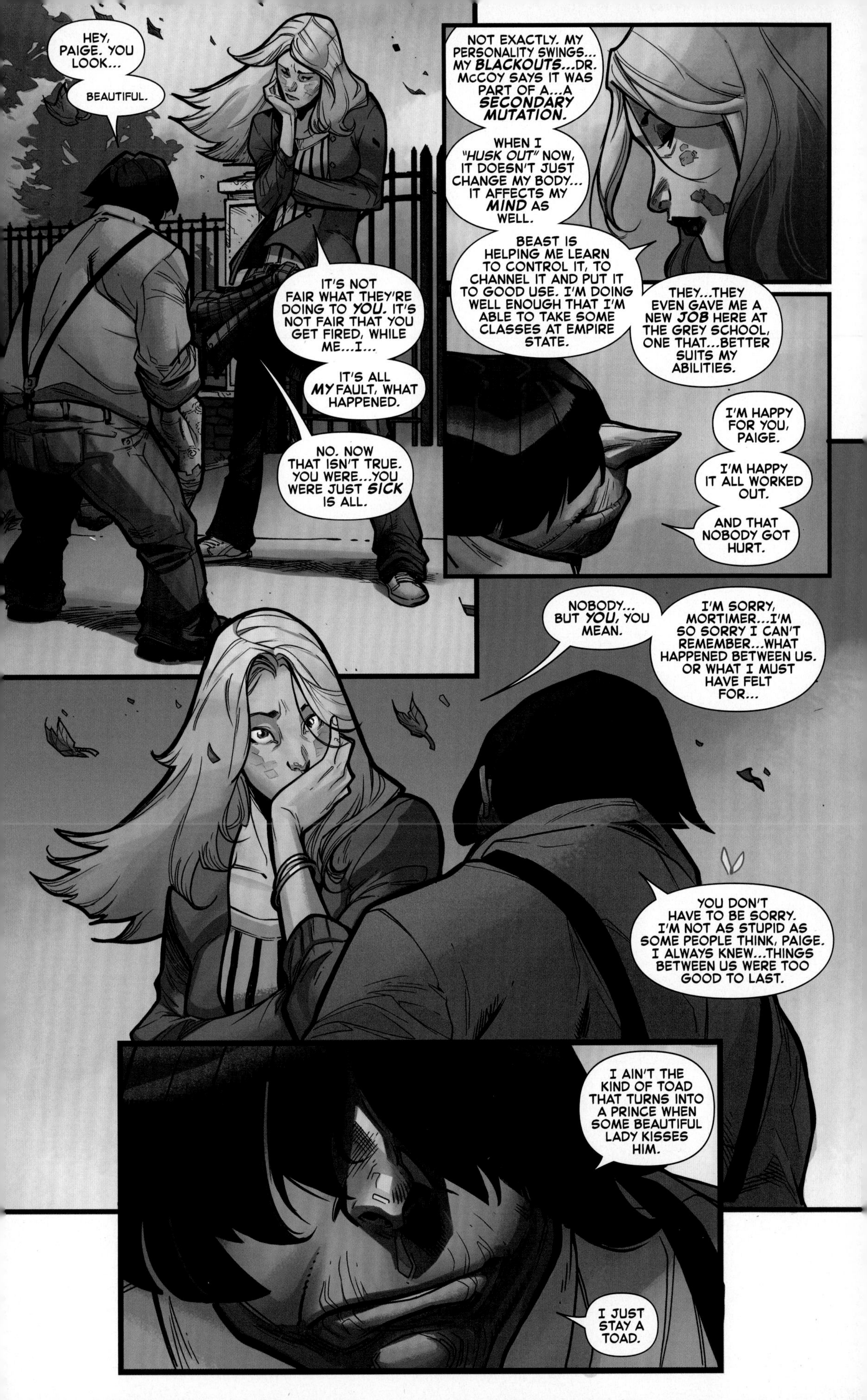
HEY, PAIGE. YOU LOOK...
BEAUTIFUL.
NOT EXACTLY. MY PERSONALITY SWINGS... MY BLACKOUTS...DR. McCOY SAYS IT WAS PART OF A...A SECONDARY MUTATION.
WHEN I "HUSK OUT" NOW, IT DOESN'T JUST CHANGE MY BODY... IT AFFECTS MY MIND AS WELL.
BEAST IS HELPING ME LEARN TO CONTROL IT, TO CHANNEL IT AND PUT IT TO GOOD USE. I'M DOING WELL ENOUGH THAT I'M ABLE TO TAKE SOME CLASSES AT EMPIRE STATE.
THEY...THEY EVEN GAVE ME A NEW JOB HERE AT THE GREY SCHOOL, ONE THAT...BETTER SUITS MY ABILITIES.
IT'S NOT FAIR WHAT THEY'RE DOING TO YOU. IT'S NOT FAIR THAT YOU GET FIRED, WHILE ME...I...
IT'S ALL MY FAULT, WHAT HAPPENED.
NO. NOW THAT ISN'T TRUE. YOU WERE...YOU WERE JUST SICK IS ALL.
I'M HAPPY FOR YOU, PAIGE.
I'M HAPPY IT ALL WORKED OUT.
AND THAT NOBODY GOT HURT.
NOBODY... BUT YOU, YOU MEAN.
I'M SORRY, MORTIMER...I'M SO SORRY I CAN'T REMEMBER...WHAT HAPPENED BETWEEN US. OR WHAT I MUST HAVE FELT FOR...
YOU DON'T HAVE TO BE SORRY. I'M NOT AS STUPID AS SOME PEOPLE THINK, PAIGE. I ALWAYS KNEW...THINGS BETWEEN US WERE TOO GOOD TO LAST.
I AIN'T THE KIND OF TOAD THAT TURNS INTO A PRINCE WHEN SOME BEAUTIFUL LADY KISSES HIM.
I JUST STAY A TOAD.

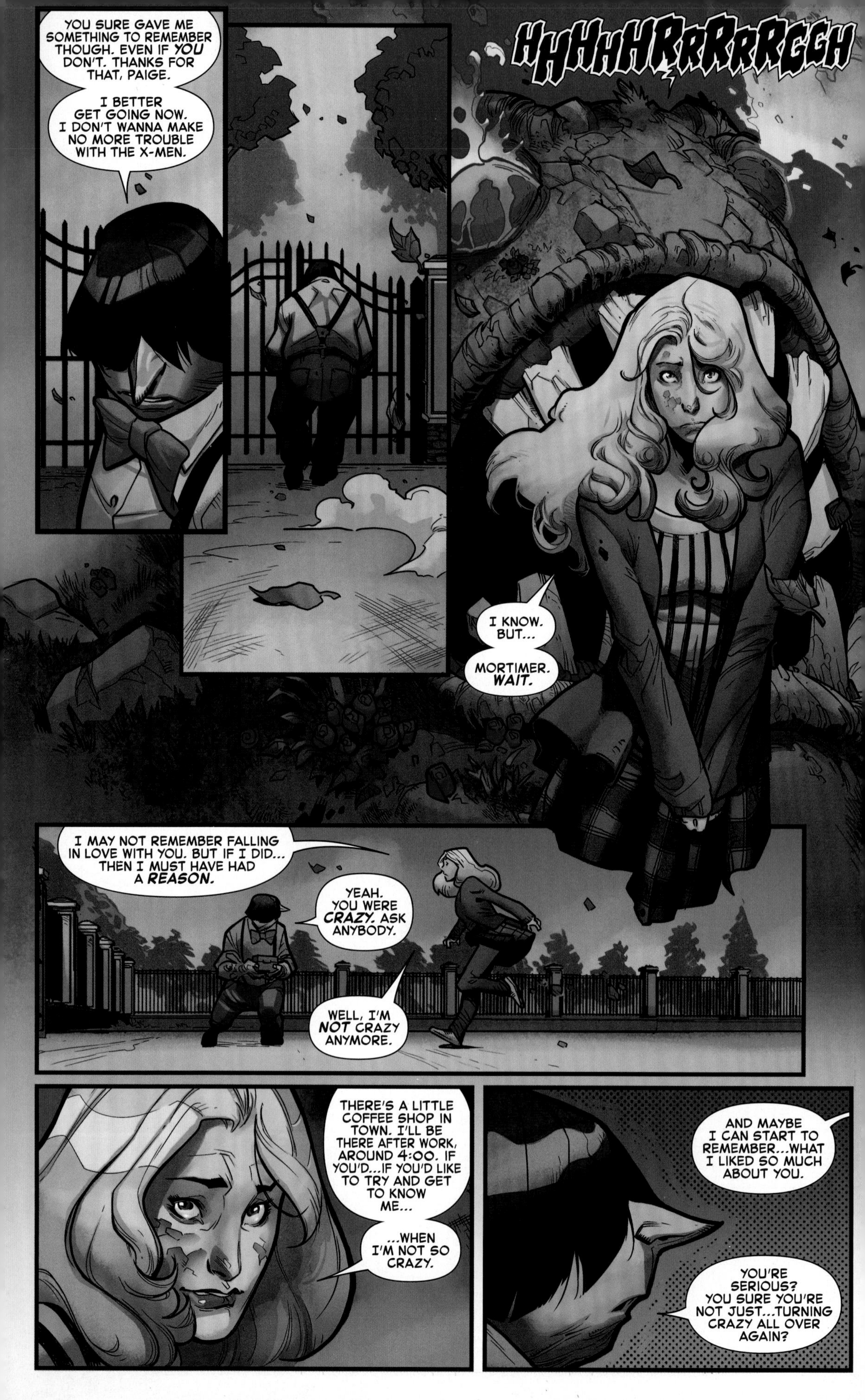
YOU SURE GAVE ME SOMETHING TO REMEMBER THOUGH. EVEN IF YOU DON'T. THANKS FOR THAT, PAIGE.
I BETTER GET GOING NOW. I DON'T WANNA MAKE NO MORE TROUBLE WITH THE X-MEN.
HHHHHRRRRRRGGH
I KNOW. BUT...
MORTIMER. WAIT.
I MAY NOT REMEMBER FALLING IN LOVE WITH YOU. BUT IF I DID... THEN I MUST HAVE HAD A REASON.
YEAH. YOU WERE CRAZY. ASK ANYBODY.
WELL, I'M NOT CRAZY ANYMORE.
THERE'S A LITTLE COFFEE SHOP IN TOWN. I'LL BE THERE AFTER WORK, AROUND 4:00. IF YOU'D...IF YOU'D LIKE TO TRY AND GET TO KNOW ME...
...WHEN I'M NOT SO CRAZY.
AND MAYBE I CAN START TO REMEMBER...WHAT I LIKED SO MUCH ABOUT YOU.
YOU'RE SERIOUS? YOU SURE YOU'RE NOT JUST...TURNING CRAZY ALL OVER AGAIN?

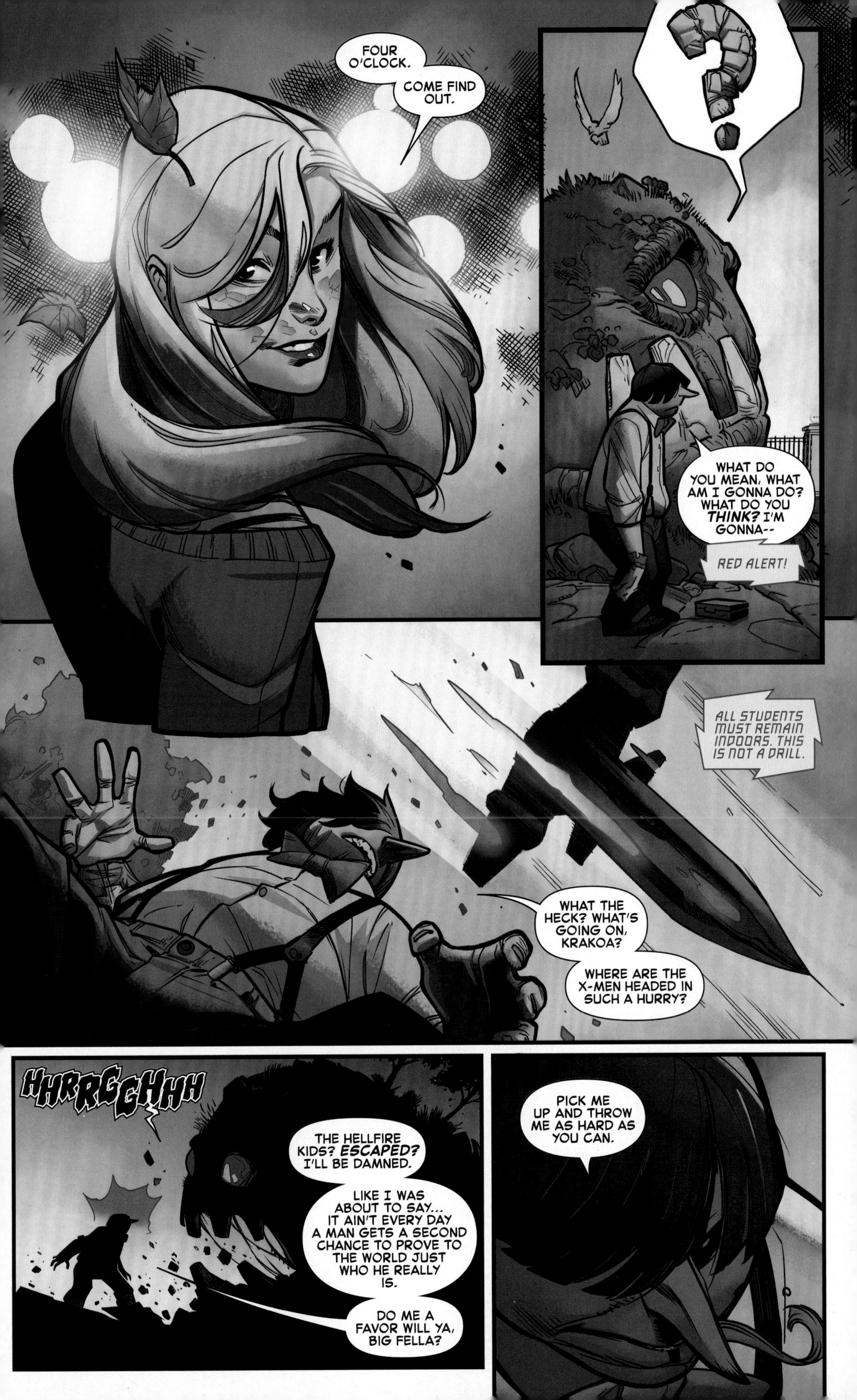
FOUR O'CLOCK.
COME FIND OUT.
?
WHAT DO YOU MEAN, WHAT AM I GONNA DO? WHAT DO YOU *THINK?* I'M GONNA--
RED ALERT!
ALL STUDENTS MUST REMAIN INDOORS. THIS IS NOT A DRILL.
WHAT THE HECK? WHAT'S GOING ON, KRAKOA?
WHERE ARE THE X-MEN HEADED IN SUCH A HURRY?
HHRRGGHHH
THE HELLFIRE KIDS? *ESCAPED?* I'LL BE DAMNED.
LIKE I WAS ABOUT TO SAY... IT AIN'T EVERY DAY A MAN GETS A SECOND CHANCE TO PROVE TO THE WORLD JUST WHO HE REALLY IS.
DO ME A FAVOR WILL YA, BIG FELLA?
PICK ME UP AND THROW ME AS HARD AS YOU CAN.

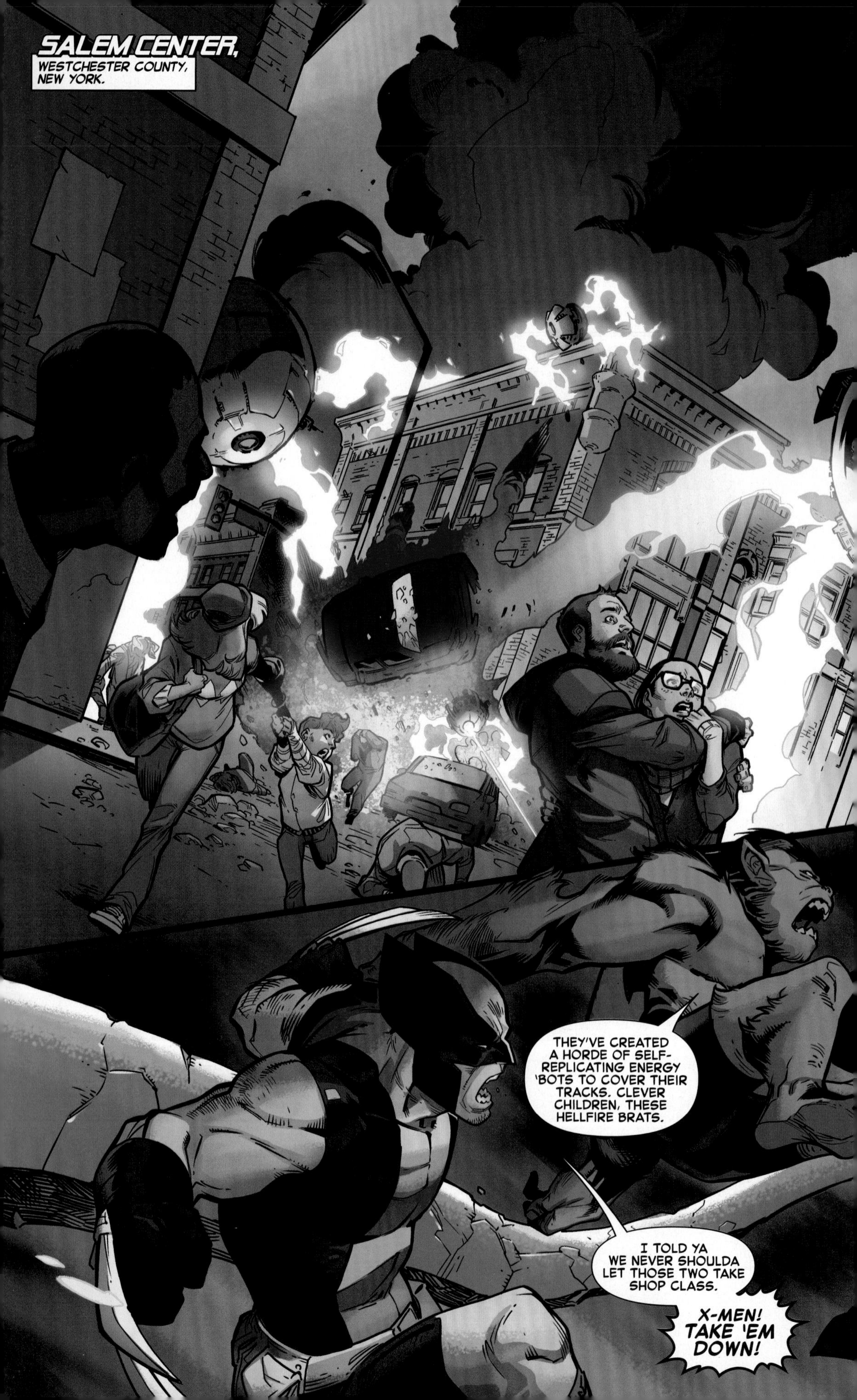
SALEM CENTER,
WESTCHESTER COUNTY, NEW YORK.
THEY'VE CREATED A HORDE OF SELF-REPLICATING ENERGY 'BOTS TO COVER THEIR TRACKS. CLEVER CHILDREN, THESE HELLFIRE BRATS.
I TOLD YA WE NEVER SHOULDA LET THOSE TWO TAKE SHOP CLASS.
X-MEN! TAKE 'EM DOWN!

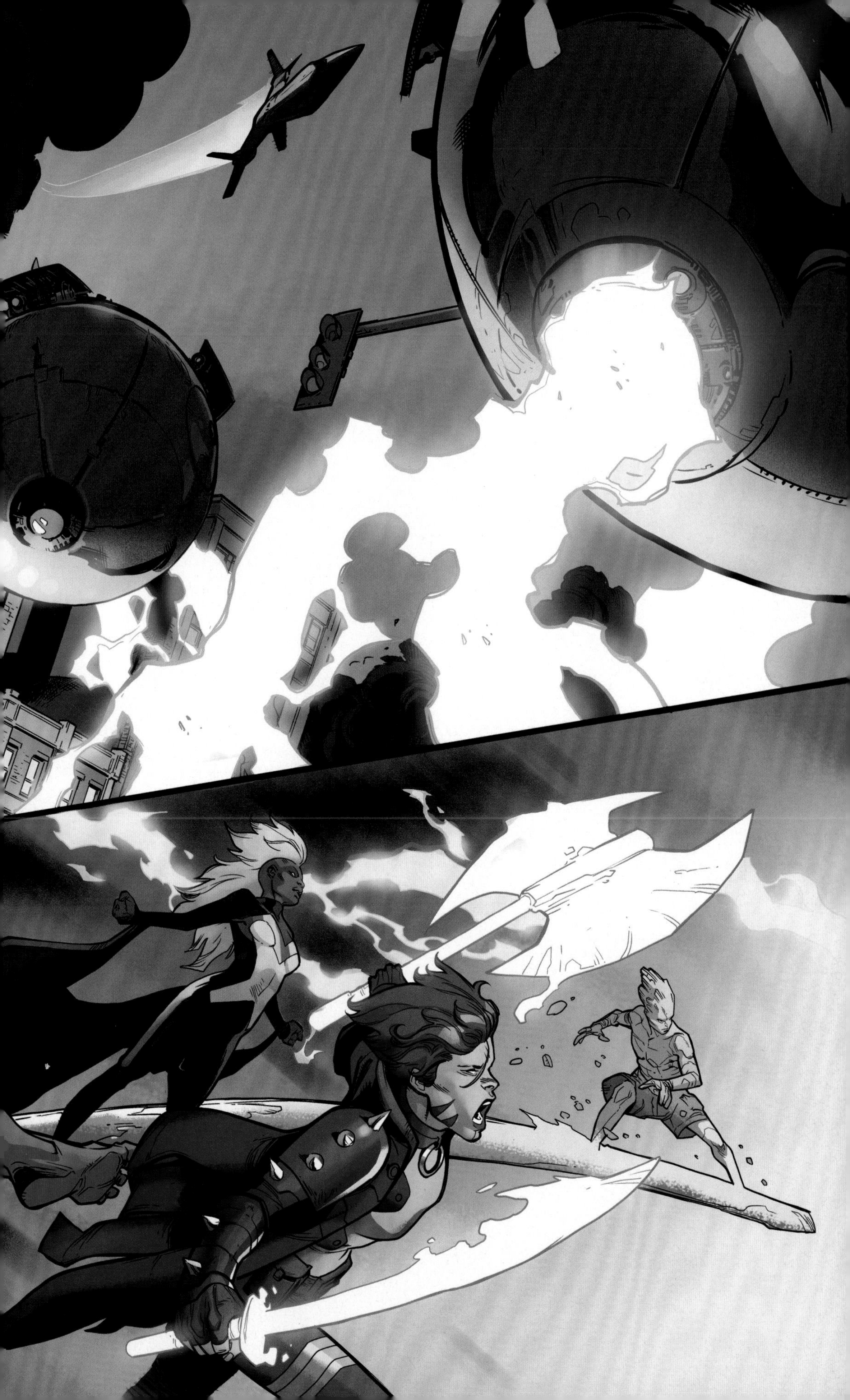

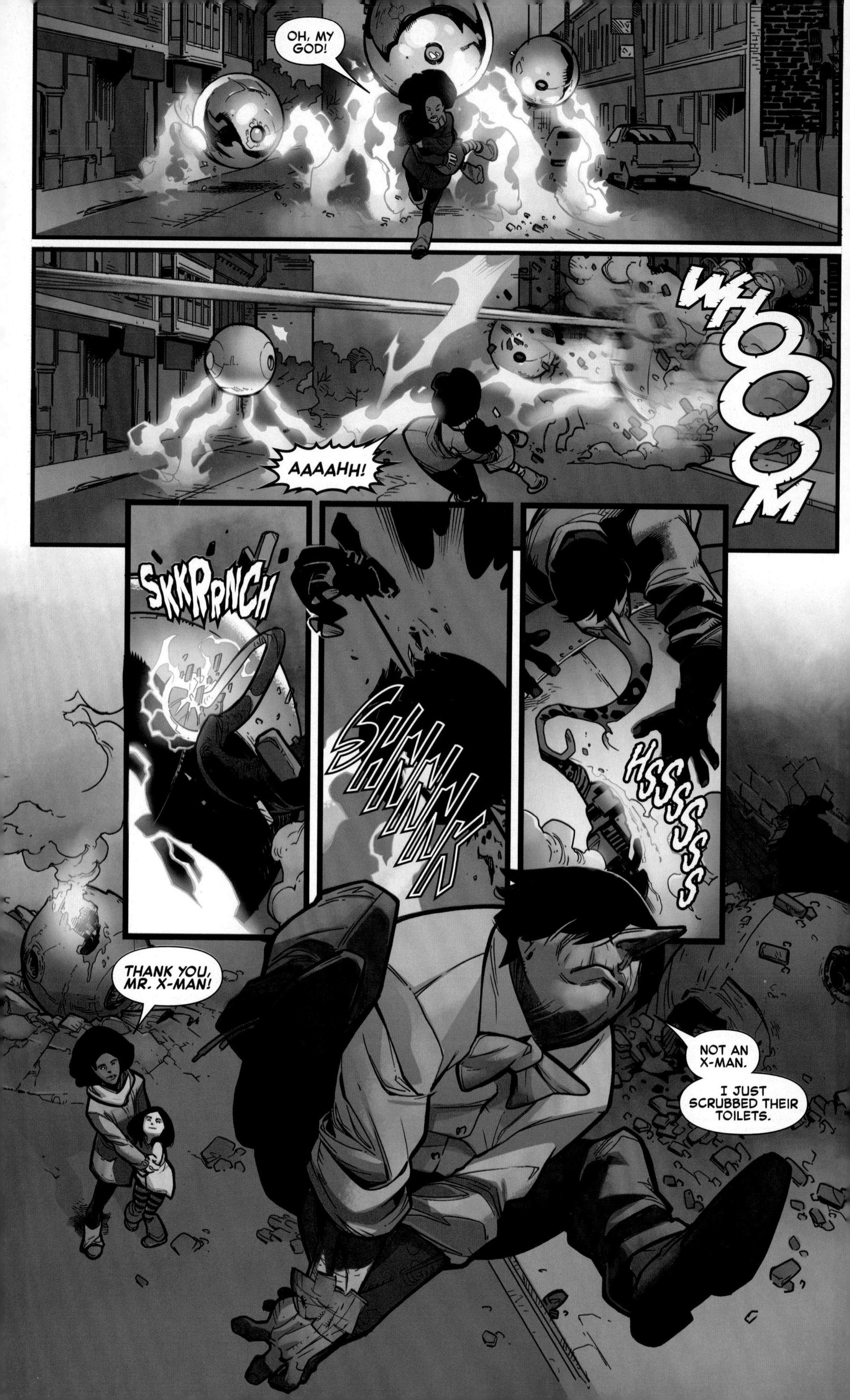
OH, MY GOD!
AAAAHH!
WHOOOOM
SKKRRNCH
SHNNNK
HSSSSSS
THANK YOU, MR. X-MAN!
NOT AN X-MAN.
I JUST SCRUBBED THEIR TOILETS.

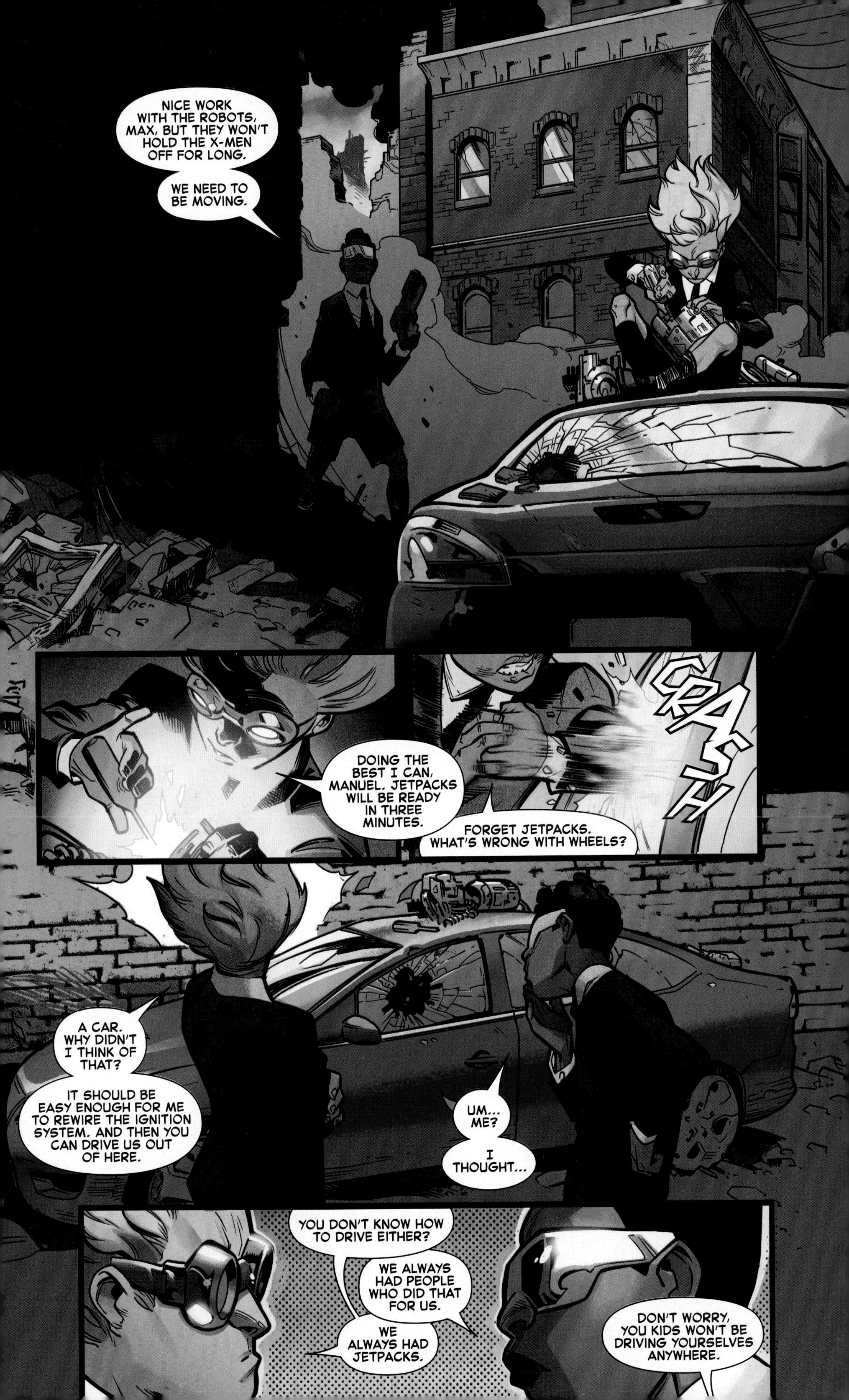
NICE WORK WITH THE ROBOTS, MAX, BUT THEY WON'T HOLD THE X-MEN OFF FOR LONG.
WE NEED TO BE MOVING.
DOING THE BEST I CAN, MANUEL. JETPACKS WILL BE READY IN THREE MINUTES.
CRASH
FORGET JETPACKS. WHAT'S WRONG WITH WHEELS?
A CAR. WHY DIDN'T I THINK OF THAT?
IT SHOULD BE EASY ENOUGH FOR ME TO REWIRE THE IGNITION SYSTEM. AND THEN YOU CAN DRIVE US OUT OF HERE.
UM... ME?
I THOUGHT...
YOU DON'T KNOW HOW TO DRIVE EITHER?
WE ALWAYS HAD PEOPLE WHO DID THAT FOR US.
WE ALWAYS HAD JETPACKS.
DON'T WORRY, YOU KIDS WON'T BE DRIVING YOURSELVES ANYWHERE.

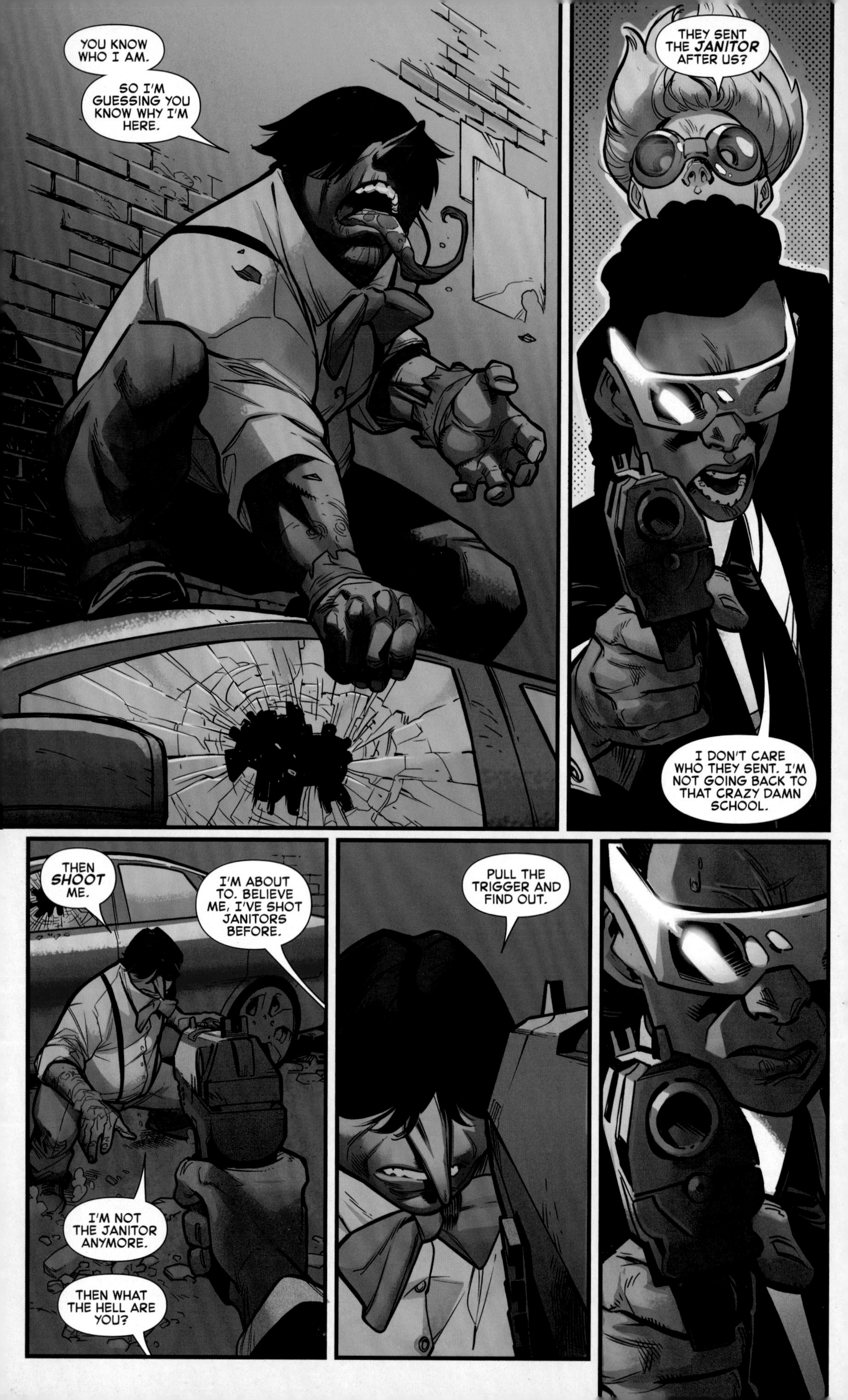
YOU KNOW WHO I AM.
SO I'M GUESSING YOU KNOW WHY I'M HERE.
THEY SENT THE *JANITOR* AFTER US?
I DON'T CARE WHO THEY SENT. I'M NOT GOING BACK TO THAT CRAZY DAMN SCHOOL.
THEN *SHOOT* ME.
I'M ABOUT TO. BELIEVE ME, I'VE SHOT JANITORS BEFORE.
I'M NOT THE JANITOR ANYMORE.
THEN WHAT THE HELL ARE YOU?
PULL THE TRIGGER AND FIND OUT.

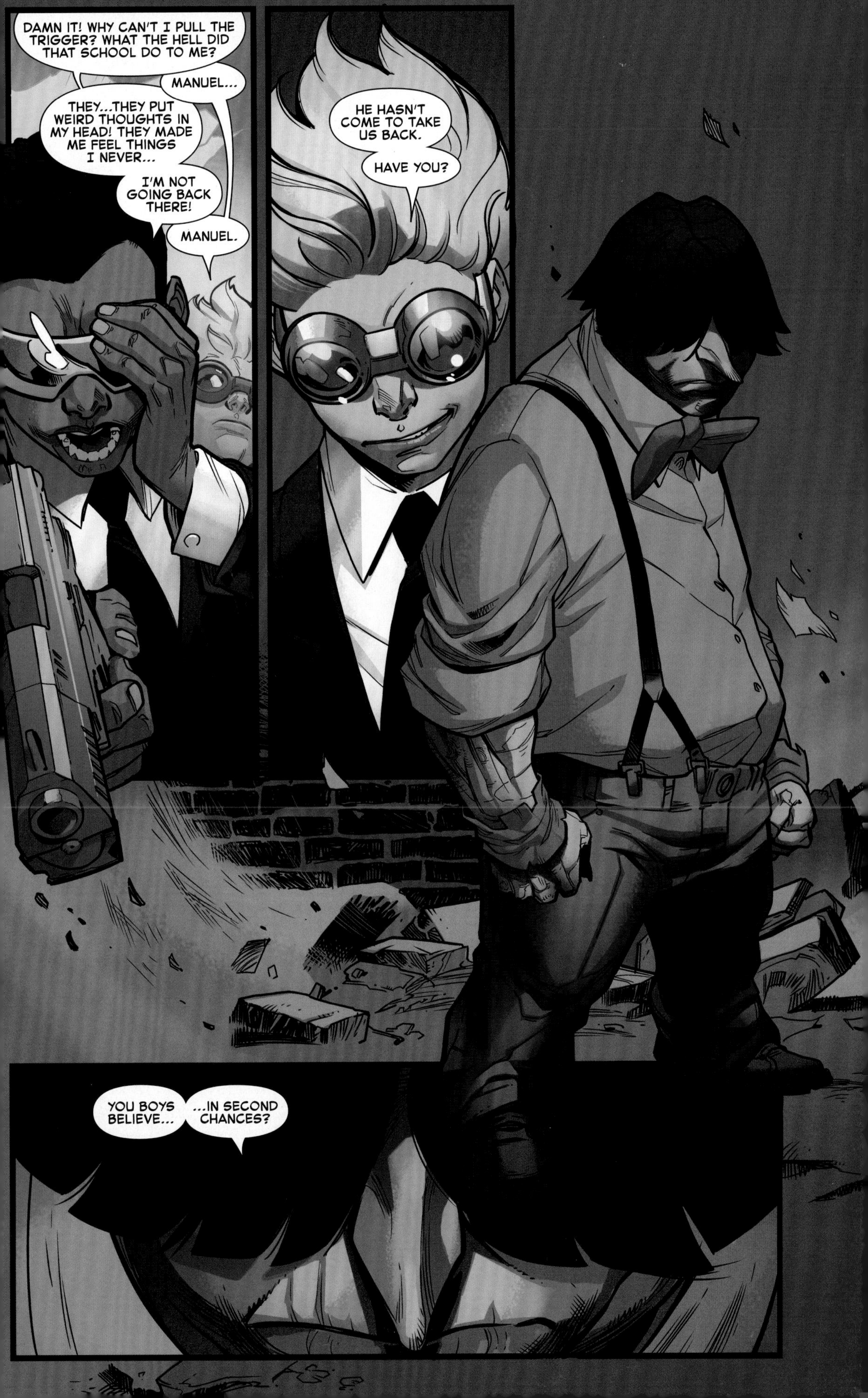
DAMN IT! WHY CAN'T I PULL THE TRIGGER? WHAT THE HELL DID THAT SCHOOL DO TO ME?
MANUEL...
THEY...THEY PUT WEIRD THOUGHTS IN MY HEAD! THEY MADE ME FEEL THINGS I NEVER...
I'M NOT GOING BACK THERE!
MANUEL.
HE HASN'T COME TO TAKE US BACK.
HAVE YOU?
YOU BOYS BELIEVE...
...IN SECOND CHANCES?

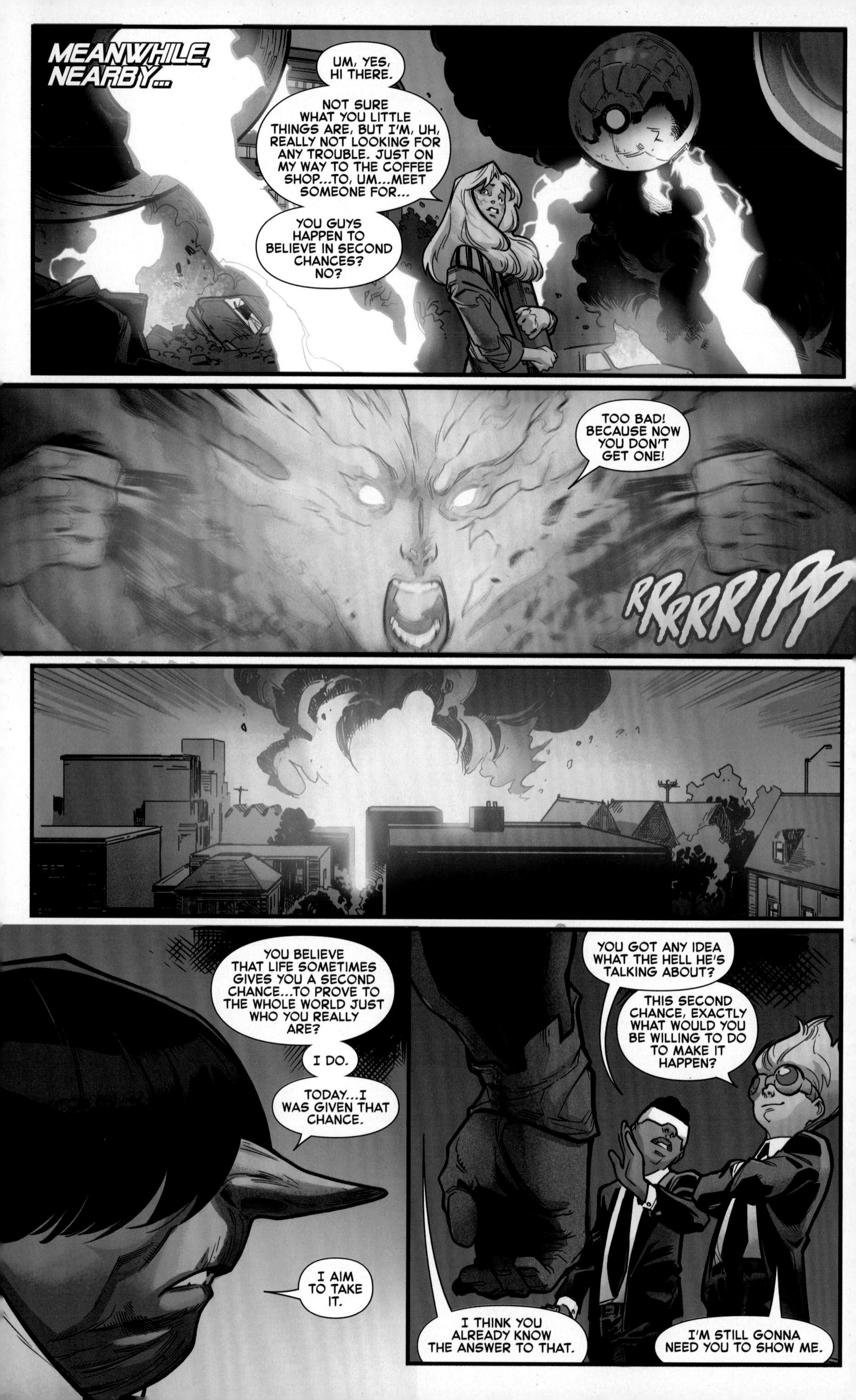
MEANWHILE, NEARBY...
UM, YES, HI THERE.
NOT SURE WHAT YOU LITTLE THINGS ARE, BUT I'M, UH, REALLY NOT LOOKING FOR ANY TROUBLE. JUST ON MY WAY TO THE COFFEE SHOP...TO, UM...MEET SOMEONE FOR...
YOU GUYS HAPPEN TO BELIEVE IN SECOND CHANCES? NO?
TOO BAD! BECAUSE NOW YOU DON'T GET ONE!
RRRRRIPP
YOU BELIEVE THAT LIFE SOMETIMES GIVES YOU A SECOND CHANCE...TO PROVE TO THE WHOLE WORLD JUST WHO YOU REALLY ARE?
I DO.
TODAY...I WAS GIVEN THAT CHANCE.
I AIM TO TAKE IT.
YOU GOT ANY IDEA WHAT THE HELL HE'S TALKING ABOUT?
THIS SECOND CHANCE, EXACTLY WHAT WOULD YOU BE WILLING TO DO TO MAKE IT HAPPEN?
I THINK YOU ALREADY KNOW THE ANSWER TO THAT.
I'M STILL GONNA NEED YOU TO SHOW ME.

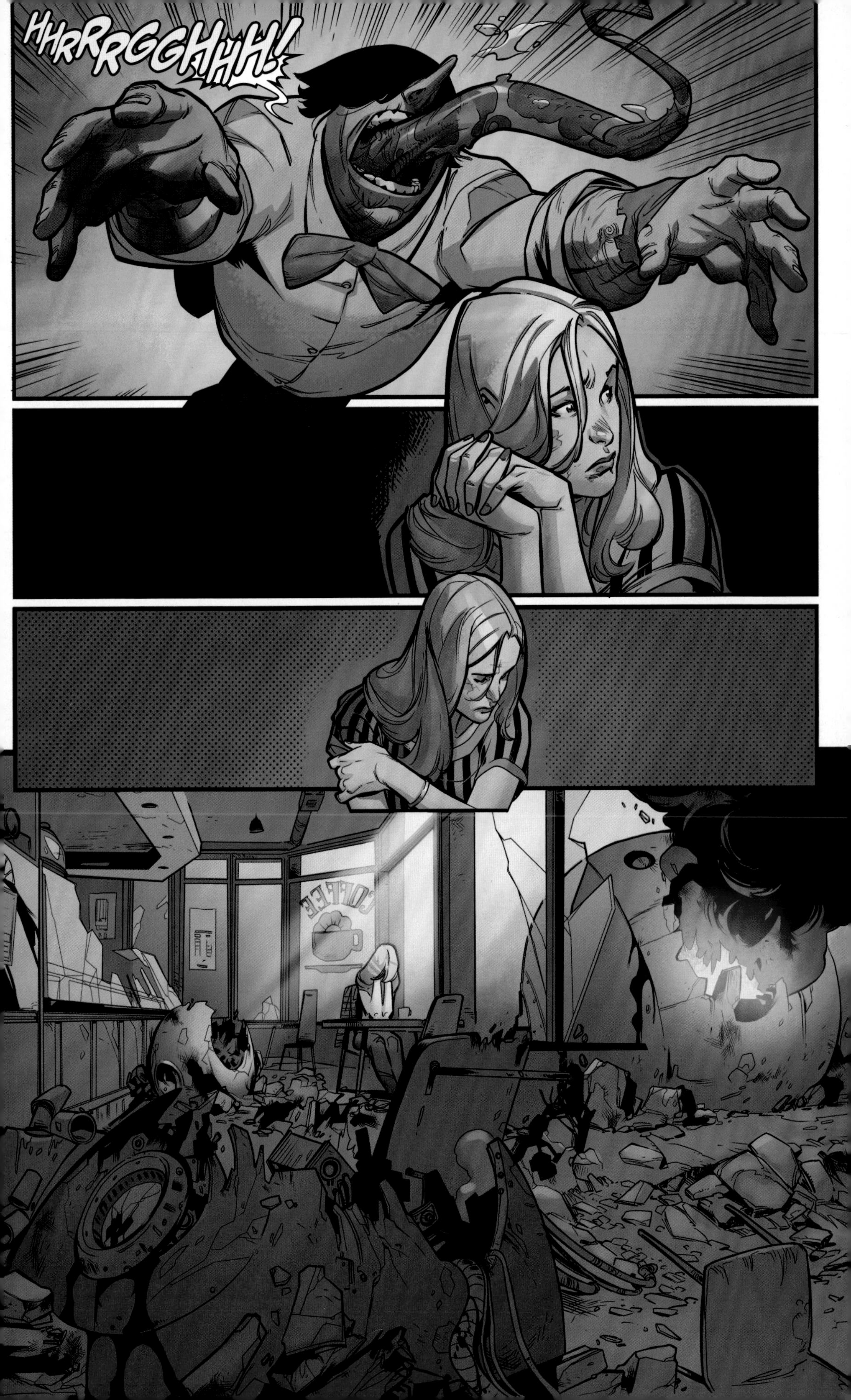
HHRRRGGHHH!
COFFEE

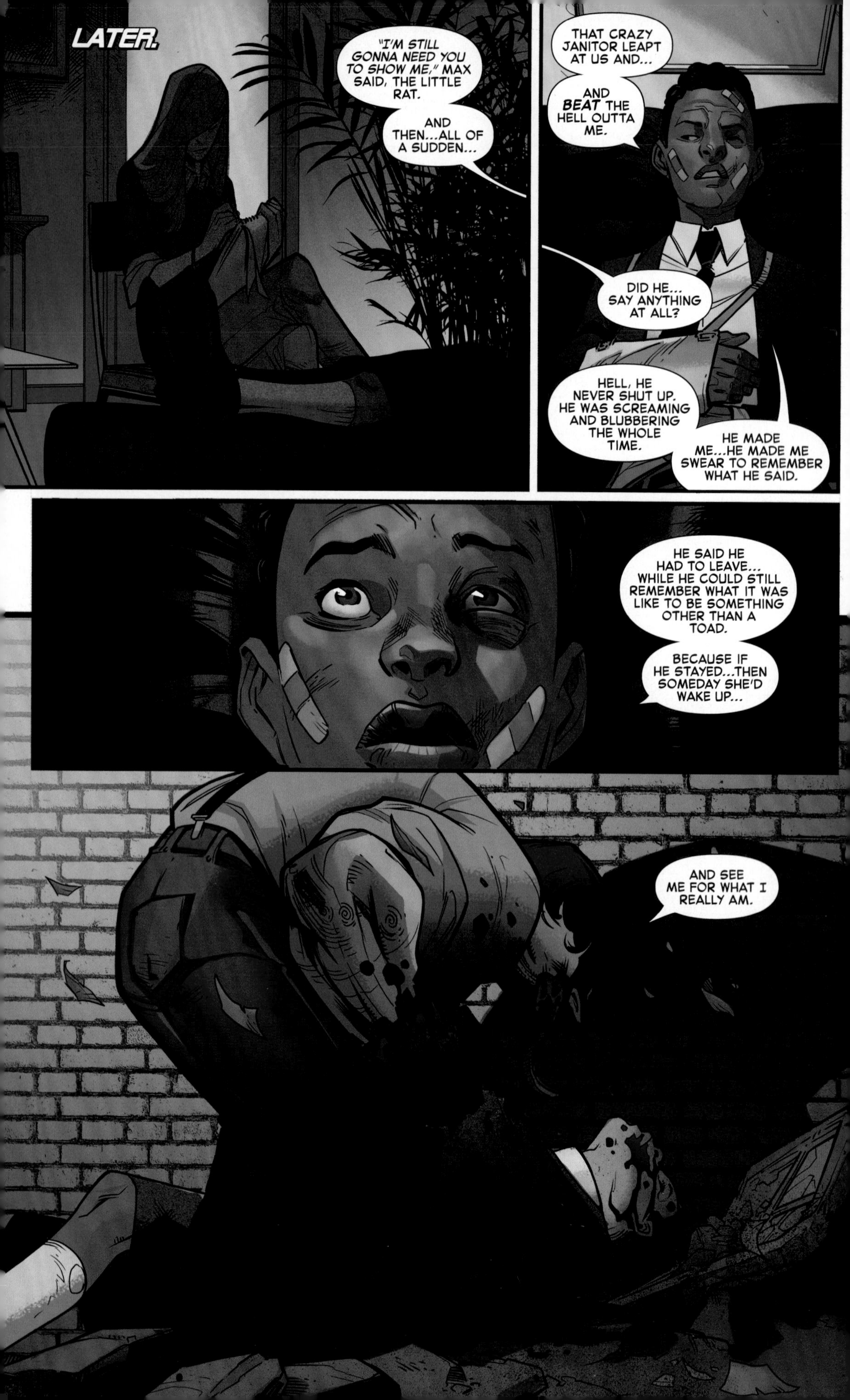
LATER.
"I'M STILL GONNA NEED YOU TO SHOW ME," MAX SAID, THE LITTLE RAT.
AND THEN...ALL OF A SUDDEN...
THAT CRAZY JANITOR LEAPT AT US AND...
AND BEAT THE HELL OUTTA ME.
DID HE... SAY ANYTHING AT ALL?
HELL, HE NEVER SHUT UP. HE WAS SCREAMING AND BLUBBERING THE WHOLE TIME.
HE MADE ME...HE MADE ME SWEAR TO REMEMBER WHAT HE SAID.
HE SAID HE HAD TO LEAVE... WHILE HE COULD STILL REMEMBER WHAT IT WAS LIKE TO BE SOMETHING OTHER THAN A TOAD.
BECAUSE IF HE STAYED...THEN SOMEDAY SHE'D WAKE UP...
AND SEE ME FOR WHAT I REALLY AM.

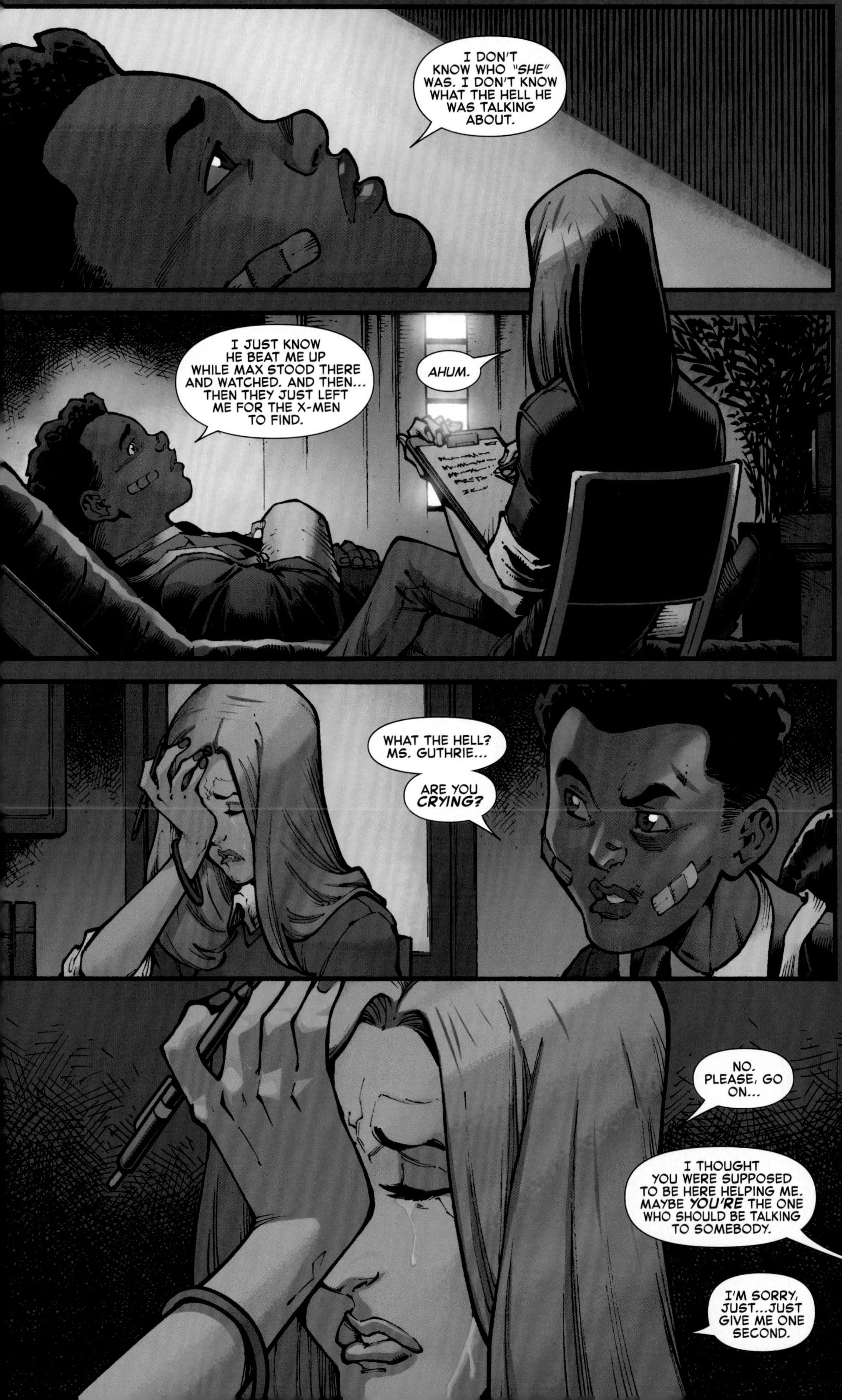
I DON'T KNOW WHO "SHE" WAS. I DON'T KNOW WHAT THE HELL HE WAS TALKING ABOUT.
I JUST KNOW HE BEAT ME UP WHILE MAX STOOD THERE AND WATCHED. AND THEN... THEN THEY JUST LEFT ME FOR THE X-MEN TO FIND.
AHUM.
WHAT THE HELL? MS. GUTHRIE...
ARE YOU CRYING?
NO. PLEASE, GO ON...
I THOUGHT YOU WERE SUPPOSED TO BE HERE HELPING ME. MAYBE YOU'RE THE ONE WHO SHOULD BE TALKING TO SOMEBODY.
I'M SORRY, JUST...JUST GIVE ME ONE SECOND.

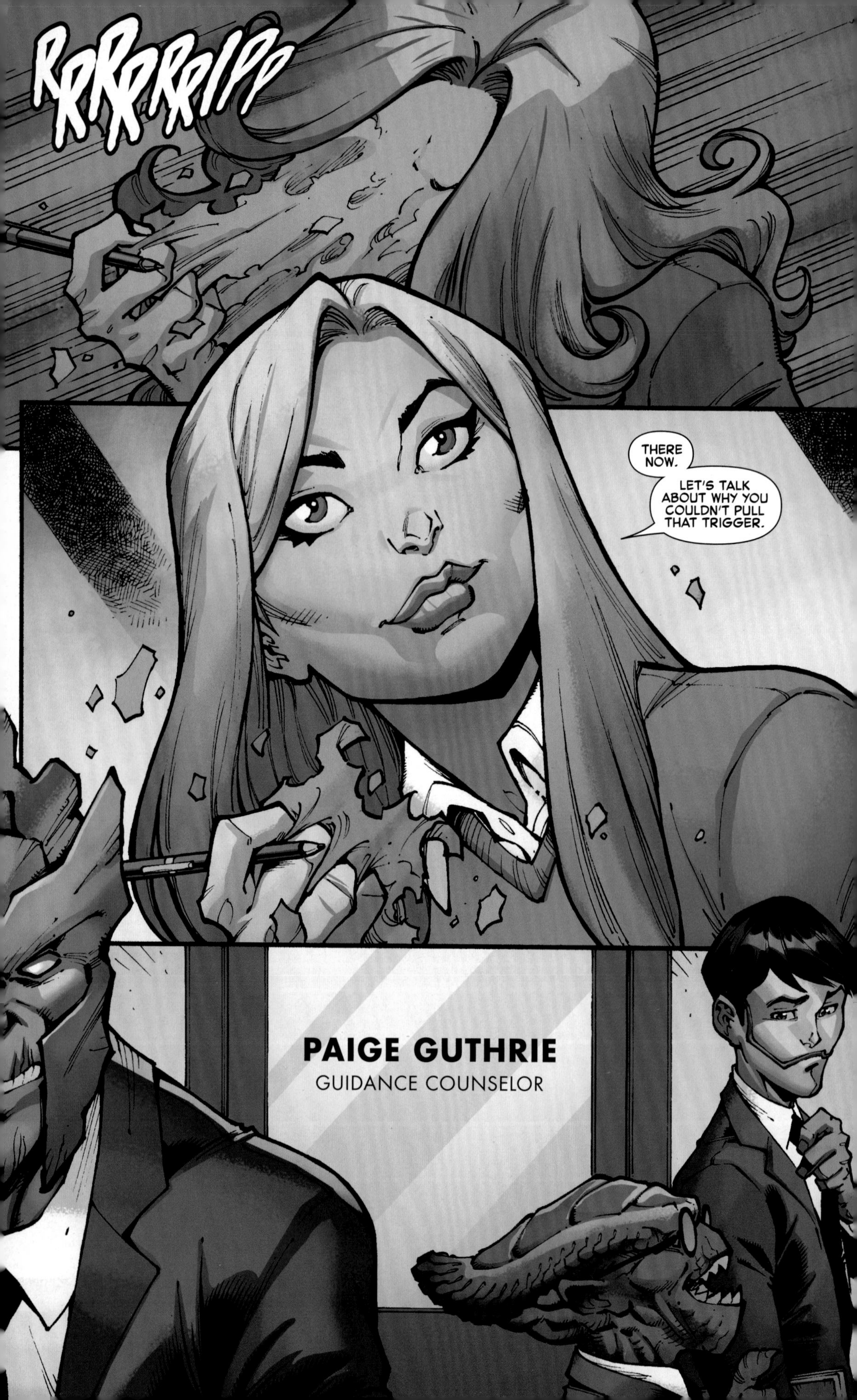
RRRRRRIPP
THERE NOW.
LET'S TALK ABOUT WHY YOU COULDN'T PULL THAT TRIGGER.
PAIGE GUTHRIE
GUIDANCE COUNSELOR

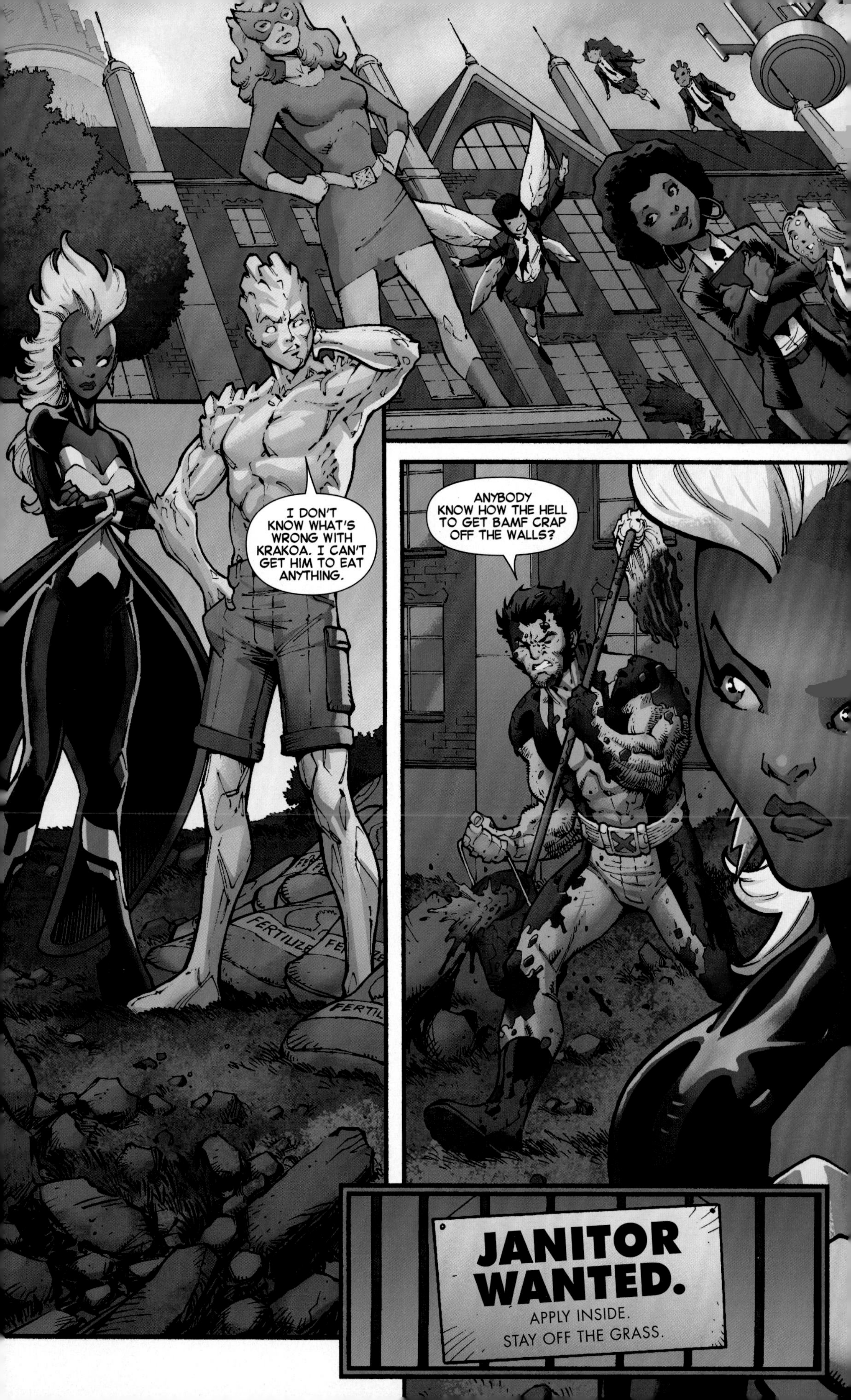
I DON'T KNOW WHAT'S WRONG WITH KRAKOA. I CAN'T GET HIM TO EAT ANYTHING.
ANYBODY KNOW HOW THE HELL TO GET BAMF CRAP OFF THE WALLS?
FERTILIZE
JANITOR WANTED.
APPLY INSIDE.
STAY OFF THE GRASS.

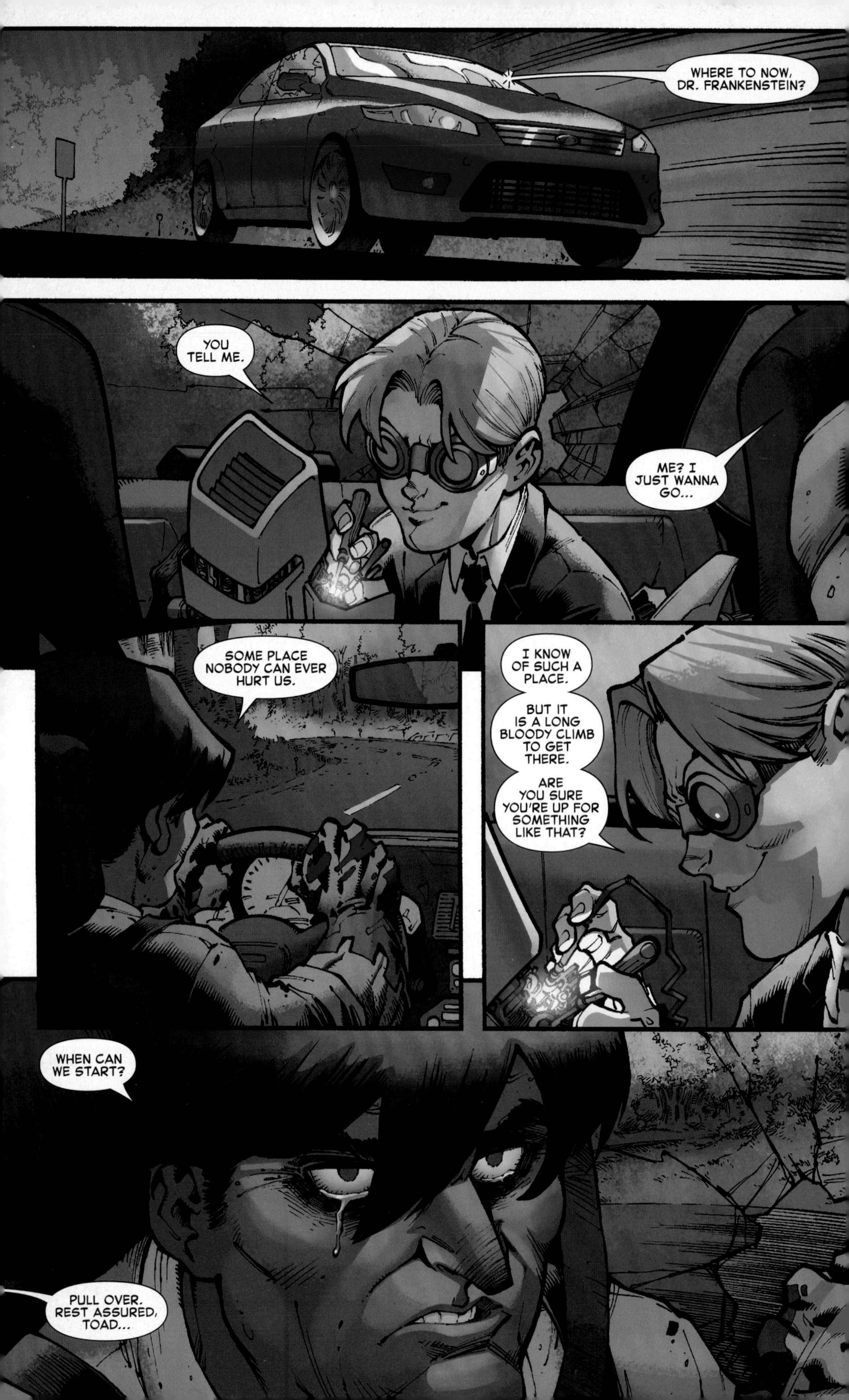
WHERE TO NOW, DR. FRANKENSTEIN?
YOU TELL ME.
ME? I JUST WANNA GO...
SOME PLACE NOBODY CAN EVER HURT US.
I KNOW OF SUCH A PLACE.
BUT IT IS A LONG BLOODY CLIMB TO GET THERE.
ARE YOU SURE YOU'RE UP FOR SOMETHING LIKE THAT?
WHEN CAN WE START?
PULL OVER. REST ASSURED, TOAD...

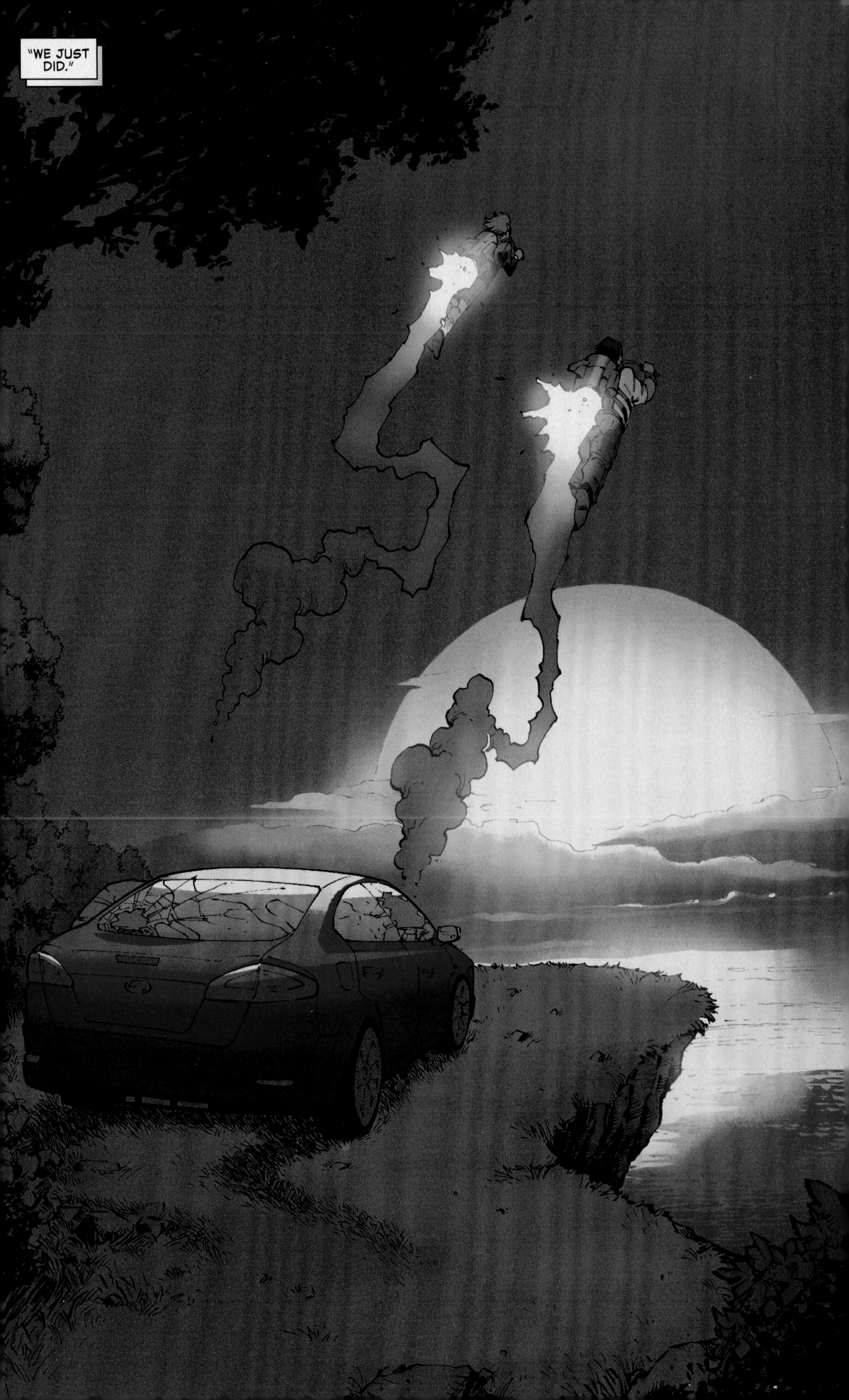
"WE JUST DID."

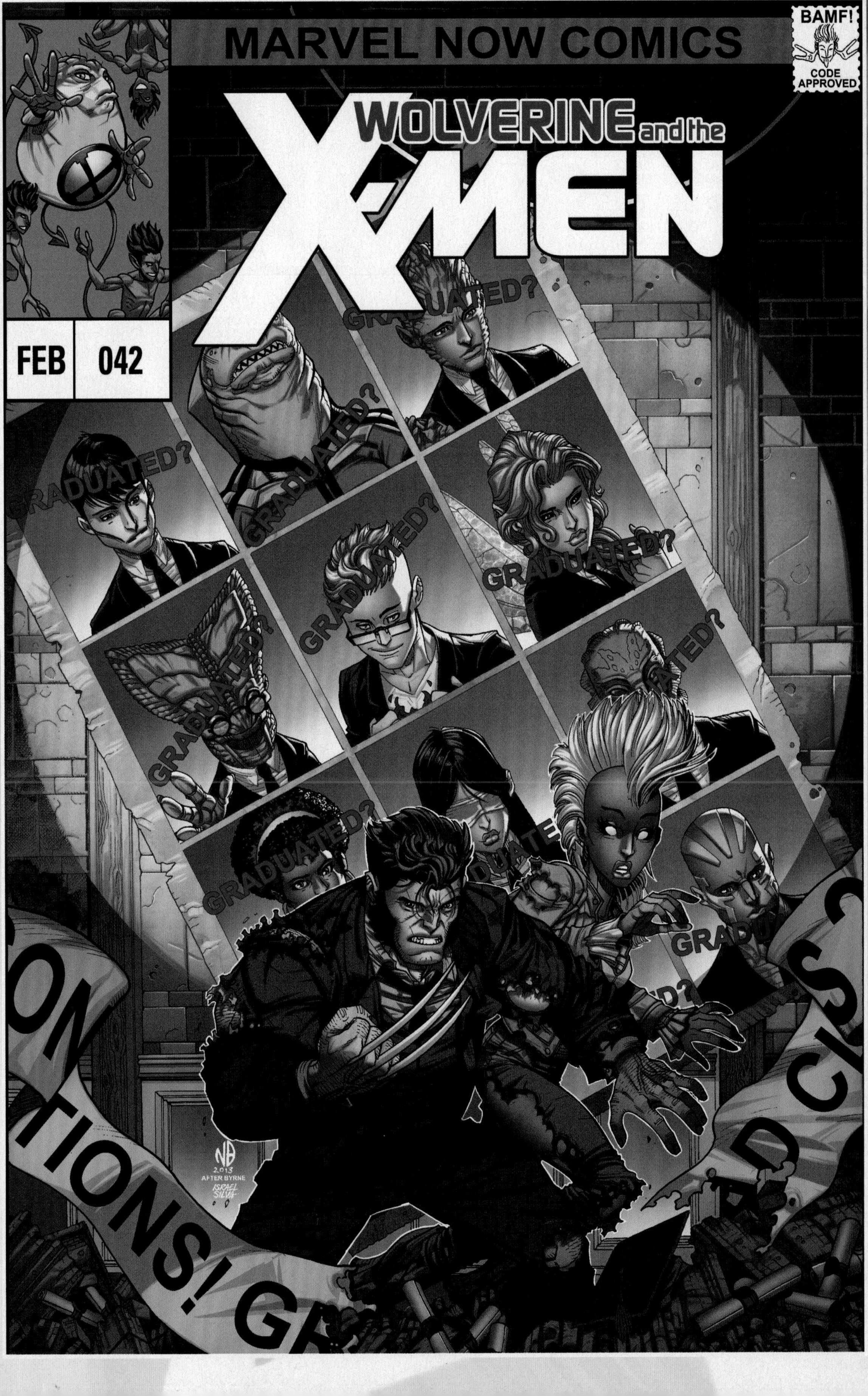
MARVEL NOW COMICS
BAMF!
CODE APPROVED
WOLVERINE and the
X-MEN
FEB
042
GRADUATED?
GRADUATED?
GRADUATED?
GRADUATED?
GRADUATED?
GRADUATED?
GRADUATED?
GRADUATED?
NB 2013 AFTER BYRNE
ISRAEL SILVA

1407 GRAYMALKIN LANE,
SALEM CENTER, WESTCHESTER COUNTY, NEW YORK. MANY DAYS AFTER.

I'M TIRED.

TIMES LIKE THIS, WHEN I GET A MOMENT TO CATCH MY BREATH, I SOMETIMES REALIZE...I CAN'T. GOD HELP ME...

I'M STARTING TO ACTUALLY FEEL MY AGE.

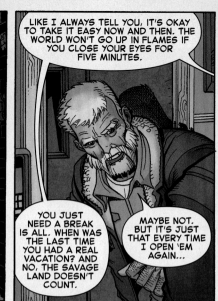

LIKE I ALWAYS TELL YOU, IT'S OKAY TO TAKE IT EASY NOW AND THEN. THE WORLD WON'T GO UP IN FLAMES IF YOU CLOSE YOUR EYES FOR FIVE MINUTES.

YOU JUST NEED A BREAK IS ALL. WHEN WAS THE LAST TIME YOU HAD A REAL VACATION? AND NO, THE SAVAGE LAND DOESN'T COUNT.

MAYBE NOT. BUT IT'S JUST THAT EVERY TIME I OPEN 'EM AGAIN...

...I CAN'T HELP BUT WONDER WHERE ALL THE YEARS HAVE GONE.

I MEAN, JUST LOOK AT YOU. SWEET LITTLE IDIE, ALL GROWN UP. WHEN THE HELL DID THAT HAPPEN?

OKAY, NOW YOU'RE JUST BEING MAUDLIN. WE BOTH KNOW I WAS NEVER THAT SWEET, EVEN WHEN I WAS LITTLE.

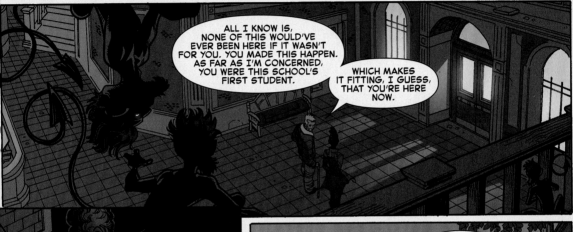

ALL I KNOW IS, NONE OF THIS WOULD'VE EVER BEEN HERE IF IT WASN'T FOR YOU. YOU MADE THIS HAPPEN. AS FAR AS I'M CONCERNED, YOU WERE THIS SCHOOL'S FIRST STUDENT.

WHICH MAKES IT FITTING, I GUESS, THAT YOU'RE HERE NOW.

TO SEE IT ALL END.

YOU'RE SERIOUS THIS TIME? YOU'RE REALLY GOING TO CLOSE IT DOWN?

LOOK AROUND YOU, IDIE. I DON'T HAVE TO CLOSE IT DOWN.

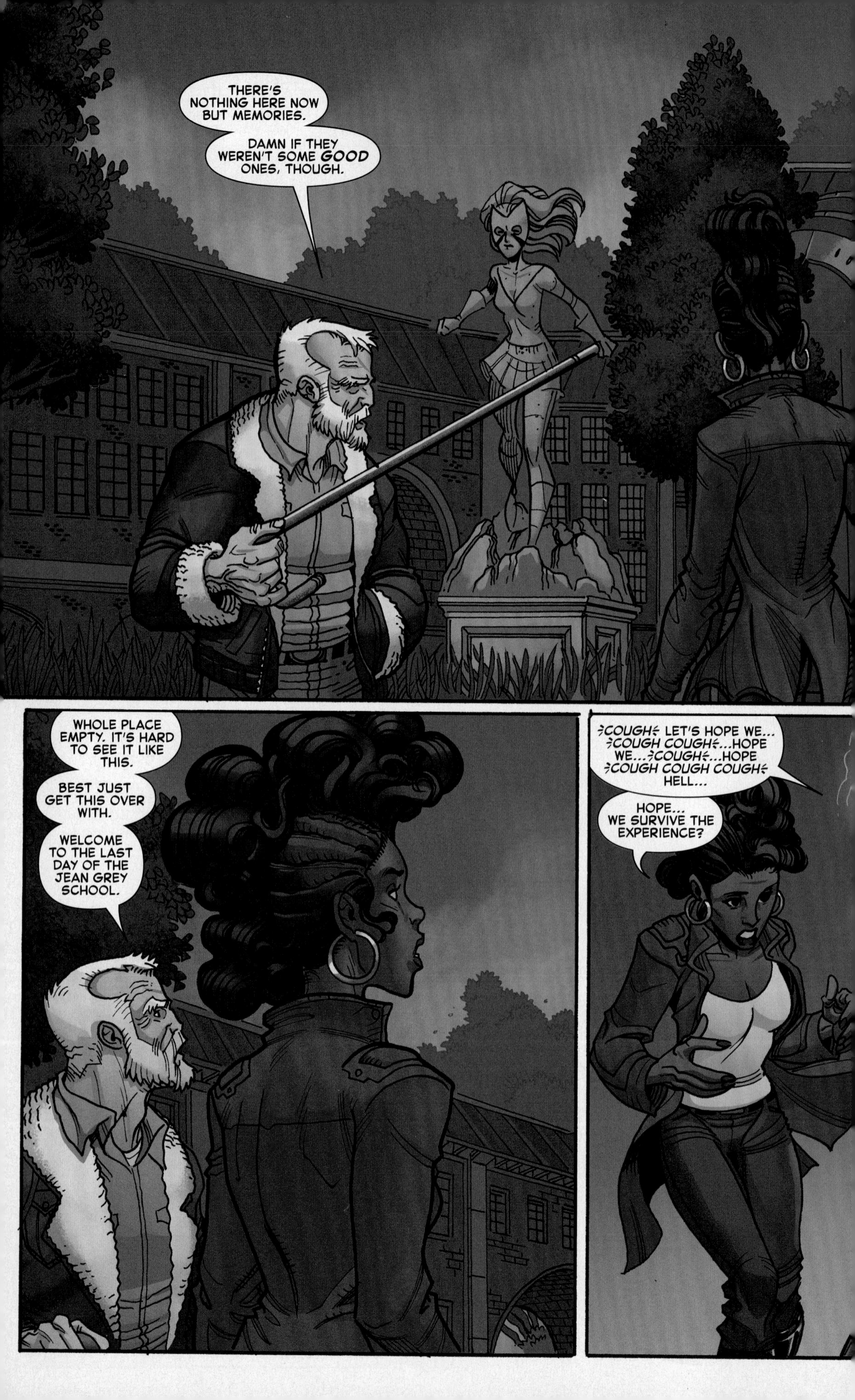
THERE'S NOTHING HERE NOW BUT MEMORIES.
DAMN IF THEY WEREN'T SOME GOOD ONES, THOUGH.
WHOLE PLACE EMPTY. IT'S HARD TO SEE IT LIKE THIS.
BEST JUST GET THIS OVER WITH.
WELCOME TO THE LAST DAY OF THE JEAN GREY SCHOOL.
COUGH LET'S HOPE WE... COUGH COUGH ...HOPE WE... COUGH ...HOPE COUGH COUGH COUGH HELL...
HOPE... WE SURVIVE THE EXPERIENCE?

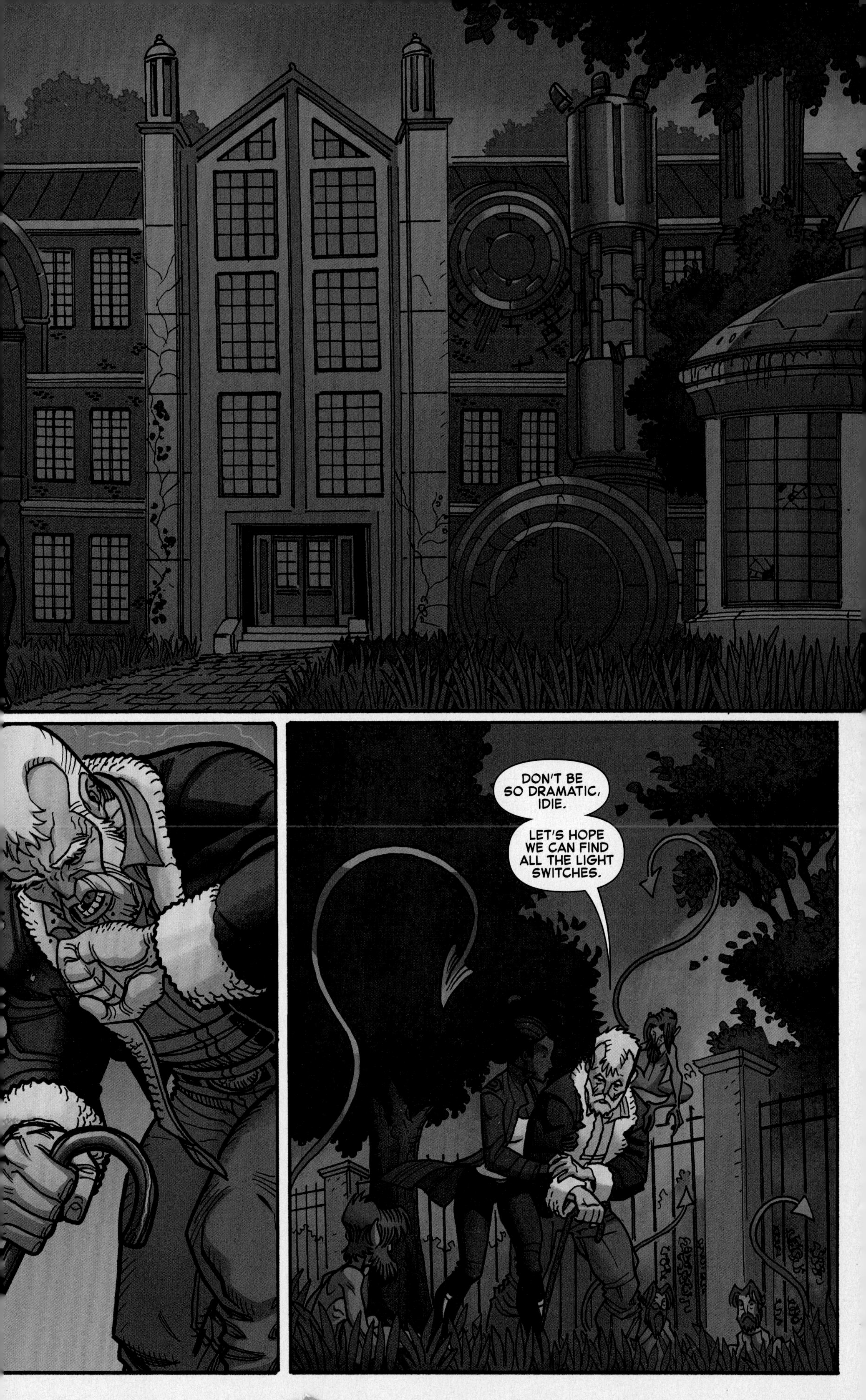
DON'T BE SO DRAMATIC, IDIE.
LET'S HOPE WE CAN FIND ALL THE LIGHT SWITCHES.

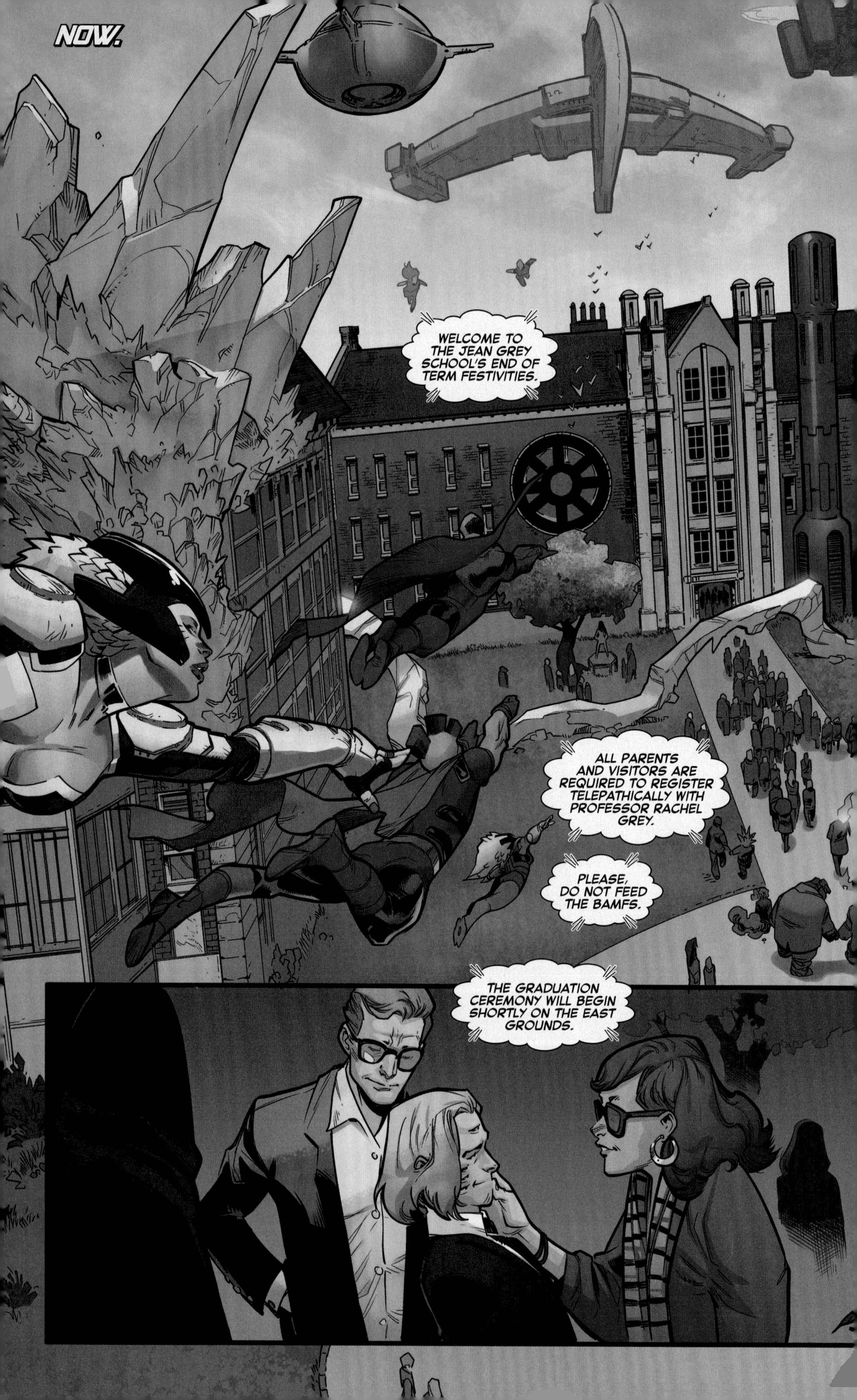
NOW.
WELCOME TO THE JEAN GREY SCHOOL'S END OF TERM FESTIVITIES.
ALL PARENTS AND VISITORS ARE REQUIRED TO REGISTER TELEPATHICALLY WITH PROFESSOR RACHEL GREY.
PLEASE, DO NOT FEED THE BAMFS.
THE GRADUATION CEREMONY WILL BEGIN SHORTLY ON THE EAST GROUNDS.

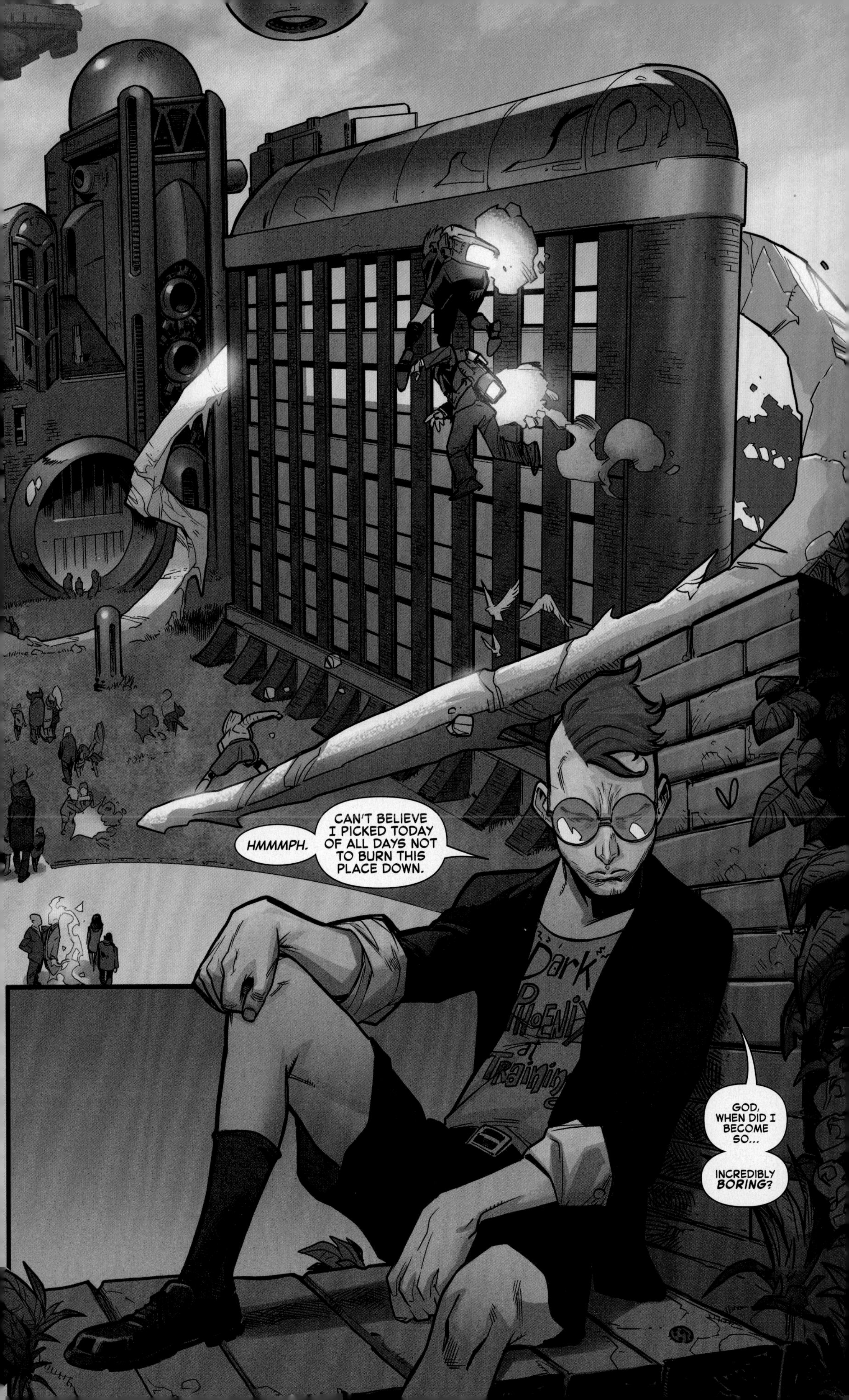
HMMMPH.
CAN'T BELIEVE I PICKED TODAY OF ALL DAYS NOT TO BURN THIS PLACE DOWN.
Dark Phoenix in Training
GOD, WHEN DID I BECOME SO...
INCREDIBLY *BORING*?

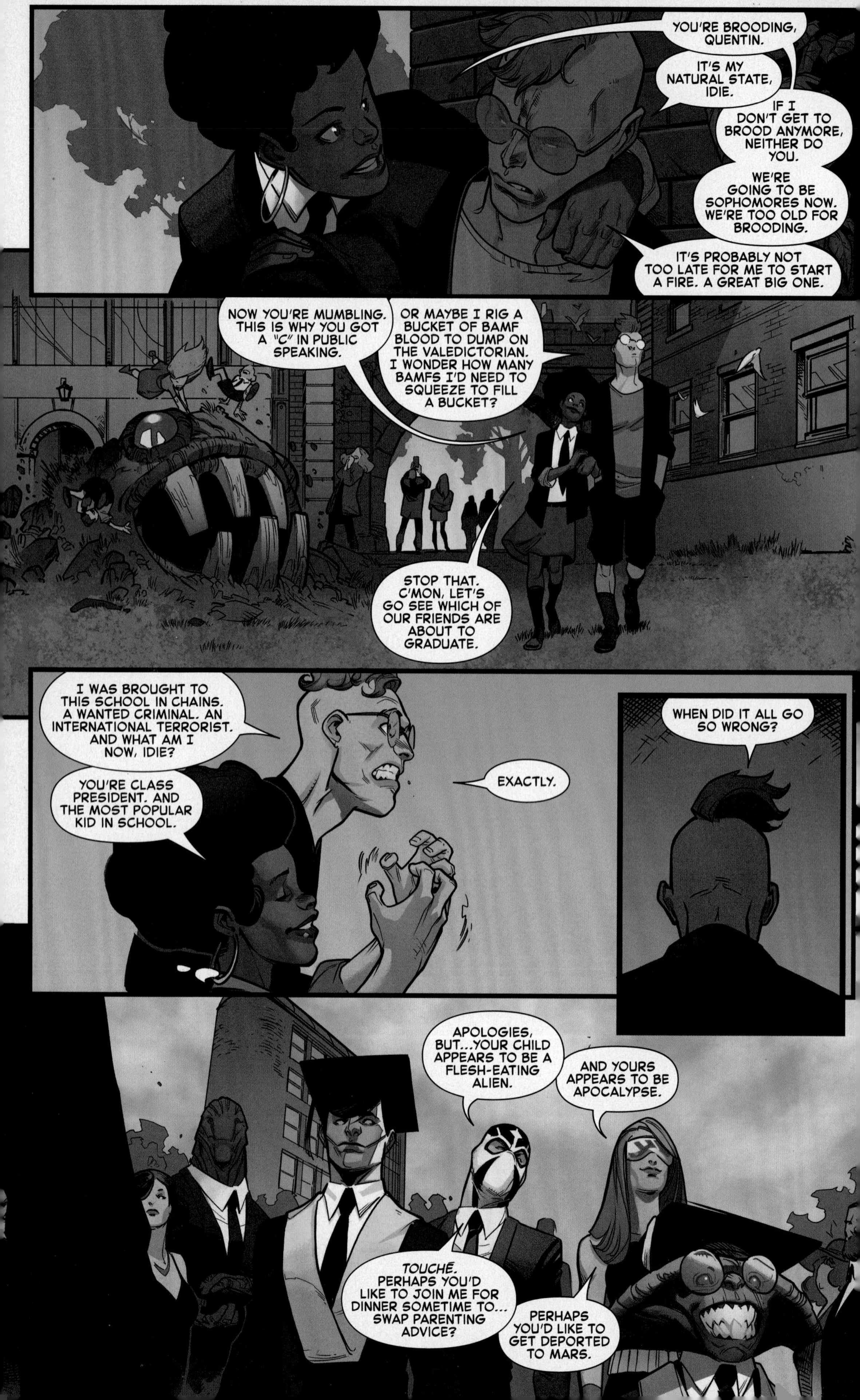
YOU'RE BROODING, QUENTIN.
IT'S MY NATURAL STATE, IDIE.
IF I DON'T GET TO BROOD ANYMORE, NEITHER DO YOU.
WE'RE GOING TO BE SOPHOMORES NOW. WE'RE TOO OLD FOR BROODING.
IT'S PROBABLY NOT TOO LATE FOR ME TO START A FIRE. A GREAT BIG ONE.
OR MAYBE I RIG A BUCKET OF BAMF BLOOD TO DUMP ON THE VALEDICTORIAN. I WONDER HOW MANY BAMFS I'D NEED TO SQUEEZE TO FILL A BUCKET?
NOW YOU'RE MUMBLING. THIS IS WHY YOU GOT A "C" IN PUBLIC SPEAKING.
STOP THAT. C'MON, LET'S GO SEE WHICH OF OUR FRIENDS ARE ABOUT TO GRADUATE.
I WAS BROUGHT TO THIS SCHOOL IN CHAINS. A WANTED CRIMINAL. AN INTERNATIONAL TERRORIST. AND WHAT AM I NOW, IDIE?
YOU'RE CLASS PRESIDENT. AND THE MOST POPULAR KID IN SCHOOL.
EXACTLY.
WHEN DID IT ALL GO SO WRONG?
APOLOGIES, BUT...YOUR CHILD APPEARS TO BE A FLESH-EATING ALIEN.
AND YOURS APPEARS TO BE APOCALYPSE.
TOUCHÉ. PERHAPS YOU'D LIKE TO JOIN ME FOR DINNER SOMETIME TO... SWAP PARENTING ADVICE?
PERHAPS YOU'D LIKE TO GET DEPORTED TO MARS.

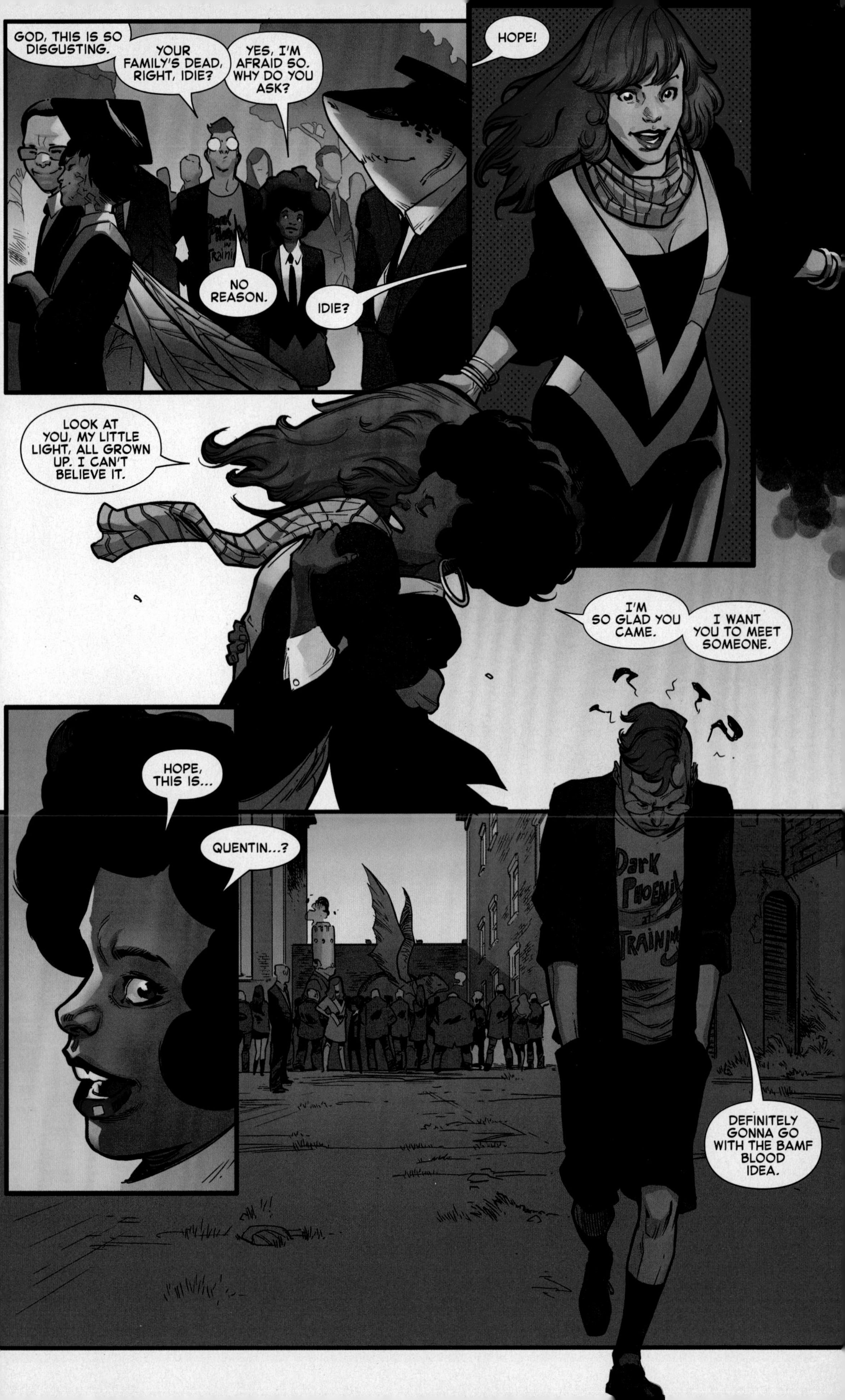
GOD, THIS IS SO DISGUSTING.
YOUR FAMILY'S DEAD, RIGHT, IDIE?
YES, I'M AFRAID SO. WHY DO YOU ASK?
NO REASON.
IDIE?
HOPE!
LOOK AT YOU, MY LITTLE LIGHT, ALL GROWN UP. I CAN'T BELIEVE IT.
I'M SO GLAD YOU CAME.
I WANT YOU TO MEET SOMEONE.
HOPE, THIS IS...
QUENTIN...?
DEFINITELY GONNA GO WITH THE BAMF BLOOD IDEA.

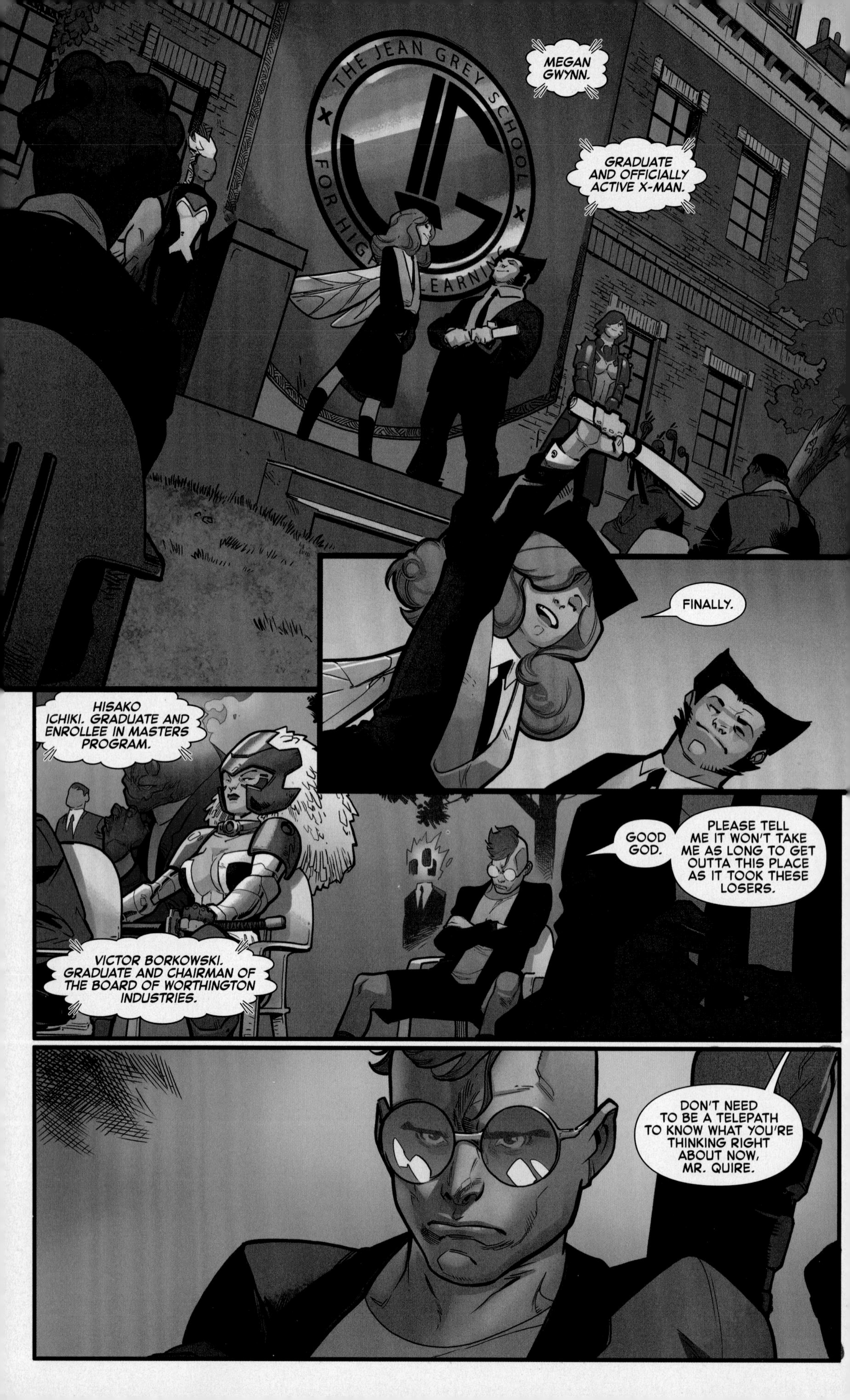

MEGAN GWYNN.
GRADUATE AND OFFICIALLY ACTIVE X-MAN.
FINALLY.
HISAKO ICHIKI. GRADUATE AND ENROLLEE IN MASTERS PROGRAM.
VICTOR BORKOWSKI. GRADUATE AND CHAIRMAN OF THE BOARD OF WORTHINGTON INDUSTRIES.
GOOD GOD.
PLEASE TELL ME IT WON'T TAKE ME AS LONG TO GET OUTTA THIS PLACE AS IT TOOK THESE LOSERS.
DON'T NEED TO BE A TELEPATH TO KNOW WHAT YOU'RE THINKING RIGHT ABOUT NOW, MR. QUIRE.

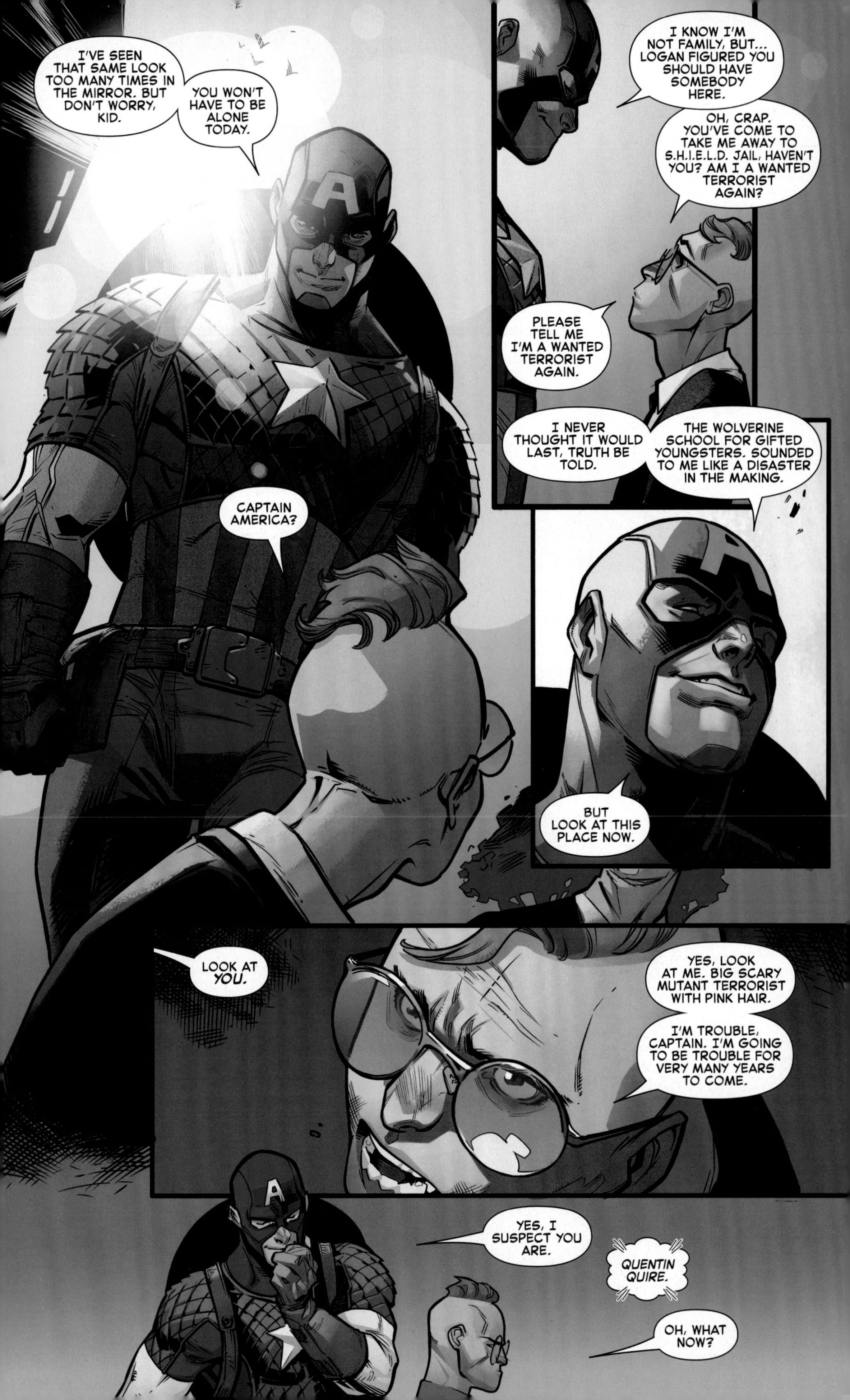
CAPTAIN AMERICA?
I'VE SEEN THAT SAME LOOK TOO MANY TIMES IN THE MIRROR. BUT DON'T WORRY, KID.
YOU WON'T HAVE TO BE ALONE TODAY.
I KNOW I'M NOT FAMILY, BUT... LOGAN FIGURED YOU SHOULD HAVE SOMEBODY HERE.
OH, CRAP. YOU'VE COME TO TAKE ME AWAY TO S.H.I.E.L.D. JAIL, HAVEN'T YOU? AM I A WANTED TERRORIST AGAIN?
PLEASE TELL ME I'M A WANTED TERRORIST AGAIN.
I NEVER THOUGHT IT WOULD LAST, TRUTH BE TOLD.
THE WOLVERINE SCHOOL FOR GIFTED YOUNGSTERS. SOUNDED TO ME LIKE A DISASTER IN THE MAKING.
BUT LOOK AT THIS PLACE NOW.
LOOK AT *YOU.*
YES, LOOK AT ME. BIG SCARY MUTANT TERRORIST WITH PINK HAIR.
I'M TROUBLE, CAPTAIN. I'M GOING TO BE TROUBLE FOR VERY MANY YEARS TO COME.
YES, I SUSPECT YOU ARE.
QUENTIN QUIRE.
OH, WHAT NOW?

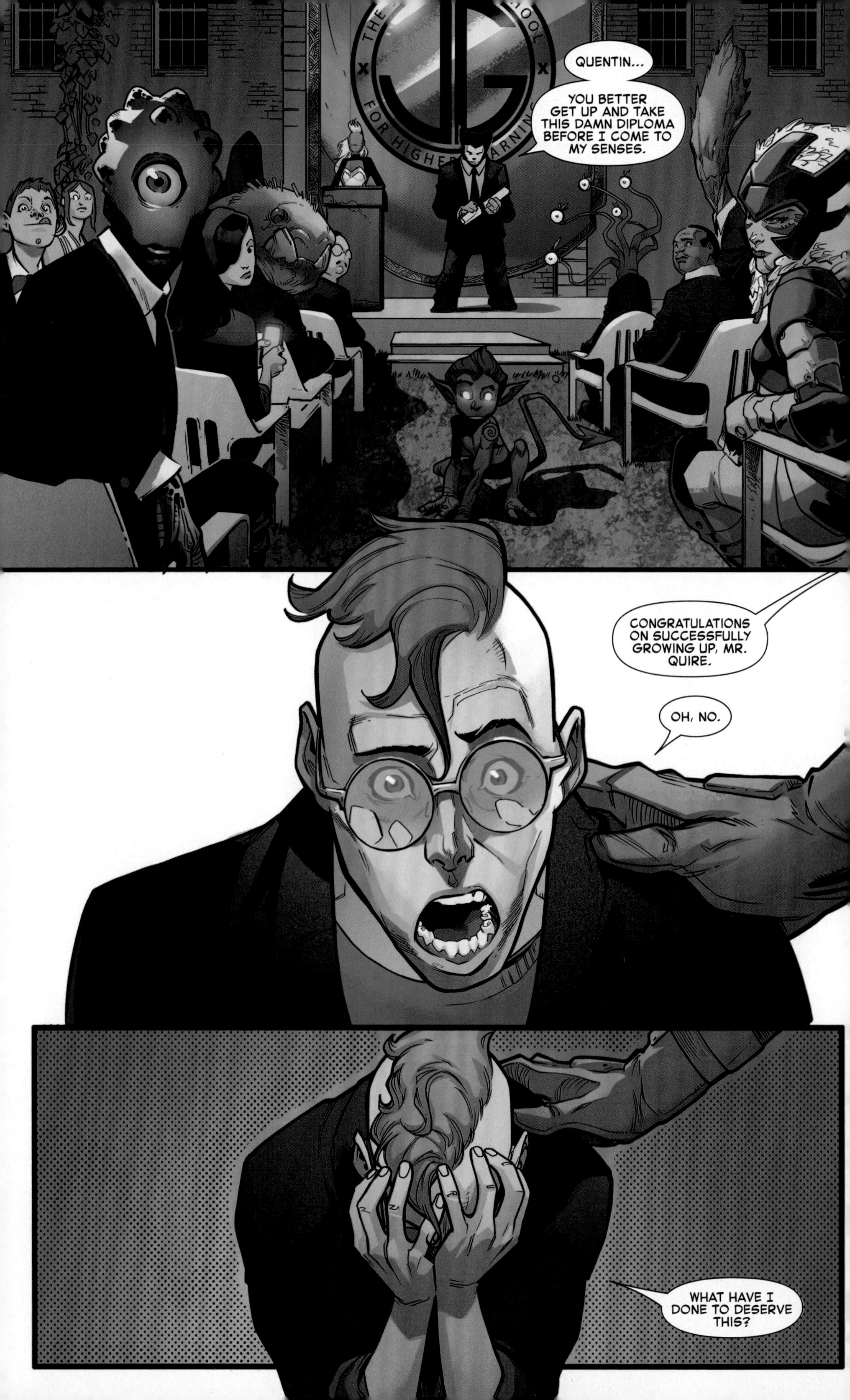
QUENTIN...
YOU BETTER GET UP AND TAKE THIS DAMN DIPLOMA BEFORE I COME TO MY SENSES.
CONGRATULATIONS ON SUCCESSFULLY GROWING UP, MR. QUIRE.
OH, NO.
WHAT HAVE I DONE TO DESERVE THIS?

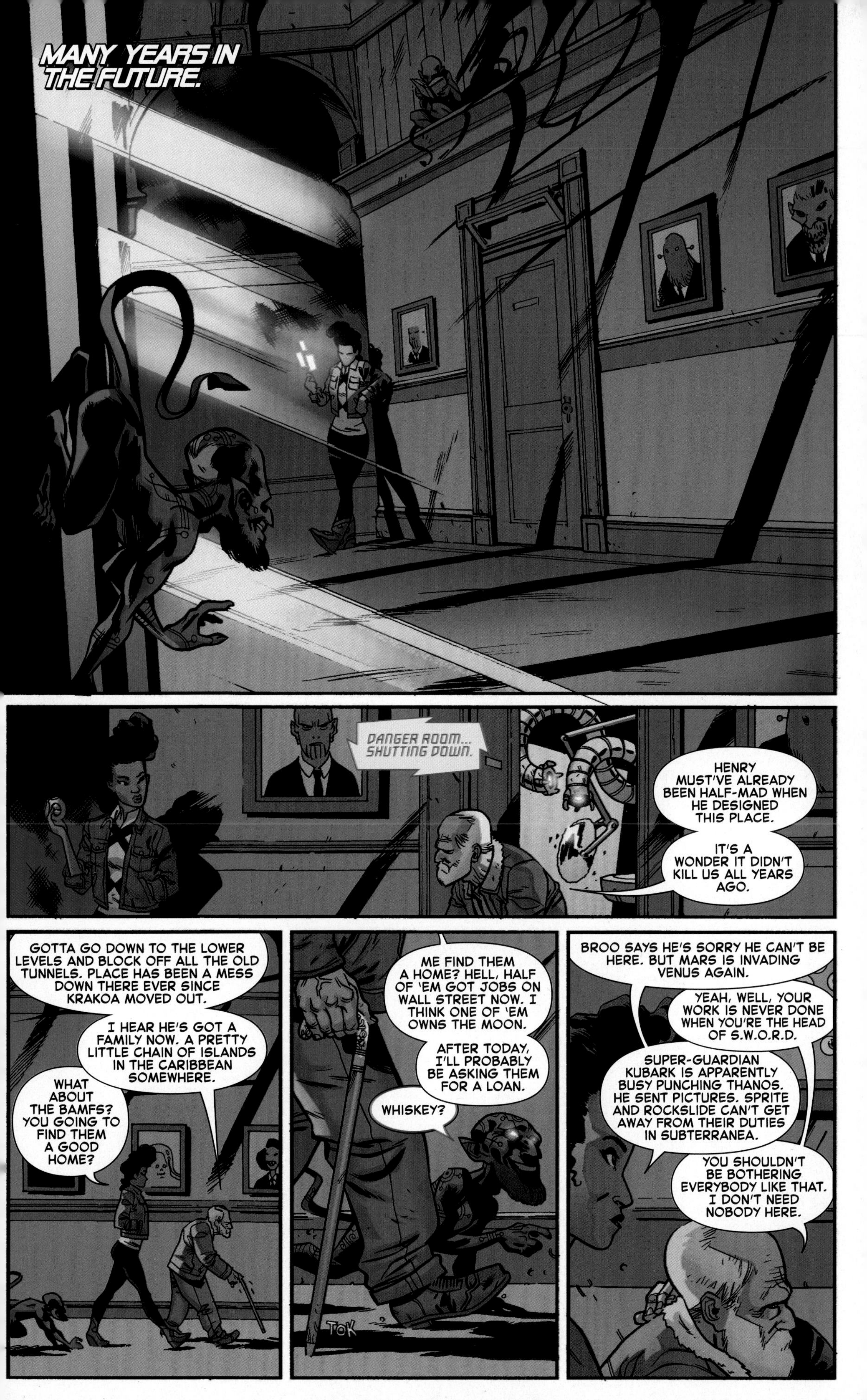
MANY YEARS IN THE FUTURE.
DANGER ROOM... SHUTTING DOWN.
HENRY MUST'VE ALREADY BEEN HALF-MAD WHEN HE DESIGNED THIS PLACE.
IT'S A WONDER IT DIDN'T KILL US ALL YEARS AGO.
GOTTA GO DOWN TO THE LOWER LEVELS AND BLOCK OFF ALL THE OLD TUNNELS. PLACE HAS BEEN A MESS DOWN THERE EVER SINCE KRAKOA MOVED OUT.
I HEAR HE'S GOT A FAMILY NOW. A PRETTY LITTLE CHAIN OF ISLANDS IN THE CARIBBEAN SOMEWHERE.
WHAT ABOUT THE BAMFS? YOU GOING TO FIND THEM A GOOD HOME?
ME FIND THEM A HOME? HELL, HALF OF 'EM GOT JOBS ON WALL STREET NOW. I THINK ONE OF 'EM OWNS THE MOON.
AFTER TODAY, I'LL PROBABLY BE ASKING THEM FOR A LOAN.
WHISKEY?
TOK
BROO SAYS HE'S SORRY HE CAN'T BE HERE. BUT MARS IS INVADING VENUS AGAIN.
YEAH, WELL, YOUR WORK IS NEVER DONE WHEN YOU'RE THE HEAD OF S.W.O.R.D.
SUPER-GUARDIAN KUBARK IS APPARENTLY BUSY PUNCHING THANOS. HE SENT PICTURES. SPRITE AND ROCKSLIDE CAN'T GET AWAY FROM THEIR DUTIES IN SUBTERRANEA.
YOU SHOULDN'T BE BOTHERING EVERYBODY LIKE THAT. I DON'T NEED NOBODY HERE.

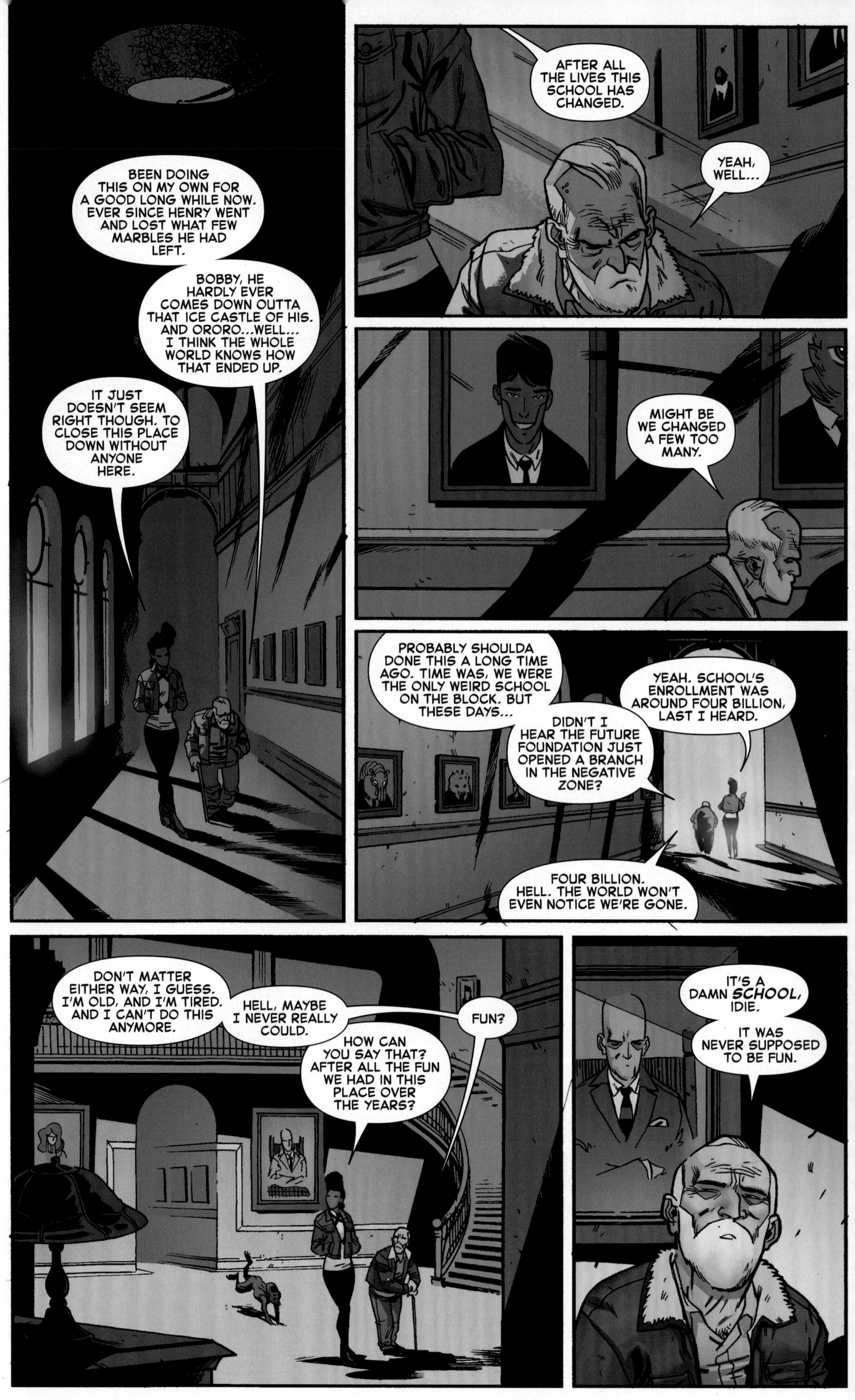
BEEN DOING THIS ON MY OWN FOR A GOOD LONG WHILE NOW. EVER SINCE HENRY WENT AND LOST WHAT FEW MARBLES HE HAD LEFT.
BOBBY, HE HARDLY EVER COMES DOWN OUTTA THAT ICE CASTLE OF HIS. AND ORORO...WELL... I THINK THE WHOLE WORLD KNOWS HOW THAT ENDED UP.
IT JUST DOESN'T SEEM RIGHT THOUGH. TO CLOSE THIS PLACE DOWN WITHOUT ANYONE HERE.
AFTER ALL THE LIVES THIS SCHOOL HAS CHANGED.
YEAH, WELL...
MIGHT BE WE CHANGED A FEW TOO MANY.
PROBABLY SHOULDA DONE THIS A LONG TIME AGO. TIME WAS, WE WERE THE ONLY WEIRD SCHOOL ON THE BLOCK. BUT THESE DAYS...
DIDN'T I HEAR THE FUTURE FOUNDATION JUST OPENED A BRANCH IN THE NEGATIVE ZONE?
YEAH. SCHOOL'S ENROLLMENT WAS AROUND FOUR BILLION, LAST I HEARD.
FOUR BILLION. HELL. THE WORLD WON'T EVEN NOTICE WE'RE GONE.
DON'T MATTER EITHER WAY, I GUESS. I'M OLD, AND I'M TIRED. AND I CAN'T DO THIS ANYMORE.
HELL, MAYBE I NEVER REALLY COULD.
HOW CAN YOU SAY THAT? AFTER ALL THE FUN WE HAD IN THIS PLACE OVER THE YEARS?
FUN?
IT'S A DAMN *SCHOOL*, IDIE.
IT WAS NEVER SUPPOSED TO BE FUN.

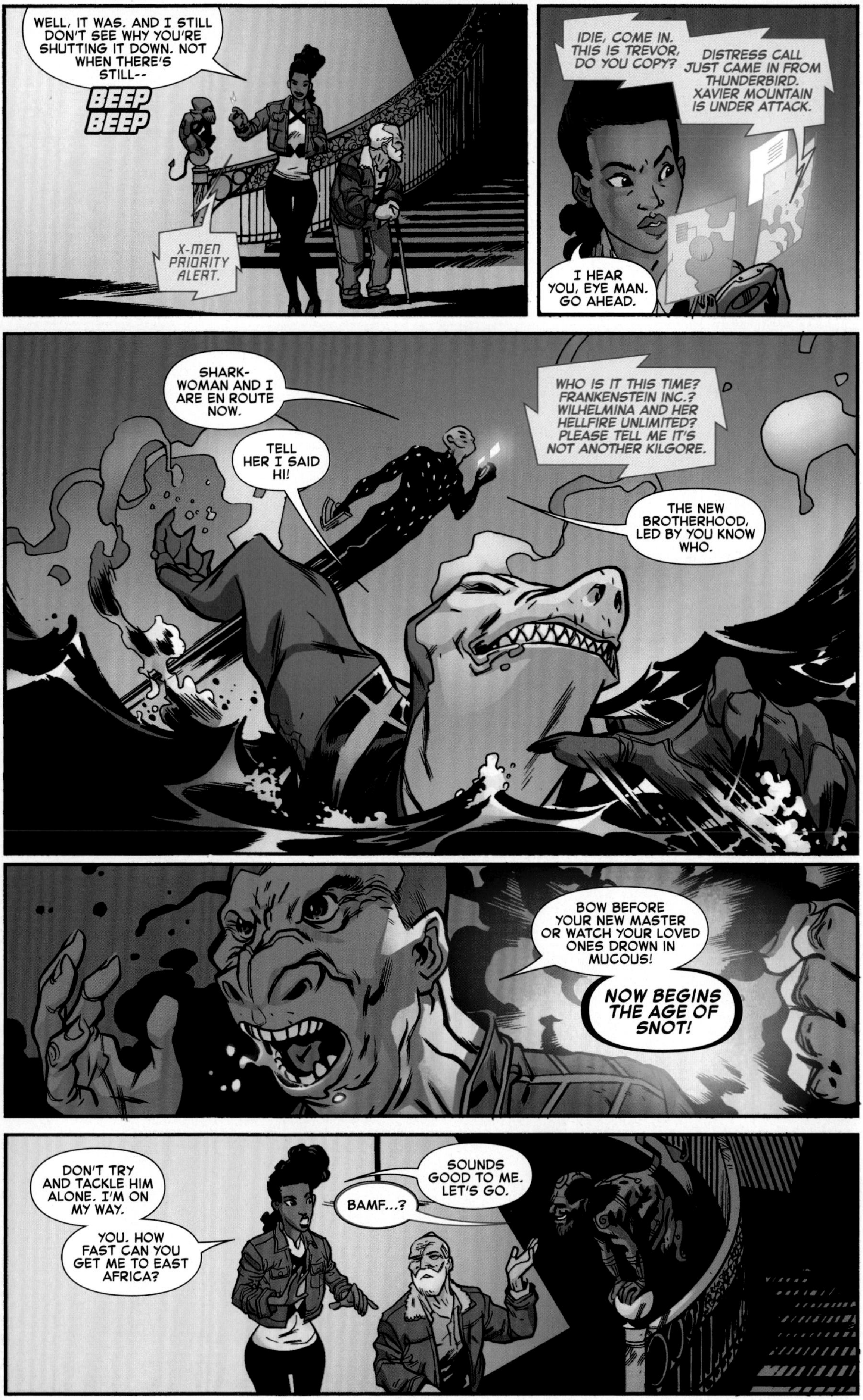
WELL, IT WAS. AND I STILL DON'T SEE WHY YOU'RE SHUTTING IT DOWN. NOT WHEN THERE'S STILL--
BEEP BEEP
X-MEN PRIORITY ALERT.
IDIE, COME IN. THIS IS TREVOR, DO YOU COPY?
DISTRESS CALL JUST CAME IN FROM THUNDERBIRD. XAVIER MOUNTAIN IS UNDER ATTACK.
I HEAR YOU, EYE MAN. GO AHEAD.
SHARK-WOMAN AND I ARE EN ROUTE NOW.
TELL HER I SAID HI!
WHO IS IT THIS TIME? FRANKENSTEIN INC.? WILHELMINA AND HER HELLFIRE UNLIMITED? PLEASE TELL ME IT'S NOT ANOTHER KILGORE.
THE NEW BROTHERHOOD, LED BY YOU KNOW WHO.
BOW BEFORE YOUR NEW MASTER OR WATCH YOUR LOVED ONES DROWN IN MUCOUS!
NOW BEGINS THE AGE OF SNOT!
DON'T TRY AND TACKLE HIM ALONE. I'M ON MY WAY.
YOU. HOW FAST CAN YOU GET ME TO EAST AFRICA?
BAMF...?
SOUNDS GOOD TO ME. LET'S GO.

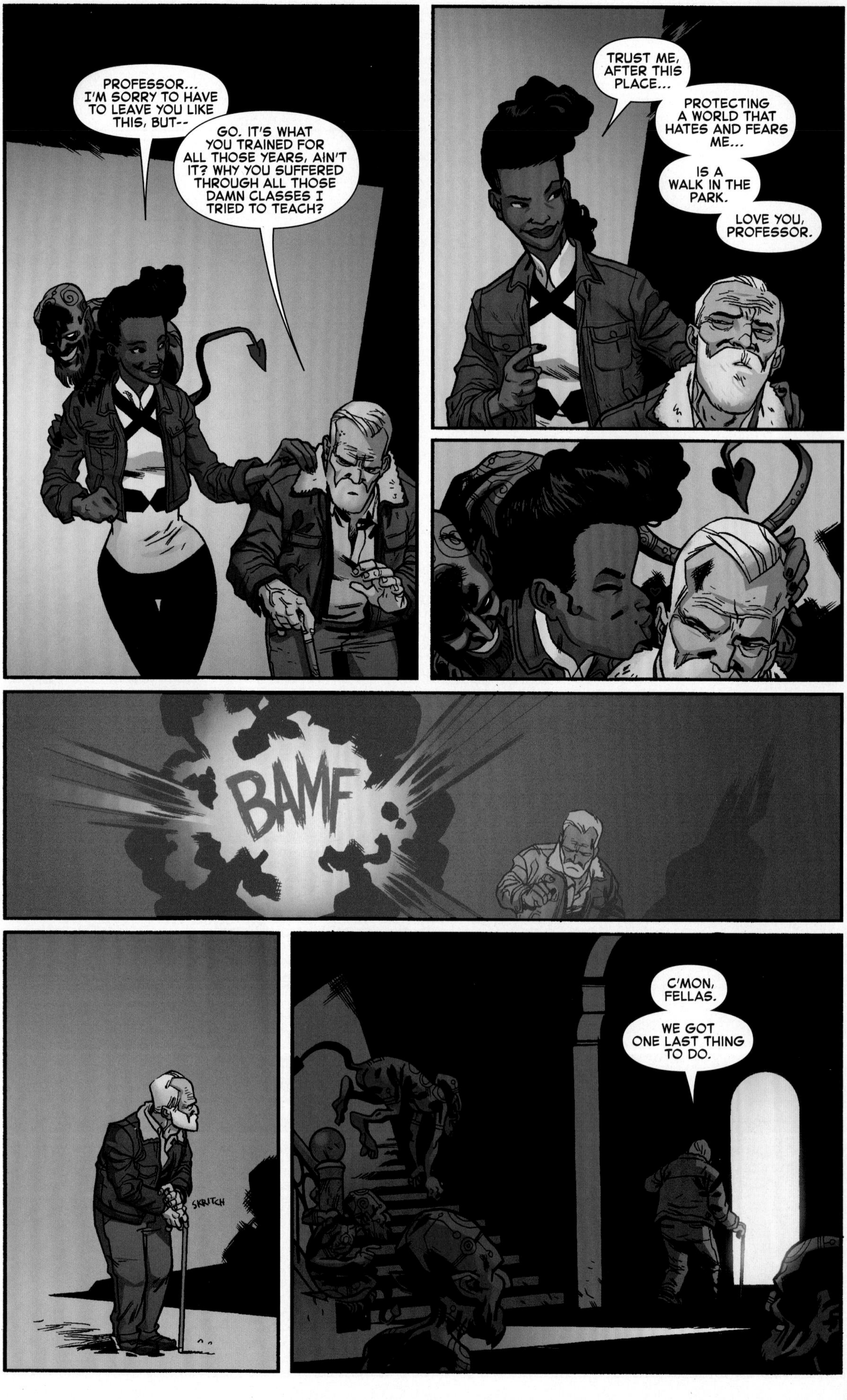
PROFESSOR... I'M SORRY TO HAVE TO LEAVE YOU LIKE THIS, BUT--
GO. IT'S WHAT YOU TRAINED FOR ALL THOSE YEARS, AIN'T IT? WHY YOU SUFFERED THROUGH ALL THOSE DAMN CLASSES I TRIED TO TEACH?
TRUST ME, AFTER THIS PLACE...
PROTECTING A WORLD THAT HATES AND FEARS ME...
IS A WALK IN THE PARK.
LOVE YOU, PROFESSOR.
BAMF
SKRITCH
C'MON, FELLAS.
WE GOT ONE LAST THING TO DO.

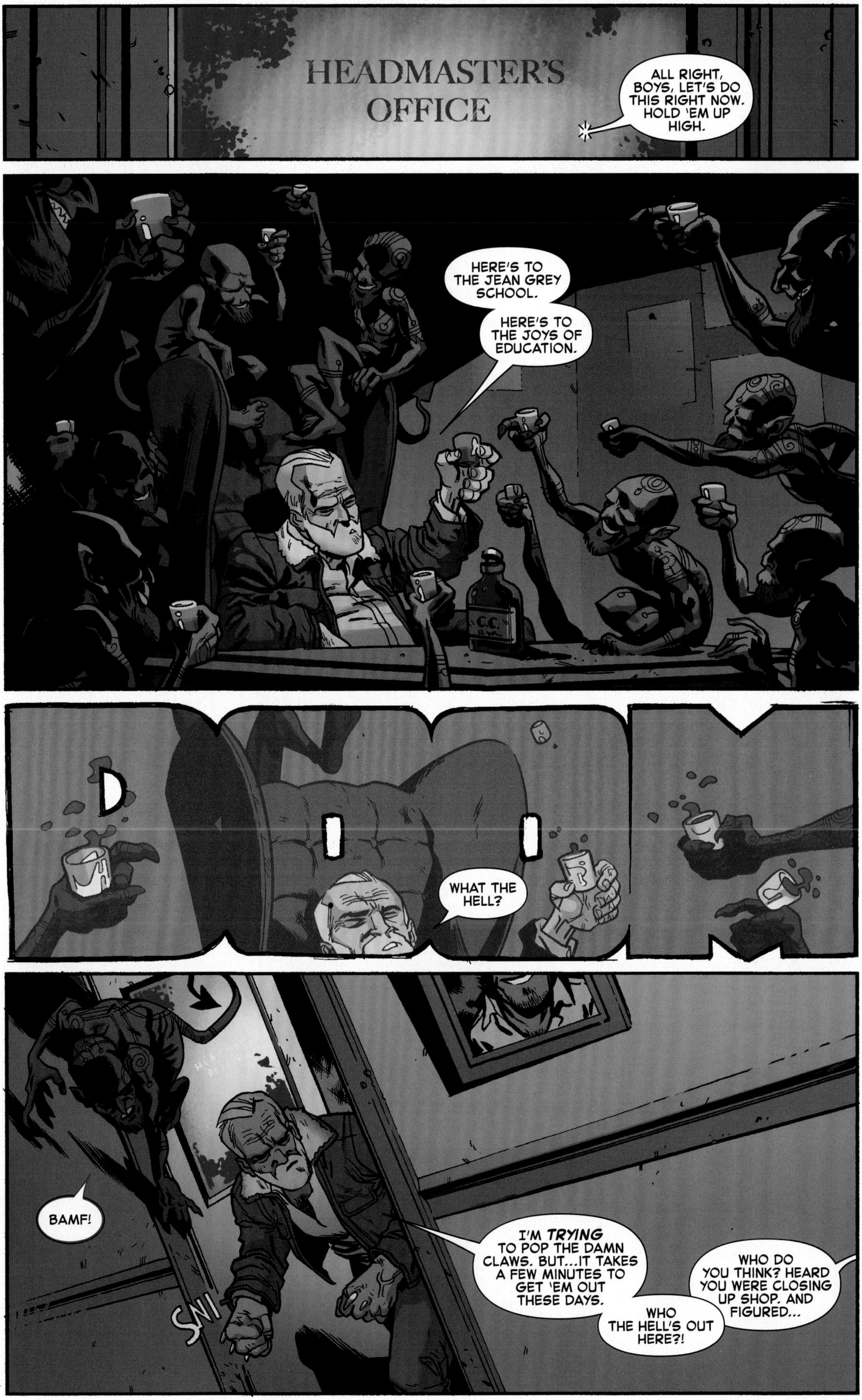
HEADMASTER'S OFFICE
ALL RIGHT, BOYS, LET'S DO THIS RIGHT NOW. HOLD 'EM UP HIGH.
HERE'S TO THE JEAN GREY SCHOOL.
HERE'S TO THE JOYS OF EDUCATION.
DOOM
WHAT THE HELL?
BAMF!
SNI
I'M *TRYING* TO POP THE DAMN CLAWS. BUT...IT TAKES A FEW MINUTES TO GET 'EM OUT THESE DAYS.
WHO THE HELL'S OUT HERE?!
WHO DO YOU THINK? HEARD YOU WERE CLOSING UP SHOP. AND FIGURED...

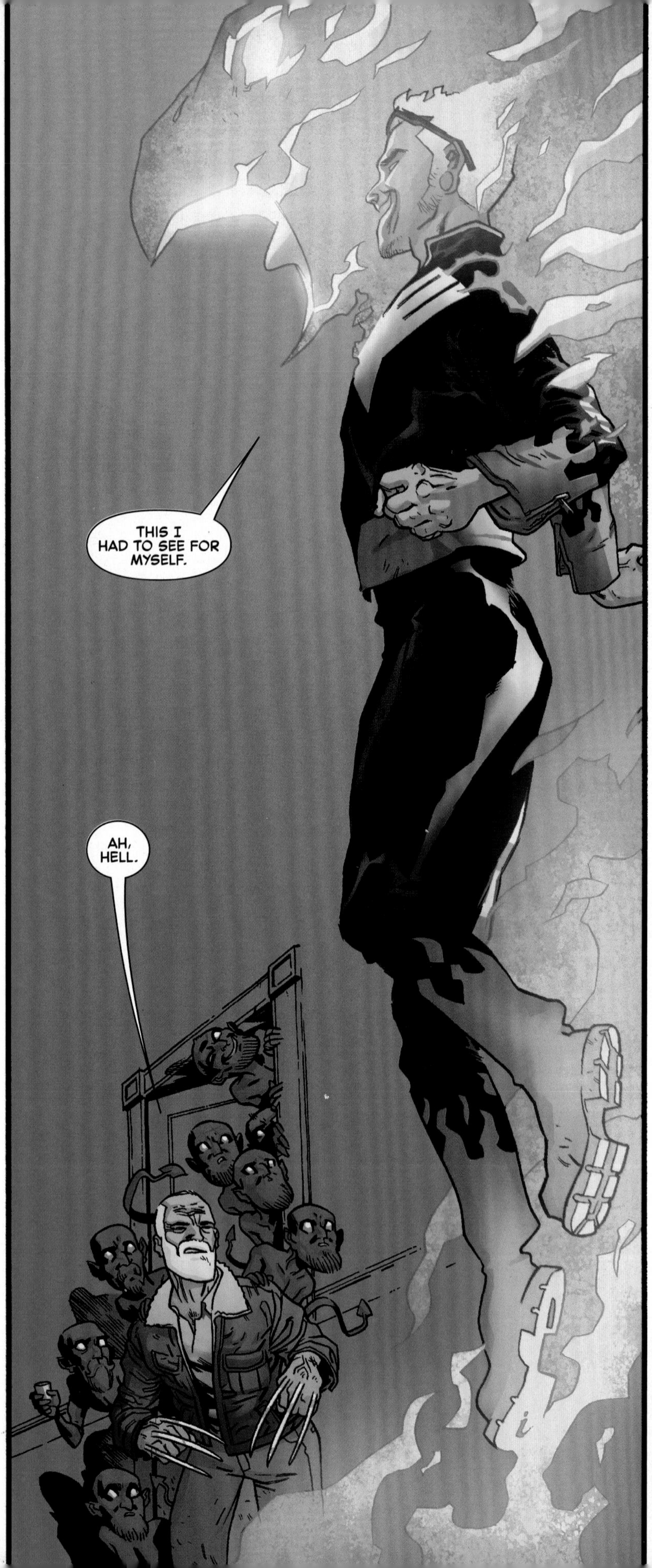
THIS I HAD TO SEE FOR MYSELF.
AH, HELL.
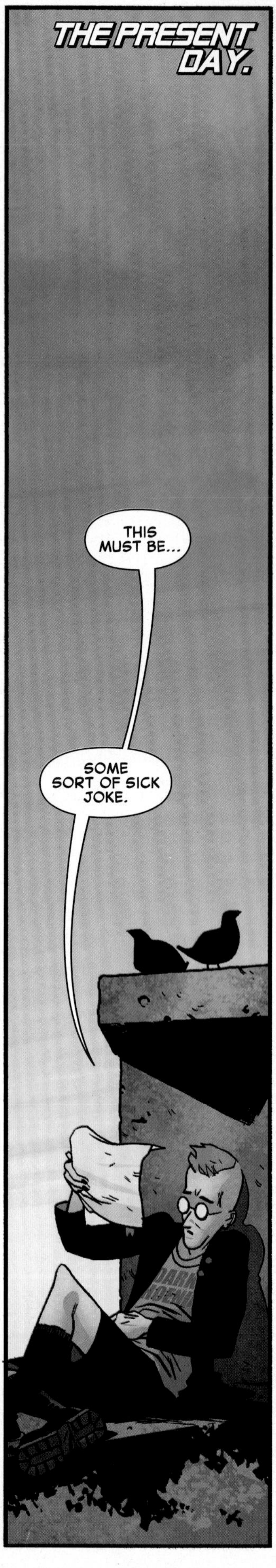
THE PRESENT DAY.
THIS MUST BE...
SOME SORT OF SICK JOKE.

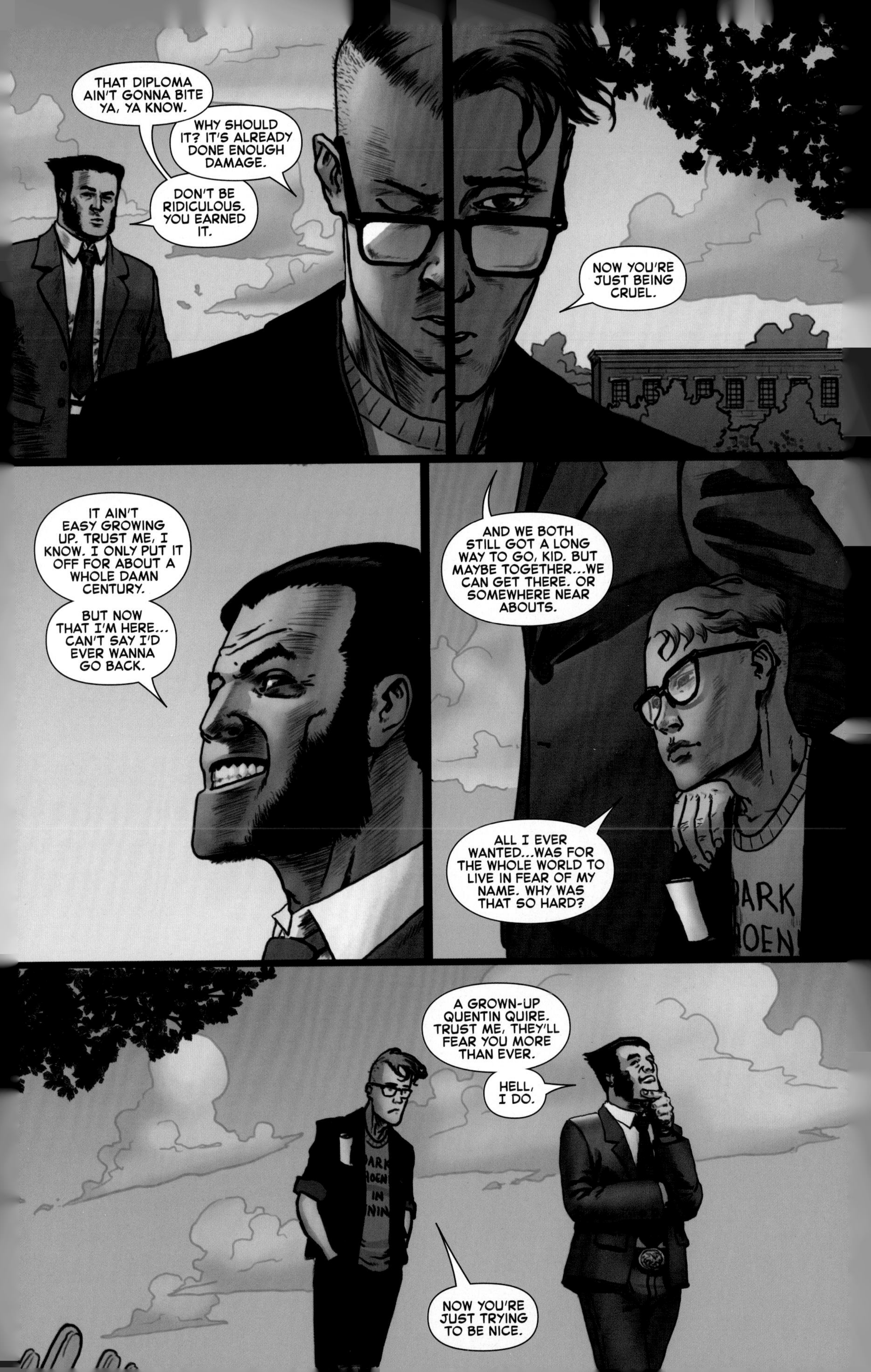
THAT DIPLOMA AIN'T GONNA BITE YA, YA KNOW.
WHY SHOULD IT? IT'S ALREADY DONE ENOUGH DAMAGE.
DON'T BE RIDICULOUS. YOU EARNED IT.
NOW YOU'RE JUST BEING CRUEL.
IT AIN'T EASY GROWING UP. TRUST ME, I KNOW. I ONLY PUT IT OFF FOR ABOUT A WHOLE DAMN CENTURY.
BUT NOW THAT I'M HERE... CAN'T SAY I'D EVER WANNA GO BACK.
AND WE BOTH STILL GOT A LONG WAY TO GO, KID. BUT MAYBE TOGETHER...WE CAN GET THERE. OR SOMEWHERE NEAR ABOUTS.
ALL I EVER WANTED...WAS FOR THE WHOLE WORLD TO LIVE IN FEAR OF MY NAME. WHY WAS THAT SO HARD?
A GROWN-UP QUENTIN QUIRE. TRUST ME, THEY'LL FEAR YOU MORE THAN EVER.
HELL, I DO.
NOW YOU'RE JUST TRYING TO BE NICE.

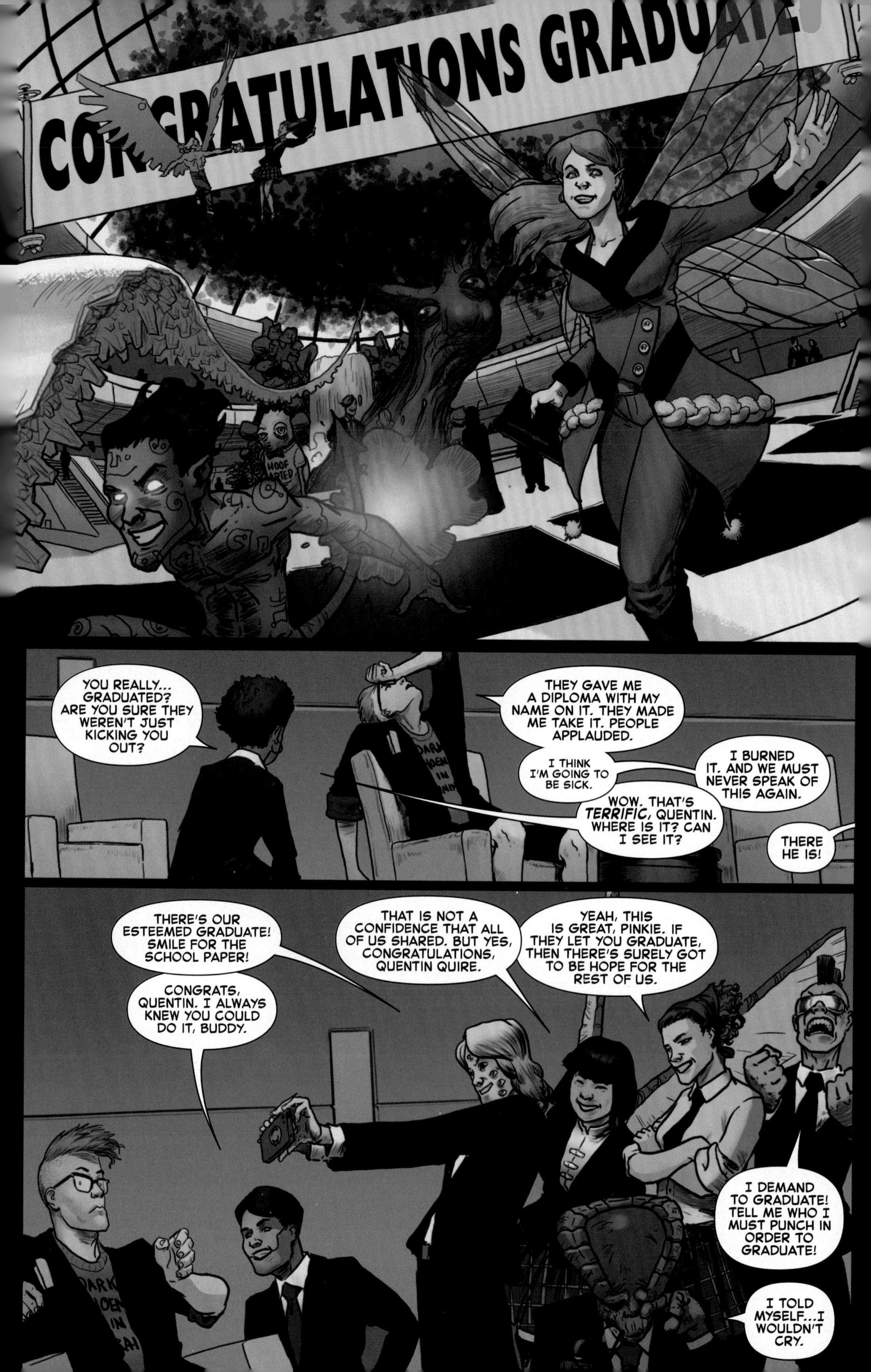
CONGRATULATIONS GRADUATE
HOOF ARTED
YOU REALLY... GRADUATED? ARE YOU SURE THEY WEREN'T JUST KICKING YOU OUT?
THEY GAVE ME A DIPLOMA WITH MY NAME ON IT. THEY MADE ME TAKE IT. PEOPLE APPLAUDED.
I THINK I'M GOING TO BE SICK.
WOW. THAT'S TERRIFIC, QUENTIN. WHERE IS IT? CAN I SEE IT?
I BURNED IT. AND WE MUST NEVER SPEAK OF THIS AGAIN.
THERE HE IS!
THERE'S OUR ESTEEMED GRADUATE! SMILE FOR THE SCHOOL PAPER!
CONGRATS, QUENTIN. I ALWAYS KNEW YOU COULD DO IT, BUDDY.
THAT IS NOT A CONFIDENCE THAT ALL OF US SHARED. BUT YES, CONGRATULATIONS, QUENTIN QUIRE.
YEAH, THIS IS GREAT, PINKIE. IF THEY LET YOU GRADUATE, THEN THERE'S SURELY GOT TO BE HOPE FOR THE REST OF US.
I DEMAND TO GRADUATE! TELL ME WHO I MUST PUNCH IN ORDER TO GRADUATE!
I TOLD MYSELF...I WOULDN'T CRY.

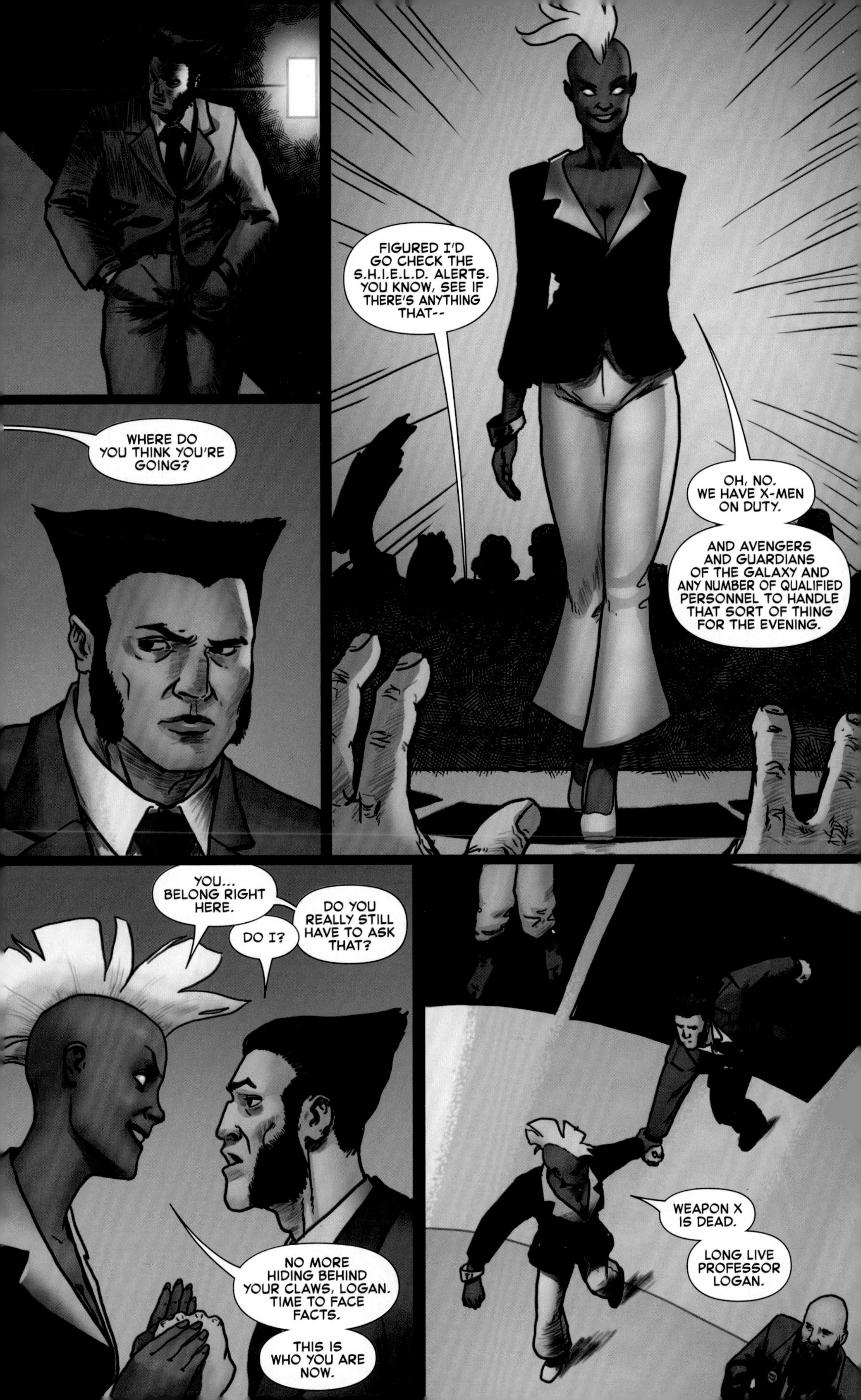
FIGURED I'D GO CHECK THE S.H.I.E.L.D. ALERTS. YOU KNOW, SEE IF THERE'S ANYTHING THAT--
WHERE DO YOU THINK YOU'RE GOING?
OH, NO. WE HAVE X-MEN ON DUTY.
AND AVENGERS AND GUARDIANS OF THE GALAXY AND ANY NUMBER OF QUALIFIED PERSONNEL TO HANDLE THAT SORT OF THING FOR THE EVENING.
YOU... BELONG RIGHT HERE.
DO I?
DO YOU REALLY STILL HAVE TO ASK THAT?
NO MORE HIDING BEHIND YOUR CLAWS, LOGAN. TIME TO FACE FACTS.
THIS IS WHO YOU ARE NOW.
WEAPON X IS DEAD.
LONG LIVE PROFESSOR LOGAN.

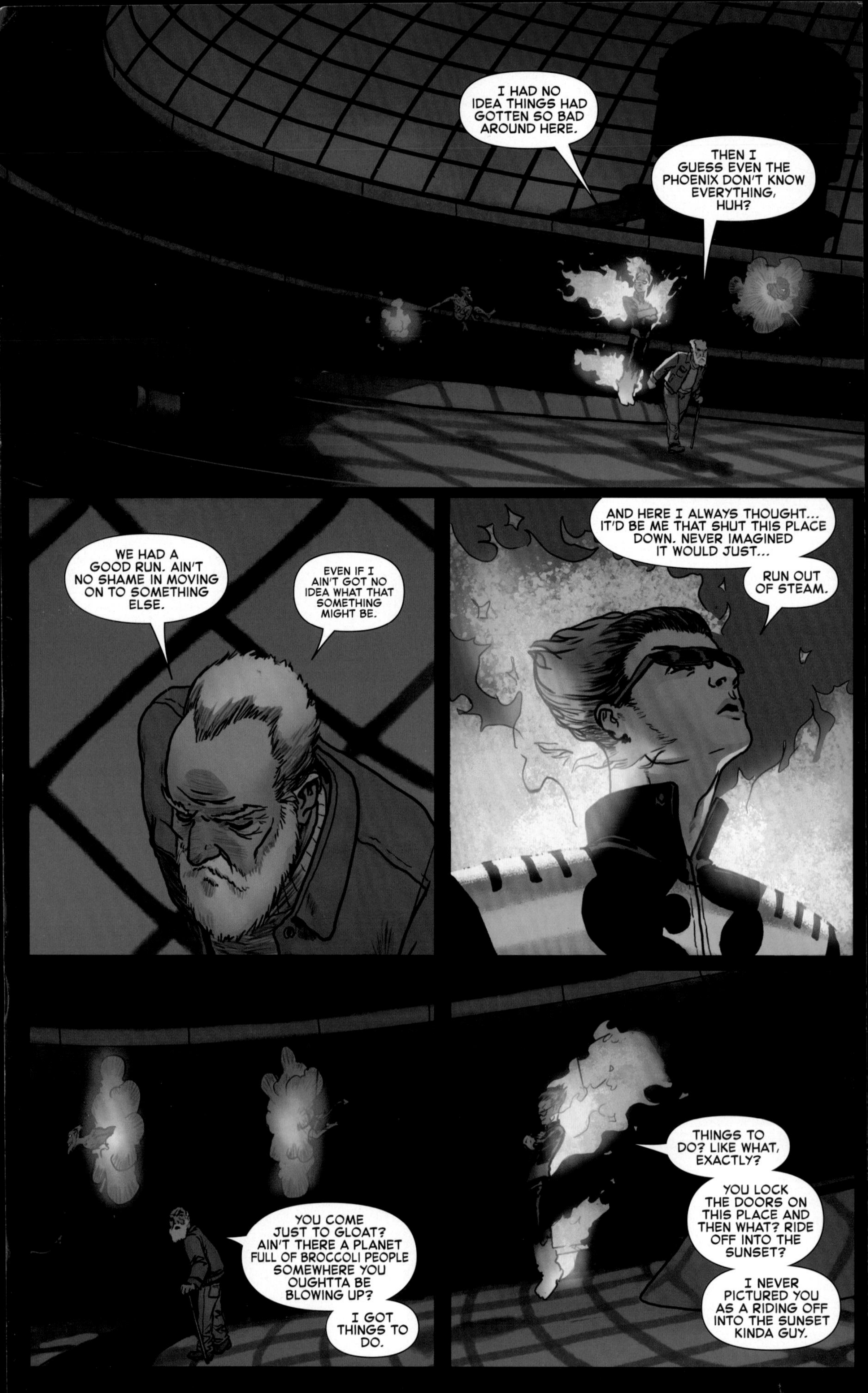
I HAD NO IDEA THINGS HAD GOTTEN SO BAD AROUND HERE.
THEN I GUESS EVEN THE PHOENIX DON'T KNOW EVERYTHING, HUH?
WE HAD A GOOD RUN. AIN'T NO SHAME IN MOVING ON TO SOMETHING ELSE.
EVEN IF I AIN'T GOT NO IDEA WHAT THAT SOMETHING MIGHT BE.
AND HERE I ALWAYS THOUGHT... IT'D BE ME THAT SHUT THIS PLACE DOWN. NEVER IMAGINED IT WOULD JUST...
RUN OUT OF STEAM.
YOU COME JUST TO GLOAT? AIN'T THERE A PLANET FULL OF BROCCOLI PEOPLE SOMEWHERE YOU OUGHTTA BE BLOWING UP?
I GOT THINGS TO DO.
THINGS TO DO? LIKE WHAT, EXACTLY?
YOU LOCK THE DOORS ON THIS PLACE AND THEN WHAT? RIDE OFF INTO THE SUNSET?
I NEVER PICTURED YOU AS A RIDING OFF INTO THE SUNSET KINDA GUY.

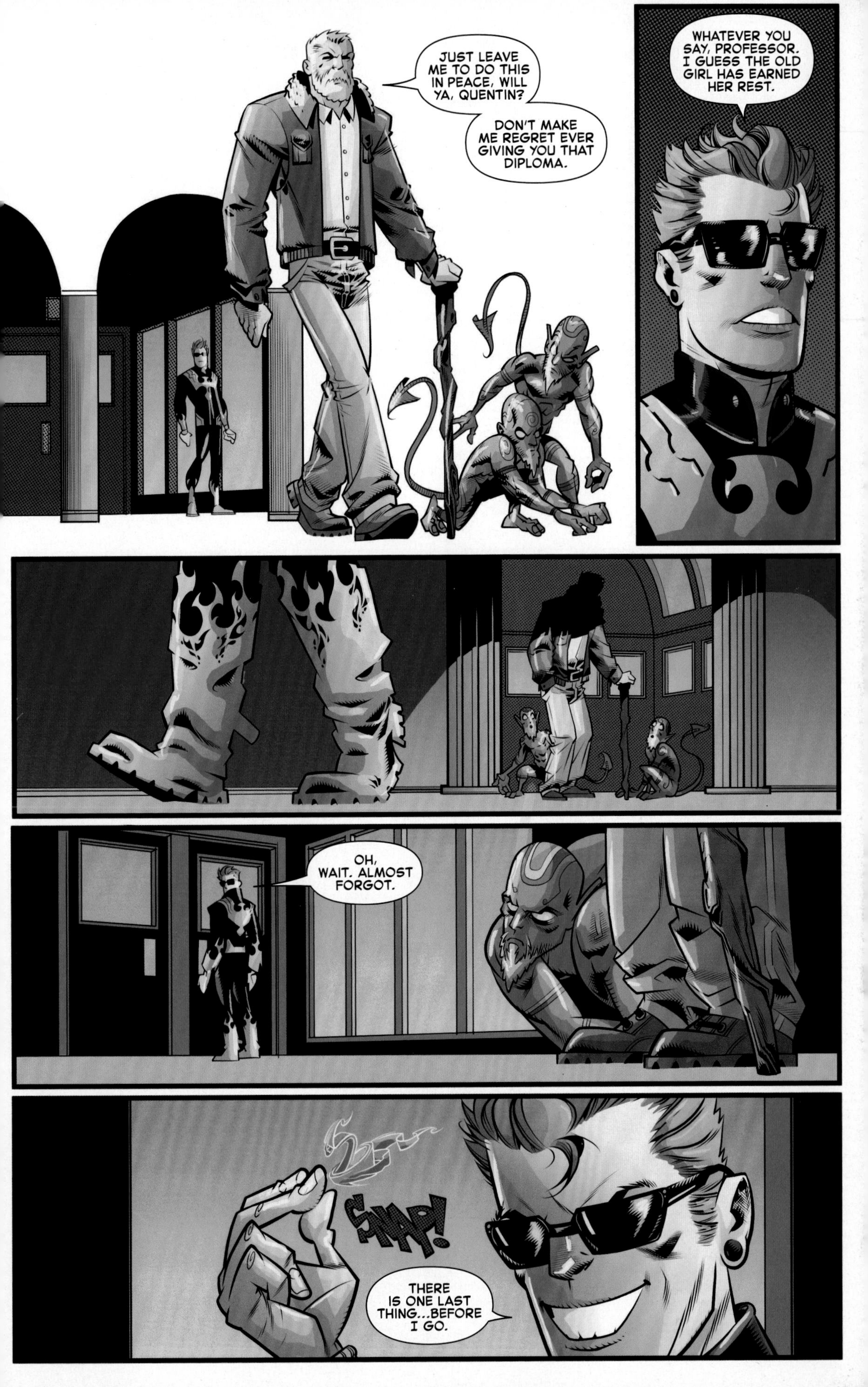
JUST LEAVE ME TO DO THIS IN PEACE, WILL YA, QUENTIN?
DON'T MAKE ME REGRET EVER GIVING YOU THAT DIPLOMA.
WHATEVER YOU SAY, PROFESSOR. I GUESS THE OLD GIRL HAS EARNED HER REST.
OH, WAIT. ALMOST FORGOT.
SNAP!
THERE IS ONE LAST THING...BEFORE I GO.

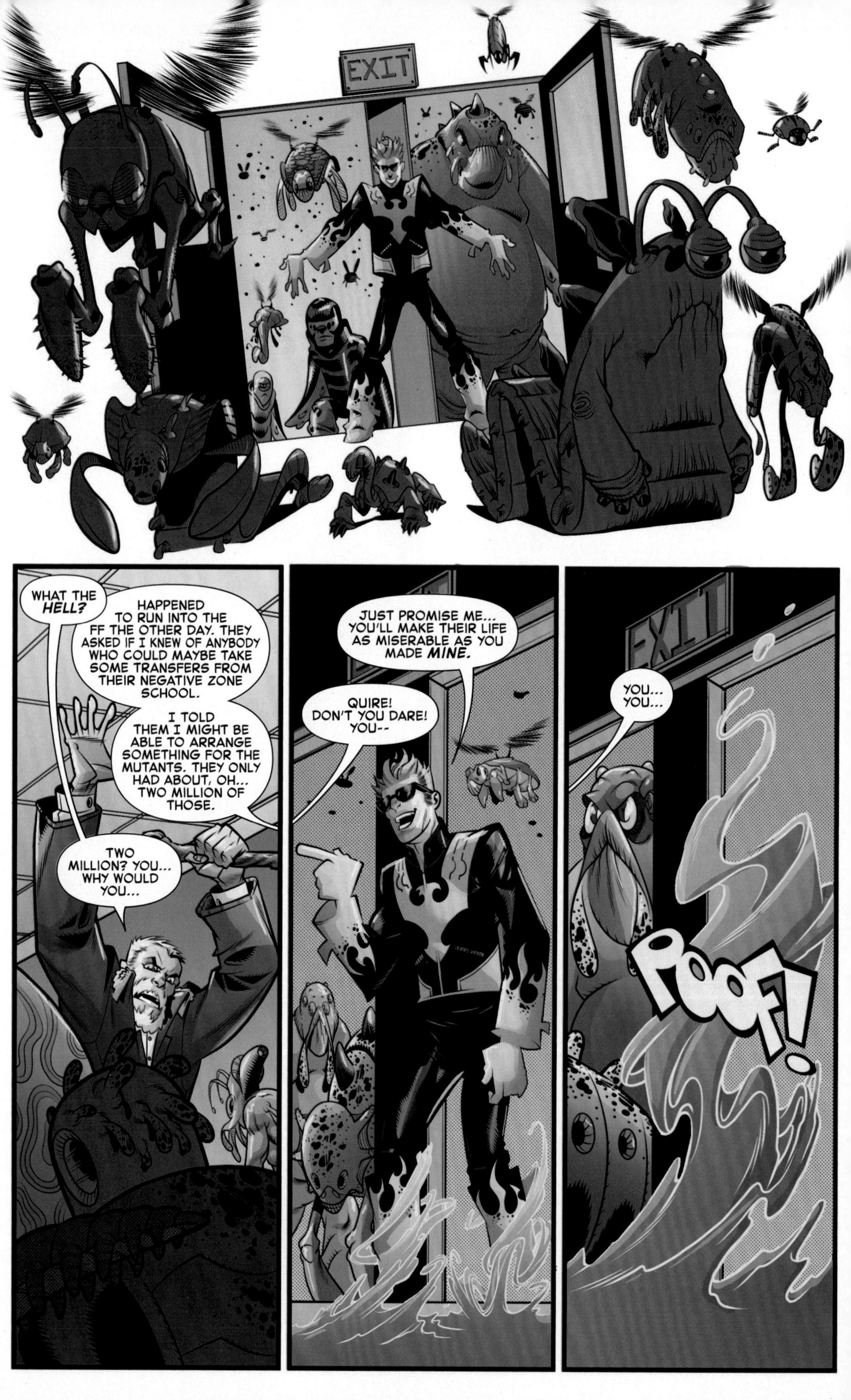
EXIT
WHAT THE HELL?
HAPPENED TO RUN INTO THE FF THE OTHER DAY. THEY ASKED IF I KNEW OF ANYBODY WHO COULD MAYBE TAKE SOME TRANSFERS FROM THEIR NEGATIVE ZONE SCHOOL.
I TOLD THEM I MIGHT BE ABLE TO ARRANGE SOMETHING FOR THE MUTANTS. THEY ONLY HAD ABOUT, OH... TWO MILLION OF THOSE.
TWO MILLION? YOU... WHY WOULD YOU...
JUST PROMISE ME... YOU'LL MAKE THEIR LIFE AS MISERABLE AS YOU MADE MINE.
QUIRE! DON'T YOU DARE! YOU--
EXIT
YOU... YOU...
POOF!

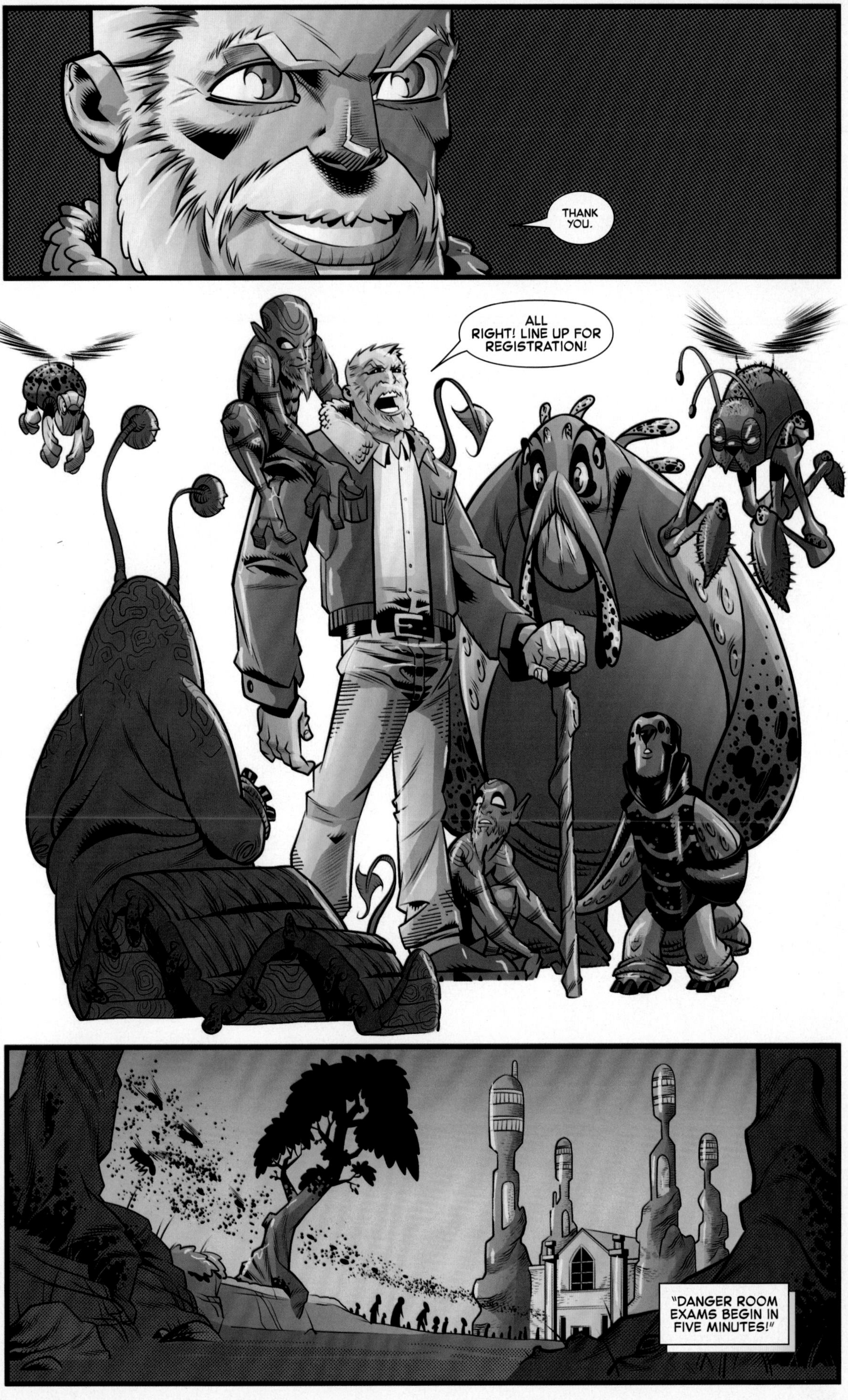
THANK YOU.
ALL RIGHT! LINE UP FOR REGISTRATION!
"DANGER ROOM EXAMS BEGIN IN FIVE MINUTES!"

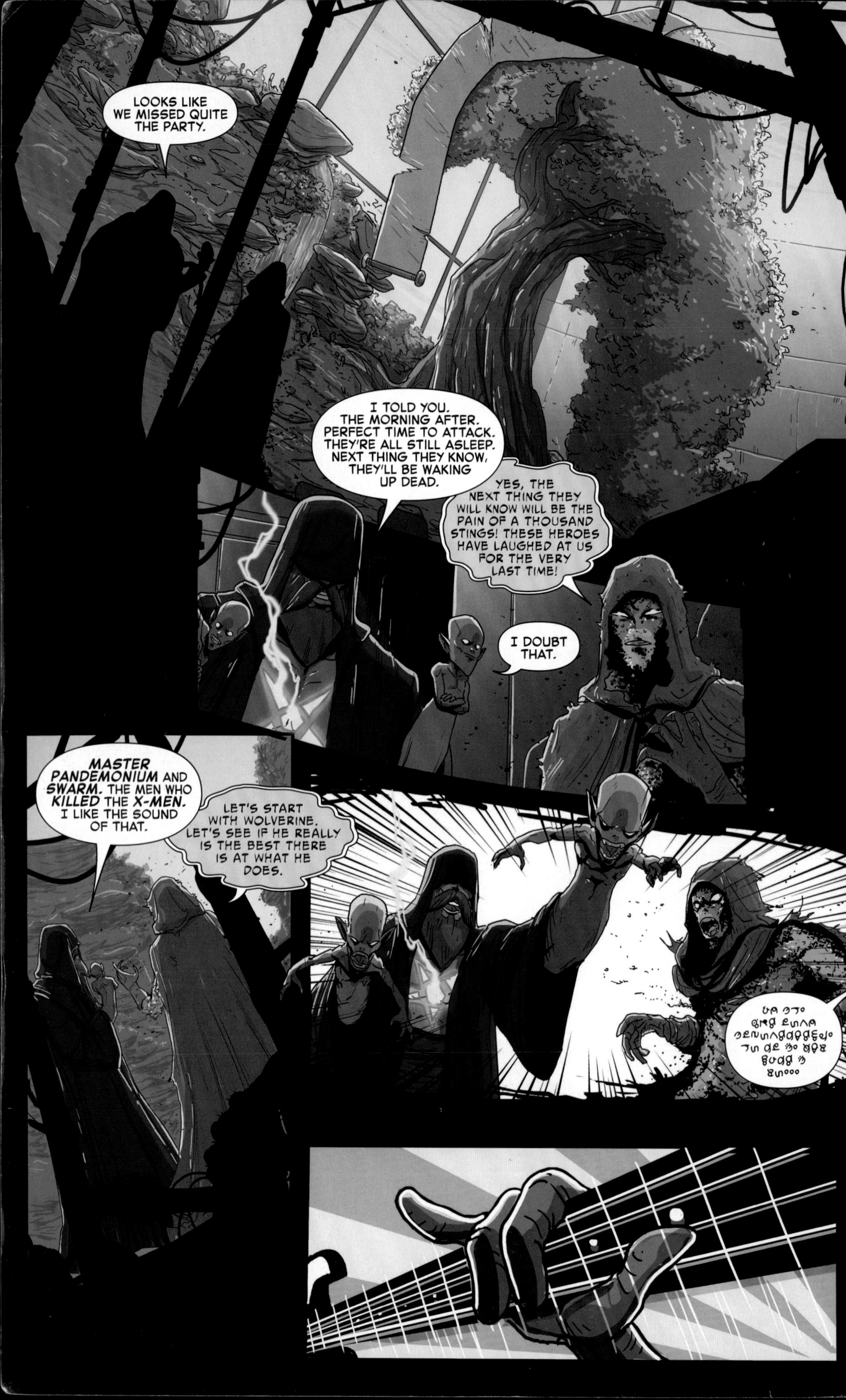
LOOKS LIKE WE MISSED QUITE THE PARTY.
I TOLD YOU. THE MORNING AFTER. PERFECT TIME TO ATTACK. THEY'RE ALL STILL ASLEEP. NEXT THING THEY KNOW, THEY'LL BE WAKING UP DEAD.
YES, THE NEXT THING THEY WILL KNOW WILL BE THE PAIN OF A THOUSAND STINGS! THESE HEROES HAVE LAUGHED AT US FOR THE VERY LAST TIME!
I DOUBT THAT.
MASTER PANDEMONIUM AND SWARM. THE MEN WHO KILLED THE X-MEN. I LIKE THE SOUND OF THAT.
LET'S START WITH WOLVERINE. LET'S SEE IF HE REALLY IS THE BEST THERE IS AT WHAT HE DOES.

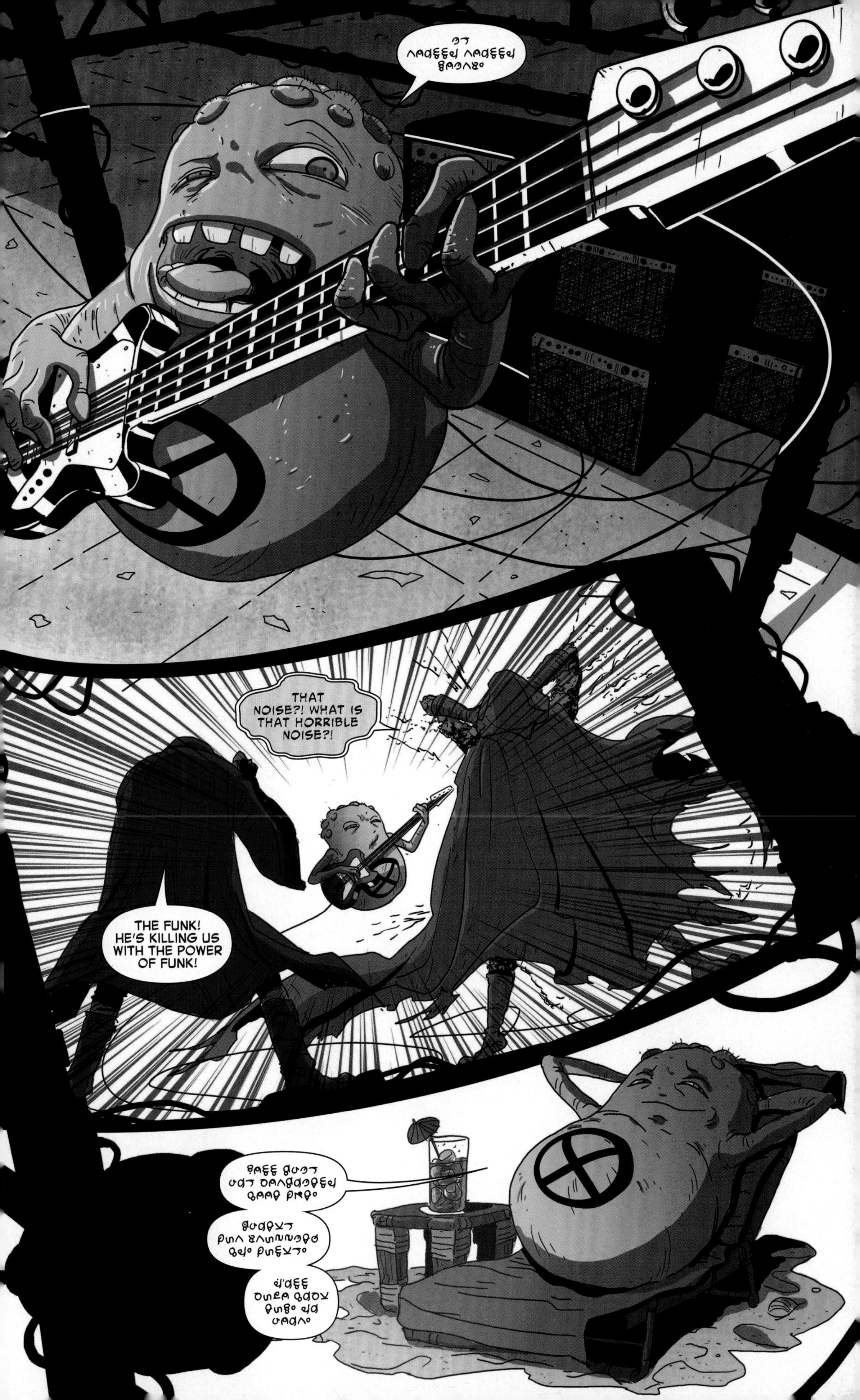
THAT NOISE?! WHAT IS THAT HORRIBLE NOISE?!
THE FUNK! HE'S KILLING US WITH THE POWER OF FUNK!

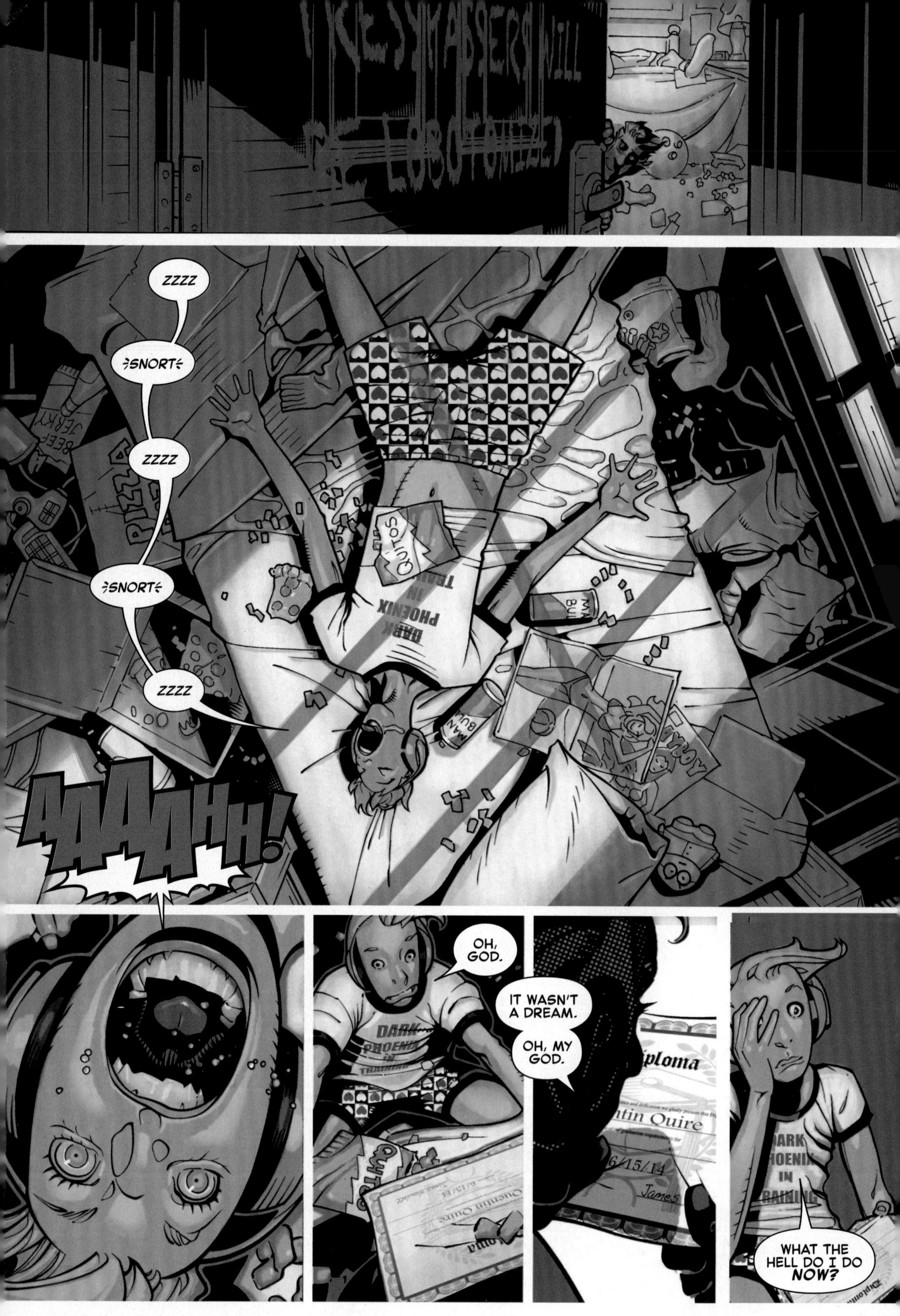
ZZZZ
SNORT
ZZZZ
SNORT
ZZZZ
AAAAAHH!
OH, GOD.
IT WASN'T A DREAM.
OH, MY GOD.
WHAT THE HELL DO I DO NOW?

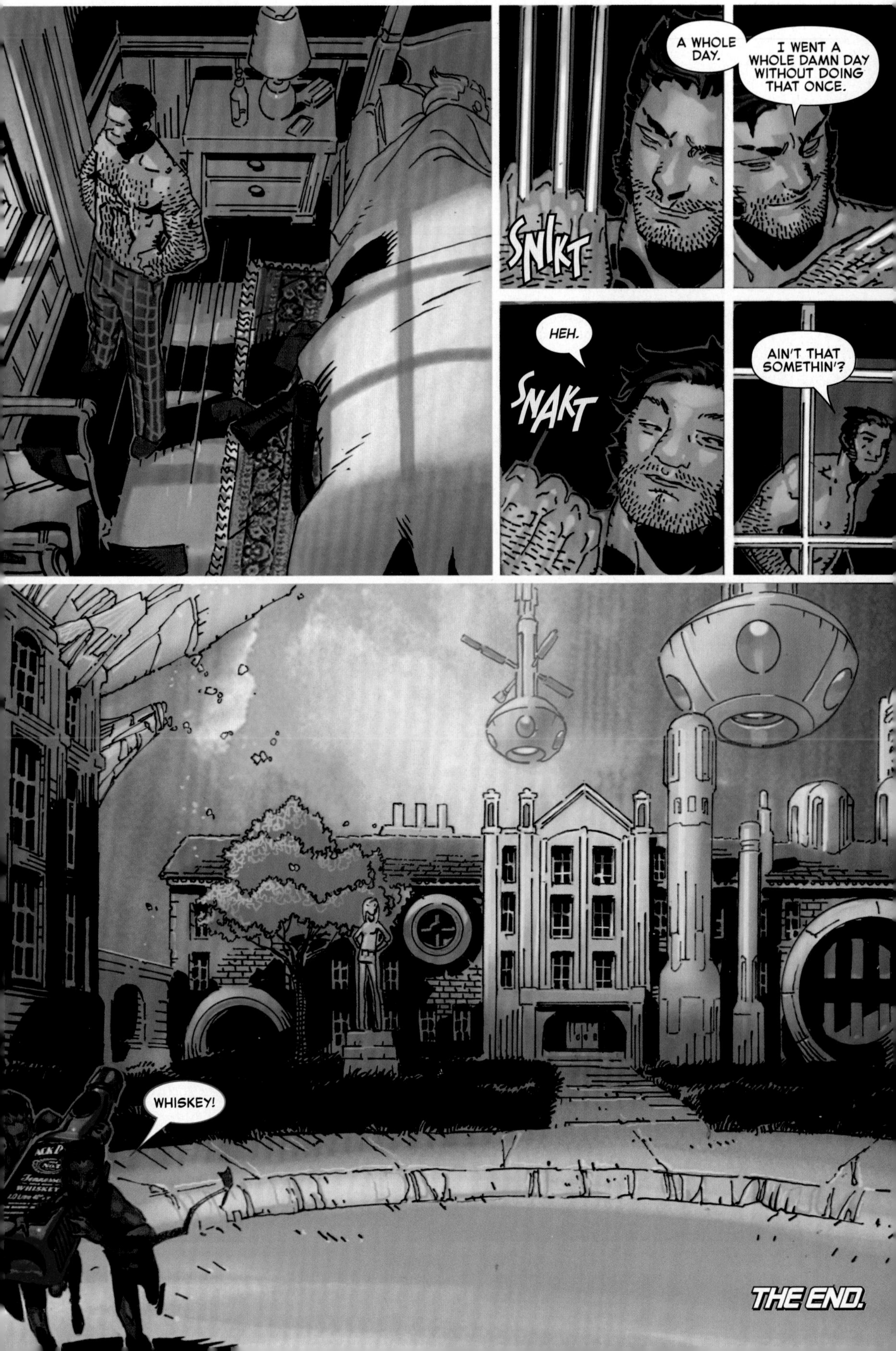

SNIKT
A WHOLE DAY.
I WENT A WHOLE DAMN DAY WITHOUT DOING THAT ONCE.
HEH.
SNAKT
AIN'T THAT SOMETHIN'?
WHISKEY!
THE END.

AFTERWORD

"Fun" is not a dirty word.

That was my mantra coming into this series.

The X-Men had just gone through an ideological split, a Schism, which prompted Wolverine to head back to Westchester, to the X-Men's old home base, where he reopened the school for young mutants. I was given the chance by my esteemed editors, Nick Lowe and Axel Alonso, to create that new school.

I knew right away, I wanted it to be the wildest, craziest school the Marvel Universe had ever seen.

I wanted to reclaim the tag line that once ran above the title of the original X-Men series: "The Strangest Teens of All!"

And above all else, I wanted it to be fun.

The X-Men over the years have at times had a penchant for being dour. I should know, I've written plenty of those stories myself. At the time of the Schism, I'd actually just finished writing the darkest, most depressing Wolverine solo story I'd ever done, where a group of his old enemies, called the Red Right Hand, literally sent Logan to hell and then tricked him into murdering his own... well, let's just say it was dark and leave it at that.

Perhaps it was because I was coming off that story, which was enough to disturb even me, that I wanted to swing the pendulum in the opposite direction. I didn't want to write about dark and serious X-Men. I wanted to write something that was full of joy and laughs but was more than just a series of jokes. Something that was about growing up, about what it means to be an oddball kid in school, to be a parent.

And that all started with Wolverine.

Having Logan become the headmaster of this new school was an idea I felt seemed inevitable, something that his character had been building toward for years, while at the same time, it was a direction that felt fresh and opened up all sorts of new story possibilities.

The Wolverine School for Gifted Youngsters. That was where the series began. And from there, we were off.

Now here we are, 42 issues and an Annual later, and I still can't believe I got away with some of this stuff. Krakoa as the school's yard. The world's most dangerous bathroom. Kitty pregnant with a billion Brood and making out with Iceman. Wolverine fighting Frankenstein. Dog, Snot, Glob, Broo and Doop. Quentin Quire: future Phoenix.

All thanks (or blame) go to Nick Lowe for allowing this series to be such an all-new, all-different sort of X-Men tale and for making each story better with his passion and insights. Thank you to the entire cast of insanely talented folks who brought this series to life, but most especially the ones who did the bulk of the heavy lifting, namely artists Chris Bachalo, Nick Bradshaw, Ramon Perez and Pepe Larraz, and our amazing colorists, Justin Ponsor and Laura Martin. And some special shout-outs go to Irene Lee for the awesome cast pages and class lists sprinkled throughout the series and to the great Mike Allred for... well, for Doop.

I don't imagine I'll get to do another book quite like this one anytime soon. Which just makes me all the more grateful for the fans who supported WOLVERINE & THE X-MEN along the way. Thanks for giving me the chance to have some fun.

Hope you had some too.

JGS Forever.

JASON AARON
FEBRUARY 2014